# 1,001 EASY POTLUCK RECIPES

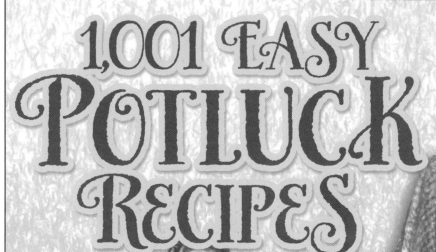

## Easy to Make, Easy to Take, Budget-Friendly Family Recipes

Cookbook Resources, LLC
Highland Village, Texas

**1,001 Easy Potluck Recipes**
*Easy to Make, Easy to Take, Budget-Friendly Family Recipes*

Printed January 2013

© Copyright 2012 by Cookbook Resources, LLC

International Standard Book Number: 978-1-59769-198-7

Library of Congress Control Number:

Library of Congress Cataloging-in-Publication Data

1,001 easy potluck recipes. Variant title: One thousand one easy potluck recipes
One thousand and one easy potluck recipes

    pages cm

    Includes bibliographical references and index.

    ISBN 978-1-59769-202-1

    1. Cooking, American. Cookbook Resources, LLC.

    TX715 .A11438 2012

    641.5973

2012027496

Cover and design by Rasor Advertising & Interactive Design

Illustrations by Nancy Griffith

Edited, Designed and Published in the United States of America
and Manufactured in China by
Cookbook Resources, LLC
541 Doubletree Drive
Highland Village, Texas 75077

Toll free 866-229-2665

www.cookbookresources.com

Bringing Family and Friends to the Table

# 1,001 EASY POTLUCK RECIPES

## Takes the "luck" out of Potluck…

### *You Know Your Dish Will Be One of the Best!*

Recipes in *1,001 Easy Potluck Recipes* are simple and easy with everyday ingredients… no trips to specialty stores for rare ingredients you'll never use again. All are recipes that families call their favorites and enjoy around their kitchen tables.

When you go to any kind of gathering, take a "covered dish" you know will be a hit. These recipes are special enough for company and delicious enough to become family favorites.

These are home-run recipes that become frequently requested and create family memories. We all remember some of the regular dishes we ate when we were growing up. Food and family meals have been imprinted in our minds and just the thought of them can often bring a heartwarming feeling about a simpler life.

Some dishes even remind us of certain people. When I was growing up, Mary Katherine made the Incredible Broccoli-Cheese Soup on page 88. She took it to families before funerals, to people who were sick and to people who just moved to town. Sometimes she just shared half of it with friends because it makes a lot. I always think of Mary Katherine whenever I make that Incredible Broccoli-Cheese Soup and even sometimes when I don't.

A recipe can bring on one of those beloved memories that are just fun to recollect. We can go to those memories anytime, anywhere and relive a special time, a special person or just get a "warm and fuzzy" feeling.

And that's what really good recipes are all about… nourishment… not only for the body, but for our minds and hearts.

Enjoy these recipes and find your special recipes that will last a lifetime.

Thank you for reading this cookbook and thank you for cooking! Cooking is a highly valued effort that is packed with rewards for all.

*The Editor*

*Memories Are Made in the Kitchen.*

# CONTENTS

# APPETIZERS

## ARTICHOKE-BLUE CHEESE DIP

*½ cup (1 stick) butter*
*1 (14 ounce) can artichoke hearts, drained, chopped*
*1 (4 ounce) package blue cheese*
*2 teaspoons lemon juice*

- In skillet, melt butter and mix in artichoke hearts. Add blue cheese and lemon juice. Mix well and serve hot. Serves 8 to 10.

## BLACK BEAN DIP

*2 (15 ounce) cans black beans, rinsed, drained*
*1 sweet onion, finely chopped*
*1 green bell pepper, finely chopped*
*1 (4 ounce) can chopped pimentos*

- Place half beans in bowl and mash with fork. Add remaining beans, onion, bell pepper and pimentos.

### DRESSING:

*3 tablespoons olive oil*
*2 tablespoons red wine vinegar*
*2 teaspoons minced garlic*
*2 teaspoons sugar*

- In small bowl, combine olive oil, vinegar, garlic and sugar; season with a little salt and pepper and mix well. Stir into bean mixture. Serve at room temperature with tortilla chips. Serves 8 to 10.

## BROCCOLI-CHEESE DIP

*1 (10 ounce) can broccoli-cheese soup*
*1 (10 ounce) package frozen, chopped broccoli, thawed*
*½ cup sour cream*
*2 teaspoons dijon-style mustard*

- In saucepan, combine soup, broccoli, sour cream, ½ teaspoon salt and mustard and mix well. Cook on low until hot throughout and serve. Serves 8 to 10.

# SOUTHWESTERN DIP

*Try this one – you'll love it!*

2 (8 ounce) packages cream cheese, softened
¼ cup lime juice
1 tablespoon cumin
1 teaspoon cayenne pepper
1 (8 ounce) can whole kernel corn, drained
1 cup chopped walnuts
1 (4 ounce) can chopped green chilies, drained
3 green onions with tops, chopped
Tortilla chips

- Beat cream cheese in bowl until fluffy. Beat in lime juice, cumin, 1 teaspoon salt and cayenne pepper. Stir in corn, walnuts, green chilies and onions.
- Refrigerate before serving. Serve with tortilla chips. Serves 14 to 16.

# WONDER DIP

⅓ cup finely chopped green onions
½ cup very finely cut broccoli (tiny florets)
1 (8 ounce) can water chestnuts, drained, coarsely chopped
¾ cup mayonnaise
¾ cup sour cream
1 (2.7 ounce) jar crystallized ginger, finely chopped
½ cup finely chopped pecans
2 tablespoons soy sauce
Wheat crackers

- Combine all ingredients plus ½ teaspoon salt in bowl and mix well. Prepare day ahead and refrigerate. Serve with wheat crackers. Serves 10 to 12.

# SASSY ONION DIP

1 (8 ounce) package cream cheese, softened
1 (8 ounce) carton sour cream
½ cup chili sauce
1 (1 ounce) packet onion soup mix
Raw vegetables

- Beat cream cheese in bowl until fluffy. Add remaining ingredients and mix well.
- Cover and refrigerate. Serve with strips of raw zucchini, celery, carrots or turnips. Serves 8 to 10.

# ҒIVE-LAYER DIP

*This is really "different" -- unique flavor!*

1 (16 ounce) can refried beans
1 (8 ounce) carton sour cream
1 (1 ounce) packet ranch dressing mix
1 cup diced tomatoes, drained
1 (4 ounce) can chopped green chilies, drained
½ cup shredded cheddar cheese
½ cup shredded Monterey Jack cheese
1 (2 ounce) can chopped black olives, drained
Chips

- Spread beans on 10-inch serving platter or 9-inch glass pie pan.
- Combine and mix sour cream and dressing mix in bowl and spread over beans. As you spread each layer, make it a little smaller around so it becomes tiered.
- In separate bowl, combine diced tomatoes and green chilies and spread over sour cream. Next, sprinkle both cheeses over tomatoes and green chilies. Last, sprinkle olives over top. Refrigerate. Serve with chips. Serves 16 to 18.

# MEXICALI GUACAMOLE DIP OR SALAD

2 green onions, finely chopped
1 tomato, finely chopped
5 - 6 avocados
3 tablespoons lemon juice
3 tablespoons mayonnaise
1 teaspoon olive oil
4 dashes hot sauce
¼ cup picante sauce

- Combine onions and tomato in bowl. Chop and partially mash avocados and add to onions and tomato. Add in 2½ teaspoons salt, lemon juice, mayonnaise, oil, hot sauce and picante sauce.
- For salad, serve on bed of chopped lettuce. For dip, serve with chips. Serves 6 to 8.

# CUCUMBER DIP

1 (8 ounce) package cream cheese, softened
1 (1 ounce) packet ranch dressing mix
1½ cucumbers, peeled, seeded, grated
¼ cup mayonnaise
1 teaspoon lemon juice
½ cup finely chopped pecans
¼ teaspoon garlic powder
½ teaspoon cayenne pepper
Chips

- Combine all ingredients plus ½ teaspoon salt in bowl and refrigerate. Serve with chips. Serves 8 to 10.

# SPINACH-VEGETABLE DIP

1 (10 ounce) package frozen, chopped spinach, thawed
1 (1 ounce) packet vegetable soup mix
½ onion, very finely chopped
1 rib celery, finely chopped
1 cup mayonnaise
1 cup sour cream
Crackers or chips

- Squeeze spinach between paper towels to complete remove excess moisture. (The dip will be too thin if you don't remove excess water.)
- Combine all ingredients in bowl and mix well. Cover and refrigerate overnight. Serve with crackers or chips. Serves 10 to 12.

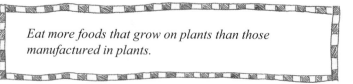

*Eat more foods that grow on plants than those manufactured in plants.*

# DIPPER'S DELIGHT

*This is so good you'll want to make it into a sandwich.*

1 (8 ounce) package cream cheese, softened
2 tablespoons milk
1 (2.5 ounce) package smoked, sliced, pressed pastrami
3 green onions with tops, finely sliced
3 tablespoons finely chopped green bell peppers
⅓ cup mayonnaise
½ cup finely chopped pecans
½ teaspoon hot sauce
¼ teaspoon garlic powder
½ teaspoon Italian herbs
Crackers

- Beat cream cheese and milk in bowl until creamy. Cut pastrami into very fine pieces.
- Add onions, bell pepper, mayonnaise, pecans, hot sauce, garlic powder, Italian herbs and ¼ teaspoon each of salt and pepper and mix well. Refrigerate. Serve with crackers. Serves 8 to 10.

# QUICK TUNA DIP

1 (7 ounce) can white meat tuna, drained, separated
1 (1 ounce) packet onion soup mix
1 cup sour cream
⅓ cup finely chopped pecans
⅛ teaspoon cayenne pepper
Crackers

- Combine all ingredients in bowl and mix well. Refrigerate for several hours before serving. Serve with crackers. Serves 6 to 8.

# EASY CRAB DIP

*This is really delicious and easy too!*

1 (6.5 ounce) can white crabmeat, drained, flaked
1 (8 ounce) package cream cheese
½ cup (1 stick) butter
Chips

- In saucepan, combine crabmeat, cream cheese and butter. Cook over low until mixture blends. Serve with chips. Serves 4 to 6.

# HOT CRAB DIP

1 (8 ounce) package cream cheese
1 (8 ounce) can crabmeat, picked, drained
1 clove garlic, finely minced
½ cup mayonnaise
½ teaspoon mustard
1 teaspoon powdered sugar
2 tablespoons dry white wine
Tortilla chips

- Place all ingredients plus ½ teaspoon salt in double boiler. Stir frequently until cream cheese melts. Serve warm with tortilla chips. Serves 8 to 10.

# SHRIMP DIP

3 cups cooked, veined shrimp, finely chopped
2 tablespoons horseradish
¼ cup chili sauce
⅔ cup mayonnaise
½ teaspoon white pepper
Cucumber or zucchini slices

- Combine shrimp, horseradish, chili sauce, mayonnaise, white pepper and ½ teaspoon salt in bowl, mix well and refrigerate. Serve with cucumber or zucchini slices. Serves 14 to 16.

TIP: *If shrimp are frozen, be sure to drain well after thawing.*

# HORSEY SHRIMP DIP

1 (8 ounce) package cream cheese, softened
⅔ cup mayonnaise
1 tablespoon lemon juice
3 tablespoons creamy horseradish
¼ cup chili sauce
½ teaspoon Creole seasoning
¼ teaspoon garlic powder
2 (8 ounce) cans shrimp, chopped, drained
2 green onions with tops, chopped
Chips

- Beat cream cheese, mayonnaise, lemon juice, horseradish, chili sauce, Creole seasoning and garlic powder in bowl.

- Chop shrimp and onions and add to cream cheese mixture and blend. Refrigerate. Serve with chips. Serves 10 to 12.

# PEANUTTY FRUIT DIP

*1 (8 ounce) package cream cheese, softened*
*1 cup packed brown sugar*
*1 teaspoon vanilla*
*½ cup chopped dry roasted peanuts*

- Combine cream cheese, brown sugar and vanilla with mixer. Beat until creamy. Stir in peanuts. Store in refrigerator. Serve with crisp apple slices. Serves about 4.

# MARSHMALLOW FRUIT DIP

*1 (8 ounce) package cream cheese, softened*
*1 (7 ounce) cartons marshmallow cream*
*¼ teaspoon ground ginger*
*Fruit*

- Blend cream cheese and marshmallow cream with mixer and fold in ginger. Refrigerate. Serve with apple slices, pineapple sticks, honeydew slices, etc. Serves about 4.

# CREAMY ORANGE DIP

*1 (8 ounce) package cream cheese, softened*
*1 (8 ounce) carton orange yogurt*
*½ cup orange marmalade*
*¼ cup finely chopped pecans*

- Beat cream cheese until smooth. Fold in remaining ingredients and refrigerate. Serve with fruit slices. Serves about 4.

*The ornaments of a house are the friends who frequent it.*
—Ralph Waldo Emerson

# Hot Artichoke Spread

1 (14 ounce) can artichoke hearts, drained, chopped
1 (4 ounce) can chopped green chilies, drained
1 cup mayonnaise
1 cup shredded mozzarella cheese
¼ teaspoon white pepper
½ teaspoon garlic salt
Paprika
Tortilla chips or crackers

- Preheat oven to 300°. Remove spikes or tough leaves from artichoke hearts. Combine all ingredients, except paprika in bowl and mix well.

- Place in sprayed 9-inch baking dish and sprinkle paprika over top. Bake for 30 minutes. Serve warm with tortilla chips or crackers. Serves 10 to 12.

# Black Olive Spread

1 (8 ounce) package cream cheese, softened
½ cup mayonnaise
1 (4 ounce) can chopped black olives
3 fresh green onions, minced

- Blend cream cheese and mayonnaise until smooth. Add olives and onions and refrigerate. Spread on slices of party rye bread. Serves 4 to 6.

# Deluxe Pimento Cheese Spread

1 (16 ounce) package shredded sharp cheddar cheese
2 (4 ounce) jars diced pimentos, drained
1 cup salsa
3 tablespoons mayonnaise

- Combine cheese, pimentos and salsa in large bowl and mix well. Add ¼ teaspoon pepper and mayonnaise and blend well. Refrigerate. Spread on wheat crackers or use to make sandwiches. Serves 6.

# OLIVE-CHEESE SPREAD

2 (8 ounce) packages cream cheese, softened
½ cup (1 stick) butter, softened
5 green onions and tops, chopped
2½ tablespoons sweet pickle relish
3 tablespoons finely chopped ripe olives
1 teaspoon garlic powder
1 teaspoon paprika
⅛ teaspoon cayenne pepper

- Combine cream cheese and butter in bowl and beat until fluffy. Add remaining ingredients and mix well. Cover and refrigerate for 24 hours or more.
- Serve with fancy crackers or make small sandwiches with pumpernickel bread. Serves 10 to 12.

# SEAFOOD SPREAD

1 (8 ounce) package cream cheese, softened
⅓ cup mayonnaise
⅓ cup sour cream
3 eggs, hard-boiled, mashed
1 (8 ounce) can crabmeat, flaked
1 (8 ounce) can thinly cut shrimp, drained, chopped
¼ onion, minced
1 rib celery, minced
1 teaspoon Creole seasoning
Several dashes hot sauce

- Combine cream cheese, mayonnaise, sour cream and eggs in bowl. Beat until fairly smooth.
- Add crabmeat, shrimp, onion, celery, Creole seasoning and hot sauce and mix well. Serves 14 to 16.

TIP: This recipe can also be used as a dip or to make good sandwiches.

# JIFFY TUNA SPREAD

*1 (6 ounce) can white tuna, drained, flaked*
*½ cup chopped ripe olives*
*1 (.04 ounce) packet Italian salad dressing mix*
*1 (8 ounce) carton sour cream*
*Paprika*

* Combine tuna, olives, dressing mix and sour cream in bowl and mix well. Sprinkle with a little paprika for color and serve on crackers. Serves 6.

# CRAB-ARTICHOKE SPREAD

*1½ cups freshly grated parmesan cheese*
*1 (14 ounce) can artichoke, drained, chopped*
*1½ cups mayonnaise*
*½ cup finely minced onion*
*½ teaspoon Worcestershire sauce*
*¼ cup seasoned breadcrumbs*
*⅛ teaspoon garlic powder*
*2 drops hot sauce*
*1 (6 ounce) can crabmeat, drained, flaked*
*Paprika*
*Crackers*

* Preheat oven to 350°.

* Combine parmesan cheese, artichoke, mayonnaise, onion, Worcestershire sauce, breadcrumbs, garlic powder, hot sauce and crabmeat in bowl. Mix well and spread into sprayed 9-inch glass pie pan.

* Sprinkle good amount of paprika over spread and bake for 20 minutes. Serve with crackers. Serves 6 to 8.

# BASIC DEVILED EGGS

*12 eggs, hard-boiled, peeled*
*1 teaspoon lemon juice*
*1 teaspoon garlic powder*
*1 tablespoon mustard*
*2 tablespoons mayonnaise*
*Paprika*

- Cut eggs in half lengthwise. Separate egg whites from yolks and place egg white halves on plate. Place yolks in bowl, mash with fork, but leave lumpy.

- Add lemon juice, garlic powder, mustard and mayonnaise and stir. The filling should be rough, not smooth. Fill white halves with egg yolk mixture. Sprinkle paprika on top lightly for decoration. Serves 10 to 12.

*TIP: To make peeling eggs easier, add a little salt and vinegar to the water before boiling.*

*TIP: To change up Basic Deviled Eggs, garnish eggs differently and you'll have a whole new recipe with new flavors: crumbled bacon bits, chopped chives, chopped pimentos, chopped parsley, chopped green or black olives, dash of red pepper flakes, minced salad shrimp, shredded cheddar cheese, radish slices, chopped red or green bell pepper.*

*TIP: Or – add one of the following to the yolk mixture: 2 tablespoons drained sweet pickle relish, 1 tablespoon chopped celery, 1 teaspoon horseradish, 1 (4 ounce) can deviled ham, 1 (6 ounce) can crabmeat, flaked, drained.*

# DEVILED EGGS DIJON

*12 eggs, hard-boiled, peeled*
*1 - 2 tablespoons mayonnaise*
*1 tablespoon dijon-style mustard*
*1 teaspoon chopped onion or chives*
*2 - 3 dashes hot sauce*

- Cut eggs in half and remove yolks. Mash yolks with fork and mix with remaining ingredients plus a little salt and pepper. Drop spoonfuls of mixture into egg white shells. Makes 24 halves.

# SPINACH PINWHEELS

*1 (8 ounce) can crescent dinner rolls*
*1 (8 ounce) package garlic-herb spreadable cheese, softened*
*6 thin slices cooked deli ham*
*30 fresh spinach leaves, stems removed*

- Separate crescent dough into 4 rectangles and press perforations to seal. Generously spread rectangles with cheese, leaving ¼-inch around edge without cheese. Top with ham slices and spinach leaves.

- Starting at short side of dough, roll each rectangle and press edges to seal. Refrigerate rolls for 30 minutes to 1 hour and slice each roll into 6 slices.

- Place slices on baking sheet and bake at 350° for about 15 minutes or until lightly brown. Serves 6 to 8.

# PIGS IN A BLANKET

*1 (10 count) package wieners*
*3 (10 count) cans biscuits*
*Dijon-style mustard*

- Preheat oven to 400°. Cut each wiener into thirds. Flatten each biscuit slightly and spread with mustard. Wrap each wiener piece in biscuit and pinch to seal. Bake for 10 to 12 minutes. Makes 30 small pieces.

# OLIVE PUFFS

*2 cups shredded sharp cheddar cheese*
*½ cup (1 stick) butter, very soft*
*1 teaspoon paprika*
*½ teaspoon garlic powder*
*1 cup flour*
*48 green stuffed olives*

- Preheat oven to 375°. Combine cheese and butter in bowl. Stir in paprika, garlic powder, flour and ½ teaspoon salt and mix well.

- Wrap teaspoon of mixture around each olive and place on baking sheet. Bake for 15 to 16 minutes. Serves 12 to 16.

# COCKTAIL HAM ROLL-UPS

*1 (3 ounce) package cream cheese, softened*
*1 teaspoon finely grated onion*
*Mayonnaise*
*1 (3 ounce) package sliced ham*
*1 (15 ounce) can asparagus spears, drained*

- Beat cream cheese, grated onion and enough mayonnaise to make spreading consistency in bowl.

- Separate sliced ham, spread mixture on slices and place 1 asparagus spear on each ham slice and roll. Cut each roll into 4 pieces.

- Spear each piece with toothpick for serving. Refrigerate. Serves 8 to 10.

# SAUSAGE-PINEAPPLE BITS

*1 pound cooked link sausage*
*1 pound hot bulk sausage*
*1 (8 ounce) can crushed pineapple with juice*
*1 cup apricot preserves*
*1 cup packed brown sugar*
*1 tablespoon marinade for chicken*

- Slice link sausage into ¼ inch pieces. Shape bulk sausage into 1 inch balls and brown in skillet.

- In separate large saucepan, combine pineapple, preserves, brown sugar and marinade for chicken. Add sausages and simmer for 30 minutes.

- Serve in chafing dish with cocktail picks. Serves 8 to 10.

# PARTY SAUSAGES

*1 cup ketchup*
*1 cup plum jelly*
*1 tablespoon lemon juice*
*¼ cup mustard*
*2 (15 ounce) packages tiny smoked sausages*

- Combine all ingredients except sausages in saucepan and heat well. Add sausages and simmer for 15 minutes.

- Serve with cocktail toothpicks. (You may substitute smoked sausages for sliced wieners.) Serves 8 to 10.

# SAUSAGE BALLS

*1 pound hot pork sausage, uncooked*
*1 (16 ounce) package shredded cheddar cheese*
*3 cups biscuit mix*
*⅓ cup milk*

- Preheat oven to 375°.
- Combine all ingredients and form into small balls. If dough is a little too sticky, add 1 teaspoon more biscuit mix. Bake for 13 to 15 minutes. Serves 8.

# SWEET-AND-SOUR SAUSAGE BALLS

*1 pound hot ground pork sausage*
*1 pound mild ground pork sausage*
*2 eggs*
*2 cups soft breadcrumbs*

- Mix sausage, eggs, ½ teaspoon salt and breadcrumbs and from into small balls. Brown sausage balls in skillet, cook over medium-high heat and drain..

## SAUCE:

*1 (12 ounce) bottle cocktail sauce*
*¾ cup packed brown sugar*
*½ cup wine vinegar*
*½ cup soy sauce*

- Combine all sauce ingredients and pour over sausage balls. Simmer uncovered for about 1 hour. Serves 6 to 8

*TIP: You could also use a slow cooker to simmer the sausage balls and serve in the slow cooker.*

# ROASTED MIXED NUTS

*1 pound mixed nuts*
*¼ cup maple syrup*
*2 tablespoons brown sugar*
*1 (.04 ounce) packet ranch salad dressing mix*

- Preheat oven to 300°.
- Combine nuts and maple syrup in bowl and mix well. Sprinkle with brown sugar and salad dressing mix and stir gently to coat. Spread in sprayed 10 x 15-inch baking pan. Bake for 25 minutes or until light brown and cool. Serves 8 to 10.

# SMOKED SALMON LOG

*This is so good. You'll make it all year long!*

1 (15 ounce) can red salmon
1 (8 ounce) package cream cheese, softened
1 tablespoon lemon juice
2 tablespoons grated onion
¼ teaspoon liquid smoke
6 tablespoons very finely crushed crackers
Flour
1 cup very finely chopped pecans
3 tablespoons minced fresh parsley
Crackers

- Drain salmon. Remove skin and bones and flake with fork to remove shells.

- Beat cream cheese and lemon juice in bowl. Add onion, ¼ teaspoon salt, liquid smoke, crackers and salmon. (Add another spoonful of cracker crumbs, if your mixture seems too sticky).

- Refrigerate for several hours or overnight. Spread light coat of flour on wax paper sheet. Make roll with salmon mixture and roll in pecans and parsley mixture.

- Roll onto another piece of wax paper to be able to lift roll. Refrigerate for several hours and serve with crackers. Serves 6 to 8.

# CHEESE CRISPS

1 cup (2 sticks) butter, softened
2 cups shredded sharp cheddar cheese
2 cups flour
2 cups rice crispy cereal
¼ teaspoon garlic powder
¼ teaspoon cayenne pepper

- Preheat oven to 350°.

- Combine butter and cheese in bowl and beat well. Add remaining ingredients plus ½ teaspoon salt and mix well.

- Drop spoonfuls of mixture onto unsprayed baking sheet. Bake for 15 minutes or until slightly brown. Cool and store in covered container. Serves 6 to 8.

# SPINACH-CRAB BALLS

1 tablespoon butter
1 onion, minced
2 (10 ounce) packages frozen chopped spinach, thawed, well drained*
4 eggs
2 tablespoons flour
4 slices bacon, cooked, crumbled
½ cup (1 stick) butter, softened
1 (7.5 ounce) can crabmeat, drained, flaked
2 cups seasoned stuffing, crumbled
½ teaspoon dill weed
¼ teaspoon garlic powder

- Preheat oven to 325°.

- Melt butter in skillet and saute onion. Mix thoroughly with remaining ingredients plus ½ teaspoon salt and ¼ teaspoon pepper.

- Form into ½ inch balls and place on baking sheet. Bake for 15 minutes. Serve warm. Serves 8 to 10.

*TIP: Squeeze spinach between paper towels to completely remove excess moisture.*

*TIP: If you want to make ahead and bake when you're ready to serve, just freeze spinach balls on the baking sheet and remove to resealable plastic bag to store frozen.*

# RANCH CHEESE BALL

1 (1 ounce) packet dry ranch-style salad dressing mix
2 (8 ounce) packages cream cheese, softened
¼ cup finely chopped pecans
1 (3 ounce) jar real bacon bits

- Mix dressing mix and cream cheese with mixer. Roll into ball. Roll cheese ball in pecans and bacon bits. Refrigerate several hours before serving. Serves 4 to 6.

*If celery gets limp, place it in a tall container filled with cold water. Refrigerate and the celery will become crisp again.*

# CHILI-CHEESE LOG

*1 (8 ounce) package cream cheese, softened*
*2 cups shredded cheddar cheese, softened*
*2 tablespoons mayonnaise*
*1 tablespoon lemon juice*
*½ teaspoon garlic powder*
*½ cup finely chopped pecans*
*1 teaspoon chili powder*
*1 teaspoon paprika*
*Crackers*

- Combine cream cheese, cheddar cheese, mayonnaise, lemon juice and garlic powder in bowl and beat with until smooth and creamy. Stir in pecans.

- Shape mixture into a roll that is 1½ inches in diameter. Mix chili powder and paprika in bowl and sprinkle roll with mixture. Roll cheese log in wax paper and refrigerate. Serve with crackers. Serves 4 to 6.

# CHEESE STRAWS

*1 (9 ounce) package piecrust mix, divided*
*¾ cup shredded cheddar cheese*
*Cayenne pepper*
*¼ teaspoon garlic powder*

- Preheat oven to 350°.

- Prepare piecrust for 1 pie according to package directions. Roll into rectangular shape. Sprinkle cheese over dough and press into dough.

- Sprinkle cayenne pepper and garlic powder over cheese. Fold dough over once and cover cheese. Roll to make ¼-inch thick.

- Cut dough into ½ x 3-inch pieces and place on sprayed baking sheet. Bake for 12 to 15 minutes. Serves about 6 to 8.

# BEVERAGES

## LEMONADE TEA

*2 family-size tea bags*
*½ cup sugar*
*1 (12 ounce) can frozen lemonade*
*1 quart ginger ale, chilled*

- Steep tea in 3 quarts water and mix with sugar and lemonade. Add ginger ale just before serving. Makes 3 quarts.

## VICTORIAN ICED TEA

*4 individual tea bags*
*¼ cup sugar*
*1 (12 ounce) can frozen cranberry-raspberry juice concentrate, thawed*

- Place tea bags in teapot and add 4 cups boiling water. Cover and steep for 5 minutes. Remove and discard tea bags. Add sugar and mix. Refrigerate tea.

- Just before serving, combine cranberry-raspberry concentrate and cold water according to concentrate directions in 2½-quart pitcher.

- Stir in tea and serve with ice cubes. Makes 2½ quarts.

## BEST TROPICAL PUNCH

*1 (46 ounce) can pineapple juice*
*1 (46 ounce) can apricot nectar*
*3 (6 ounce) cans frozen limeade concentrate, thawed*
*3 quarts ginger ale, chilled*

- Combine pineapple juice, apricot nectar and limeade in container and refrigerate.

- When ready to serve, add ginger ale. Makes 1½ gallons.

# PINA COLADA PUNCH

1 (46 ounce) can pineapple juice, chilled
1 (20 ounce) can crushed pineapple with juice
1 (15 ounce) can cream of coconut
1 (32 ounce) bottle lemon-lime carbonated drink, chilled

- Combine all ingredients in punch bowl.
- Serve over ice cubes. Makes 1 gallon.

# FROSTY ORANGE-PINEAPPLE PUNCH

2 (46 ounce) cans pineapple juice, chilled
1 (½ gallon) carton orange sherbet
1 (2 liter) bottle ginger ale, chilled

- Pour juice in punch bowl and stir in sherbet. Add ginger ale and serve immediately. Makes 32 to 36 punch cups.

# SLUSHY PINEAPPLE PUNCH

1 (46 ounce) can pineapple juice
1 (46 ounce) can apple juice
2 (28 ounce) bottles 7UP®, chilled

- Freeze pineapple juice and apple juice in cans. Set out juices 1 hour before serving. When ready to serve, combine all ingredients in punch bowl. Makes 32 to 36 punch cups.

# CHRISTMAS PUNCH

1 (46 ounce) can pineapple juice, chilled
1 (1 liter) bottle ginger ale, chilled
1 (2 liter) bottle strawberry soda, chilled

- Combine all ingredients in punch bowl. Use extra ginger ale or 7UP®, if desired. Makes 20 punch cups.

# PINEAPPLE DELIGHT PUNCH

*1 (2 quart) can pineapple-coconut juice, chilled*
*2 (1 liter) bottles 7UP®, chilled*
*1 (20 ounce) can pineapple rings with juice*

- Combine pineapple-coconut juice, 7UP® and juice from pineapple rings in punch bowl. Float pineapple rings in punch bowl. Makes 24 punch cups.

# RECEPTION PUNCH

*4 cups sugar*
*5 ripe bananas, mashed*
*Juice of 2 lemons*
*1 (46 ounce) can pineapple juice*
*1 (6 ounce) can frozen concentrated orange juice*
*2 quarts ginger ale*

- Boil sugar and 6 cups water in saucepan for 3 minutes. Cool.
- Blend bananas with lemon juice. Add in pineapple and orange juice. Combine remaining ingredients except ginger ale.
- Freeze in large container. To serve, thaw for 1 hour 30 minutes and then add ginger ale. Punch will be slushy. Serves 40.

# PINEAPPLE PUNCH

*4 (1 quart) bottles ginger ale, chilled*
*1 (½ gallon) carton pineapple sherbet*
*1 (15 ounce) can pineapple tidbits, chilled*

- Combine ginger ale, pineapple sherbet and pineapple tidbits and mix. Serve in punch bowl. Makes 28 (4-ounce) punch cups.

# PINEAPPLE-CITRUS PUNCH

*1 (46 ounce) can pineapple juice, chilled*
*1 quart apple juice, chilled*
*1 (2 liter) bottle lemon-lime soda, chilled*
*1 (6 ounce) can frozen lemonade concentrate, thawed*
*1 orange, sliced*

- Combine pineapple juice, apple juice, lemon-lime soda and lemonade in punch bowl. Add orange slices for decoration. Serves 48.

# QUICK STRAWBERRY PUNCH

2 (10 ounce) boxes frozen strawberries, thawed
2 (6 ounce) cans frozen pink lemonade concentrate
2 (2 liter) bottles ginger ale, chilled

- Process strawberries through blender. Pour lemonade into punch bowl and stir in strawberries. Add chilled ginger ale and stir well. Serves 24.

# CREAMY STRAWBERRY SLUSH

1 (10 ounce) package frozen strawberries, thawed
½ gallon strawberry ice cream, softened
2 (2 liter) bottles ginger ale, chilled
Fresh strawberries

- Process frozen strawberries through blender. Combine strawberries, chunks of ice cream and ginger ale in punch bowl.
- Stir and serve immediately with fresh strawberries. Serves 24.

# STRAWBERRY SPRITZER

1 (10 ounce) package frozen strawberries in syrup, thawed
1 (24 ounce) bottle white grape juice, chilled
1 (12 ounce) can club soda, chilled

- Process strawberries and syrup in blender until smooth, but stop once to scrape down sides.
- Mix strawberry puree and white grape juice in pitcher and add club soda. Serves 7.

# PURPLE PASSION PUNCH

3 (1 quart) bottles grape juice, chilled
1 (1 quart) bottle cranberry juice, chilled
1 (1 quart) carton raspberry sherbet

- Combine juices in punch bowl and mix well. Stir in sherbet and serve immediately. Makes 20 to 26 punch cups.

# EASIEST GRAPE PUNCH

*½ gallon ginger ale*
*Red seedless grapes*
*Sparkling white grape juice, chilled*

- Fill circular gelatin mold with hole in center with ginger ale and seedless grapes and freeze. (Use any shape for ice mold.) When ready to serve, pour sparkling white grape juice in punch bowl with ice ring. Serves 24.

# FROSTY GRAPE FIZZ

*1 (2 quart) bottle grape juice, chilled*
*1 (½ gallon) carton raspberry sherbet*
*2 (2 liter) bottles ginger ale, chilled*

- Combine grape juice and sherbet in punch bowl. When ready to serve, add ginger ale. Makes 32 to 36 punch cups.

# APRICOT-ORANGE PUNCH

*1 (46 ounce) can apricot juice, chilled*
*1 (2 liter) bottle ginger ale, chilled*
*1 (½ gallon) carton orange sherbet*

- When ready to serve, combine juice and ginger ale in punch bowl. Stir in scoops of orange sherbet. Serve in 4-ounce punch cups. Makes 32 to 36 punch cups.

# PEACH NECTAR PUNCH

*1 (46 ounce) can apricot nectar, chilled*
*1 (2 liter) bottle peach soda, chilled*
*1 (½ gallon) carton peach ice cream*

- When ready to serve, combine apricot nectar and peach soda in punch bowl. Stir in peach ice cream. Makes 32 to 36 punch cups.

# GINGER ALE NECTAR PUNCH

*1 (12 ounce) can apricot nectar*
*1 (6 ounce) can frozen orange juice concentrate, thawed, undiluted*
*2 tablespoons lemon juice*
*1 (2 liter) bottle ginger ale, chilled*

- Combine apricot nectar, orange juice concentrate, 1 cup water and lemon juice in pitcher and refrigerate. When ready to serve, stir in ginger ale and pour into punch bowl. Serves 24.

# SUNNY HAWAIIAN PUNCH

*1 (46 ounce) can Hawaiian Punch®, chilled*
*1 (2 liter) bottle ginger ale or 7UP®, chilled*
*1 (12 ounce) can frozen lemonade concentrate*

- Combine ingredients in punch bowl. Mix in 2 cups cold water and serve immediately. Serves about 32 to 36 punch cups.

# RUBY PUNCH

*The Cran-Apple juice™ in this punch really makes it a "Christmas" special!*

*2 (6 ounce) cans frozen orange juice concentrate*
*2 (46 ounce) cans red Hawaiian punch*
*1 (46 ounce) can pineapple juice*
*1 (46 ounce) bottle Cran-Apple™ juice*
*2 liters ginger ale, chilled*

- Combine orange juice, 4 cups water, Hawaiian punch, pineapple juice and Cran-Apple™ juice in 2 (1 gallon) bottles and stir well. Refrigerate.
- Place in punch bowl. Just before serving, add ginger ale. Makes 2 gallons.

# PARTY PUNCH

*The almond extract really gives this punch a special taste!*

3 cups sugar
1 (6 ounce) package lemon gelatin
1 (3 ounce) can frozen orange juice concentrate, thawed
⅓ cup lemon juice
1 (46 ounce) can pineapple juice
3 tablespoons almond extract
2 quarts ginger ale, chilled

- Combine sugar and 1 quart water in saucepan. Heat until sugar dissolves. Add gelatin and stir until dissolved.
- Add fruit juices, 1½ quarts water and almond extract. Refrigerate.
- When ready to serve, place in punch bowl and add chilled ginger ale. Serves 50.

# FIVE ALIVE PUNCH

2 (12 ounce) cans frozen Five Alive® juice concentrate
1 (12 ounce) can frozen pink lemonade concentrate
1 (2 liter) bottle ginger ale, chilled

- Dilute frozen concentrates according to can directions and mix in punch bowl. When ready to serve, add ginger ale. Makes 32 to 36 punch cups.

# PINK CRANBERRY PUNCH

2 (28 ounce) bottles ginger ale
1 (46 ounce) can pineapple juice
1 (1 quart) jar cranberry juice
1 (1 quart) carton pineapple sherbet, softened

- Chill all ingredients. Mix in punch bowl. Serves 30 to 36.

# CRANBERRY-LEMON PUNCH

2 quarts cranberry juice
1 (6 ounce) can lemonade concentrate, thawed
⅔ cup maraschino cherry juice
1 (2 liter) lemon-lime soda, chilled

- Combine all ingredients and mix well. Serves 16 to 20.

# SPARKLING CRANBERRY PUNCH

*Ice mold for punch bowl*
*Red food coloring, optional*
*2 quarts cranberry juice cocktail*
*1 (6 ounce) can frozen lemonade, thawed*
*1 quart ginger ale, chilled*

- Pour water in mold for ice ring and add red food coloring to make mold brighter and prettier.
- Mix cranberry juice and lemonade in pitcher and refrigerate until ready to serve. When serving, pour cranberry mixture into punch bowl, add ginger ale and stir well.
- Add decorative ice mold to punch bowl. Serves 24 cups.

# CAPPUCCINO ICE CREAM PUNCH

*¼ cup instant coffee granules*
*¾ cup sugar*
*3 pints milk*
*1 (1 pint) carton half-and-half cream*
*1 quart chocolate ice cream, softened*
*1 quart vanilla ice cream, softened*

- Combine coffee granules and sugar in bowl and stir in 1 cup boiling water. Cover and refrigerate. When ready to serve, pour coffee mixture into 1-gallon punch bowl.
- Stir in milk and half-and-half cream. Add scoops of both ice creams and stir until most of ice cream melts. Serves 16 to 22.

# VERY SPECIAL COFFEE PUNCH

*I promise that this will be a hit. Everyone will be back for seconds!*

*1 (2 ounce) jar instant coffee granules*
*2¼ cups sugar*
*2 quarts half-and-half cream*
*1 quart ginger ale, chilled*
*1 (1 pint) carton whipping cream, whipped*
*½ gallon French vanilla ice cream*

- Dissolve instant coffee in 2 quarts hot water in saucepan. When cool, add sugar and half-and-half cream and mix well. Refrigerate.
- When ready to serve, pour coffee-sugar mixture in punch bowl, add chilled ginger ale, whipped cream and ice cream. Let some chunks of ice cream remain. Serves 60.

# MOCHA MAGIC

*4 cups brewed coffee*
*¼ cup sugar*
*4 cups milk*
*4 cups chocolate ice cream, softened*

- Combine coffee and sugar in container and stir until sugar dissolves. Refrigerate for 2 hours.

- Just before serving, pour into small punch bowl. Add milk and mix well. Top with scoops of ice cream and stir well. Makes 3 quarts.

# PINK GRAPEFRUIT PUNCH

*1 (46 ounce) can pink grapefruit juice, chilled*
*1 (46 ounce) can pineapple juice, chilled*
*1 (1 liter) bottle 7UP®, chilled*

- Mix juices and 7UP® in punch bowl. Serve immediately. Makes 32 to 36 punch cups.

# ENGLISH TEA PUNCH

*1 (12 ounce) can frozen orange juice concentrate, thawed*
*1 (½ gallon) container prepared lemon tea, chilled*
*1 (46 ounce) can pineapple juice, chilled*

- Dilute orange juice with water according to can directions. Combine all ingredients in punch bowl and stir. Makes 32 to 36 punch cups.

# HOLIDAY PUNCH

*1 (1 ounce) package cherry fruit-flavored drink mix*
*1 (2 liter) bottle ginger ale, chilled*
*1 (46 ounce) can pineapple juice, chilled*

- Combine all ingredients and mix well. Add more ginger ale, if needed. Serve in punch bowl. Makes 24 to 36 punch cups.

# GREEN PARTY PUNCH

*This punch would also be a good one to use when the party is close to St. Patrick's Day!*

*1 (3 ounce) package lime gelatin*
*1 (6 ounce) can frozen limeade*
*1 (6 ounce) can frozen lemonade*
*1 quart orange juice*
*1 quart pineapple juice*
*1 tablespoon almond extract*
*2 - 3 drops green food coloring*
*1 liter ginger ale, chilled*

- Dissolve lime gelatin in 1 cup boiling water in bowl and stir well. Combine dissolved gelatin, limeade, lemonade, orange juice, pineapple juice, almond extract and food coloring in gallon bottle. Refrigerate.
- When ready to serve, add ginger ale. Serves 32.

# EMERALD PUNCH

*2 (1 ounce) packages lime fruit-flavored drink mix*
*1 (46 ounce) can pineapple juice, chilled*
*1 (2 liter) bottle ginger ale, chilled*

- Prepare drink mix according to package directions. Refrigerate several hours. Pour into punch bowl and stir in pineapple juice.
- When ready to serve, add ginger ale. Makes 32 to 36 punch cups.

*TIP: Make an ice ring with additional ginger ale and add to punch bowl. If you don't have a round gelatin mold, pour ginger ale into any nicely shaped container and freeze.*

# LIME PUNCH

*2 (2 liter) bottles 7UP®, chilled*
*1 (2 liter) bottle ginger ale, chilled*
*1 (½ gallon) carton lime sherbet*

- Combine 7UP® and ginger ale. When ready to serve, add lime sherbet and stir until it mixes well. Makes 32 to 36 punch cups.

# PERFECT PARTY PUNCH

*1 (12 ounce) can frozen limeade concentrate*
*1 (46 ounce) can pineapple juice, chilled*
*1 (46 ounce) apricot nectar, chilled*
*1 quart ginger ale, chilled*

- Dilute limeade concentrate according to can directions. Add pineapple juice and apricot nectar and stir well.
- When ready to serve, add ginger ale. Makes 1½ gallons.

# SUNNY LIMEADE COOLER

*1½ pints lime sherbet, divided*
*1 (6 ounce) can frozen limeade concentrate*
*3 cups milk*
*Lime slices*

- Beat lime sherbet in bowl and add concentrated limeade and milk. Blend all ingredients.
- Pour into glasses and top each with an additional scoop lime sherbet. Serve immediately. Garnish with lime slices. Makes 1½ quarts.

# APPLE PARTY PUNCH

*3 cups sparkling apple cider*
*2 cups apple juice*
*1 cup pineapple juice*
*½ cup brandy*

- Combine all ingredients and freeze. Remove punch from freezer 30 minutes before serving. Place in small punch bowl and break into chunks. Stir until slushy. Serves 12.

# APRICOT PUNCH

*1 (12 ounce) can apricot nectar*
*1 (6 ounce) can frozen orange juice concentrate, thawed*
*2 tablespoons lemon juice*
*1 (2 liter) bottle ginger ale, chilled*

- Combine apricot nectar, orange juice concentrate, lemon juice and 1 cup water. Refrigerate. When ready to serve stir in ginger ale. Serves 10 to 12.

# Spiced Mulled Cider

*½ cup packed brown sugar*
*1 gallon apple cider*
*2 teaspoons whole allspice*
*2 teaspoons whole cloves*
*2 (3 inch) sticks cinnamon*
*Whole nutmeg*

- Mix brown sugar, apple cider and ¼ teaspoon salt in saucepan. Put spices in tea ball or cheesecloth sack and add to cider.
- Bring to a boil, reduce heat and simmer for about 15 to 20 minutes. Remove spices and serve hot. Serves about 20.

# Old-Fashioned Hot Chocolate

*2½ cups sugar*
*1¼ cups cocoa powder*
*1 gallon plus 1 quart milk*
*1 tablespoon plus 2 teaspoons vanilla*

- Mix sugar and cocoa with ⅓ cup water in saucepan over medium heat until sugar and cocoa dissolve and mixture begins to boil.
- Add milk, stirring constantly, and simmer until hot. (Do not boil.) Remove from heat, add vanilla and stir briskly with whisk until frothy. Serve immediately. Serves 20.

# Instant Cocoa Mix for 48

*1 (8 quart) box dry milk powder*
*1 (12 ounce) jar non-dairy creamer*
*1 (16 ounce) can instant chocolate-flavored drink mix*
*1¼ cups powdered sugar*

- Combine all ingredients and store in airtight container. To serve, use ¼ cup cocoa mix for each cup of hot water. Serves 48.

34

# SPARKLING WINE PUNCH

6 oranges with peels, thinly sliced
1 cup sugar
2 (750 ml) bottles dry white wine
3 (750 ml) bottles sparkling wine, chilled

- Place orange slices in large plastic or glass container and sprinkle with sugar.
- Add white wine, cover and refrigerate for at least 8 hours.
- Stir in sparkling wine. Makes 1 gallon.

# CHAMPAGNE PUNCH

1 (750 ml) bottle champagne, chilled
1 (32 ounce) bottle ginger ale, chilled
1 (6 ounce) can frozen orange juice concentrate
Orange slices

- Mix champagne, ginger ale and orange juice in punch bowl. Refrigerate and serve. Garnish with orange slices. Makes 1½ quarts.

# AMARETTO COOLER

1¼ cups amaretto liqueur
2 quarts orange juice
1 (15 ounce) bottle club soda, chilled
Orange slices

- Combine amaretto, orange juice and club soda in container and stir well.
- Serve over ice. Garnish with orange slices. Makes 2½ quarts.

*You can't change the past, but you can ruin the present by worrying over the future.*
—Anonymous

# Sparkling Pink Party Punch

*3 (6 ounce) cans frozen pink lemonade concentrate*
*1 (750 ml) bottle pink sparkling wine*
*3 (2 liter) bottles lemon-lime carbonated beverage, divided*
*Lime slices*

- Combine pink lemonade, sparkling wine and 1 bottle carbonated beverage in airtight container, cover and freeze for 8 hours or until firm.
- Let stand at room temperature 10 minutes and place in punch bowl.
- Add remaining bottle carbonated beverage and stir until slushy. Garnish with lime slices. Makes 3 quarts.

# Holiday Eggnog

*1 gallon eggnog*
*1 (1 pint) carton whipping cream*
*1 quart brandy*
*½ gallon vanilla ice cream, softened*

- Mix all ingredients in bowl.
- Pour into individual cups and serve immediately. Makes 1½ gallons.

*Optional: Sprinkle with ground nutmeg for a nice touch.*

*I cldnuot blviee that I cluod aulaclty uesdnatnrd waht I was rdanieg. The phaonmneal pweor of the hmuan mnid. Aoccdrnig to rscheearch at Cmabrigde Uinervtisy, it deosn't mttaer in waht odrer the ltteers in a wrod are, the olny iprmoatnt tnhig is taht the frist and lsat ltteer be in the rghit pclae.*

# Breads & Sandwiches

## Mom's Quick Never-Fail Bread

*This whole process takes less than 5 hours.*

1½ yeast cakes
½ cup milk, room temperature
1 tablespoon sugar
2 tablespoons butter, melted
5 - 6 cups flour

- Dissolve yeast in 1½ cups warm water and warm milk in large bowl. Mix in sugar, 1½ teaspoons salt and butter until it blends well.

- Slowly pour flour into mixture and stir after each addition. Add flour until dough is stiff enough to knead. Place on lightly floured board and knead until dough is smooth and springs back when touched.

- Cover and set aside in warm place until dough doubles in size. Punch down lightly and divide into 2 equal parts. Place in sprayed, floured loaf pans, cover and let stand in warm place until dough doubles in size again.

- When ready to bake, preheat oven to 450°. Bake for 15 minutes. Reduce heat to 350° and bake for 30 minutes or until golden brown on top. Makes 2 loaves.

# SOURDOUGH STARTER AND BREAD

## STARTER:

*1 package yeast*
*2 cups flour*

- Dissolve yeast in 2 cups warm water in glass bowl. Add flour and mix well. (Use only glass bowl for mixing and do NOT leave metal utensils in starter.)
- Place starter in warm place overnight. Next morning, cover container and refrigerate. Use only glass container to store starter. Refrigerate starter when not in use and keep covered. Every 5 days add and stir into starter:

    *1 cup milk*
    *¼ cup sugar*
    *1 cup flour*

- Do not use starter on day it is "fed." Always keep at least 2 cups mixture in container. Starter may be fed more frequently than every 5 days.

## SOURDOUGH BREAD:

*2 cups flour*
*1 tablespoon baking powder*
*2 tablespoons sugar*
*1 egg*
*2 cups Sourdough Starter*

- Mix flour, baking powder, 1 teaspoon salt and sugar in bowl, add egg and starter and mix well. Pour into loaf pan and place in warm place. Allow to double in bulk.
- When ready to bake, preheat oven to 350°. Bake for 30 to 35 minutes. Makes 1 loaf.

# WILLIAMSBURG SALLY LUNN BREAD

*1 package yeast or yeast cake*
*1 cup warm milk*
*½ cup (1 stick) butter, softened*
*⅓ cup sugar*
*3 eggs, beaten*
*4 cups flour*

- Dissolve yeast in warm milk. Cream butter, sugar and eggs in bowl. Add yeast-milk mixture. Sift flour into mixture and mix well. Let rise in warm place.
- Punch down and place into sprayed mold or 3-quart ring mold. Let rise again. When ready to bake, preheat oven to 350°. Bake for 45 minutes or until done. Serve hot. Serves 6 to 8.

# EVERYDAY BUTTER ROLLS

*2 cups biscuit mix*
*1 (8 ounce) carton sour cream*
*½ cup (1 stick) butter, melted*

- Preheat oven to 400°. Combine all ingredients in bowl and mix well. Spoon into sprayed muffin cups (or cups with paper liners) and fill only half full. Bake for 12 to 14 minutes or light brown. Serves 6 to 8.

# NO-NEED-TO-KNEAD ROLLS

*2 packages dry yeast*
*1 egg*
*¼ cup shortening*
*6½ cups flour*

- Combine 2 cups lukewarm water, 1½ teaspoons salt and remaining ingredients in bowl, mix well and shape into rolls. Place rolls in sprayed round cake pans. Cover and let rise for 1 hour 30 minutes to 2 hours.
- When ready to bake, preheat oven to 400°. Bake for 15 to 20 minutes. Makes 30.

# BUTTERMILK REFRIGERATOR ROLLS

*3 packages dry yeast*
*5 cups flour*
*¼ cup sugar*
*¾ cup shortening, melted*
*2 cups buttermilk\**

- Dissolve yeast in ¼ cup warm water in bowl and set aside. In separate bowl, combine flour, sugar and shortening. Add buttermilk and yeast mixture and mix thoroughly by hand. Add more flour, if needed. Cover and refrigerate.
- About 1 hour 30 minutes before baking, shape dough pieces into 1-inch balls and place in muffin cups, three to a cup. Prepare as many rolls as needed and refrigerate remaining dough.
- Cover rolls and let rise in warm place for 1 hour before baking. When ready to bake, preheat oven to 425°.
- Bake for 12 minutes or until brown. Dough will last 10 days in plastic container in refrigerator. Makes 24 to 30 rolls.

*\*TIP: To make buttermilk, mix 1 cup milk with 1 tablespoon lemon juice or vinegar and let milk stand for about 10 minutes.*

# STICKY SWEET ROLLS

*1 (12 count) package frozen dinner rolls, partially thawed*
*¼ cup (½ stick) butter, melted*
*¾ cup packed brown sugar*
*½ teaspoon ground cinnamon*
*1 cup chopped pecans*

- Place 1 roll in each of 12 sprayed muffin cups and cut a deep "x" in top of each roll. Spray tops of rolls with cooking spray and place sheet of plastic wrap over rolls.
- Let rise about 3 hours or until double in size.
- Preheat oven to 350°.
- In bowl, combine butter, brown sugar and cinnamon and mix well.
- Stir in pecans and spoon sugar mixture over rolls. Pull "x" open and let sugar mixture seep into rolls.
- Bake for 15 to 20 minutes or until light brown. Serve 6 to 8.

# QUICK AND EASY LUNCHEON MUFFINS

*1 cup (2 sticks) butter, softened*
*2 cups flour*
*1 (8 ounce) carton sour cream*

- Preheat oven to 350°. Combine all ingredients in bowl and mix well. Pour mixture into sprayed muffin cups and bake for 20 to 25 minutes. Serves 8.

# EASY DROP BISCUITS

*1⅓ cups self-rising flour*
*1 (8 ounce) carton whipping cream*
*2 tablespoons sugar*
*Butter*

- Preheat oven to 400°. Combine all ingredients and stir until they blend. Drop biscuits by spoon onto sprayed baking sheet. Bake for about 10 minutes or until light brown. Serve with butter. Serves 6 to 8.

# SOUR CREAM BISCUITS

2 cups plus 1 tablespoon flour
3 teaspoons baking powder
½ teaspoon baking soda
½ cup shortening
1 (8 ounce) carton sour cream

- Preheat oven to 400°. Combine dry ingredients and add pinch of salt. Cut in shortening. Gradually add sour cream and mix lightly.

- Turn onto lightly floured board and knead a few times. Roll to ½-inch thick. Cut with biscuit cutter and place on sprayed baking sheet. Bake 15 minutes or until light brown. Makes about 2 dozen.

# ANGEL BISCUITS

5 cups flour
¼ cup sugar
3 teaspoons baking powder
1 teaspoon baking soda
⅔ cup shortening
1½ packages dry yeast
2 cups buttermilk*
Canola oil

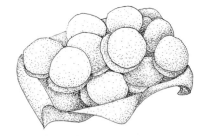

- Preheat oven to 400°

- Sift flour, sugar, baking powder, baking soda and 1 teaspoon salt in bowl and cut in shortening.

- In separate bowl, dissolve yeast in ¼ cup warm water and add with buttermilk to dry ingredients. Mix well but only until dough moistens well. Place in covered bowl and refrigerate to use as needed.

- To bake biscuits, remove amount desired, roll out on floured board to ½ inch thickness and cut with biscuit cutter.

- Place on oiled baking pan and turn once to grease both sides. Bake for 12 to 15 minutes or until nicely brown.

- Remaining dough will keep in refrigerator for 2 weeks. Makes about 2 dozen.

*TIP: To make buttermilk, mix 1 cup milk with 1 tablespoon lemon juice or vinegar and let stand for about 10 minutes.

# Old South Sweet Potato Biscuits

1 (16 ounce) can sweet potatoes, drained
1 tablespoon sugar
¼ cup milk
1½ cups biscuit mix

- Preheat oven to 450°.

- In mixing bowl, mash sweet potatoes, add sugar and milk and beat until creamy. Stir in biscuit mix with fork until most lumps dissolve.

- Pour mixture onto floured, wax paper and knead 5 to 6 times. Press down to about ½-inch thick and cut out biscuits with biscuit cutter or small glass. Bake for 10 to 12 minutes on baking sheet. Serves 6 to 8.

# French Bread Monterey

1 loaf French bread, sliced
Butter, softened
1 cup mayonnaise
½ cup grated parmesan cheese
½ onion, finely chopped
½ teaspoon Worcestershire sauce
Paprika

- Preheat oven to 200°.

- Spread bread slices completely with butter and place on baking sheet. Combine mayonnaise, cheese, onion and Worcestershire sauce in bowl.

- Spread mixture on buttered bread and then sprinkle with paprika. Place bread in oven for 15 minutes then turn on broiler and brown lightly. Serve immediately. Serves 8 to 10.

## Morton Salt

*Before 1911, salt clumped in damp weather and dispensing was difficult. In 1911 the Morton Salt Company added magnesium carbonate to its salt so that it would flow freely. The girl with umbrella, illustrating that the salt flows even in the rain, was introduced in 1914.*

# GARLIC-HERB BREAD

*While cooking, the aroma from this recipe is heavenly!*

1 loaf French bread
½ cup (1 stick) butter, melted
1 teaspoon dried parsley flakes
½ teaspoon dried crushed oregano
¼ teaspoon dried dill weed
¼ teaspoon garlic powder
Freshly grated parmesan cheese

- Preheat oven to 375°.

- Slice bread into thick slices. Combine butter, parsley, oregano, dill weed and garlic in bowl and mix well.

- Spread each slice generously with butter mixture with brush and sprinkle ½ teaspoon parmesan cheese on each slice.

- Reassemble into loaf shape and spread remaining butter mixture over top.

- Place on baking sheet and wrap foil halfway up loaf, leaving top exposed. Bake for 20 minutes. Serves 8 to 10.

# CRUNCHY BREADSTICKS

*Try these for lunch or dinner. You'll be surprised.*

1 (8 count) package hot dog buns
1 cup (½ stick) butter, melted
Garlic powder
Paprika

- Preheat oven to 225°.

- Slice each bun in half lengthwise. Use pastry brush to butter breadsticks and sprinkle with a little garlic powder and paprika on each.

- Place on sprayed baking sheet and bake for 45 minutes. Serves 8.

# GARLIC TOAST

*1 loaf thick-sliced bread*
*1 tablespoon garlic powder*
*¼ cup finely chopped parsley*
*1 teaspoon marjoram leaves*
*½ cup (1 stick) butter, melted*
*1 cup parmesan cheese*

- Preheat oven to 225°.

- Combine garlic powder, parsley, marjoram leaves and butter in small bowl and mix well.

- Use brush liberally to spread mixture on bread slices and sprinkle with parmesan cheese. Place on baking sheet and bake for about 1 hour. Serves 8 to 10.

# SESAME TOAST

*2 tablespoons sesame seeds*
*½ cup (1 stick) plus 2 tablespoons (¼ stick) butter*
*¼ teaspoon basil*
*½ teaspoon rosemary*
*¼ teaspoon marjoram*
*½ teaspoon garlic powder*
*½ loaf French bread, sliced*

- Brown sesame seeds in 2 tablespoons butter in saucepan. Add ½ cup butter, melt and add seasonings. Refrigerate overnight.

- When ready to bake, preheat oven to 300°.

- Stir butter mixture and spread on bread slices. Bake for 20 minutes or until slightly brown. Serves 6 to 8.

# CHEDDAR-BUTTER TOAST

*½ cup (1 stick) butter, softened*
*1¼ cups shredded cheddar cheese*
*1 teaspoon Worcestershire sauce*
*¼ teaspoon garlic powder*
*Thick sliced bread*

- Combine all ingredients except bread in bowl and spread on thick sliced bread. Turn on broiler to preheat, turn off broiler and put toast in oven for about 15 minutes. Serves 6.

# GREEN CHILI-CHEESE BREAD

*1 loaf unsliced Italian bread*
*½ cup (1 stick) butter, melted*
*1 (4 ounce) can diced green chilies, drained*
*¾ cup shredded Monterey Jack cheese*

- Preheat oven to 350°.

- Slice bread almost all the way through. Combine melted butter, chilies and cheese. Spread between bread slices. Cover loaf with foil. Bake for 25 minutes. Serves 8 to 10.

# CORN STICKS

*2 cups biscuit mix*
*2 tablespoons minced green onions*
*1 (8 ounce) can cream-style corn*
*Melted butter*

- Preheat oven to 400°.

- Combine biscuit mix, green onions and cream-style corn. Place dough on floured surface and cut into 3 x 1-inch strips. Roll in melted butter. Bake for 15 to 16 minutes. Serves 4.

# EASY CHEDDAR CORNBREAD

*2 (8.5 ounce) packages cornbread-muffin mix*
*2 eggs, beaten*
*1 cup plain yogurt*
*1 (14 ounce) can cream-style corn*
*½ cup shredded cheddar cheese*

- Preheat oven to 400°. Combine cornbread mix, eggs and yogurt in bowl and blend well. Stir in corn and cheese.

- Pour into sprayed 9 x 13-inch baking dish. Bake for 18 to 20 minutes or until slightly brown. Serves 8 to 10.

# SPICY CORNBREAD TWISTS

*3 tablespoons butter*
*½ cup cornmeal*
*¼ teaspoon cayenne pepper*
*1 (11 ounce) can refrigerated soft breadsticks*

- Preheat oven to 350°.

- Melt butter in pie pan in oven. Remove from oven as soon as butter melts. Mix cornmeal and cayenne pepper on wax paper.

- Roll breadsticks in butter and in cornmeal mixture. Twist breadsticks according to label directions and place on large baking sheet. Bake for 15 to 18 minutes. Serves 6.

# NUT BREAD

*1 cup milk*
*2 tablespoons butter*
*¼ cup sugar*
*1 yeast cake*
*2 cups white flour*
*⅔ cup chopped walnuts*
*1½ - 2 cups whole wheat flour*

- Heat milk in saucepan and add butter, sugar and 1 teaspoon salt. Dissolve yeast in 2 tablespoons lukewarm water. When milk mixture cools, add yeast. Add white flour and walnuts and beat until smooth. Cover and set in warm place to rise for about 1 hour.

- Add whole wheat flour and knead or mix in stand mixer until elastic to touch and does not stick to unfloured board. Cover and set in warm place to rise until double in bulk.

- Knead or mix again until free from air bubbles. Place in sprayed loaf pan. Cover and set in warm place to rise until doubled in bulk. Bake at 350° for 50 to 60 minutes. Serves 6 to 8.

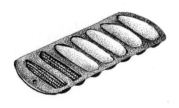

# BANANA-NUT BREAD

*½ cup (1 stick) butter, softened*
*1 cup sugar*
*2 eggs*
*2 cups flour*
*1 teaspoon baking soda*
*1 teaspoon ground cinnamon*
*4 ripe bananas*
*1 cup chopped pecans*

- Preheat oven to 350°.

- Cream butter and sugar in bowl and add eggs one at a time. Stir vigorously. In separate bowl, combine flour, baking soda and cinnamon and stir into butter mixture a little at a time.

- Mash bananas and add to mixture. Stir well and add pecans. Pour into sprayed loaf pan and bake for 50 to 60 minutes. Serves 8 to 12. (Makes loaf with about 13 to 15 slices.)

# VERY BERRY STRAWBERRY BREAD SANDWICHES

*3 cups sifted flour*
*2 cups sugar*
*1 teaspoon baking soda*
*1 tablespoon ground cinnamon*
*3 large eggs, beaten*
*1 cup canola oil*
*1¼ cups chopped walnuts*
*2 (10 ounce) packages frozen sweetened strawberries with juice, thawed*
*1 (8 ounce) package cream cheese, softened, optional*

- Preheat oven to 350°. Combine flour, sugar, 1 teaspoon salt, baking soda and cinnamon in large bowl. Add remaining ingredients except cream cheese.

- Pour in 2 sprayed, floured 9 x 5-inch loaf pans. Bake for 1 hour or when toothpick inserted in center comes out clean. Cool for several minutes before removing from pan.

- To serve, slice bread and spread with cream cheese or Pineapple-Pecan Spread (page 47); top with second slice. For finger sandwiches, cut in smaller pieces. Serves 12 to 16.

# PINEAPPLE-PECAN SPREAD

*2 (8 ounce) packages cream cheese, softened*
*1 (8 ounce) can crushed pineapple with juice*
*¾ cup chopped pecans*

- Beat cream cheese in bowl until smooth. Drain pineapple and save juice. Add crushed pineapple to cream cheese.

- Stir with spoon and add just enough juice to make mixture spreadable. Add pecans and refrigerate. Spread on slices of Very Berry Strawberry Bread (page 46). Cut sandwiches into thirds lengthwise for finger sandwiches. Makes 3 cups.

# GLAZED LEMON BREAD

*¾ cup (1½ sticks) butter*
*2 cups sugar*
*4 eggs, slightly beaten*
*½ teaspoon baking soda*
*3 cups flour*
*1 cup buttermilk\**
*2 tablespoons grated lemon peel*
*1 cup chopped pecans*

- Preheat oven to 325°.

- Cream butter and sugar in large bowl and mix in eggs. Mix dry ingredients and ½ teaspoon salt and add alternately with buttermilk and lemon peel.

- Stir in pecans and pour into sprayed, floured 9 x 5-inch loaf pan. Bake for 40 minutes or until toothpick inserted in center comes out clean. Serves 10 to 12. (Makes about 13 to 15 slices.)

## GLAZE:

*Juice of 2 lemons*
*1 cup powdered sugar*

- Remove from oven and punch holes in bread with toothpick and pour glaze over bread while it is still hot. Cool completely.

*\*TIP: To make buttermilk, mix 1 cup milk with 1 tablespoon lemon juice or vinegar and let stand for about 10 minutes.*

# ḪOLIDAY CRANBERRY BREAD

*2 cups flour*
*1 cup sugar*
*1½ teaspoons baking powder*
*½ teaspoon baking soda*
*¼ cup shortening*
*¾ cup orange juice*
*1 tablespoon grated orange peel*
*1 egg, well beaten*
*½ cup chopped nuts*
*1 (16 ounce) can whole cranberry sauce*

- Preheat oven to 350°.

- Sift flour, sugar, baking powder, baking soda and 1 teaspoon salt in bowl. Cut in shortening until mixture resembles coarse cornmeal.

- In separate bowl, combine orange juice, orange peel and egg and pour into dry ingredients. Mix just enough to dampen; fold in nuts and cranberry sauce. Spoon mixture into sprayed loaf pan and spread corners and sides slightly higher than center.

- Bake for 1 hour until crust is brown and center is done. Remove, cool and store overnight for easy slicing. Serves 10 to 12. (Makes about 13 to 15 slices.)

# QUICK PUMPKIN BREAD

*1 (16 ounce) package pound cake mix*
*1 cup canned pumpkin*
*2 eggs*
*⅓ cup milk*
*1 teaspoon allspice*

- Preheat oven to 350°. Beat all ingredients in bowl and blend well. Pour into sprayed, floured 9 x 5-inch loaf pan.

- Bake for 1 hour. Bread is done when toothpick inserted in center comes out clean. Cool and turn out onto cooling rack. Serves 15.

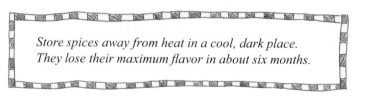

*Store spices away from heat in a cool, dark place.*
*They lose their maximum flavor in about six months.*

# ZUCCHINI BREAD

*3 eggs*
*2 cups sugar*
*1 cup canola oil*
*3 teaspoons vanilla*
*2 cups grated zucchini*
*2 cups flour*
*1 tablespoon ground cinnamon*
*¼ teaspoon baking powder*
*2 teaspoons baking soda*
*1 cup chopped pecans*

- Preheat oven to 325°.

- Beat eggs in bowl until fluffy and add sugar, oil and vanilla. Beat until thick and lemon colored. Stir in zucchini, flour, cinnamon, baking powder, 1 teaspoon salt and baking soda.

- Fold in pecans and spoon into 2 sprayed, floured (9 x 5-inch) loaf pans. Bake for 55 minutes. Cool in pan for about 10 minutes before removing from loaf pan. Serves about 20 to 24. (Makes about 26 to 30 slices.)

# PARTY CHEESE FINGERS

*12 slices whole wheat bread*
*2½ cups shredded sharp cheddar cheese*
*⅓ cup chili sauce*
*¾ cup mayonnaise*
*½ cup chopped olives*
*½ cup chopped pecans*
*1 (2 ounce) jar chopped pimentos, drained*
*¼ teaspoon garlic powder*

- Trim crusts off bread. Combine all remaining ingredients in bowl and mix well.

- Spread mixture on 6 slices of bread and top with remaining bread slices. Cut each sandwich into 3 strips and refrigerate. Serves about 8 to 10.

# ISLAND MANGO BREAD

*This is wonderful, moist and delicious bread – great toasted for breakfast.*

*2 cups flour*
*1 teaspoon baking soda*
*1 teaspoon ground cinnamon*
*1 cup sugar*
*3 eggs, beaten*
*¾ cup plus 1 tablespoon canola oil*
*2 cups peeled, seeded and finely diced mangoes (2 ripe mangoes)*
*1 teaspoon lemon juice*
*⅓ cup shredded coconut*
*⅔ cup chopped pecans*

- Preheat oven to 350°.

- Combine flour, baking soda, cinnamon, ¼ teaspoon salt and sugar in large bowl and mix well.

- In separate bowl, combine eggs, oil, mangoes and lemon juice. Pour into flour mixture and mix well with spoon.

- Stir in coconut and pecans and pour into 2 sprayed, floured 8 x 4-inch loaf pans.

- Bake for 40 to 45 minutes. Bread is done when toothpick inserted in center comes out clean. Serves about 16 to 18.

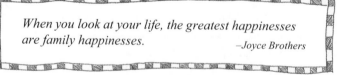

*When you look at your life, the greatest happinesses are family happinesses.*
                                                    *–Joyce Brothers*

# SWEET APPLE LOAF

⅔ cup (1⅓ sticks) butter
2 cups sugar
4 eggs
2 cups applesauce
⅓ cup milk
1 tablespoon lemon juice
4 cups flour
1 teaspoon ground cinnamon
2 teaspoons baking powder
1 teaspoon baking soda
1½ cups chopped pecans
¾ cup chopped maraschino cherries, well drained

- Preheat oven to 325°. Cream butter, sugar and eggs in bowl and beat for several minutes. Stir in applesauce, milk and lemon juice.
- In separate bowl, sift flour, cinnamon, baking powder, baking soda and 1 teaspoon salt, add to first mixture and mix well. Fold in pecans and cherries.
- Pour into 3 sprayed, floured loaf pans and bake for 1 hour. Bread is done when toothpick inserted in center comes out clean. Set aside for 10 to 15 minutes, remove from pans and cool on rack. Freezes well. Serve toasted for breakfast or spread with cream cheese for lunch. Serves about 20 to 24.

*How many times during our childhoods did we hear the adage "An apple a day keeps the doctor away"? As it turns out, the truth is the apple is a very nutritious food. Apples contain vitamin C plus many other antioxidants which are cancer fighters.*

# MINCEMEAT BREAD

*1¾ cups flour*
*1¼ cups sugar*
*2½ teaspoons baking powder*
*2 eggs, beaten*
*1 teaspoon vanilla*
*1½ cups mincemeat*
*¾ cups chopped pecans*
*⅓ cup shortening, melted*

- Preheat oven to 350°.
- Combine flour, sugar, baking powder and ½ teaspoon salt in large bowl.
- In separate bowl, combine eggs, vanilla, mincemeat and pecans and mix well. Stir in shortening and mix quickly. Batter will be stiff.
- Pour egg mixture into dry ingredients and stir only enough to moisten flour.
- Spoon batter into sprayed, floured loaf pan and bake for 1 hour or until toothpick inserted in center comes out clean. Cool for 15 minutes and remove from pan to cool completely. Serves about 6 to 8.

## GLAZE:

*1 cup powdered sugar*
*1 tablespoon milk*
*¼ cup finely chopped pecans*

- Combine powdered sugar and milk in bowl and stir until smooth. Stir in pecans and spread over loaf. Slice bread and spread a little butter on each slice and toast.
- This bread is well worth the cost of the prepared mincemeat. It usually comes in a large jar so you will have enough left to make mincemeat cookies. They are delicious.

# Applesauce-Pecan Bread

*1 cup sugar*
*1 cup applesauce*
*⅓ cup canola oil*
*2 eggs*
*2 tablespoons milk*
*1 teaspoon almond extract*
*2 cups flour*
*1 teaspoon baking soda*
*½ teaspoon baking powder*
*¾ teaspoon ground cinnamon*
*¼ teaspoon ground nutmeg*
*¾ cup chopped pecans*

- Preheat oven to 350°.
- Combine sugar, applesauce, oil, eggs, milk and almond extract in bowl and mix well.
- In separate bowl, combine baking soda, baking powder, cinnamon, nutmeg and ¼ teaspoon salt and add to sugar mixture. Mix well and fold in pecans. Pour into sprayed, floured loaf pan.

## Topping:

*½ cup chopped pecans*
*½ teaspoon ground cinnamon*
*½ cup packed brown sugar*

- Combine pecans, cinnamon and brown sugar in bowl and sprinkle over batter. Bake for 1 hour 5 minutes. Bread is done when toothpick inserted in center comes out clean. Cool on rack. Serves 6 to 8.

Mankind has not only valued apples for their taste but also for their shelf life. For centuries, so-called winter apples prevalent in Asia and Europe could be picked in late autumn and stored at temperatures as low as just above freezing, therefore serving as an important food source during winter. Europeans who settled America and Argentina repeated that pattern.

# APRICOT BREAD EXTRAORDINAIRE

*This is "it" for apricot lovers!*

3 cups flour
1½ teaspoons baking soda
2 cups sugar
1½ cups canola oil
4 eggs
1 teaspoon vanilla
1 (5 ounce) can evaporated milk
Apricot Butter (recipe follows)
1¼ cups chopped pecans

- Preheat oven to 350°.

- Combine flour, baking soda and ½ teaspoon salt in bowl. Add sugar, oil, eggs, vanilla and evaporated milk. Mix thoroughly. Add apricot butter and pecans and blend.

- Pour into 2 sprayed, floured loaf pans and bake for 1 hour 10 minutes or until toothpick inserted in center comes out clean.

## APRICOT BUTTER:

1¼ cups finely chopped apricots
1 cup sugar

- Cover apricots with water in bowl and soak overnight. Combine apricots and sugar in saucepan and simmer for 10 minutes or until soft. Cool completely before adding to recipe. Serves 12 to 16.

*Apricots are full of beta-carotene, fiber and potassium. Fresh apricots are loaded with vitamins A and C and are available from May through August.*

# APPLE-BANANA BREAD

3 apples, peeled, grated
3 bananas, mashed
2 teaspoons lemon juice
½ cup (1 stick) butter, softened
2 cups sugar
2 eggs
3 cups flour
1½ teaspoons baking powder
1½ teaspoons baking soda
1 teaspoon vanilla

- Preheat oven to 350°. Sprinkle apples and bananas with lemon juice in bowl.

- In separate bowl, cream butter, sugar and eggs and beat well. Stir in fruit. Add flour, baking powder, baking soda, vanilla and ¼ teaspoon salt and stir.

- Pour into 2 sprayed, floured loaf pans and bake for 50 to 55 minutes or until golden brown. Bread is done when toothpick inserted in center comes out clean. Serves 12 to 16.

# GINGER MUFFINS

¾ cup (1½ sticks) butter, softened
¾ cup sugar
¼ cup corn syrup
¼ cup sorghum molasses
2 eggs
1 teaspoon baking soda
½ cup buttermilk*
2 cups flour
1 teaspoon ground ginger
¼ teaspoon ground cinnamon
¼ cup raisins
½ cup chopped pecans

- Preheat oven to 350°. Combine butter, sugar, corn syrup and molasses in bowl and mix well. Add eggs and beat well.

- In separate bowl, combine baking soda into buttermilk, add to butter-sugar mixture and beat. Add flour, pinch of salt, ginger and cinnamon and beat. Stir in raisins and pecans and mix well.

- Pour into 20 to 24 sprayed muffin cups and bake for 16 to 18 minutes or more depending on size of muffins. Serves 20 to 24.

*TIP: To make buttermilk, mix 1 cup milk with 1 tablespoon lemon juice or vinegar and let stand for about 10 minutes.*

# TURKEY ON A MUFFIN

*4 slices Swiss cheese*
*2 English muffins, split, toasted*
*½ pound thinly sliced deli turkey*
*1 (15 ounce) can asparagus spears, well drained*
*1 (1 ounce) packet hollandaise sauce mix*

- Place cheese slice on each muffin half and top with turkey slices. Cut asparagus spears to fit muffin halves and top each sandwich with 3 or 4 asparagus spears. (Save remaining asparagus for another use.)

- Prepare hollandaise sauce according to package directions and pour generous amount over each open-face sandwich. Serve immediately. Serves 4.

# TURKEY-CRANBERRY CROISSANTS

*1 (8 ounce) package cream cheese, softened*
*½ cup orange marmalade*
*6 large croissants, split*
*Shredded lettuce*
*1 pound thinly sliced deli turkey*
*1 cup whole berry cranberry sauce*

- With mixer, beat cream cheese, orange marmalade and 1 tablespoon water. Spread small amount evenly on cut sides of croissants.

- Top with lettuce and slices of turkey. Place cranberry sauce in bowl and stir for easy spreading. Spread 2 or 3 tablespoons cranberries over turkey and place top of croissant over cranberry sauce. Serves 6.

# GUACAMOLE-HAM WRAP

*¾ cup prepared guacamole*
*4 (8 inch) spinach tortillas*
*¾ cup salsa*
*½ (8 ounce) package shredded 4-cheese blend*
*¾ pound deli ham, cut in thin strips*
*Shredded lettuce*

- Spread guacamole over half of each tortilla and layer salsa, cheese, ham strips and lettuce to within 2 inches of edges. Roll tightly. Refrigerate. Serves 4.

# CHICKEN-BACON SANDWICHES

*1 (12 ounce) can chicken breast, drained*
*⅓ cup mayonnaise*
*1 tablespoon dijon-style mustard*
*1 celery rib, finely chopped*
*3 tablespoons finely diced green onions*
*¼ cup cooked, crumbled bacon*
*Whole wheat bread*

- In medium bowl, combine chicken, mayonnaise, mustard, celery, green onions, bacon and a little salt and pepper in medium bowl.

- Spread chicken mixture on bread (crust removed) and top with shredded lettuce. Place second slice of bread on top and cut to make 4 little "bites". Serves 4 to 8.

# HOT BUNWICHES

*8 hamburger buns*
*8 slices Swiss cheese*
*8 slices deli ham*
*8 slices deli turkey*
*8 slices American cheese*

- Lay out all 8 buns and place slices of Swiss cheese, ham, turkey and American cheese on bottom buns.

- Place top bun over American cheese, wrap each bunwich individually in foil and place in freezer. Remove from freezer 2 to 3 hours before serving.

- When ready to heat, preheat oven to 325°. Heat for about 30 minutes and serve hot. Serves 8.

# PARTY SANDWICH STRIPS

*1 (4 ounce) package pre-cooked crumbled bacon*
*½ cup ripe olives, chopped*
*½ cup chopped pecans*
*1¼ cups mayonnaise*
*Thinly sliced bread*

- In bowl, combine bacon, olives, pecans, mayonnaise and a little salt and pepper. Spread mixture on bread and cut sandwiches into three strips. Serves 8 to 12.

*TIP: These ingredients can be spread on croissants and baked for 5 minutes at 350°.*

# SPINACH SANDWICHES

1 (10 ounce) package frozen chopped spinach, thawed, well drained
1 cup mayonnaise
1 (8 ounce) carton sour cream
½ cup finely minced onion
1 (1 ounce) packet vegetable soup mix
White bread

- Squeeze spinach between paper towels to completely remove excess moisture. Combine all ingredients in bowl except bread and mix well. (If you like, ¾ cup finely chopped pecans may be added.)
- Refrigerate for 3 to 4 hours before making sandwiches. To make sandwiches, spread on thin white bread. Serves 6 to 10.

# PARTY SANDWICHES

1 (8 ounce) package cream cheese, softened
⅓ cup chopped stuffed olives
2 tablespoons olive juice
⅓ cup chopped pecans
6 slices bacon, cooked, crumbled
Party rye bread

- Beat cream cheese in bowl until smooth. Add remaining ingredients. Spread on party rye bread. Serves 6.

# CUCUMBER SANDWICHES

1 (8 ounce) package cream cheese, softened
1 tablespoon mayonnaise
1 teaspoon lemon juice
1 (1 ounce) packet ranch dressing mix
⅛ teaspoon cayenne pepper
½ teaspoon garlic powder
1 tablespoon dry parsley flakes
2 cucumbers, peeled, grated, seeded
White sandwich bread

- Beat cream cheese, mayonnaise and lemon juice in bowl until creamy. Add dressing mix, ½ teaspoon salt, cayenne pepper, garlic powder and parsley flakes and mix well.
- Prepare cucumbers and combine all ingredients. Cut crusts off bread and spread sandwiches. Store in refrigerator. Serves 8 to 14.

# SALADS

## CREAMY FRUIT SALAD

*You'll get requests for this salad and it's so
easy. It looks really nice in a glass bowl.*

*1 (14 ounce) can sweetened condensed milk*
*¼ cup lemon juice*
*1 (20 ounce) can peach pie filling*
*1 (15 ounce) can pineapple chunks, drained*
*2 (15 ounce) cans fruit cocktail, drained*
*1 cup chopped pecans*
*1 (8 ounce) carton frozen whipped topping, thawed*

- In large bowl, combine condensed milk and lemon juice and stir well. Add pie filling, pineapple chunks, fruit cocktail and pecans and mix. Fold in whipped topping. Serves 12 to 14.

*TIP: You may substitute any pie filling.*

## FANTASTIC FRUIT SALAD

*If you try just one recipe from this cookbook, make
it this one. You'll make it over and over again.*

*2 (11 ounce) cans mandarin oranges*
*2 (15 ounce) cans pineapple chunks*
*1 (16 ounce) carton frozen strawberries, thawed*
*1 (20 ounce) can peach pie filling*
*1 (20 ounce) can apricot pie filling*

- Drain oranges, pineapple and strawberries. Combine all ingredients and fold together gently. (If you like, add 2 sliced bananas to salad.) Serves 8 to 10.

# PASTA TOSS WITH BALSAMIC DRESSING

*1 (8 ounce) package bow-tie pasta*
*2 cups diagonally sliced carrots*
*2 cups broccoli florets*
*1 red bell pepper, seeded, chopped*
*1 yellow bell pepper, seeded, chopped*
*2 cups cooked, cubed ham*

- Cook pasta according to package directions. Drain pasta and add 1 tablespoon olive oil and cool. Add carrots, broccoli, bell peppers and cubed ham.

## BALSAMIC DRESSING:

*¾ cup creamy Italian salad dressing*
*2 tablespoons balsamic vinegar*
*1 tablespoon sugar*
*½ teaspoon seasoned salt*
*½ teaspoon seasoned pepper*

- Combine dressing ingredients and pour over vegetables and toss. Refrigerate for several hours before serving. Serves 6 to 8.

# FUSILLI PASTA SALAD

*1 (16 ounce) package fusilli or corkscrew pasta*
*1 (16 ounce) package frozen broccoli-cauliflower combination*
*1 (8 ounce) package cubed mozzarella cheese*
*1 (8 ounce) bottle of Catalina salad dressing*

- Cook pasta according to package directions. Drain and cool. Cook vegetables in microwave according to package directions. Drain and cool.

- In large bowl, combine pasta, vegetables and cheese chunks. Toss with Catalina dressing. Refrigerate several hours before serving. Serves 6 to 8.

# TERRIFIC TORTELLINI SALAD

*2 (14 ounce) packages frozen cheese tortellini*
*1 green bell pepper, seeded, diced*
*1 red bell pepper, seeded, diced*
*1 cucumber, chopped*
*1 (14 ounce) can artichoke hearts, rinsed, drained*
*1 (8 ounce) bottle creamy Caesar salad dressing*

- Prepare tortellini according to package directions and drain. Rinse with cold water, drain and refrigerate.

- Combine tortellini, bell peppers, cucumber, artichoke hearts and dressing in large bowl. (You may want to add a little black pepper). Cover and refrigerate for at least 2 hours before serving. Serves 8 to 10.

# LEMON PASTA-PEA SALAD

*1 pound bow-tie pasta*
*1 (10 ounce) package frozen baby green peas, thawed*
*½ cup mayonnaise*
*2 tablespoons lemon juice*
*½ cup whipping cream*
*2 cups cubed ham*

- Cook pasta according to package directions. Add peas in last 2 minutes of cooking time. Drain pasta and peas, rinse in cold water and drain again. Transfer to large salad bowl.

- Combine mayonnaise with lemon juice, 1 teaspoon salt, a little pepper and stir in cream and cubed ham carefully in salad bowl.

- Fold mayonnaise mixture into pasta and peas and toss to coat well. Refrigerate several hours before serving. Serves 6 to 8.

*Pasta has been a very popular food from its beginning, but it was not served on the tables of the rich and famous because it was eaten with the hands. Then a member of the Spanish court of King Ferdinand II in the 1400's invented the fork especially for eating pasta and history was made.*

# MACARONI-VEGETABLE SALAD

*1 (16 ounce) package tri-colored macaroni*
*1 sweet red bell pepper, seeded, julienned*
*1 small zucchini, sliced*
*2 cups small broccoli florets*
*1 cup refrigerated Caesar salad dressing*

- Cook macaroni according to package directions and drain. Place in container with lid and add bell pepper, zucchini, broccoli and a little salt and pepper.

- Toss with salad dressing. Use more if needed to coat salad well. Cover and refrigerate several hours before serving. Serves 6 to 8.

# CALICO SALAD

*1 (15 ounce) can whole kernel white corn, drained*
*1 (15 ounce) can green peas, drained*
*1 (8 ounce) can whole green beans, drained*
*1 (15 ounce) can garbanzo beans, drained*
*1 cup chopped celery*
*1 red bell pepper, seeded, chopped*
*1 bunch fresh green onion with tops, sliced*

- Combine all vegetables in bowl with lid.

## DRESSING:

*½ cup sugar*
*½ cup wine vinegar*
*½ cup olive oil*
*½ teaspoon basil*

- In separate bowl, combine dressing ingredients with 1 teaspoon salt and ½ teaspoon pepper, mix thoroughly and pour over vegetables. Cover and refrigerate overnight. This will keep for several days in refrigerator. Serves 6 to 8.

*Pasta, whether macaroni, noodles, spaghetti or any of the fun shapes, is a great way to make leftovers into a fresh and economic meal. Adding bits of meat or tuna stretches macaroni and cheese.*

# LAYERED SPINACH SALAD

*This is a very pretty salad. Serving it in a large crystal bowl*
*about 10 inches in diameter will make this a spectacular dish.*

*1 (10 ounce) package fresh spinach, torn into pieces*
*1 cup sliced fresh mushrooms*
*1 bunch green onions with tops, chopped*
*1 (10 ounce) box frozen green peas, thawed*
*1½ cups shredded cheddar cheese*
*4 eggs, hard-boiled, grated*
*½ head cauliflower, chopped*
*1 cup shredded Monterey Jack cheese*

- Layer half spinach in bottom of large bowl, then place layer of mushrooms, green onions, peas and half cheddar cheese.

## DRESSING:

*1½ cups mayonnaise*
*1½ cups sour cream*
*2 teaspoons sugar, divided*

- For dressing, combine mayonnaise and sour cream in bowl and spread half over top of cheese. Sprinkle with 1 teaspoon sugar, a little salt and lots of pepper.

- Next layer remaining spinach, eggs, cauliflower and remaining cheddar cheese. Spread remaining dressing on top.

- Sprinkle 1 teaspoon sugar, a little salt and pepper over salad. Top with Monterey Jack cheese. Cover and refrigerate overnight. Serves 6 to 8.

# BROCCOLI SALAD

*5 cups broccoli florets, stemmed*
*1 sweet red bell pepper, julienned*
*1 cup chopped celery*
*8 - 12 ounces Monterey Jack cheese, cubed*

- Combine all ingredients and mix well. Toss with Italian or favorite dressing. Refrigerate. Serves 6 to 8.

# Wonderful Broccoli Salad

*1 large bunch fresh broccoli*
*½ purple onion, sliced, separated*
*½ cup golden raisins*
*½ cup slivered almonds, toasted*
*½ cup chopped celery*

- Wash broccoli ahead of time and drain well on paper towels. (The broccoli needs to be well drained.) Cut into small bite-size florets.
- Combine broccoli, onion, raisins, almonds and celery in bowl and mix well. (The sliced, separated onion looks better, but chopped onion is easier to eat.)

## Dressing:

*1 cup mayonnaise*
*¼ cup sugar*
*2 tablespoons vinegar*
*Bacon bits*

- Combine dressing ingredients with 1 teaspoon salt and ½ teaspoon pepper in bowl. Spoon over broccoli mixture and toss. Refrigerate for several hours before serving.
- Sprinkle bacon bits over salad just before serving. Serves 6.

*TIP: You can make this salad a day ahead. Remarkably the broccoli stays crisp for several days, but I wouldn't keep it longer than 2 or 3 days.*

# Broccoli-Cauliflower Salad

*1 small head cauliflower*
*3 stalks broccoli*
*1 cup mayonnaise*
*1 tablespoon vinegar*
*1 tablespoon sugar*
*1 bunch fresh green onions with tops, chopped*
*8 ounces mozzarella cheese, cubed*

- Cut up cauliflower and broccoli into bite-size florets in bowl. In separate bowl, combine mayonnaise, vinegar and sugar.
- Combine cauliflower, broccoli, mayonnaise mixture, onions and cheese. (Add a little salt, if you like.) Toss and refrigerate. Serves 10.

# BROCCOLI-NOODLE CRUNCH SALAD

*People are intrigued with this salad. It is delicious and it will last in the refrigerator for several days.*

1 cup slivered almonds, toasted
1 cup sunflower seeds, toasted
2 (3 ounce) packages chicken-flavored ramen noodles
1 (12 ounce) package broccoli slaw

- Preheat oven to 275°.
- Toast almonds and sunflower seeds in baking pan in oven for 15 minutes. Break up ramen noodles (but do not cook) and mix with slaw, almonds and sunflower seeds.

## DRESSING:

¾ cup oil
½ cup white vinegar
½ cup sugar
Ramen noodles seasoning packet

- In separate bowl, combine dressing ingredients and noodle seasoning packet. Pour over slaw mixture and mix well. Prepare at least 1 hour before serving. Serves 6 to 8.

# CALYPSO COLESLAW

1 (16 ounce) package shredded cabbage
1 bunch green onions with tops, sliced
2 cups cubed cheddar or mozzarella cheese
¼ cup sliced ripe olives
1 (15 ounce) can whole kernel corn with peppers, drained

- Combine all slaw ingredients and add a few sprinkles of salt.

## DRESSING:

1 cup mayonnaise
2 tablespoons sugar
1 tablespoon prepared mustard
2 tablespoons vinegar

- Combine dressing ingredients and mix well. Add dressing to slaw, toss, cover and refrigerate. Serves 6 to 8.

# CRUNCHY CHINESE SLAW

*This recipe is so good and it will go with just about any main dish.*

1 cup slivered almonds
1 cup sunflower seeds
2 (16 ounce) packages shredded slaw mix
1 bunch green onions, sliced
1 red bell pepper, seeded, finely diced
1 cup sliced celery
1 (11 ounce) can mandarin oranges, drained
2 (3 ounce) packages chicken-flavored ramen noodles, crumbled

- Preheat oven to 275°.

- Toast slivered almonds and sunflower seeds on baking sheet for about 12 minutes. Combine slaw mix, almonds, sunflower seeds, green onions, bell pepper, celery, oranges and ramen noodles in bowl and mix well.

## DRESSING:

1 cup olive oil
¾ cup white vinegar
¾ cup sugar
2 dashes hot sauce
Ramen noodles' seasoning packet

- Combine oil, vinegar, sugar, hot sauce, seasoning packet and 2 teaspoons salt and 1 teaspoon pepper in pint jar with lid and mix well. Pour over slaw ingredients and toss well. Refrigerate at least 1 hour. Serves 16 to 18.

*TIP: This slaw can be made ahead of time and it will keep in the refrigerator for several days.*

# CARROT SALAD

3 cups finely grated carrots
1 (8 ounce) can crushed pineapple, drained
¼ cup shredded coconut
1 tablespoon sugar
⅓ cup mayonnaise

- Combine all ingredients and toss well. Refrigerate. Serves 6.

# MARINATED CUCUMBERS

*⅓ cup vinegar*
*2 tablespoons sugar*
*1 teaspoon dried dill weed*
*3 cucumbers, peeled, sliced*

- Combine vinegar, sugar, 1 teaspoon salt, dill weed and ¼ teaspoon pepper. Pour over cucumbers. Refrigerate 1 hour before serving. Serves 8.

# CUCUMBER SALAD

*1 (3 ounce) package lime gelatin*
*2 medium cucumbers*
*1 tablespoon minced onion*
*½ cup mayonnaise*
*½ cup sour cream*

- Dissolve gelatin in ¾ cup boiling water and mix well. Bring to room temperature.

- Slice cucumber in half and remove seeds. Grate cucumber and add to cool gelatin with onion, mayonnaise and sour cream. Pour into serving dish. Refrigerate until set. Serves 6 to 8.

# MARINATED CORN SALAD

*3 (15 ounce) cans whole kernel corn, drained*
*1 red bell pepper, chopped*
*1 cup chopped walnuts*
*¾ cup chopped celery*
*1 (8 ounce) bottle Italian salad dressing*

- In bowl with lid, combine corn, bell pepper, walnuts and celery. (For a special little zip, add several dashes hot sauce.)

- Pour salad dressing over vegetables and refrigerate several hours before serving. Serves 10 to 12.

# Winter Salad

*It's good to keep these ingredients on hand because it's so quick and easy to put together. If you don't have an ingredient, just leave it out. No one will notice!*

1 (16 ounce) can French-style green beans, drained
1 (16 ounce) can jalapeno black-eyed peas, drained
1 (16 ounce) can shoe-peg white corn, drained
1 (2 ounce) jar chopped pimentos, drained
1 bell pepper, chopped
1 onion, sliced, broken into rings

- In 3-quart container with lid, combine all salad ingredients plus 2 teaspoons salt and 1 teaspoon pepper and gently mix. (Be sure to drain vegetables well before combining.)

## Dressing:

¾ cup sugar
½ teaspoon garlic powder
½ cup oil
¾ cup vinegar

- To prepare dressing, combine all dressing ingredients and mix well. Pour mixture over vegetables and stir. Cover and refrigerate. Serves 14 to 16.

# Zesty Bean Salad

1 (15 ounce) can kidney beans
1 (15 ounce) can pinto beans
1 (16 ounce) package frozen whole kernel corn, thawed, drained
1 red onion, chopped
1 bell pepper, seeded, chopped
1 (7 ounce) can chopped green chilies
2 cups cubed deli ham

- Rinse and drain kidney beans and pinto beans; place in salad bowl. Add corn, onion, bell pepper, green chilies, cubed ham and mix well.

## Dressing:

1 (8 ounce) bottle cheddar-parmesan ranch dressing
2 tablespoons lemon juice

- Pour ranch dressing into small bowl and stir in lemon juice. Pour over salad and toss. Refrigerate several hours before serving for flavors to blend. Serves 8 to 10.

# BLACK-EYED PEA SALAD

2 (15 ounce) cans jalapeno black-eyed peas, drained
1 purple onion, chopped
1 cup chopped celery
1 red bell pepper, seeded, chopped
1 green bell pepper, seeded, chopped

- Mix all salad ingredients in large bowl.

## DRESSING:

⅓ cup olive oil
⅓ cup white vinegar
3 tablespoons sugar
¼ teaspoon garlic powder

- In separate bowl, combine dressing ingredients with ½ teaspoon salt and mix well. Add dressing to vegetables and toss. Cover and refrigerate. Serves 6.

# COLORFUL ENGLISH PEA SALAD

2 (16 ounce) packages frozen green peas, thawed, drained
1 (8 ounce) package cubed mozzarella cheese
1 red and 1 orange bell pepper, seeded, chopped
1 small purple onion, cut in rings
2 eggs, hard-boiled, chopped
1¼ cups mayonnaise

- In large salad bowl, combine uncooked peas, cheese, bell peppers, onion rings and chopped eggs. Stir in mayonnaise and 1 teaspoon each of salt and pepper. Refrigerate and when ready to serve. Serves 8 to 10.

# GREEN AND WHITE SALAD

1 (16 ounce) package frozen green peas, thawed
1 head cauliflower, cut into bite-size pieces
1 (8 ounce) carton sour cream
1 (1 ounce) package dry ranch-style salad dressing

- In large bowl, combine peas and cauliflower. Combine sour cream and salad dressing. Toss with vegetables. Refrigerate. Serves 6 to 8.

# WARM GERMAN POTATO SALAD

8 slices bacon
1 - 2 pounds red potatoes
1 teaspoon flour
¼ cup cider vinegar
1½ - 2 tablespoons sugar
⅓ cup chopped celery
⅓ cup chopped onion
1 - 2 eggs, hard-boiled

- Cook bacon in skillet, crumble and set aside. Save bacon drippings. Gently cook potatoes in boiling water in saucepan until just tender. Drain and set aside.

- Return ¼ cup bacon drippings to skillet over low heat, add flour and stir until flour dissolves. Add vinegar and ¼ cup water, stir constantly and simmer for about 1 minute or until it thickens. Turn heat off and add sugar and stir until it dissolves.

- When potatoes are just cool enough to handle, slice one-half into large baking dish and add one-half each of celery, onion and bacon.

- Sprinkle lightly with a little salt and pepper and drizzle several spoonfuls of dressing over top. Repeat this process 1 more time, but set aside 2 spoonfuls of dressing. Slice eggs over top and drizzle remaining dressing over eggs. Serve warm. Serves 4 to 6.

# MEDITERRANEAN POTATO SALAD

2 pounds red new potatoes, quartered
¾ - 1 cup Caesar dressing
½ cup grated parmesan cheese
¼ cup chopped fresh parsley
½ cup chopped roasted red peppers

- Cook potatoes in boiling water until fork-tender, drain and place in large bowl. Pour dressing over potatoes, add cheese, parsley and peppers and toss lightly. Serve warm or chilled. Serves 12 to 14.

*An excellent health tip: Read More Books Than You Did Last Year.*

# SOUR CREAM POTATO SALAD

12 medium red potatoes with peel
¼ cup vinegar
4 eggs, hard-boiled
2 cups sour cream
2 tablespoons mustard
1 clove garlic, minced
1 small onion, diced

- Boil red potatoes until tender about 20 minutes. Cube potatoes and refrigerate. Combine vinegar, eggs, sour cream and mustard.
- Add garlic, onion, and 1 to 2 teaspoons each of salt and pepper. When potatoes are cool, toss with sour cream mixture. Serves 4 to 6.

# BARBECUED CHICKEN SALAD

*Here's a quickie with that "it-takes-a-long-time" flavor.*

¾ cup ranch dressing
3 tablespoons barbecue sauce
2 tablespoons salsa
3 grilled boneless, skinless chicken breast halves
1 (9 ounce) package romaine lettuce
1 (15 ounce) can seasoned black beans, rinsed, drained
12-15 cherry tomatoes

- Combine ranch dressing, barbecue sauce and salsa and refrigerate.
- Cut grilled chicken breasts in strips and place in oven just enough to warm thoroughly. Place chicken strips, cut-up romaine, black beans and cherry tomatoes in large bowl. Toss with enough dressing to lightly coat. Serves 4 to 6.

TIP: *The next time you grill, just grill some extra chicken breasts and freeze them to use for this dish. Or, if you don't have time to grill chicken, just use deli smoked turkey.*

# CAESAR SALAD WITH CHICKEN

2 - 3 boneless, skinless chicken breast halves, grilled
1 (10 ounce) package romaine salad greens
½ cup shredded parmesan cheese
1 cup seasoned croutons
¾ cup Caesar salad dressing

- Cut chicken breasts into strips. Combine chicken, salad greens, cheese and croutons in large bowl. When ready to serve, toss with Caesar or Italian salad dressing. Serves 4 to 6.

# BLACK BEAN CHICKEN SALAD

*3 - 4 boneless, skinless chicken breast halves, cooked, cubed*
*1 (15 ounce) can black beans, drained*
*1 bunch green onions, chopped*
*1 cup chopped celery*

- Combine chicken, black beans, onions and celery.

## CUMIN-VINAIGRETTE DRESSING:

*¾ cup virgin olive oil*
*¼ cup lemon juice*
*2 teaspoons dijon-style mustard*
*2 teaspoons ground cumin*

- Combine all dressing ingredients and mix well. Pour dressing over black bean-chicken salad, toss and refrigerate. Serves 8.

# CHICKEN-GRAPEFRUIT SALAD SUPPER

*1 (10 ounce) package romaine salad mix*
*1 (24 ounce) jar grapefruit sections, well-drained*
*1 rotisserie chicken, boned, cubed*
*½ red onion, sliced*

- Combine salad mix, grapefruit sections, chicken and onion in salad bowl.

## DRESSING:

*2 tablespoons orange juice*
*2 tablespoons white wine vinegar*
*2 tablespoons extra-virgin olive oil*
*1 teaspoon seasoned salt and pepper*

- In small bowl, combine all dressing ingredients, pour over salad and toss. Serves 6 to 8.

# HAWAIIAN CHICKEN SALAD

*3 cups cooked, diced chicken breasts*
*1 (20 ounce) can pineapple tidbits, well-drained*
*1 cup halved red grapes*
*1 cup chopped celery*
*1 large banana*
*½ cup salted peanuts*

- Combine diced chicken, pineapple, grapes and celery and toss. Cover and refrigerate.

## DRESSING:

*¾ cup mayonnaise*
*½ cup poppy seed dressing*

- Combine mayonnaise, poppy seed dressing and a sprinkle of salt for dressing. When ready to serve, slice bananas and add to salad. Top with mayonnaise-poppy seed dressing and toss. Just before serving, sprinkle peanuts over top of salad. Serves 6 to 8.

# HERBED CHICKEN SALAD

*1 rotisserie-cooked chicken*
*¼ cup chopped fresh chives*
*2 tablespoons capers*
*1 cup chopped celery*
*1 cup chopped sweet pickles*

- Skin chicken and cut meat from bones. Slice chicken in thin strips and place in bowl. Add fresh chives, capers, celery and sweet pickles and mix well.

## DRESSING:

*¼ cup extra-virgin olive oil*
*3 tablespoons white wine vinegar*
*1 teaspoon chopped fresh thyme*
*1 teaspoon oregano*
*1 tablespoon honey*

- Whisk olive oil, vinegar, thyme, oregano, honey and a little salt and pepper to taste in bowl. Spoon over chicken salad and toss. Refrigerate. Serves 6 to 8.

# MEXICAN CHICKEN SALAD

*3 - 4 boneless, skinless chicken breast halves, cooked, cubed*
*1 (15 ounce) can chick-peas, drained*
*1 red and 1 green bell peppers, seeded, diced*
*1 cup chopped celery*

- Combine all ingredients and serve with dressing below.

## DRESSING :

*1½ cups sour cream*
*2 tablespoons chili sauce*
*2 teaspoons ground cumin*
*1 small bunch cilantro, minced*

- Combine all ingredients for dressing and add a little salt and pepper. Pour over chicken salad and toss. Refrigerate before serving. Serves 6 to 8.

# APPLE-WALNUT CHICKEN SALAD

*3 - 4 boneless, skinless chicken breast halves, cooked, cubed*
*2 tart green apples, peeled, chopped*
*½ cup chopped pitted dates*
*1 cup finely chopped celery*
*½ cup chopped, toasted walnuts*

- Combine chicken, apples, dates and celery. Toast walnuts at 300° for 10 minutes. Cool and add to chicken.

## DRESSING:

*⅓ cup sour cream*
*⅓ cup mayonnaise*
*1 tablespoon lemon juice*

- Combine sour cream, mayonnaise and lemon juice and mix well. Add in walnuts. Pour dressing over chicken salad, toss and refrigerate. Serves 6 to 8.

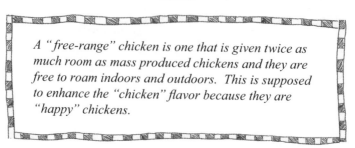

A "free-range" chicken is one that is given twice as much room as mass produced chickens and they are free to roam indoors and outdoors. This is supposed to enhance the "chicken" flavor because they are "happy" chickens.

# SIMPLE CHICKEN SALAD

*3 cups chicken breast halves, cooked, finely chopped*
*1½ cups chopped celery*
*½ cup sweet pickle relish*
*2 hard-boiled eggs, chopped*
*¾ cup mayonnaise*

- Combine all ingredients and several sprinkles of salt and pepper.  Serves 6 to 8.

*TIP:  Adding ½ cup chopped pecans gives the chicken salad a special taste.*

# FAVORITE CHICKEN SALAD WITH GRAPES AND WALNUTS

*1 rotisserie-cooked chicken*
*1 cup red grapes, halved*
*1 cup green grapes, halved*
*2 cups chopped celery*
*⅔ cup whole walnuts*
*⅔ cup sliced fresh onion*

- Skin chicken and cut chicken breast in thin strips.  (Save dark meat for another meal or use frozen, grilled chicken breasts.)  Place in bowl with lid.  Add red and green grapes, celery, walnuts and sliced onions.

## DRESSING:

*½ cup mayonnaise*
*1 tablespoon orange juice*
*2 tablespoons red wine vinegar*
*1 teaspoon chili powder*

- Combine all dressing ingredients, add a little salt and pepper to taste and mix well. Spoon over salad mixture and toss.  Refrigerate.  Serves 8 to 10.

*The next best thing to your own garden is the farmer's market.  Find one near you and look for farms and markets where you can pick your own produce.  Not only will kids like picking their own foods, but you'll save money and improve the quality of foods you put on the table.*

# STRAWBERRY-CHICKEN SALAD

*1 pound boneless, skinless chicken breast halves*
*1 (10 ounce) package spring greens mix*
*1 pint fresh strawberries, sliced*
*½ cup chopped walnuts*

- Cut chicken into strips and place in large skillet with a little oil. Cook on medium to high heat for about 10 minutes and stir occasionally.

## DRESSING:

*¾ cup honey*
*⅔ cup red wine vinegar*
*1 tablespoon soy sauce*
*½ teaspoon ground ginger*

- While chicken cooks, combine all dressing ingredients and mix well. After chicken strips cook for 10 minutes, pour ½ cup dressing into skillet with chicken and cook 2 minutes longer or until liquid evaporates and chicken cooks.
- In salad bowl, combine spring greens mix, strawberries and walnuts, pour on remaining dressing and toss. Top with chicken strips. Serves 4 to 6.

# TARRAGON-CHICKEN SALAD

*1 cup chopped pecans*
*3 - 4 boneless, skinless chicken breast halves, cooked, cubed*
*1 cup chopped celery*
*¾ cup peeled, chopped cucumber*

- Place pecans in shallow pan and toast at 300° for 10 minutes. Combine chicken, celery and cucumbers.

## DRESSING:

*⅔ cup mayonnaise*
*1 tablespoon lemon juice*
*2 tablespoons tarragon vinegar*
*1¼ teaspoons crumbled, dried tarragon*

- Combine all dressing ingredients and mix well. When ready to serve, toss with chicken mixture and add pecans. Serves 6 to 8.

# SOUTHWESTERN CHICKEN SALAD

4 cups cubed, cooked chicken breasts
1 (16 ounce) can black beans, drained
¾ red onion, chopped
¼ cup chopped fresh cilantro
½ cup sour cream
¼ cup mayonnaise
½ teaspoon garlic powder
1 teaspoon lime juice

- Combine chicken, beans, onion and cilantro in large bowl. Whisk sour cream and mayonnaise in small bowl.
- Stir in garlic powder and lime juice and add to chicken. Add a little salt and pepper to taste and toss. Refrigerate at least 1 hour, just before serving. Serve on bed of lettuce. Serves 8.

# CASHEW-CHICKEN SALAD

3 cups cooked, cubed chicken
1 cup chopped celery
1½ cups halved green grapes
¾ cup cashews
¾ cup mayonnaise
1 cup chow mein noodles

- Combine chicken, celery, grapes and cashews and toss with mayonnaise. Just before serving, mix in noodles and serve on cabbage leaf. Serves 4.

*TIP: Turkey is great for this salad as well.*

# CHICKEN OR TURKEY SALAD WITH RICE

3 cups cooked, cubed chicken or turkey
1 (6 ounce) box long-grain, wild rice, cooked, drained
1 bunch fresh green onions with tops, chopped
1 cup chopped walnuts
1 (8 ounce) can sliced water chestnuts
1 cup mayonnaise
¾ teaspoon curry powder

- Combine chicken, rice, onions, walnuts and water chestnuts. Toss with mayonnaise and curry powder and refrigerate. Serve on bed of lettuce. Serves 4.

# CHICKEN OR TURKEY SALAD

*3 cups cooked, cubed chicken or turkey*
*⅔ cup chopped celery*
*¾ cup sweet pickle relish*
*1 bunch fresh green onions with tops, chopped*
*3 hard-boiled eggs, chopped*
*¾ cup mayonnaise*

- Combine chicken, celery, relish, onions and eggs. Toss with mayonnaise and refrigerate. Serve on lettuce leaf. Serves 4.

# SPINACH-TURKEY SALAD SUPPER

*2 (8 ounce) packages baby spinach*
*⅓ cup chopped walnuts*
*⅓ cup Craisins®*
*2 red delicious apples with peel, sliced*
*¾ pound deli smoked turkey*
*½ cup honey-mustard salad dressing*

- In large salad bowl, combine spinach, walnuts, Craisins®, apples and turkey. Toss with dressing. Serves 6 to 8.

# CREAMY TURKEY SALAD

*2 (10 ounce) packages chopped romaine lettuce*
*2½ - 3 cups cooked, sliced turkey*
*1 (8 ounce) jar baby corn, quartered, drained*
*2 tomatoes, chopped*
*1 (8 ounce) package shredded colby cheese*

- In large salad bowl, combine romaine lettuce, turkey, baby corn, tomatoes and cheese.

## DRESSING:

*⅔ cup mayonnaise*
*⅔ cup prepared salsa*
*¼ cup cider vinegar*
*2 tablespoons sugar*

- Combine all dressing ingredients in bowl and mix well. When ready to serve, sprinkle on a little salt and pepper, pour dressing over salad and toss to coat well. Serves 8 to 10.

*TIP: If you want to make this leftover dish an even "bigger and better" salad, just add some ripe olives, red onion, black beans or cooked bacon bits.*

# TURKEY-NOODLE SALAD

*1 (3 ounce) package oriental-flavor ramen noodle soup mix*
*1 (16 ounce) package finely shredded coleslaw mix*
*¾ pound deli smoked turkey, cut into strips*
*½ cup vinaigrette salad dressing*

- Coarsely crush noodles and place in bowl with lid. Add coleslaw mix and turkey strips.
- Combine vinaigrette salad dressing and seasoning packet from noodle mix in small bowl. Pour over noodle-turkey mixture and toss to coat mixture well. Refrigerate. Serves 6 to 8.

# FIESTA HOLIDAY SALAD

*This is great for leftover holiday turkey!*

*1 (10 ounce) package torn romaine lettuce*
*3 cups diced smoked turkey*
*1 (15 ounce) can black beans, rinsed, drained*
*2 tomatoes, quartered, drained*

- Combine lettuce, turkey, beans and tomatoes in large salad bowl.

## DRESSING:

*⅔ cup mayonnaise*
*¾ cup chunky salsa*

- When ready to serve, combine mayonnaise and salsa. Spoon dressing over salad and toss. Serves 6 to 8.

*TIP: If you want a little something extra, you might sprinkle crumbed bacon over top of salad or add sliced purple onion.*

> *The first Thanksgiving was held at Plymouth Colony located on Cape Cod in Massachusetts in 1621. George Washington declared a one-time national holiday to give thanks in 1789, but Thanksgiving Day did not become a permanent national holiday until 1863 under Abraham Lincoln.*

# Gourmet Couscous Salad

1 (10 ounce) box chicken-flavored couscous
2 tomatoes, coarsely chopped
2 zucchini, coarsely chopped
4 fresh green onions, sliced
1 cup cubed deli turkey
1 cup crumbled feta cheese

- Cook couscous according to package directions, but do not use butter. In salad bowl combine tomatoes, zucchini, green onions, cubed turkey and couscous.

## Dressing:

1 tablespoon lemon juice
¼ cup olive oil
½ teaspoon dried basil
½ teaspoon seasoned black pepper

- Combine dressing ingredients in pint jar with lid and shake until they blend well. When ready to serve, add feta cheese, pour dressing over salad, toss and refrigerate. Serves 6 to 8.

# Mixed Greens Toss

1 (10 ounce) package mixed salad greens
1½ cups halved cherry tomatoes
1 cucumber, sliced
1 red onion, sliced in rings
1 pound seasoned, cooked chicken breasts, cut into strips
Italian salad dressing
Seasoned black pepper
¼ teaspoon cayenne pepper

- Combine greens, tomatoes, cucumber and onion rings in large salad bowl and toss. Top with strips of chicken.
- When ready to serve, toss with salad dressing and sprinkle with seasoned black pepper and cayenne pepper. Serves 6 to 8.

# ROAST BEEF AND BEAN SALAD

*¾ pound deli roast beef, cut in strips*
*2 (15 ounce) can kidney beans, rinsed, drained*
*1 cup chopped onion*
*1 cup chopped celery*
*3 hard-boiled eggs, chopped*

• Combine beef strips, beans, onion, celery and chopped eggs in salad bowl.

## DRESSING:

*⅓ cup mayonnaise*
*⅓ cup chipotle mayonnaise*
*¼ cup ketchup*
*¼ cup sweet pickle relish*
*2 tablespoons olive oil*

• In small bowl, combine mayonnaise, chipotle mayonnaise, ketchup, pickle relish and oil and mix well. Spoon over beef-bean mixture and toss.

• Refrigerate several hours before serving. Serves 6 to 8.

*TIP: Rather than serving in salad bowl, shred lettuce on serving plate and serve beef-bean salad over lettuce.*

# SUPER SUMMER SALAD SUPREME

*⅓ pound cooked deli roast beef*
*1 (15 ounce) can 3-bean salad, chilled, drained*
*1 (8 ounce) package mozzarella cheese, cubed*
*1 (10 ounce) bag mixed salad greens with Italian dressing*

• In large salad bowl, lightly toss beef, 3-bean salad, cheese and greens. Pour in just enough salad dressing to moisten greens. Serves 4.

*TIP: Substitute turkey or ham for beef and Swiss cheese for mozzarella for completely different salads.*

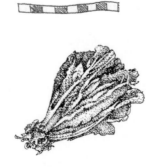

# COLORFUL VEGGIE SALAD

*4 cups fresh broccoli florets*
*4 cups fresh cauliflower florets*
*1 red onion, sliced*
*1 (4 ounce) can sliced ripe olives*
*3 small zucchini, sliced*
*2 cups chopped ham*

- In large bowl, combine broccoli, cauliflower, onion, olives, zucchini, chopped ham and toss.

## DRESSING:

*1 envelope zesty Italian dry dressing mix*
*1½ cups bottled zesty Italian salad dressing*
*2 tablespoons extra-virgin olive oil*

- In small bowl, combine dry dressing mix, bottled dressing and olive oil and mix well.
- Pour over vegetables and toss to coat. Refrigerate several hours before serving or make 1 day in advance. Serves 4.

# HONEY HAM SALAD

*3 cups cooked, chopped ham*
*¾ cup chopped celery*
*1 cup small-curd cottage cheese, drained*
*1 cup chopped cauliflower florets*
*1 cup chopped broccoli florets*
*Honey-mustard salad dressing*

- Combine ham, celery, cottage cheese, cauliflower and broccoli; toss with salad dressing and refrigerate. Serve on lettuce leaves. Serves 4 to 6.

# SUMMERTIME HAM SALAD

*3 cups cooked, chopped ham*
*1 bunch fresh green onions with tops, chopped*
*½ cup slivered almonds, toasted*
*½ cup sunflower seeds*
*2 cups chopped fresh broccoli florets*
*¾ cup mayonnaise*

- Combine chopped ham, green onions, almonds, sunflower seeds and broccoli florets; toss with mayonnaise and refrigerate. Serve on lettuce leaf. Serves 4.

# PORK TENDERLOIN SALAD

1 (10 ounce) package fresh green salad mix
2 cups halved, seedless green grapes
1 cup fresh strawberries
1 cup refrigerated red grapefruit sections with juice, drained but set aside juice
½ - ¾ pound cooked pork tenderloin, thinly sliced, chilled

- Toss salad mix, green grapes, strawberries and grapefruit sections in salad bowl. Arrange salad on individual plates and place tenderloin slices over top.

## DRESSING:

¼ cup juice from grapefruit sections
2 tablespoons red wine vinegar
2 tablespoons oil
1 teaspoon poppy seeds
2 teaspoons honey

- Mix all dressing ingredients well and pour dressing over top of salads. Serves 6.

# SPINACH-VEGGIE TOSS WITH HAM

2 (8 ounce) packages baby spinach, stems removed
1 small head cauliflower, cut into small florets
1 sweet red bell pepper, cut in strips
¾ cup chopped walnuts
½ cup roasted sunflower seeds
2 cups chopped ham
Berry vinaigrette dressing

- In large salad bowl, combine spinach, cauliflower, bell pepper strips, walnuts, chopped ham, sunflower seeds and a generous amount of salt.
- Toss with strawberry or raspberry vinaigrette salad dressing. Serves 8 to 10.

*Cut loss; don't toss. Bits of leftovers can easily go into soups, stews, stir-fry, sandwiches, etc., later in the week.*

# VEGETABLE SALAD

1 head cauliflower
1 head broccoli
1 (10 ounce) package frozen green peas, thawed
2 ribs celery, diagonally sliced
1 bunch fresh green onions, sliced
2 cups cubed deli ham

- Wash and drain cauliflower and broccoli and break into florets.  Place in large mixing bowl.  Add peas, celery, green onions, cubed ham and toss.

## DRESSING:

2 cups mayonnaise
¼ cup sugar
1 tablespoon white vinegar
1 cup shredded mozzarella cheese

- Combine all dressing ingredients and pour over vegetables and toss.  Refrigerate for several hours before serving.  Serves 6 to 8.

# TUNA-SPAGHETTI SALAD

1 (7 ounce) package spaghetti
¼ cup (½ stick) butter
1 (12 ounce) can tuna, drained
1 (4 ounce) can sliced ripe olives

- Cook spaghetti according to package directions and drain.  Add butter and stir until butter melts.  Add tuna and olives.

## DRESSING:

¾ cup whipping cream
1 teaspoon dried basil leaves
2 tablespoons parmesan cheese
1 teaspoon seasoned salt

- Combine whipping cream, basil, cheese and seasoned salt for dressing.  Pour over spaghetti-tuna mixture and toss.  Serves 6 to 8.

## WACKY TUNA SALAD

*1 (7 ounce) package cooked, light tuna in water*
*1 red apple with peel, cored, chopped*
*1 (10 ounce) package frozen green peas, thawed, drained*
*1 red bell pepper, chopped*

- Place tuna in bowl, add chopped apple, green peas and bell pepper and mix well.

### DRESSING:

*½ (8 ounce) bottle sweet honey Catalina salad dressing*
*½ cup mayonnaise*

- Combine dressing and mayonnaise, pour over tuna salad and stir to blend well. Refrigerate at least 2 hours and serve over bed of shredded lettuce. Serves 4 to 6.

## READY SHRIMP SALAD

*1 (14 ounce) package frozen, cooked tortellini, thawed*
*1 pound cooked, peeled, veined shrimp*
*½ cup sliced ripe olives*
*½ cup chopped celery*
*½ cup zesty Italian salad dressing*

- Combine tortellini, shrimp, olives and celery in salad bowl. Pour salad dressing over salad and toss. Serve immediately or refrigerate until ready to serve. Serves 4.

# SOUPS & STEWS

## POTATO-BACON SOUP

*2 (14 ounce) cans chicken broth seasoned with garlic*
*2 potatoes, peeled, cubed*
*1 onion, finely chopped*
*6 slices bacon, cooked, crumbled*

- In large saucepan, combine broth, potatoes and onion. Bring to a boil, reduce heat to medium-high and cook about 10 minutes or until potatoes are tender.
- Season with pepper. Ladle into bowls and sprinkle with crumbled bacon. Serves 6 to 8.

# CHEESY CORN CHOWDER

2 baking potatoes, peeled, diced
½ cup shredded carrots
½ cup finely chopped onion
1 (15 ounce) can cream-style corn
1 (8 ounce) can whole kernel corn, drained
1 (10 ounce) can cream of celery soup
1 cup milk
1 (8 ounce) package cubed Velveeta® cheese

- Cook potatoes, carrots and onion in 1½ cups water in large saucepan for about 15 minutes or until potatoes are tender; do not drain.

- Stir in cream-style corn, whole kernel corn, soup, milk and a little salt and pepper. Heat and stir constantly until mixture is thoroughly hot; stir in cheese and serve when cheese melts. Serves 6.

# CREAM OF ZUCCHINI SOUP

1 small onion, finely chopped
2 tablespoons butter
3½ cups grated zucchini with peel
1 (14 ounce) can chicken broth
1 teaspoon seasoned salt
1 teaspoon dill weed
½ teaspoon white pepper
1 (8 ounce) carton sour cream

- Saute onion in butter in soup pot until onion cooks lightly but not brown. Add zucchini, broth, seasoned salt, dill weed and white pepper to onion. Bring to a boil, reduce heat and simmer for 15 minutes.

- Stir in sour cream, mix well and bring to a boiling point, but do not boil. Remove from heat and serve. Serves 4 to 8.

*When your family is hungry and the budget is tight, few dishes are so satisfying as a hearty soup or stew.*

# ASPARAGUS SOUP

¼ cup (½ stick) butter
3 (14 ounce) cans chicken broth
¾ teaspoon garlic powder
1 bunch green onions with tops, diced
1 large potato, cut in small chunks
½ (8 ounce) carton cubed Velveeta® cheese
1 (15 ounce) can extra long asparagus spears
1 (8 ounce) carton sour cream
Bacon bits

- Combine butter, broth, garlic powder, green onions and potato in large soup pot. Heat and cook for 15 minutes or until potatoes are tender. Add cheese and heat long enough for cheese to melt.

- Cut asparagus spears into 1 inch lengths and add to soup. Fold in sour cream and heat (do not boil) just enough to make soup hot. Sprinkle bacon bits over top of soup before serving. Serves 6 to 8.

*TIP:  This may be made day before.  If you want a spicy soup, use mild Mexican Velveeta® instead of original Velveeta®.*

# CHEESE SOUP SUPREME

*This recipe is a great one.*

½ cup(1 stick) butter
½ cup shredded carrots
⅓ cup flour
¼ cup minced onion
1 teaspoon instant chicken bouillon
¼ teaspoon dry mustard
3 cups milk
2 cups shredded processed American cheese
¼ cup beer

- Melt butter in large saucepan. Add carrots and sauté; pour in flour, onion, instant chicken bouillon, dry mustard and a little salt and pepper. Remove from heat, stir well and slowly add milk, stirring constantly.

- Return to medium heat, add cheese and stir constantly. Bring to a soft boil for 1 minute, stirring constantly. (Do not burn.) Reduce heat to simmer and after it stops boiling, add beer. Cook for about 5 minutes and serve immediately. Serves 4.

# CHEESY POTATO SOUP

1 (16 ounce) package frozen hash-brown potatoes
1 cup chopped onion
1 (14 ounce) can chicken broth
1 (10 ounce) can fiesta nacho cheese soup
1 (10 ounce) can cream of chicken soup
2 cups milk

- Combine potatoes, onion and 2 cups water in large saucepan and bring to a boil. Cover, reduce heat and simmer for 30 minutes. Stir in broth, soups and milk and heat thoroughly. Serves 6 to 8.

# INCREDIBLE BROCCOLI-CHEESE SOUP

*Wonderful, wonderful soup!*

1 (10 ounce) package frozen chopped broccoli
3 tablespoons butter
¼ onion, finely chopped
¼ cup flour
1 (16 ounce) carton half-and-half cream
1 (14 ounce) can chicken broth
⅛ teaspoon cayenne pepper
1 (8 ounce) package cubed mild Mexican Velveeta® cheese

- Punch several holes in broccoli package and microwave for 5 minutes. Turn package in microwave and cook for additional 4 minutes. Leave in microwave for 3 minutes.

- Melt butter in large saucepan over low heat and saute onion but do not brown. Add flour, stir and gradually add half-and-half cream, chicken broth, ½ teaspoon salt, ¼ teaspoon pepper and cayenne pepper.

- Stir constantly and heat until mixture is slightly thick. Do NOT let mixture come to a boil. Add cheese, stir and heat until cheese melts. Add cooked broccoli. Serve piping hot. Serves 6 to 8.

*Read the introduction on page 3 for a true story about Incredible Broccoli-Cheese Soup.*

# FIESTA SOUP

*1 (15 ounce) can Mexican-style stewed tomatoes*
*1 (15 ounce) can whole kernel corn*
*1 (15 ounce) can pinto beans*
*1 (14 ounce) can chicken broth*
*1 (10 ounce) can fiesta nacho cheese soup*

- In soup pot or kettle, on high heat, combine tomatoes, corn, pinto beans, chicken broth and a little salt and mix well.
- Stir in nacho soup and heat just until it heats thoroughly. Serves 4 to 6.

*TIP: If you feel that soup needs a touch of meat, just add 1 (12 ounce) can white chicken chunks.*

# MEXICAN-STYLE MINESTRONE SOUP

*1 (16 ounce) package frozen garlic-seasoned pasta and vegetables*
*1 (16 ounce) jar thick and chunky salsa*
*1 (15 ounce) can pinto beans with liquid*
*1 teaspoon chili powder*
*1 teaspoon cumin*
*1 (8 ounce) package shredded Mexican 4-cheese blend*

- Combine pasta and vegetables, salsa, pinto beans, chili powder, cumin and 1 cup water in large saucepan.
- Heat to boiling, reduce heat to low and simmer for about 8 minutes, stirring occasionally, or until vegetables are tender. When ready to serve, top each serving with cheese. Serves 6 to 8.

# OLD-FASHIONED TOMATO SOUP

*2½ pounds fresh tomatoes, peeled, seeded, chopped or 4 cups canned stewed, chopped tomatoes*
*3 - 4 cups chicken stock*
*2 ribs celery, minced*
*1 carrot, minced*
*1 onion, minced*
*2 tablespoons basil*

- In large soup pot, combine tomatoes, chicken stock, celery, carrot and onion on high heat. After soup begins to boil, reduce heat to low and simmer for 15 to 30 minutes. Add basil, salt and pepper to taste. Serves 4.

# CREAM OF TOMATO SOUP

- Use recipe for Old-Fashioned Tomato Soup (page 89). Omit chicken stock and onion and add 2 to 3 cups half-and-half cream. Bring to almost boiling and reduce heat to simmer. Serves 4.

# RAINY DAY LENTIL SOUP

*¼ cup apple juice*
*1 cup chopped onions*
*½ cup diced celery*
*2 (14 ounce) cans chicken broth*
*1 cup shredded carrots*
*½ cup shredded sweet potatoes*
*1 cup dry lentils, rinsed*
*1 - 2 tablespoons minced garlic*
*½ teaspoon cumin*

- Bring apple juice to a boil in large saucepan. Add onions and celery and return to boil. Add chicken broth, carrots, sweet potatoes, lentils and garlic and bring to a boil.

- Reduce heat to medium, add cumin and cover. Cook for about 30 minutes or until flavors mix. Add a little salt and pepper. Serves 4.

# TACO SOUP OLÉ

*2 pounds lean ground beef*
*2 (15 ounce) cans ranch-style beans with liquid*
*1 (15 ounce) can whole kernel corn, drained*
*2 (15 ounce) cans stewed tomatoes*
*1 (10 ounce) can tomatoes and green chilies*
*1 (1 ounce) package ranch-style dressing mix*
*1 (1 ounce) package taco seasoning*

- In large skillet, brown ground beef, drain and transfer to slow cooker. Add remaining ingredients and stir well. Cover and cook on LOW for 6 to 8 hours. Serves 6 to 8.

# SPICY BEAN SOUP

1 (15 ounce) can refried beans
1 (14 ounce) can chicken broth
2 (4 ounce) cans chopped green chilies
2 cloves garlic, minced
1 - 3 jalapeno chilies, seeded, chopped
1 teaspoon chili powder
6 slices bacon
5 ribs celery, chopped
1 bunch green onions with tops, chopped, divided
1 (8 ounce) package shredded cheddar cheese

- Heat refried beans and chicken broth in large saucepan and whisk beans and broth together. Add green chilies, garlic, jalapenos, ¼ teaspoon black pepper and chili powder and stir well. Reduce heat to low and stir occasionally.

- Fry bacon in skillet until crisp and drain. In pan drippings saute celery and about three-fourths of onions until onions are translucent.

- Crumble bacon and put into bean soup. Add celery, onions and pan drippings and stir well. Bring to a boil, reduce heat to low and serve immediately. Garnish with remaining onions and cheese. Serves 4.

# QUICK BRUNSWICK STEW

*This is great with cornbread!*

1 (15 ounce) can beef stew
1 (15 ounce) can chicken stew
1 (15 ounce) can lima beans, with liquid
2 (15 ounce) cans stewed tomatoes, with liquid
1 (15 ounce) can whole kernel corn, drained
½ teaspoon hot sauce, optional

- Combine beef stew, chicken stew, beans, tomatoes and corn in large stew pot. On medium to high heat, bring stew to boil, reduce heat and simmer for 35 minutes. Serves 6 to 8.

TIP: *Brunswick stew needs to be a little spicy, so stir in hot sauce. If you don't want the "spicy", add 1 tablespoon Worcestershire sauce.*

# BEEFY VEGGIE SOUP

1 pound lean ground beef
2 teaspoons minced garlic
2 (15 ounce) cans Italian stewed tomatoes
2 (14 ounce) cans beef broth
2 teaspoons Italian seasoning
1 (16 ounce) package frozen mixed vegetables
⅓ cup shell macaroni
Shredded mozzarella cheese

- Cook beef and garlic in large soup pot for 5 minutes. Stir in tomatoes, broth, 1 cup water, seasoning, mixed vegetables, macaroni and a little salt and pepper.

- Bring to a boil, reduce heat and simmer for 10 to 15 minutes or until macaroni is tender. Ladle into individual serving bowls and sprinkle several tablespoons cheese over top of soup. Serves 8.

# BLUE NORTHER STEW

*When cold weather comes from the north to the south, it is called a "norther" in the south.*

1½ pounds lean ground beef
1 onion, chopped
1 (1 ounce) packet taco seasoning
1 (1 ounce) packet ranch dressing mix
1 (15 ounce) can whole kernel corn, drained
1 (15 ounce) can kidney beans with liquid
2 (15 ounce) cans pinto beans
2 (15 ounce) cans Mexican stewed tomatoes
1 (10 ounce) can tomatoes and green chilies

- Brown ground beef and onion in large roasting pan. Add both packets of seasonings and mix well. Add corn, kidney beans, pinto beans, stewed tomatoes, tomatoes and green chilies and 1 cup water, mix well and simmer for about 30 minutes. Serves 8.

*Soups and stews have been around probably as long as fire. Combining ingredients in a large pot is a ritual enjoyed by all cultures and cuisines. It's as simple or as complicated as you want to make it and it's always a pleasing and comforting dish.*

# BLUE RIBBON BEEF STEW

*1 (2½ pound) boneless beef chuck roast, cubed*
*⅓ cup flour*
*2 (14 ounce) cans beef broth*
*2 teaspoons minced garlic*
*1 pound red potatoes with peel, sliced*
*2 large carrots, chopped*
*3 ribs celery, chopped*
*2 onions, finely chopped*
*1 (10 ounce) package frozen green peas, thawed*

- Dredge beef in flour mixed with 1 teaspoon salt; reserve leftover flour. Brown half beef in a little oil in stew pot over medium heat for about 10 minutes and transfer to plate. Repeat with remaining beef.

- Add a little of reserved flour to stew pot and cook, stir constantly, for 1 minute. Stir in beef broth, ½ cup water and garlic and boil. Reduce heat, simmer for 50 minutes and stir occasionally.

- Add potatoes, carrots, celery and onion and cook for 30 minutes. Stir in green peas, a little salt and pepper just before serving; heat to boiling. Serve immediately. Serves 6.

# CHILI

*2 pounds beef chuck, cubed*
*2 tablespoons oil*
*1 onion, chopped*
*3 cloves garlic, chopped*
*1 (8 ounce) can tomato sauce*
*1 cup beef broth*
*3 - 5 tablespoons chili powder*
*2 teaspoons ground cumin*

- Brown beef in hot oil in large, heavy saucepan. Stir in onion, garlic, tomato sauce and beef broth. Stir to mix well.

- Add chili powder, cumin, ½ teaspoon each of salt and pepper and stir to mix. Cover and simmer for 1 to 2 hours and stir occasionally. If liquid is too thin, remove cover and continue simmering. Serves 4 to 6.

*TIP:  To make chili hotter, add more chili powder or slices of seeded jalapenos. Add additional seasonings a little at a time, cook 10 minutes and taste.*

# ᏚASY CHILI

2 pounds lean ground beef
1 onion, chopped
4 (15 ounce) cans chili-hot beans with liquid
1 (1 ounce) packet chili seasoning mix
1 (46 ounce) can tomato juice

- Brown beef and onion in large, heavy pan, stir until meat crumbles and drain. Stir in remaining ingredients.

- Bring mixture to a boil, reduce heat and simmer, stirring occasionally for 2 hours. Serves 6 to 8.

# CHILI-SOUP WARMER

1 (10 ounce) can tomato bisque soup
1 (24 ounce) can chili with beans
1 (15 ounce) can chicken broth

- In saucepan, combine all ingredients. Add amount of water to produce desired thickness of soup. Heat and serve hot with crackers. Serves 4.

# ᏚASY ᏚEEFY VEGETABLE SOUP

1 pound lean ground beef
1 (46 ounce) can vegetable juice
1 (1 ounce) packet onion soup mix
1 (3 ounce) package beef-flavored ramen noodles
1 (16 ounce) package frozen mixed vegetables

- In large soup pot or kettle over medium heat, brown beef and drain. Stir in juice, soup mix, contents of noodle seasoning packet and mixed vegetables.

- Heat mixture to boiling, reduce heat and simmer uncovered 6 minutes or until vegetables are tender-crisp. Return to boiling, stir in noodles and cook 3 minutes. Serves 6 to 8.

# ENCHILADA SOUP

*1 pound lean ground beef, browned, drained*
*1 (15 ounce) can Mexican stewed tomatoes*
*1 (15 ounce) can pinto beans with liquid*
*1 (15 ounce) can whole kernel corn, with liquid*
*1 onion, chopped*
*2 (10 ounce) cans enchilada sauce*
*1 (8 ounce) package shredded 4-cheese blend*

- Spray 5 to 6-quart slow cooker with cooking spray. Combine beef, tomatoes, beans, corn, onion, enchilada sauce and 1 cup water and mix well.

- Cover and cook on LOW for 6 to 8 hours or on HIGH for 3 to 4 hours. Stir in shredded cheese. If desired, top each serving with a few crushed tortilla chips. Serves 6 to 8.

# HAMBURGER–VEGETABLE SOUP

*2 pounds lean ground beef*
*2 (15 ounce) cans chili without beans*
*1 (16 ounce) package frozen mixed vegetables, thawed*
*3 (14 ounce) cans beef broth*
*2 (15 ounce) cans stewed tomatoes*
*1 teaspoon seasoned salt*

- In skillet, brown ground beef and place in 6-quart slow cooker. Add chili, vegetables, broth, tomatoes, 1 cup water and seasoned salt and stir well. Cover and cook on LOW for 6 to 7 hours. Serves 8 to 10.

# MEAT AND POTATO STEW

*2 pounds beef stew meat*
*2 (15 ounce) cans new potatoes, drained*
*1 (15 ounce) can sliced carrots, drained*
*2 (10 ounce) cans French onion soup*

- Season meat with a little salt and pepper and cook with 2 cups water in large pot for 1 hour over medium-low heat.

- Add potatoes, carrots and onion soup and mix well. Bring to a boil, reduce heat and simmer for 30 minutes. Serves 6 to 8.

# STEAKHOUSE STEW

*1 pound boneless beef sirloin steak, cubed*
*1 (15 ounce) can stewed tomatoes*
*1 (10 ounce) can French onion soup*
*1 (10 ounce) can tomato soup*
*1 (16 ounce) package frozen stew vegetables, thawed*

- Cook steak cubes in skillet with a little oil until juices evaporate. (Sirloin steak will cook and get tender fairly fast.) Transfer to soup pot.

- Add 1 cup water, tomatoes, soups and vegetables and start boiling. Reduce heat to low and cook on medium for about 15 minutes or until vegetables are tender. Serves 4 to 6.

# TACO SOUP

*1½ pounds lean ground beef*
*1 (1 ounce) envelope taco seasoning*
*2 (15 ounce) cans Mexican stewed tomatoes*
*2 (15 ounce) cans chili beans with liquid*
*1 (15 ounce) can whole kernel corn, drained*
*Crushed tortilla chips*
*Shredded cheddar cheese*

- Brown ground beef in skillet, drain and place in 5 to 6-quart slow cooker. Add taco seasoning, tomatoes, chili beans, corn and 1 cup water and mix well.

- Cover and cook on LOW for 4 to 5 hours or on HIGH for 2 to 3 hours. Serve over crushed tortilla chips and sprinkle shredded cheddar cheese on top. Serves 4 to 6.

*It is a fact that most people have a dozen or so meals that they eat for breakfast, lunch and dinner. They usually rotate these and introduce some minor variations throughout most of their lives. Choose your meals wisely.*

# TORTILLA SOUP

*3 - 4 flour tortillas*
*1 (1.8 ounce) package tomato with basil soup mix*
*1 (14 ounce) can chicken broth*
*2 cups salsa*
*1 (10 ounce) can enchilada sauce*
*2 cups cooked, diced chicken breast*
*1 avocado, sliced*
*1 (8 ounce) package shredded Monterey Jack cheese*

- Preheat oven to 325°. Cut tortillas in thin strips and bake for 10 to 15 minutes or until crisp.

- In large saucepan, combine soup mix, broth, salsa, enchilada sauce and 1 cup water. Bring to boil, stirring constantly, and add diced chicken. Serve in shallow bowls.

- Place diced avocado, cheese and toasted tortilla strips in separate bowls so each person can garnish as they wish. Serves 4 to 6.

# TASTY CHICKEN AND RICE SOUP

*1 pound boneless skinless chicken breasts*
*½ cup uncooked brown rice*
*1 (10 ounce) can cream of chicken soup*
*1 (10 ounce) can cream of celery soup*
*1 (14 ounce) can chicken broth with roasted garlic*
*1 (16 ounce) package frozen sliced carrots, thawed*
*1 cup half-and-half cream*

- Cut chicken into 1-inch pieces. Place pieces in sprayed 4 or 5-quart slow cooker.

- In large saucepan, mix rice, both soups, chicken broth and carrots. Cook over medium heat until ingredients mix well.

- Pour over chicken, cover and cook on LOW 7 to 8 hours. Turn heat to HIGH, add half-and-half cream and cook another 15 to 20 minutes. Serves 4 to 6.

# QUICK CHICKEN-NOODLE SOUP

4 *(14 ounce) cans chicken broth*
4 *boneless, skinless chicken breast halves, cooked, cubed*
2 *(8 ounce) cans sliced carrots, drained*
4 *ribs celery, sliced*
1 *(8 ounce) package medium egg noodles*

- Combine broth, chicken, carrots, celery and generous dash of pepper in large saucepan. Boil and cook for 3 minutes.

- Stir in noodles, reduce heat and cook for 10 minutes or until noodles are done; stir often. Serves 8 to 12.

# CONFETTI CHICKEN SOUP

1 *pound skinless, boneless chicken thighs*
1 *(6 ounce) package chicken and herb-flavored rice*
3 *carrots, sliced*
3 *(14 ounce) cans chicken broth*
1 *(10 ounce) can cream of chicken soup*
1½ *tablespoons chicken seasoning*
1 *(10 ounce) package frozen whole kernel corn, thawed*
1 *(10 ounce) package frozen baby green peas, thawed*

- Cut thighs in thin strips. In 5 or 6-quart slow cooker, combine chicken, rice, carrots and 1 cup water.

- Combine chicken broth, cream of chicken soup and chicken seasoning in saucepan and heat to mix well. Pour over chicken in slow cooker. Cover and cook on LOW for 8 to 9 hours.

- About 30 minutes before serving, turn heat to HIGH and add corn and peas to cooker. Continue cooking for another 30 minutes. Serves 6 to 8.

*More statistical studies are finding that family meals play a significant role in childhood development. Children who eat with their families four or more nights per week are healthier, make better grades in school, score higher on aptitude tests and are less likely to have problems with drugs.*

# CHICKEN-VEGETABLE STEW

*1 (16 ounce) package frozen, chopped onions and bell peppers*
*2 tablespoons minced garlic*
*2 tablespoons chili powder*
*3 teaspoons ground cumin*
*2 pounds chicken cutlets, cubed*
*2 (14 ounce) cans chicken broth*
*3 (15 ounce) cans pinto beans with jalapenos, divided*

- Cook onions and bell peppers about 5 minutes in large, heavy pot over medium-high heat with little oil and stir occasionally,

- Add garlic, chili powder, cumin and cubed chicken and cook another 5 minutes. Stir in broth and a little salt. Bring to boil, reduce heat, cover and simmer for 15 minutes.

- Place 1 can beans in shallow bowl and mash with fork. Add mashed beans and remaining 2 cans of beans to pot. Bring to boil, reduce heat and simmer for 10 minutes. Serves 8 to 10.

*TIP: Delicious served with hot, buttered flour tortillas or spooned over small, original corn chips.*

# CHICKEN-PASTA SOUP

*1½ pounds boneless, skinless chicken thighs, cubed*
*1 onion, chopped*
*3 carrots, sliced*
*½ cup halved pitted ripe olives*
*1 teaspoon prepared minced garlic*
*3 (14 ounce) cans chicken broth*
*1 (15 ounce) can Italian stewed tomatoes*
*1 teaspoon Italian seasoning*
*½ cup uncooked small shell pasta*
*Parmesan cheese*

- In slow cooker, combine all ingredients except shell pasta and parmesan cheese. Cover and cook on LOW for 8 to 9 hours.

- About 30 minutes before serving, add pasta and stir. Increase heat to HIGH and cook another 20 to 30 minutes. Serve with parmesan. Serves 8 to 10.

# CHICKEN-NOODLE SUPPER

*1 (3 ounce) package chicken-flavored ramen noodles, broken*
*1 (10 ounce) package frozen green peas, thawed*
*2 tablespoons butter*
*1 (4 ounce) jar sliced mushrooms*
*3 cups cooked, cubed chicken or deli turkey*

- In large saucepan, heat 2¼ cups water to boiling and add ramen noodles, contents of seasoning packet, peas and butter.

- Heat to boiling, reduce heat to medium and cook about 5 minutes. Stir in mushrooms, chicken and ¾ teaspoon black pepper. Continue cooking over medium heat until all ingredients heat through. Serves 4.

# CHICKEN AND RICE GUMBO

*3 (14 ounce) cans chicken broth*
*1 pound boneless, skinless chicken, cubed*
*2 (15 ounce) cans whole kernel corn, drained*
*2 (15 ounce) cans stewed tomatoes with liquid*
*¾ cup uncooked white rice*
*1 teaspoon Cajun seasoning*
*2 (10 ounce) packages frozen okra, thawed, chopped*

- In soup pot on high heat, combine chicken broth and chicken pieces and cook for 15 minutes.

- Add remaining ingredients plus 1 teaspoon pepper and bring to boil. Reduce heat and simmer for 20 minutes or until rice is done. Serves 10 to 12.

# JAMBALAYA

*1 (8 ounce) package jambalaya mix*
*1 (6 ounce) package frozen chicken breast strips, thawed*
*1 (11 ounce) can Mexicorn®*
*1 (2 ounce) can chopped black olives*

- Combine jambalaya mix and 2¼ cups water in soup or large saucepan. Heat to boiling, reduce heat and cook slowly 5 minutes.

- Add chopped chicken, corn and black olives. Heat to boiling, reduce heat and simmer about 20 minutes. Serves 4.

*TIP: You could also add leftover ham or sausage and 1 tablespoon lemon juice to change it up some.*

*TIP: If you want to serve more than 5 people, just double the recipe.*

# COUNTRY CHICKEN CHOWDER

*1½ pounds boneless, skinless chicken breast halves*
*2 tablespoons butter*
*2 (10 ounce) cans cream of potato soup*
*1 (14 ounce) can chicken broth*
*1 (8 ounce) package frozen whole kernel corn*
*1 onion, sliced*
*2 ribs celery, sliced*
*1 (10 ounce) package frozen peas and carrots, thawed*
*½ teaspoon dried thyme*
*½ cup half-and-half cream*

- Cut chicken into 1-inch strips. Brown chicken strips in butter in skillet and transfer to large slow cooker. Add soup, broth, corn, onion, celery, peas and carrots, and thyme and stir.

- Cover and cook on LOW for 3 to 4 hours or until vegetables are tender. Turn off heat, stir in half-and-half cream and set aside for about 10 minutes before serving. Serves 6.

# FIFTEEN-MINUTE TURKEY SOUP

*1 (14 ounce) can chicken broth*
*3 (15 ounce) cans navy beans, rinsed, drained*
*1 (28 ounce) can diced tomatoes with liquid*
*2 - 3 cups small chunks white turkey meat*
*2 teaspoons minced garlic*
*Freshly grated parmesan cheese*

- Mix all ingredients except cheese in saucepan and heat. Garnish with parmesan cheese before serving. Serves 6.

*TIP: A little cayenne pepper gives this a nice kick.*

*The American Medical Association's* Archives of Family Medicine *published in March 2000 stated that eating meals at home during the week is directly associated with better nutrition in children. They got more nutrients such calcium, iron, fiber, vitamin B6, vitamin C, vitamin E and consumed less fat eating at home than eating out.*

# TURKEY-MUSHROOM SOUP

*Here's another great way to use leftover chicken or turkey.*

2 cups sliced mushrooms
2 ribs celery, chopped
1 small onion, chopped
2 tablespoons butter
1 (15 ounce) can sliced carrots, drained
2 (14 ounce) cans chicken broth
2 cups cooked, chopped turkey (Do not use smoked turkey.)

* Saute mushrooms, celery and onion in butter in skillet. Transfer to slow cooker and add carrots, broth and turkey. Cover and cook on LOW for 2 to 3 hours or on HIGH for 1 to 2 hours. Serves 6.

# SPICY TURKEY SOUP

*This is spicy – but not too much, just right! Try it with chicken too.*

3 - 4 cups cooked, chopped turkey
3 (10 ounce) cans chicken broth
2 (10 ounce) cans diced tomatoes and green chilies
1 (16 ounce) can whole corn
1 large onion, chopped
1 (10 ounce) can tomato soup
1 teaspoon garlic powder
1 teaspoon dried oregano
3 tablespoons cornstarch

* Combine turkey, broth, tomatoes and green chilies, corn, onion, tomato soup, garlic powder and oregano in soup pot.
* Combine cornstarch with 3 tablespoons water in bowl and add to soup mixture.
* Bring mixture to a boil, reduce heat and simmer for 2 hours. Stir occasionally. Makes about 2½ quarts.

*Os Guinness wrote in his book* Time for Truth *that "in a postmodern world, the question is no longer 'Is it true?' but rather 'Whose truth is it?' and 'Which power stands to gain?'"*

# ITALIAN VEGETABLE SOUP

*1 pound bulk Italian sausage*
*2 onions, chopped*
*2 teaspoons minced garlic*
*1 (1 ounce) envelope beefy recipe soup mix*
*1 (15 ounce) can sliced carrots, drained*
*2 (15 ounce) cans Italian stewed tomatoes*
*1 cup elbow macaroni*

- In large soup pot, brown sausage, onions and garlic. Drain fat and add 4 cups water, soup mix, carrots and tomatoes. Bring to boil, reduce heat to low and simmer for 25 minutes.

- Add elbow macaroni and continue cooking another 15 to 20 minutes or until macaroni is tender. Serves 6.

# BLACK BEAN SOUP

*2 (14 ounce) cans chicken broth*
*3 (15 ounce) cans black beans, rinsed, drained*
*2 (10 ounce) cans tomatoes and green chilies*
*1 onion, chopped*
*1 teaspoon ground cumin*
*½ teaspoon dried thyme*
*½ teaspoon dried oregano*
*2 - 3 cups finely diced, cooked ham*

- In slow cooker, combine chicken broth and black beans and turn cooker to HIGH. Cook, covered, just long enough for ingredients to get hot.

- With potato masher, mash about half of beans in slow cooker. Reduce heat to LOW and add tomatoes, onion, spices, diced ham and ¾ cup water. Cover and cook for 5 to 6 hours. Serves 6 to 8.

# QUICK NAVY BEAN SOUP

*3 (16 ounce) cans navy beans with juice*
*1 (14 ounce) can chicken broth*
*1 cup chopped ham*
*1 large onion, chopped*
*½ teaspoon garlic powder*

- In large saucepan, combine all ingredients with 1 cup water and bring to a boil. Simmer until onion is tender-crisp and serve hot with cheese muffins or cornbread. Serves 4 to 6.

# TATER TALK SOUP

5 medium potatoes, peeled, cubed
2 cups cooked, cubed ham
1 cup fresh broccoli florets, cut very, very fine
1 (10 ounce) can cheddar cheese soup
1 (10 ounce) can fiesta nacho cheese soup
1 (14 ounce) can chicken broth
2½ soup cans milk

- Place potatoes, ham and broccoli in slow cooker sprayed with vegetable cooking spray. In saucepan, combine soups, broth and milk. Heat just enough to mix until smooth.

- Stir into ingredients already in slow cooker. Cover and cook on LOW for 7 to 9 hours. When serving, sprinkle a little paprika over each serving, if desired. Serves 6 to 8.

# BLACK BEAN STEW SUPPER

1 (16 ounce) pork and beef sausage ring, thinly sliced
2 onions, chopped
3 ribs celery, chopped
3 (15 ounce) cans black beans, drained, rinsed
2 (10 ounce) cans diced tomatoes and green chilies
2 (14 ounce) cans chicken broth

- Place sausage slices, onion and celery in soup pot with a little oil and cook until sausage is slightly brown and onion is soft. Drain fat.

- Add beans, tomatoes and broth. Bring mixture to boiling, reduce heat and simmer for 30 minutes.

- Take out about 2 to 3 cups soup mixture, place in blender and pulse until almost smooth. Return mixture to pot and stir to thicken stew. Return heat to high until stew is thoroughly hot. Serves 4.

# EASY MEATY MINESTRONE

2 (20 ounce) cans minestrone soup
1 (15 ounce) can pinto beans with liquid
1 (18 ounce) package frozen Italian meatballs, thawed
1 (5 ounce) package grated parmesan cheese

- In large saucepan, combine soup, beans, meatballs and ½ cup water. Bring to boil, reduce heat to low and simmer about 15 minutes. To serve, sprinkle each serving with parmesan cheese. Serves 6 to 8.

# MEATBALL STEW

*1 (18 ounce) package frozen prepared Italian meatballs, thawed*
*1 (14 ounce) can beef broth*
*1 (15 ounce) can cut green beans*
*1 (16 ounce) package baby carrots*
*2 (15 ounce) cans stewed tomatoes*
*1 tablespoon Worcestershire sauce*
*½ teaspoon ground allspice*

- Combine all ingredients in slow cooker. Cover and cook on LOW for 3 to 5 hours. Serves 4 to 6.

# SPAGHETTI SOUP

*1 (7 ounce) package spaghetti*
*1 (18 ounce) package frozen, cooked meatballs, thawed*
*1 (28 ounce) jar spaghetti sauce*
*1 (15 ounce) can Mexican stewed tomatoes*

- In soup pot or kettle with 3 quarts boiling water and a little salt, break spaghetti and cook about 6 minutes (no need to drain).

- When spaghetti is done, add meatballs, spaghetti sauce and stewed tomatoes and cook until mixture heats through. Serves 8 to 10.

*TIP: To garnish each soup bowl, sprinkle with 2 tablespoons mozzarella cheese or any cheese you have in the refrigerator.*

# MEXICAN MEATBALL SOUP

*3 (14 ounce) cans beef broth*
*1 (16 ounce) jar hot salsa*
*1 (16 ounce) package frozen whole kernel corn, thawed*
*1 (16 ounce) package frozen meatballs, thawed*
*1 teaspoon minced garlic*

- Combine all ingredients in slow cooker and stir well. Cover and cook on LOW for 4 to 7 hours. Serves 4 to 6.

# SAUSAGE-BEAN CHOWDER

2 pounds pork sausage
1 (15 ounce) can pinto beans with liquid
1 (15 ounce) can navy beans with liquid
1 (15 ounce) can kidney beans, drained
2 (15 ounce) cans Mexican stewed tomatoes
2 (14 ounce) cans chicken broth
1 - 2 teaspoons minced garlic

- Brown and cook sausage in soup pot and stir until sausage crumbles. Add all beans, tomatoes, broth and garlic. Bring to a boil, reduce heat to low and simmer for 20 minutes. Serves 6.

# SPICY SAUSAGE SOUP

1 pound mild bulk sausage
1 pound hot bulk sausage
2 (15 ounce) cans Mexican stewed tomatoes
3 cups chopped celery
1 cup sliced carrots
1 (15 ounce) can cut green beans, drained
1 (14 ounce) can chicken broth
1 teaspoon seasoned salt

- Combine mild and hot sausage, shape into small balls and place in non-stick skillet. Brown thoroughly and drain. Place in large slow cooker.

- Add remaining ingredients plus 1 teaspoon salt and 1 cup water. Stir gently so meatballs will not break-up. Cover and cook on LOW 6 to 7 hours. Serves 4 to 6.

# HAM AND FRESH OKRA SOUP

1 ham hock
1 cup frozen butter beans or lima beans
1½ pounds cooked, cubed ham or chicken
1 (15 ounce) can chopped stewed tomatoes
3 cups small whole okra
2 large onions, diced
Rice, cooked

- Boil ham hock in 1½ quarts water in soup pot for about 1 hour 30 minutes. Add remaining ingredients and slow-boil for additional 1 hour. Season with a little salt and pepper and serve over rice. Serves 6 to 8.

# CORN-HAM CHOWDER

1 (14 ounce) can chicken broth
1 cup whole milk
1 (10 ounce) can cream of celery soup
1 (15 ounce) can cream-style corn
1 (15 ounce) can whole kernel corn
½ cup dry potato flakes
1 onion, chopped
2 - 3 cups chopped, cooked ham

- Combine broth, milk, soup in saucepan and cook over medium heat just long enough to mix well. Pour into 6-quart slow cooker and add cream-style corn, whole kernel corn, potato flakes, onion and ham.

- Cover and cook on LOW for 4 to 5 hours. When ready to serve, season with salt and black pepper. Serves 6 to 8.

# HAM-VEGETABLE CHOWDER

*This is a great recipe for leftover ham.*

1 medium potato
2 (10 ounce) cans cream of celery soup
1 (14 ounce) can chicken broth
2 cups cooked, finely diced ham
1 (15 ounce) can whole kernel corn
2 carrots, sliced
1 onion, coarsely chopped
1 teaspoon dried basil
1 (10 ounce) package frozen broccoli florets, thawed

- Cut potato into 1-inch pieces. Combine all ingredients except broccoli florets in large slow cooker.

- Cover and cook on LOW for 5 to 6 hours. Add broccoli and about ½ teaspoon each of salt and pepper and cook for additional 1 hour. Serves 4.

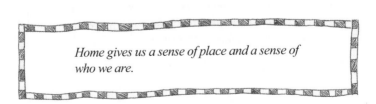

*Home gives us a sense of place and a sense of who we are.*

# Potato and Ham Chowder

*1 carrot, grated*
*2 ribs celery, sliced*
*1 onion, chopped*
*1 (4.5 ounce) package julienne potato mix*
*3 cups milk*
*2 cups cooked, cubed ham*
*Grated sharp cheddar cheese*

- In soup pot, combine 2¾ cups water with carrot, celery, onion and potato mix package. Bring to boil, reduce heat, cover and simmer 20 minutes.
- Stir in milk and packet of sauce with potatoes and mix. Stir well and return to boiling. Simmer 2 minutes and stir in ham. When serving, garnish with sharp cheddar cheese. Serves 4 to 6.

# Slow-Cook Navy Bean and Ham Soup

*1½ cups dry navy beans*
*1 carrot, finely chopped*
*¼ cup finely chopped celery*
*1 small onion, finely chopped*
*1 (¾ pound) ham hock*

- Soak beans for 8 to 12 hours and drain. Place all ingredients, 5 cups water, ½ teaspoon salt and a dash of pepper in 2-quart slow cooker. Cook for 8 to 10 hours on LOW setting.
- Remove ham hock and discard skin, fat and bone. Cut meat in small pieces and place in soup. Serves 6 to 8.

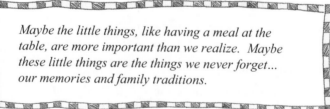

*Maybe the little things, like having a meal at the table, are more important than we realize. Maybe these little things are the things we never forget... our memories and family traditions.*

# Southern Soup

1½ cups dry black-eyed peas
2 - 3 cups cooked, cubed ham
1 (15 ounce) can whole kernel corn
1 (10 ounce) package frozen cut okra, thawed
1 onion, chopped
1 large potato, cubed
2 teaspoons Cajun seasoning
1 (14 ounce) can chicken broth
2 (15 ounce) cans Mexican stewed tomatoes

- Rinse peas and drain. Combine peas and 5 cups water in large saucepan. Bring to boil, reduce heat, simmer about 10 minutes and drain.

- Combine peas, ham, corn, okra, onion, potato, seasoning, broth and 2 cups water in 5 or 6-quart slow cooker.

- Cover and cook on LOW for 6 to 8 hours. Add stewed tomatoes and continue cooking for 1 more hour. Serves 6 to 8.

# Easy Pork Tenderloin Stew

*This is great with leftover pork, steak or beef.*

2 - 3 cups cubed, cooked pork
1 (12 ounce) jar pork gravy
¼ cup chili sauce
1 (16 ounce) package frozen stew vegetables

- In soup pot, combine cubed pork, gravy, chili sauce, stew vegetables and ½ cup water.

- Bring to boiling and boil for 2 minutes; reduce heat and simmer for 10 minutes. Serve with cornbread or hot biscuits. Serves 4 to 6.

*The highest form of discipline in eating is not will power. It's paying attention to how you respond to what you eat. How will you feel the next time you eat that food? If you eat a pastry in the morning for breakfast, how do you feel afterwards? How about in an hour? In 2 hours?*

# MAMA'S SEAFOOD GUMBO

¼ cup (½ stick) butter
¼ cup flour
1½ - 2 pounds okra, sliced
6 firm tomatoes
½ cup minced onion
2 pounds shrimp
1 pound crabmeat
1 pound fish fillets
Cayenne pepper
1 pint fresh oysters with liquor
Rice, cooked

- Melt butter in heavy skillet and add flour. Stir well over medium heat to make smooth, paste-like roux. Add 2 quarts water, okra, tomatoes and onion and cook on low for 45 minutes.

- Wash, clean and peel shrimp. Flake crabmeat and remove any pieces of shell. Remove all bones and skin from fish.

- When roux is rich brown color, add a little salt, pepper and cayenne pepper and mix well. Add all seafood and cook on medium-low heat for 30 minutes or until desired consistency. Serve over rice. Serves 6 to 8.

# SHRIMP AND SAUSAGE JAMBALAYA

1 pound cooked, smoked sausage links
1 onion, chopped
1 green bell pepper, chopped
2 teaspoons minced garlic
1 (28 ounce) can diced tomatoes
1 tablespoon parsley flakes
½ teaspoon dried thyme leaves
2 teaspoons Cajun seasoning
½ teaspoon cayenne pepper
1 pound peeled, veined shrimp
Rice, cooked

- Combine all ingredients except shrimp and rice in sprayed slow cooker. Cover and cook on LOW for 6 to 8 hours or on HIGH for 3 to 4 hours. Stir in shrimp and cook on LOW for additional 1 hour. Serve over rice. Serves 4 to 6.

# SIDE DISHES

## CHEESY VEGETABLE SAUCE

*½ cup shredded cheddar cheese*
*½ cup sour cream*
*¼ cup (½ stick) butter*
*2 tablespoons chopped fresh parsley*
*½ teaspoon garlic powder*

* Combine all ingredients in 3-quart glass bowl. Microwave on MEDIUM-HIGH for 2 minutes or until cheese melts, stirring at 1-minute intervals with wire whisk. Serve over cooked broccoli, cauliflower or even potatoes. Serves 6.

## ARTICHOKE SQUARES

*These artichoke squares can be served hot or at room temperature.*

*2 (6 ounce) jars marinated artichoke hearts with liquid*
*1 onion, finely chopped*
*½ teaspoon minced garlic*
*4 eggs, beaten*
*⅓ cup breadcrumbs*
*1 (8 ounce) package cheddar cheese*
*1 tablespoon dried parsley flakes*

* Preheat oven to 325°.

* Drain liquid (marinade) from 1 jar artichoke hearts into skillet, heat and saute onion and garlic. (Discard marinade from remaining jar.) Chop artichoke hearts in bowl and set aside.

* In separate bowl, combine eggs, breadcrumbs, and ¼ teaspoon each of salt and pepper. Fold in cheese and parsley. Add artichokes and onion-garlic mixture and mix well.

* Spoon into sprayed 9-inch square baking dish. Bake for 30 minutes. Let stand for several minutes before cutting into squares. Serves 6 to 8.

# ARTICHOKE FETTUCCINE

*1 (12 ounce) package fettuccine*
*1 (14 ounce) can water-packed artichoke hearts, drained, chopped*
*1 (10 ounce) box frozen green peas, thawed*
*1 (16 ounce) jar alfredo sauce*
*2 heaping tablespoons crumbled blue cheese*

- Cook fettuccine according to package directions. Drain and place in serving bowl to keep warm.

- Combine heat artichoke hearts, peas and alfredo sauce in large saucepan. Stir well, spoon into bowl with fettuccine and toss. Sprinkle with blue cheese and serve hot. Serves 10.

# ASPARAGUS-CHEESE BAKE

*3 (15 ounce) cans cut asparagus spears with liquid*
*3 eggs, hard-boiled, chopped*
*½ cup chopped pecans*
*1 (10 ounce) can cream of asparagus soup*
*¼ cup (½ stick) butter*
*2 cups cracker crumbs*
*1 (8 ounce) package shredded Monterey Jack cheese*

- Preheat oven to 350°.

- Drain asparagus and save liquid. Arrange asparagus spears in sprayed 2-quart baking dish. Top with chopped eggs and pecans.

- Heat asparagus soup, liquid from asparagus, butter and a little pepper in saucepan. Pour over asparagus, eggs and pecans. Combine cracker crumbs and cheese in bowl. Sprinkle over casserole. Bake for 25 minutes. Serves 4 to 6.

# ALMOND ASPARAGUS

*⅓ cup butter*
*1 - 1½ pounds fresh asparagus*
*⅔ cup slivered almonds*
*1 tablespoon lemon juice*

- Melt butter in skillet and add asparagus and almonds. Saute for 3 to 4 minutes. Cover and steam for about 2 minutes or until tender-crisp. Sprinkle lemon and a little salt and pepper over asparagus. Serve hot. Serves 5.

# ASPARAGUS BAKE

*4 (10 ounce) cans asparagus*
*3 eggs, hard-boiled, sliced*
*⅓ cup milk*
*1½ cups shredded cheddar cheese*
*1¼ cups cheese cracker crumbs*

- Preheat oven to 350°.

- Place asparagus in sprayed 7 x 11-inch baking dish, layer hard-boiled eggs on top and pour milk over casserole. Sprinkle cheese on top and add cracker crumbs. Bake for 30 minutes. Serves 8.

# ASPARAGUS CAESAR

*3 (15 ounce) cans asparagus spears, drained*
*¼ cup (½ stick) butter, melted*
*3 tablespoons lemon juice*
*½ cup grated parmesan cheese*

- Preheat oven to 400°.

- Place asparagus in 2-quart baking dish. Drizzle on butter and lemon juice. Sprinkle with cheese and a little paprika, if you like. Bake for 15 to 20 minutes. Serves 8.

# JAZZY CHEESY BROCCOLI

*1 (24 ounce) package frozen broccoli florets, thawed*
*1 (10 ounce) can cream of celery soup*
*¾ cup milk*
*½ teaspoon garlic powder*
*⅛ teaspoon cayenne pepper*
*1½ cups cubed Velveeta® cheese*

- Place broccoli in microwave-safe bowl and microwave on HIGH about 4 minutes or until tender. Keep warm.

- In saucepan, combine celery soup, milk, garlic powder and cayenne pepper. Heat and stir to mix well. On low heat, stir in cheese until it melts. Remove from heat.

- Place broccoli in serving bowl and spoon cheese sauce over broccoli. Serves 8 to 10.

# BAKED BROCCOLI

2 (10 ounce) packages frozen broccoli spears
1 (10 ounce) can cream of chicken soup
⅔ cup mayonnaise
¾ cup breadcrumbs
Paprika

- Preheat oven to 325°.

- Place broccoli spears in baking dish. Combine soup and mayonnaise in saucepan, heat and pour over broccoli. Sprinkle with breadcrumbs and paprika. Bake for 45 minutes. Serves 6.

# BROCCOLI-CHEESE POTATO TOPPER

1 (10 ounce) can fiesta nacho cheese soup
2 tablespoons sour cream
½ teaspoon dijon-style mustard
1 (10 ounce) box frozen broccoli florets, cooked
4 medium potatoes, baked, fluffed

- Stir soup, sour cream, mustard and broccoli in 1-quart microwave-safe baking dish. Heat in microwave for 2 to 2½ minutes and spoon over potato. Serves 4.

# CHEDDAR-BROCCOLI-BELL PEPPER BAKE

1 (10 ounce) can cheddar cheese soup
1 (8 ounce) package shredded cheddar-Jack cheese
⅓ cup milk
1 cup chopped celery
1 red bell pepper, seeded, julienned
1 (16 ounce) bag frozen broccoli florets, cooked
1 (6 ounce) can french-fried onions

- Preheat oven to 325°.

- Combine soup, cheese, milk, celery, bell pepper, broccoli, and ½ teaspoon each of salt and pepper in bowl and mix well. Pour into sprayed 3-quart baking dish. Cover and bake for 25 minutes.

- Sprinkle fried onions over casserole and bake uncovered for 15 minutes or until onions are golden brown. Serves 6 to 8.

# BROCCOLI FRITTATA

*3 tablespoons butter*
*½ cup chopped onion*
*4 cups fresh broccoli florets without stems*
*6 large eggs*
*1 (1 ounce) packet cream of broccoli soup mix*
*½ cup shredded cheddar cheese*
*½ cup milk*

- Preheat oven to 350°.

- Melt butter in skillet and saute onion. Add broccoli and 1 tablespoon water. Cook, stirring occasionally, on low heat for about 5 minutes until tender-crisp, but still bright green.

- Whisk eggs, soup mix, cheese, milk, and ½ teaspoon each of salt and pepper in bowl. Fold in broccoli-onion mixture.

- Pour into sprayed 10-inch deep-dish pie pan. Bake uncovered for 20 to 25 minutes or until center sets. Let frittata cool for 5 or 10 minutes before cutting into wedges. Serves 6 to 8.

# BROCCOLI SOUFFLE

*4 cups fresh broccoli florets*
*5 tablespoons butter, melted*
*2 tablespoons flour*
*3 eggs, beaten*
*1 cup small curd cottage cheese, drained*
*½ cup half-and-half cream*
*1 cup shredded cheddar cheese, divided*
*½ cup minced onion*

- Preheat oven to 350°.

- Cut broccoli into very small florets with very little stem. Place florets and 2 tablespoons water in microwave-safe bowl. Microwave on HIGH for 3 minutes.

- Remove from microwave, add butter, sprinkle flour over broccoli and toss. Combine eggs, cottage cheese, half-and-half cream, half cheese, onion, and ½ teaspoon each of salt and pepper in bowl and mix well.

- Combine broccoli and egg mixture and pour into sprayed 7 x 11-inch baking dish or souffle dish. Sprinkle remaining cheese over top. Cover and bake for 30 to 35 minutes or until center sets. Serves 6 to 8.

# BROCCOLI SUPREME

*2 (10 ounce) packages frozen broccoli spears*
*1 stick garlic cheese roll*
*1 (10 ounce) can cream of mushroom soup*
*1 (3 ounce) can sliced mushrooms, drained*
*¾ cup seasoned breadcrumbs*

- Preheat oven to 350°.

- Boil broccoli in saucepan for 3 minutes and drain. Place broccoli in 2-quart baking dish. In saucepan, combine cheese roll, soup and mushrooms. Heat on medium, stirring constantly, until cheese melts.

- Spoon cheese-mushroom mixture over broccoli. Sprinkle breadcrumbs over top of casserole. Bake uncovered for 30 minutes. Serves 4 to 6.

# BROCCOLI-RICE WHIZ

*So easy and so good! And it gives us a vegetable and rice all in one dish.*

*2 cups instant rice*
*¾ cup chopped onion*
*¾ cup chopped red bell pepper*
*¾ cup chopped celery*
*¼ cup (½ stick) butter*
*1 (8 ounce) jar Mexican Velveeta® cheese spread*
*1 (10 ounce) can cream of chicken soup*
*½ cup milk*
*2 (10 ounce) packages frozen chopped broccoli, thawed, drained*

- Preheat oven to 350°.

- Cook rice in large saucepan according to package directions. Saute onions, bell pepper and celery in butter in skillet. Add onion-celery mixture to rice. Fold in cheese, chicken soup and milk and mix well.

- Heat on low until cheese and soup blend well. Fold in chopped broccoli. Pour into sprayed 3-quart baking dish. Cover and bake for 35 minutes. Serves 6 to 8.

# BROCCOLI-STUFFED TOMATOES

4 medium tomatoes
1 (10 ounce) package frozen chopped broccoli
1 (6 ounce) roll garlic cheese, softened
½ teaspoon garlic salt

- Preheat oven to 375°.

- Cut tops off tomatoes and scoop out flesh. Cook broccoli in saucepan according to package directions and drain well.

- Combine broccoli, cheese and garlic salt and heat just until cheese melts. Stuff broccoli mixture into tomatoes and place on baking sheet. Bake for about 10 minutes. Serves 4.

# HEAVENLY BROCCOLI

2 (16 ounce) packages frozen broccoli spears
1 (8 ounce) container cream cheese and chives
2 (10 ounce) cans cream of shrimp soup
2 teaspoons lemon juice
¼ cup (½ stick) butter, melted

- Preheat oven to 350°.

- Trim some stems off broccoli and discard. Cook broccoli in microwave according to package directions and place in 2-quart baking dish.

- Combine cream cheese, soup, lemon juice and butter in saucepan. Heat just enough to mix thoroughly and pour over broccoli. Bake just until hot and bubbly. Serves 8 to 10.

# PARMESAN BROCCOLI

1 (16 ounce) package frozen broccoli spears
½ teaspoon garlic powder
½ cup breadcrumbs
¼ cup (½ stick) butter, melted
½ cup grated parmesan cheese

- Cook broccoli in saucepan according to package directions. Drain and add garlic powder, breadcrumbs, butter and cheese. Add salt, if you like and toss. Heat and serve. Serves 6.

# Pine Nut Broccoli

1 bunch fresh broccoli
¼ cup (½ stick) butter
½ cup pine nuts
⅓ cup golden raisins
2 tablespoons lemon juice

- Trim broccoli into florets and steam until tender-crisp. Combine butter, pine nuts and raisins in saucepan and saute for about 3 minutes. When ready to serve, add lemon juice to nut mixture and pour over broccoli. Serves 6.

# Cheddar-Broccoli Bake

1 (10 ounce) can cheddar cheese soup
½ cup milk
1 (16 ounce) bag frozen broccoli florets, cooked
1 (6 ounce) can french-fried onions

- Preheat oven to 350°. Mix soup, milk, broccoli and dash of pepper in 2-quart baking dish. Bake for 25 minutes.

- Stir and sprinkle fried onions over broccoli mixture. Bake for additional 5 minutes or until onions are golden. Serves 6 to 8.

# Easy Broccoli Pie

1 (16 ounce) package frozen broccoli spears, thawed
1 (12 ounce) package shredded cheddar cheese, divided
½ cup chopped onion
3 eggs, slightly beaten
¾ cup buttermilk biscuit mix
1½ cups milk

- Preheat oven to 350°. Cut broccoli into smaller pieces and discard some stems. Combine broccoli, two-thirds cheese and onion in bowl and mix well. Spoon into sprayed 10-inch deep-dish pie pan.

- In same bowl, combine eggs and biscuit mix and beat for several minutes. Add milk and ¾ teaspoon each of salt and pepper and mix until fairly smooth. Pour over broccoli and cheese mixture.

- Bake uncovered for 35 to 40 minutes or until knife inserted in center comes out clean. Top with remaining cheese and bake just until cheese melts. Let stand for 5 minute before slicing. Serves 6 to 8.

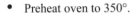

# BROCCOLI-CAULIFLOWER CASSEROLE

1 (10 ounce) package frozen broccoli florets
1 (10 ounce) package frozen cauliflower
1 egg, beaten
⅔ cup mayonnaise
1 (10 ounce) can cream of chicken soup
¼ cup milk
1 onion, chopped
1 red bell pepper, seeded, chopped
1 cup shredded Swiss cheese
1 cup seasoned breadcrumbs
2 tablespoons butter, melted

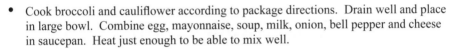

- Preheat oven to 350°.

- Cook broccoli and cauliflower according to package directions. Drain well and place in large bowl. Combine egg, mayonnaise, soup, milk, onion, bell pepper and cheese in saucepan. Heat just enough to be able to mix well.

- Spoon into bowl with broccoli-cauliflower and mix well. Pour into sprayed 2½-quart baking dish. Combine breadcrumbs and butter in bowl and sprinkle over broccoli and cauliflower mixture. Bake for 35 minutes. Serves 6 to 8.

# BAKED CAULIFLOWER

1 (16 ounce) package frozen cauliflower, thawed
1 egg
⅔ cup mayonnaise
1 (10 ounce) can cream of chicken soup
4 ounces Swiss cheese, shredded
2 ribs celery, sliced
1 green bell pepper, seeded, chopped
1 onion, chopped
1½ cups round buttery cracker crumbs

- Preheat oven to 350°.

- Place cauliflower in sprayed 9 x 13-inch glass baking dish and cover loosely with plastic wrap. Cook on HIGH in microwave for 3 minutes. Turn dish and cook for additional 3 minutes.

- Combine egg, mayonnaise, soup and cheese in saucepan. Heat just until ingredients mix. Add celery, bell pepper, onion and 1 teaspoon pepper to cauliflower and mix well. Pour soup mixture over vegetables and spread out.

- Sprinkle cracker crumbs on top. Bake for 35 to 40 minutes or until crumbs are light brown. Serves 8 to 10.

# BEST CAULIFLOWER

1 (16 ounce) package frozen cauliflower
1 (8 ounce) carton sour cream
1½ cups shredded American or cheddar cheese
4 teaspoons sesame seeds, toasted

• Preheat oven to 350°.

• Cook cauliflower in saucepan according to package directions. Drain and place half of cauliflower in sprayed 2-quart baking dish.

• Sprinkle a little salt and pepper on cauliflower and spread half of sour cream and half of cheese. Top with 2 teaspoons sesame seeds and repeat layers. Bake for about 15 to 20 minutes. Serves 6 to 8.

# CAULIFLOWER MEDLEY

1 head cauliflower, cut into florets
1 (15 ounce) can Italian stewed tomatoes with liquid
1 onion, finely chopped
1 green bell pepper, seeded, sliced
1 tablespoon sugar
1 tablespoon cornstarch
¼ cup (½ stick) butter, melted
1 cup shredded cheddar cheese
1 cup Italian seasoned breadcrumbs

• Preheat oven to 350°.

• Cook cauliflower in salted water in large saucepan for about 10 minutes or until tender-crisp and drain well. Add stewed tomatoes, onion, bell pepper, sugar, cornstarch, butter, and ½ teaspoon each of salt and pepper and mix well.

• Transfer cauliflower-tomato mixture to 2-quart baking dish and sprinkle cheese and breadcrumbs over top. Bake for 35 minutes. Serves 4 to 6.

*To enhance the flavor of veggies, you may want to put fat, salt, condiments and seasonings on them. High quality fat such as olive or canola oil or even a little butter not only helps your food taste good, it also reduces cravings for fat from junk food, improves the assimilation of fat-soluble vitamins in the veggies and satisfies more completely.*

# GRAND CAULIFLOWER

*¾ cup cooked, finely chopped ham*
*2 cloves garlic, finely minced*
*1 red bell pepper, seeded, chopped*
*6 tablespoons (¾ stick) butter, divided*
*1 (16 ounce) package frozen cauliflower, thawed*
*2 tablespoons flour*
*1½ cups whipping cream*
*1½ cups shredded cheddar cheese*
*½ cup slivered almonds, toasted*

- Preheat oven to 350°.

- Saute ham, garlic and red bell pepper in 2 tablespoons butter in large skillet over medium heat. Add cauliflower and 2 tablespoons water, cover and steam until tender-crisp.

- In separate skillet, melt remaining butter. Add flour, a little salt and pepper, and a little bit of cream and stir well to blend. Add remaining cream, heat and cook, stirring constantly, until mixture thickens. Add cheese and stir.

- Spoon cauliflower-ham mixture into sprayed 2-quart baking dish. Pour cream mixture over cauliflower. Sprinkle almonds on top of casserole. Cover and bake for 20 minutes, just until casserole is hot. Serves 4 to 6.

# CAULIFLOWER CON QUESO

*1 large head cauliflower, broken into florets*
*¼ cup (½ stick) butter*
*½ onion, chopped*
*2 tablespoons flour*
*1 (15 ounce) can Mexican stewed tomatoes*
*1 (4 ounce) can diced green chilies, drained*
*1½ cups shredded Monterey Jack cheese*

- Preheat oven to 325°.

- Cook cauliflower florets in saucepan until just tender-crisp, drain and place in sprayed 2-quart baking dish. Melt butter in medium saucepan. Saute onion just until clear, but not brown.

- Blend in flour and stir in tomatoes. Cook, stirring constantly, until mixture thickens. Add green chilies and ¾ teaspoon each of salt and pepper.

- Fold in cheese and stir until it melts. Pour sauce over cauliflower. Cover and bake for about 15 minutes. Serves 4 to 6.

# CAULIFLOWER-VEGGIE CASSEROLE

*1 large head cauliflower, cut into florets*
*1 red bell pepper, sliced*
*½ cup chopped celery*
*½ cup (1 stick) butter, divided*
*1 (10 ounce) package frozen green peas, thawed*
*1 (8 ounce) package shredded Mexican 4-cheese blend, divided*
*⅓ cup flour*
*1 (1 pint) carton half-and-half cream*
*½ cup milk*

- Preheat oven to 325°.

- Cook cauliflower in covered saucepan with small amount of water until tender-crisp. Don't overcook. Saute bell pepper and celery in 3 tablespoons butter in skillet.

- Add bell pepper, celery and peas to drained cauliflower and toss with half cheese. Spoon into sprayed 3-quart baking dish.

- In separate saucepan, combine remaining butter, flour, and ½ teaspoon each of salt and pepper and heat on medium-high. Gradually add half-and-half cream and milk. Cook, stirring constantly, until mixture thickens. Pour over vegetables.

- Cover and bake for 20 minutes. Sprinkle remaining cheese over top of casserole. Bake uncovered for 5 minutes. Serves 6 to 8.

# SUNSHINE CASSEROLE

*This is one of the prettiest casserole you will place on your table!*

*2½ cups finely shredded carrots*
*2 cups cooked rice*
*2 eggs, beaten*
*2 cups cubed Velveeta® cheese*
*1 (15 ounce) can cream-style corn*
*¼ cup half-and-half cream*
*2 tablespoons butter, melted*
*2 tablespoons dried minced onion*

- Preheat oven to 350°.

- Combine all ingredients and ½ teaspoon each of salt and pepper in large bowl. Spoon into sprayed 3-quart baking dish. Bake uncovered for 40 minutes or until set. Serves 6 to 8.

# MAPLE-RAISIN CARROTS

*¼ cup (½ stick) butter*
*½ cup packed brown sugar*
*2 tablespoons maple syrup*
*1 (16 ounce) package baby carrots*
*⅓ cup golden raisins*

- In large saucepan, combine butter, brown sugar, maple syrup and a little salt. Cook, uncovered, over medium heat for 3 to 4 minutes or until it thickens slightly.

- Stir in carrots and raisins and cook 10 more minutes or until carrots are tender. Serves 6 to 8.

# SOUR CREAM CABBAGE

*2 tablespoons (¼ stick) butter*
*1 tablespoon sugar*
*¼ teaspoon ground nutmeg*
*1 (4 ounce) jar pimentos, drained*
*1 (8 ounce) package cream cheese*
*1 medium head cabbage, cooked tender-crisp, drained*

- Combine butter, sugar, nutmeg and pimentos in saucepan. Add cream cheese while on low heat and stir until it melts. Add cabbage, mix well and cook until it is tender-crisp but don't overcook. Serves 6 to 8.

# EVERYBODY'S FAVORITE CORN

*1 (15 ounce) can whole kernel corn*
*1 (15 ounce) can cream-style corn*
*½ cup (1 stick) butter, melted*
*2 eggs, beaten*
*1 (8 ounce) carton sour cream*
*1 (6 ounce) package jalapeno cornbread mix*
*½ cup shredded cheddar cheese*

- Preheat oven to 350°. Mix all ingredients, except cheese in large bowl and pour into sprayed 9 x 13-inch baking dish.

- Bake for 35 minutes or until light brown on top. Uncover, sprinkle cheese on top and return to oven for 5 minutes. Serves 8 to 10.

# Cook's Best Cornbread

*This is moist, much like spoon bread. It's also*
*very good reheated and great with maple syrup.*

2 eggs
1 (8 ounce) carton sour cream
½ cup vegetable oil
1 (8 ounce) can cream-style corn
1 cup cornmeal
3 teaspoons baking powder

- Preheat oven to 375°. Beat eggs, sour cream, oil and corn in bowl. Blend in cornmeal, baking powder and 1½ teaspoons salt. Pour in sprayed 9 x 9-inch pan. Bake for 30 to 50 minutes. Serves 8 to 9.

# Corn Pudding

1 (8 ounce) package corn muffin mix
1 (15 ounce) can cream-style corn
½ cup sour cream
3 eggs, slightly beaten

- Combine all ingredients and pour into buttered 2-quart baking dish. Bake uncovered at 350° for about 35 minutes. Serves 4 to 6.

# Fantastic Fried Corn

*Yes, it has lots of calories, but it's worth it.*

2 (16 ounce) packages frozen whole kernel corn
½ cup (1 stick) butter
1 cup whipping cream
1 tablespoon sugar

- Place corn in large skillet and turn on medium heat. Add butter, whipping cream, sugar and 1 teaspoon salt. Stirring constantly, heat until most of whipping cream and butter absorbs into corn. Serves 10.

# Shoe-Peg Corn

*1 (8 ounce) package cream cheese, softened*
*½ cup (1 stick) butter, softened*
*3 (15 ounce) cans shoe-peg corn*
*1 (4 ounce) can diced green chilies*

- Preheat oven to 350°.

- Beat cream cheese and butter in bowl. Add corn and green chilies and mix well. Spoon into sprayed 9 x 13-inch baking dish. Cover and bake for 30 minutes. Serves 12.

# Stuffed Corn

*1 (15 ounce) can cream-style corn*
*1 (15 ounce) can whole kernel corn, drained*
*½ cup (1 stick) butter, melted*
*1 (6 ounce) package chicken stuffing mix*

- Preheat oven to 350°.

- Combine all ingredients and ½ cup water and mix well. Spoon into buttered 9 x 13-inch baking pan. Bake for 30 minutes. Serves 6 to 8.

# Corn and Green Chili Casserole

*2 (10 ounce) packages frozen whole kernel corn*
*2 tablespoons butter*
*1 (8 ounce) package cream cheese*
*1 tablespoon sugar*
*1 (4 ounce) can diced green chilies*

- Preheat oven to 350°.

- Cook corn according to package directions, drain and set aside. Melt butter in saucepan over low heat, add cream cheese and stir until it melts.

- Stir in corn, sugar and green chilies. Spoon into sprayed 2-quart baking dish. Cover and bake for 25 minutes. Serves 8.

# CREAMY MEXICAN CORN CASSEROLE FOR 20

2 (15 ounce) cans cream-style corn
2 (15 ounce) cans whole kernel corn, drained
1 bell pepper, seeded, chopped
1 onion, chopped
1 (10 ounce) can tomatoes and green chilies
¼ cup (½ stick) butter, melted
3 eggs, beaten
1 teaspoon sugar
1 cup buttery cracker crumbs
1 (8 ounce) package shredded Mexican 4-cheese blend

- Preheat oven to 350°. Mix cans of corn, bell pepper, onion, tomatoes and green chilies, butter, eggs, sugar, 1 teaspoon salt and cracker crumbs in large mixing bowl. Pour into sprayed 10 x 15-inch baking dish.

- Bake uncovered for 45 minutes. Remove from oven, sprinkle cheese over casserole and return to oven for 5 minutes. Serves 20.

# EASY CORN AND OKRA GUMBO

¼ pound bacon
1 pound fresh okra, sliced
2 onions, chopped
1 (15 ounce) can stewed tomatoes
1 (15 ounce) can whole kernel corn, drained
Rice, cooked

- Fry bacon in large skillet until crisp, drain and set aside. In same skillet with bacon drippings, saute okra and onions but do not brown.

- Add tomatoes and corn and bring to a boil. Simmer for about 5 to 10 minutes. Serve over hot rice. Sprinkle bacon over top of each serving. Serves 6 to 8.

# SPICY HOMINY

1 (15 ounce) can yellow hominy, drained
1 (8 ounce) carton sour cream
1 (4 ounce) can diced green chilies
1¼ cups shredded cheddar cheese

- Preheat oven to 350°.

- Combine all ingredients in bowl and add a little salt. Pour into 1-quart baking dish and bake for about 20 minutes. Serves 4 to 6.

# Vegetable-Corn Medley

*1 (8 ounce) can whole kernel corn, drained*
*2/3 cup milk*
*2 cups broccoli florets*
*2 cups cauliflower florets*
*1 cup shredded cheddar cheese*

- Heat corn and milk in large saucepan over medium heat to boiling and stir often. Stir in broccoli and cauliflower florets and return to boiling. Reduce heat to low and cover.

- Cook for 20 minutes or until vegetables are tender and stir occasionally. Stir in cheese and heat until cheese melts. Serves 8.

# Eggplant Frittata

*This is a delicious way to serve eggplant for a light lunch and*
*it is rich enough to be served as the main course. You could put it*
*together the day before the lunch, then bake just before serving.*

*3 cups peeled, finely chopped eggplant*
*1/2 cup chopped green bell pepper*
*3 tablespoons extra light olive oil*
*1 (8 ounce) jar roasted red peppers, drained, chopped*
*10 eggs*
*1/2 cup half-and-half cream*
*1 teaspoon Italian seasoning*
*1/3 cup grated parmesan cheese*

- Preheat oven to 325°.

- Cook eggplant and bell pepper in oil in skillet for 2 to 3 minutes, just until tender. Stir in roasted red peppers. Combine eggs, half-and-half cream, 1 teaspoon salt, Italian seasoning and 1/4 teaspoon pepper in bowl and beat just until they blend well.

- Add eggplant-pepper mixture to egg-cream mixture. Pour into sprayed 10-inch pie pan. Cover and bake for about 15 minutes or until center sets.

- Sprinkle parmesan cheese over top. Bake uncovered for about 5 minutes, just until cheese melts slightly. Cut into wedges to serve. Serve 6 to 8.

# EGGPLANT FRITTERS

*1 medium eggplant*
*1 egg, beaten*
*3 tablespoons flour*
*½ teaspoon baking powder*
*Canola oil*

- Peel and slice eggplant. Steam until tender and drain. Mash until smooth. Add egg, flour, ½ teaspoon salt and baking powder in bowl and mix well. Form into patties and fry in deep hot oil. Serves 4.

# SUNDAY GREEN BEANS

*3 (15 ounce) cans whole green beans, drained*
*1 (16 ounce) package shredded Mexican Velveeta® cheese*
*1 (8 ounce) can sliced water chestnuts, drained, chopped*
*½ cup slivered almonds*
*¾ cup chopped, roasted red bell peppers*
*1½ cups cracker crumbs*
*¼ cup (½ stick) butter, melted*

- Preheat oven to 350°.

- Place green beans in sprayed 9 x 13-inch baking dish and cover with shredded cheese. Sprinkle with water chestnuts, almonds and roasted bell peppers. Place casserole in microwave and heat just until cheese begins to melt. (Watch closely.)

- Combine cracker crumbs and melted butter in bowl, sprinkle over casserole and bake uncovered for 30 minutes. Serves 10 to 12.

# GREEN CAESAR BAKE

*2 pounds fresh green beans, snapped*
*1 (6 ounce) package garlic-flavored croutons, lightly crushed, divided*
*1½ cups bottled creamy Caesar-style salad dressing*
*⅓ cup grated parmesan cheese*
*1 tablespoon lemon juice*

- Preheat oven to 350°.

- Place beans in saucepan with ½ cup water and bring to a boil. Cook about 8 minutes or until tender. Drain and rinse with cold water.

- Transfer beans to large bowl and stir in 1 cup croutons, salad dressing, cheese and lemon juice. Spoon into sprayed 7 x 11-inch baking dish. Top with remaining croutons and bake for 30 minutes or until croutons are golden brown. Serves 10.

# FANCY GREEN BEANS

*2 (16 ounce) package frozen French-style green beans, thawed*
*½ cup (1 stick) butter*
*1 (8 ounce) package fresh mushrooms, sliced*
*2 (10 ounce) cans cream of chicken soup*
*⅔ cup sliced roasted red bell peppers*
*2 teaspoons soy sauce*
*1 cup shredded white cheddar cheese*
*⅔ cup chopped cashew*

- Preheat oven to 325°.

- Cook green beans according to package directions, drain and set aside. In large saucepan, melt butter and saute mushrooms about 5 minutes, but do not brown.

- Stir in soups, ¼ cup water, roasted peppers, soy sauce and cheese and gently mix.

- Fold in drained green beans and spoon into sprayed, deep 9 x 13-inch baking pan.

- Sprinkle cashews over top of casserole and bake uncovered for 30 minutes or until edges are hot and bubbly. Serves 10 to 12.

# BUNDLES OF GREEN

*3 (15 ounce) cans whole green beans, drained*
*1 pound bacon*
*2 (15 ounce) cans new potatoes, drained*
*2 (10 ounce) cans fiesta nacho cheese soup*
*1½ cups milk*

- Preheat oven to 350°.

- Gather 6 to 7 whole green beans in bundle, wrap with ½ strip of bacon and secure with toothpicks. Place bundles in large baking dish so bundles do not touch. Place under broiler in oven until bacon cooks on both sides.

- Spoon off bacon drippings and place potatoes around bundles. Combine nacho cheese soup and milk in saucepan and heat just enough to mix well.

- Pour over green beans and potatoes. Cover and bake for 20 minutes or just until sauce bubbles. Serves 6 to 8.

# CHEESY GREEN BEANS

*¾ cup milk*
*1 (8 ounce) package cream cheese*
*½ teaspoon garlic powder*
*½ cup grated parmesan cheese*
*2 (15 ounce) cans cut green beans*

- Combine milk, cream cheese, garlic and parmesan cheese in saucepan and heat until cheeses melt. In separate pan, heat green beans, drain and cover with cream cheese mixture. Toss to coat evenly and serve hot. Serves 6.

# ALMOND GREEN BEANS

*⅓ cup slivered almonds*
*¼ cup (½ stick) butter*
*¾ teaspoon garlic salt*
*3 tablespoons lemon juice*
*2 (16 ounce) cans French-style green beans*

- Cook almonds in butter, garlic salt and lemon juice in saucepan until slightly golden brown. Add drained green beans to almonds and heat. Serves 8.

# SNAPPY GREEN BEAN CASSEROLE

*3 (15 ounce) cans whole green beans, drained*
*1 (8 ounce) can sliced water chestnuts, drained, chopped*
*2 (5 ounce) jars jalapeno processed cheese spread, warmed*
*1½ cups cracker crumbs*
*¼ cup (½ stick) butter, melted*

- Preheat oven to 350°.

- Place green beans in sprayed 9 x 13-inch baking dish and cover with water chestnuts. Pour cheese over green beans and water chestnuts.

- Combine cracker crumbs and butter in bowl and sprinkle over casserole. Bake for 30 minutes. Serves 10.

# Green Bean Supreme

2 tablespoons butter
1 (10 ounce) can cream of mushroom soup
1 (3 ounce) package cream cheese, softened
3 (15 ounce) cans French-style green beans, drained
1 tablespoon dried onion flakes
1 (8 ounce) can sliced water chestnuts, drained
½ teaspoon garlic powder
1½ cups shredded cheddar cheese
1½ cups cracker crumbs
½ cup slivered almonds

- Preheat oven to 350°. Melt butter in large saucepan and add soup and cream cheese. Cook over low heat, stirring constantly, just until cream cheese melts and mixture is fairly smooth.

- Remove from heat and stir in green beans, onion flakes, water chestnuts, garlic powder, cheese and ½ teaspoon salt. Mix well.

- Pour into sprayed 9 x 13-inch baking dish. Top with cracker crumbs and sprinkle with almonds. Bake for 30 minutes or until casserole bubbles around edges. Serves 8 to 10.

# Green Beans with Tomatoes

2 pounds frozen, cut green beans
4 tomatoes, chopped, drained
1 bunch green onions, chopped
1 cup Italian salad dressing

- Place beans in saucepan, cover with water and bring to boil. Cook uncovered for 8 to 10 minutes or until tender crisp, drain and refrigerate. Add tomatoes, green onions and salad dressing and toss to coat. Serves 8 to 10.

# Pine Nut Green Beans

1 (16 ounce) package frozen green beans
¼ cup (½ stick) butter
¾ cup pine nuts
¼ teaspoon garlic powder

- Cook beans in water in covered 3-quart saucepan for 10 to 15 minutes or until tender-crisp and drain.

- Melt butter in skillet over medium heat and add pine nuts. Cook, stirring frequently, until golden. Add pine nuts to green beans and add garlic powder. Serve hot. Serves 6 to 8.

# CREAMED GREEN PEAS

*1 (16 ounce) package frozen English peas*
*2 tablespoons butter*
*1 (10 ounce) can cream of celery soup*
*1 (3 ounce) package cream cheese*
*1 (8 ounce) can water chestnuts, drained*

- Cook peas in microwave for 8 minutes and turn dish after 4 minutes. Combine butter, soup and cream cheese in large saucepan. Cook on medium heat and stir until butter and cream cheese melt. Add peas and water chestnuts and mix. Serve hot. Serves 8.

# SOUTHERN HOPPIN' JOHN

*Hoppin' John is a beloved southern comfort food and is*
*considered "lucky", when served on New Year's Day.*

*1 pound bulk sausage*
*1 (16 ounce) package frozen chopped onion and bell peppers*
*1 (14 ounce) can chicken broth*
*1¼ cups instant white rice*
*1 teaspoon minced garlic*
*2 (15 ounce) cans black-eyed peas*

- In large pot, brown and cook sausage, onions and bell peppers over medium-high heat. Drain and add chicken broth, rice, garlic and a little salt and pepper. Bring to a boil, reduce heat and simmer 15 minutes, stirring occasionally.

- Drain, rinse peas and add to pot. Simmer for additional 10 minutes or until liquid absorbs. Serves 6 to 8.

# BLACK-EYED PEAS AND HAM

*3 (15 ounce) cans black-eyed peas with liquid*
*1½ cups coarsely chopped ham*
*1 onion, chopped*
*1 pound small, fresh whole okra pods*

- In large saucepan, combine peas, ham and onion and bring to a boil, reduce heat and simmer 10 minutes.

- Place all okra on top of peas-ham mixture, cover and cook on medium heat about 10 minutes or until okra is tender. When serving, remove okra with slotted spoon to plate. Pour peas into serving bowl and place okra on top of peas. Serves 8 to 10.

# BLACK-EYED PEAS AND TOMATOES

*1 bell pepper, seeded, chopped*
*1 large onion, chopped*
*2 ribs celery, chopped*
*2 tablespoons butter*
*2 (15 ounce) cans jalapeno black-eyed peas, drained*
*1 (15 ounce) can stewed tomatoes with liquid*
*1 teaspoon garlic powder*
*¼ cup ketchup*
*2 teaspoons chicken bouillon granules*

- Preheat oven to 350°.

- Saute bell pepper, onion and celery in butter in saucepan until tender-crisp, but do not overcook. Remove from heat and add black-eyed peas, stewed tomatoes, garlic powder, ketchup and chicken bouillon.

- Spoon into 2-quart baking dish. Cover and bake for about 20 minutes or just until it bubbles. Serves 4 to 6.

# TASTY BLACK-EYED PEAS

*2 (10 ounce) packages frozen black-eyed peas*
*1¼ cups chopped green pepper*
*¾ cup chopped onion*
*3 tablespoons butter*
*1 (15 ounce) can stewed tomatoes with liquid*

- Cook black-eyed peas in saucepan according to package directions and drain. Saute green pepper and onion in butter in skillet. Add peas, tomatoes and a little salt and pepper. Cook over low heat until thoroughly hot and stir often. Serves 8.

# ITALIAN-STYLE RICE AND BEANS

*1 (16 ounce) package frozen chopped onions and bell peppers*
*2 tablespoons olive oil*
*1 (15 ounce) can Italian stewed tomatoes*
*1 (15 ounce) can great northern beans, drained*
*1 cup instant rice*

- In large saucepan, saute onions and bell peppers in oil. Add stewed tomatoes, beans, ½ cup water and rice and stir well.

- Over medium-high heat, cover and cook about 3 minutes. Uncover and continue cooking another 3 minutes, stirring once, or until rice is tender. Serves 8.

# ITALIAN WHITE BEANS

1 onion, coarsely chopped
1 bell pepper, seeded, chopped
2 teaspoons minced garlic
2 tablespoons olive oil
2 (15 ounce) cans great northern beans, drained
1 teaspoon sugar
1 teaspoon white wine vinegar

- In large saucepan, saute onion, bell pepper and garlic in olive oil. Stir in beans, sugar, vinegar and a little salt and pepper. Stir over medium heat several times until mixture is thoroughly hot. Serves 6 to 8.

# BAKED BEANS

2 (15 ounce) cans pork and beans, slightly drained
½ onion, finely chopped
⅔ cup packed brown sugar
¼ cup chili sauce
1 tablespoon Worcestershire sauce
2 strips bacon

- Preheat oven to 325°.

- Combine beans, onion, brown sugar, chili sauce and Worcestershire sauce in bowl. Pour into sprayed 2-quart baking dish and place bacon strips over bean mixture. Bake for 50 minutes. Serves 8.

# COUNTRY BAKED BEANS

4 (16 ounce) cans baked beans, drained
1 (12 ounce) bottle chili sauce
1 large onion, chopped
½ pound bacon, cooked, crumbled
2 cups packed brown sugar

- Preheat oven to 325°.

- Combine all ingredients in 3-quart baking dish and stir until blended. Bake for 55 minutes or until thoroughly hot. Serves 12 to 14.

# SHORTCUT BAKED BEANS

1 (1 pound) can pork and beans
¼ cup packed brown sugar
¼ cup ketchup
¼ cup chopped onion
¼ cup chopped green pepper
¼ teaspoon dry mustard
3 - 4 slices bacon, halved

- Preheat oven to 350°.

- Combine beans, sugar, ketchup, onion, green pepper and mustard and mix well. Pour into sprayed, casserole dish and top with bacon. Bake for 1 hour. Serve immediately. Serves 4 to 6.

# BETTER BUTTER BEANS

1 cup sliced celery
1 onion, chopped
¼ cup (½ stick) butter
1 (10 ounce) can diced tomatoes and green chilies
½ teaspoon sugar
2 (15 ounce) cans butter beans

- Saute celery and onion in butter in skillet for about 3 minutes. Add tomatoes and green chilies, several sprinkles of salt and sugar. Add butter beans, cover and simmer for about 20 minutes. Serve hot. Serves 8.

# BUTTER BEANS AND GREEN ONIONS

1 (10 ounce) package frozen butter beans
1 bunch fresh green onions, chopped
6 bacon slices, cooked, crumbled, drippings saved
½ teaspoon garlic powder
½ cup chopped fresh parsley

- Cook butter beans according to package directions and set aside. Saute green onions in bacon drippings. Stir in butter beans, garlic powder, parsley and a little salt and pepper. Cook just until thoroughly hot. Pour into serving bowl and sprinkle with bacon. Serves 4.

# CREAMED ONIONS AND PEAS

1 (10 ounce) can cream of celery soup
½ cup milk
3 (15 ounce) jars tiny white onions, drained
1 (10 ounce) package frozen peas
½ cup slivered almonds
3 tablespoons grated parmesan cheese

- Preheat oven to 350°. Combine soup and milk in large saucepan; heat and stir until bubbly. Gently stir in onions, peas and almonds and mix well.

- Spoon into sprayed 2-quart baking dish. Cover and bake for 30 minutes. Sprinkle parmesan cheese over top of casserole before serving. Serves 8.

# CRACKERED ONION CASSEROLE

*This is a great replacement for potatoes or rice.*

3 cups round buttery cracker crumbs
½ cup (1 stick) butter, melted, divided
2 onions, thinly sliced
1 cup milk
2 eggs, slightly beaten
1 (8 ounce) package shredded cheddar cheese

- Preheat oven to 300°.

- Combine cracker crumbs and half butter in bowl. Place in sprayed 9 x 13-inch baking dish and pat down. Saute onions in remaining butter. Spread onions over crust.

- Combine milk, eggs, cheese, and a little salt and pepper in saucepan. Heat on low just until cheese melts. Pour sauce over onions. Bake for 45 minutes or until knife inserted in center comes out clean. Serves 8 to 10.

*I totally take back all those times I didn't want to take a nap when I was younger.*

# MUSHROOM-ONION PIE

*1 large onion, halved, thinly sliced*
*2 cups sliced fresh mushrooms*
*1 tablespoon olive oil*
*4 eggs, slightly beaten*
*1 (8 ounce) carton whipping cream*
*½ teaspoon thyme*
*½ teaspoon basil*
*Ground nutmeg*
*1 (9 inch) frozen deep-dish piecrust, thawed*

- Preheat oven to 350°.

- Saute onion slices and mushrooms in oil in skillet and cook on low heat for about 10 minutes, but do not brown.

- Combine eggs, whipping cream, thyme, basil, 1½ teaspoon salt, 1 teaspoon pepper and pinch of nutmeg (if you have it) and mix well. Pour into onion-mushroom mixture and stir.

- Place piecrust in pie pan and pour in mixture. Bake for 45 minutes or until center sets. Serves 6 to 8.

# POTATO SUPREME FOR 20

*This is no time to count calories!*

*7 - 8 large baking potatoes*
*1 cup half-and-half cream*
*½ cup (1 stick) butter, sliced*
*1 (12 ounce) package shredded cheddar cheese*
*1 (16 ounce) carton sour cream*
*1 bunch green onions with tops, sliced*

- Preheat oven to 350°.

- Cook potatoes in microwave. After cooling, peel and grate. Combine cream, butter, cheese, sour cream, 2 teaspoons salt and 1 teaspoon pepper in double boiler; cook and stir just until butter and cheese melt.

- Add cheese mixture to grated potatoes and place in sprayed 10 x 15-inch baking dish. Cover and bake for 35 to 40 minutes. To serve, top with sliced green onions. Serves 20.

# CHIVE-POTATO SOUFFLE

*3 eggs, separated*
*2 cups hot instant mashed potatoes*
*½ cup sour cream*
*2 heaping tablespoons chopped chives*

- Preheat oven to 350°. Beat egg whites in bowl until stiff and set aside. In separate bowl, beat yolks until smooth and add to potatoes. Fold beaten egg whites, sour cream, chives and 1 teaspoon salt into potato-egg yolk mixture and pour into sprayed 2-quart baking dish. Bake for 45 minutes. Serves 6.

# CHEDDAR-POTATO STRIPS

*3 large potatoes, cut into ½-inch strips*
*½ cup milk*
*2 tablespoons butter*
*½ cup shredded cheddar cheese*
*1 tablespoon minced fresh parsley*

- Preheat oven to 400°. Arrange potatoes in single layer in sprayed 9 x 13-inch baking dish. Pour milk over potatoes. Dot with butter and sprinkle with a little salt and pepper.

- Cover and bake for 30 minutes or until potatoes are tender. Sprinkle with cheese and parsley. Bake uncovered for additional 5 minutes. Serves 4 to 6.

# SCALLOPED CHEESE POTATOES

*2 tablespoons butter*
*1 medium onion, thinly sliced*
*6 medium potatoes*
*1 cup shredded Velveeta® cheese*
*2 tablespoons flour*
*2½ cups milk*
*¼ cup finely crushed cracker crumbs or potato chips*

- Preheat oven to 350°. Melt butter in skillet; saute onion slices until light brown. Peel and slice potatoes; put layer in sprayed 2-quart baking dish.

- Add one-fourth onion slices; sprinkle with ¼ cup cheese, ½ tablespoon flour, 2 teaspoons salt and ⅛ teaspoon pepper. Repeat layers about 3 more times. Pour milk over top.

- Sprinkle with crumbs. Cover and bake for 1 hour. Remove cover for last 15 minutes of baking time. Serves 6.

# CREAMY MASHED POTATOES

*6 large potatoes*
*1 (8 ounce) carton sour cream*
*1 (8 ounce) package cream cheese, softened*

- Preheat oven to 325°.

- Peel, cut up and boil potatoes in large saucepan until soft. Drain. Add sour cream, cream cheese, 1 teaspoon salt and ½ teaspoon pepper (use white pepper if you don't want specks in the dish) and whip until cream cheese melts. Pour into sprayed 3-quart baking dish.

- Cover with foil and bake for about 20 minutes. (About 10 minutes longer if reheating.) Serves 8.

# FIESTA BAKED POTATOES

*4 large baking potatoes*
*1 (10 ounce) can fiesta nacho cheese soup*
*1 cup shredded Mexican 3-cheese blend*
*1 cup cooked, shredded ham*
*¼ cup sour cream*
*1 (10 ounce) package frozen broccoli florets, thawed*

- Stick potatoes with tines of fork several times. Cook potatoes in microwave until tender. In 1-quart microwave-safe bowl, stir together soup, cheese, ham, sour cream, broccoli and salt and pepper to taste.

- Heat in microwave 2 to 3 minutes or until hot and bubbly. Spoon cheese mixture over split and fluffed up potatoes. Serves 4.

# LOADED POTATOES

*6 large baking potatoes, washed*
*1 (1 pound) bulk pork sausage*
*1 (8 ounce) package cubed processed cheese*
*1 (10 ounce) can diced tomatoes and green chilies, drained*

- Stick potatoes with tines of fork. Cook potatoes in microwave until done. Brown sausage in skillet over medium heat and drain fat. Add cheese and diced tomatoes and stir well.

- With knife, cut potatoes down center and fluff insides with fork. Spoon generous amounts of sausage-cheese mixture on each potato and reheat in microwave 2 to 3 minutes if necessary. Serves 6.

# GLORY POTATOES

*Talk about a "good" potato, this is it! And you don't have to peel a single potato.*

1 (22 ounce) package frozen tater tots
2 eggs, beaten
1 (10 ounce) can cream of potato soup
1 (10 ounce) can cream of chicken soup
1 (8 ounce) carton sour cream
¾ cup milk
½ teaspoon garlic powder
1 red bell pepper, thinly sliced
1 onion, chopped
1 (12 ounce) package shredded cheddar cheese, divided

- Preheat oven to 350°.

- Arrange tater tots in sprayed 10 x 15-inch baking dish.  Combine eggs, soups, sour cream, milk, garlic powder, bell pepper, onion, and 1 teaspoon each of salt and pepper in bowl and mix well.

- Fold in half cheddar cheese.  Spoon mixture over tater tots.  Cover and bake for 50 minutes or until bubbly.  Sprinkle remaining cheese over casserole and bake uncovered for about 5 minutes.  Serves 10 to 12.

# HALLELUJAH POTATOES

*This is a super baked potato!*

6 baking potatoes
½ cup (1 stick) butter
1 (8 ounce) package cream cheese, softened
1 bunch fresh green onions with tops, sliced
1 (6 ounce) can crabmeat, drained, flaked
1 cup shredded cheddar cheese

- Preheat oven to 400°.  Bake potatoes for 1 hour or until done.  Halve potatoes lengthwise, scoop out flesh and set aside skins.  Beat hot potatoes, butter, cream cheese, and 1 teaspoon each of salt and pepper and beat well.  Stir in onions and crabmeat.

- Fill set aside skins with potato mixture.  Sprinkle cheese over top of potatoes.  Reduce oven to 350°.  Place potatoes on baking sheet and bake for 20 minutes or until it bubbles.  Serves 6.

# MASHED POTATOES SUPREME

*1 (8 ounce) package cream cheese, softened*
*½ cup sour cream*
*2 tablespoons butter, softened*
*1 (.04 ounce) packet ranch salad dressing mix*
*6 - 8 cups cooked warm instant mashed potatoes*

- Preheat oven to 350°. Beat cream cheese, sour cream, butter and dressing in bowl. Add potatoes and stir well. Transfer to 2-quart baking dish and bake for 25 minutes or until thoroughly hot. Serves 6.

# NEW POTATOES WITH HERB BUTTER

*1½ pounds new (red) potatoes with peels*
*2 tablespoon butter, sliced*
*¼ teaspoon thyme*
*½ cup chopped fresh parsley*
*½ teaspoon rosemary*

- Scrub potatoes and cut in halves. Boil potatoes in lightly salted water in medium saucepan. Cook until potatoes are tender, about 15 minutes. Drain.

- Add butter, thyme, parsley and rosemary. Toss gently until butter melts. Serves 6 to 8.

# OVEN FRIES

*5 medium baking potatoes*
*⅓ cup olive oil*
*Paprika*

- Preheat oven to 375°. Scrub potatoes, cut each in 6 lengthwise wedges and place in shallow baking dish. Combine oil, ¾ teaspoon salt and ¼ teaspoon pepper in bowl and brush potatoes with mixture.

- Sprinkle potatoes lightly with paprika. Bake for about 50 minutes or until potatoes are tender and light brown and baste twice with remaining oil mixture while baking. Serves 6 to 8.

# Potatoes Au Gratin

*1 (8 ounce) package cubed Velveeta® cheese*
*1 (16 ounce) carton half-and-half cream*
*1 cup shredded cheddar cheese*
*½ cup (1 stick) butter*
*1 (2 pound) package frozen hash-brown potatoes, thawed*

- Preheat oven to 350°. Melt Velveeta® cheese, half-and-half cream, cheddar cheese and butter in double boiler. Place hash browns in sprayed 9 x 13-inch baking dish and pour cheese mixture over potatoes. Bake for 1 hour. Serves 8 to 10.

# Scalloped Potatoes

*6 potatoes*
*½ cup (1 stick) butter*
*1 tablespoon flour*
*¾ cup milk*
*1 (8 ounce) package shredded cheddar cheese*

- Preheat oven to 350°.

- Peel and wash potatoes. Slice half of potatoes and place in sprayed 3-quart baking dish. Slice butter and place half over potatoes. Sprinkle with a little pepper and flour.

- Slice remaining potatoes and place over first layer, add remaining butter slices and pour milk over casserole. Sprinkle with a little more pepper and cover with cheese. Cover and bake for 1 hour. Serves 6 to 8.

*TIP: This must be cooked immediately or potatoes will darken. It can be frozen after baking and then reheated.*

# Terrific Taters

*5 - 6 medium potatoes*
*1 (8 ounce) carton sour cream*
*1 (.04 ounce) packet ranch dressing mix*
*1½ cups shredded cheddar cheese*
*3 pieces bacon, fried, drained, crumbled*

- Preheat oven to 350°.

- Peel, slice and boil potatoes until tender and drain. Place potatoes in 2-quart baking dish. Combine sour cream, salad dressing mix and a little pepper. Toss until potatoes are coated. Sprinkle cheese on top. Bake for about 20 minutes. Sprinkle bacon on top and serve hot. Serves 8.

# The Ultimate Potato

*This is no time to count calories!*

6 large baking potatoes, boiled
1 cup half-and-half cream
6 tablespoons (¾ stick) butter
1 (8 ounce) package shredded cheddar cheese
1 (8 ounce) carton sour cream
½ cup chopped green onions
6 strips bacon, fried, crumbled

- Preheat oven to 350°.

- Peel cooled potatoes and grate in bowl. Combine half-and-half cream, butter, cheese and sour cream in double boiler and stir just until they melt.

- Add cheese mixture to grated potatoes and place in sprayed 4-quart baking dish. Cover and bake for 30 minutes. Top with onions and crumbled bacon. Serves 8.

# Twice-Baked Potatoes

8 medium baking potatoes
2 tablespoons butter
1 (10 ounce) can cheddar cheese soup
1 tablespoon chopped dried chives

- Preheat oven to 400°.

- Bake potatoes until done. Cut potatoes in half lengthwise and scoop out flesh leaving thin shell. Whip potatoes with butter and ½ teaspoon salt in bowl.

- Gradually add soup and chives and beat until light and fluffy. Spoon into shells and sprinkle with paprika. Bake for 15 minutes. Serves 8.

*TIP: If you want a little "zip" to potatoes, add 1 (10 ounce) can fiesta nacho cheese soup instead of cheese soup.*

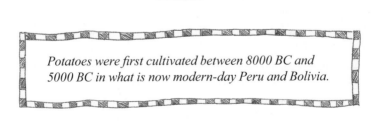

*Potatoes were first cultivated between 8000 BC and 5000 BC in what is now modern-day Peru and Bolivia.*

# POTATO-STUFFED BELL PEPPERS

*3 baking potatoes*
*6 large red bell peppers*
*Paprika*

- Preheat oven at 425°.

- Pierce each potato 3 to 4 times and place on oven rack. Bake for 1 hour 20 minutes to 1 hour 30 minutes. Cool about 20 minutes.

- While potatoes cook, cut bell peppers in half lengthwise through stem. Remove seeds and membranes, rinse and pat dry. Set aside.

## STUFFING:

*1 (8 ounce) carton sour cream*
*1 cup shredded colby Jack cheese*
*¼ cup (½ stick) butter, melted*
*3 fresh green onions, finely chopped*
*2 teaspoons dried parsley*

- Peel cooked potatoes and mash slightly with potato masher. Add sour cream, cheese, butter, chopped green onion, parsley and a little salt and pepper; mix well.

- Spoon potatoes into bell pepper halves and sprinkle with paprika.

- Bell peppers may be grilled for about 20 minutes or baked at 425° for about 10 to 15 minutes. Serves 6.

# CHEDDAR-POTATO CASSEROLE

*This is a "winner" for the best potato casserole you will ever make!*

*1 (2 pound) bag frozen hash-brown potatoes, thawed*
*1 onion, finely chopped*
*¾ cup (1½ sticks) butter, melted, divided*
*1 (8 ounce) carton sour cream*
*1 (10 ounce) can cream of chicken soup*
*1 (8 ounce) package shredded cheddar cheese*
*2 cups crushed corn flakes*

- Preheat oven to 350°.

- Combine hash browns, onion, ½ cup butter, sour cream, soup and cheese in large bowl and mix well. Pour into sprayed 9 x 13-inch baking dish.

- Combine corn flakes and remaining butter in bowl. Sprinkle over top of casserole. Bake for 45 to 50 minutes or until it bubbles around edges. Serves 8 to 10.

# MAPLE-GINGER SWEET POTATOES

*4 medium sweet potatoes*
*½ cup sour cream*
*⅓ cup maple syrup*
*¼ teaspoon ground ginger*
*¼ cup chopped pecans*

- Preheat oven to 375°.

- Pierce sweet potatoes several times with fork and place on baking sheet. Bake for 1 hour. Combine sour cream and syrup and ginger in bowl. Spoon over split potatoes and sprinkle with pecans. Serves 6.

# SPEEDY SWEET POTATOES

*2 (15 ounce) cans sweet potatoes, drained*
*1 (8 ounce) can crushed pineapple with juice*
*½ cup chopped pecans*
*⅓ cup packed brown sugar*
*1 cup miniature marshmallows, divided*

- Layer sweet potatoes, a little salt, pineapple, pecans, brown sugar and ½ cup marshmallows in 2-quart microwave-safe dish. Cover and microwave on HIGH for 6 minutes or until bubbly around edges.

- Top with remaining marshmallows and heat uncovered on HIGH for 30 seconds or until marshmallows puff. If you like, sprinkle sweet potatoes with a little nutmeg. Serves 8 to 10.

# SWEET POTATO WEDGES

*3 pounds sweet potatoes, peeled, quartered lengthwise*
*6 tablespoons (¾ stick) butter, melted*
*6 tablespoons orange juice*
*¾ teaspoon ground cinnamon*

- Preheat oven to 350°.

- Arrange sweet potatoes in sprayed 9 x 13-inch baking pan. Combine butter, orange juice, ¾ teaspoon salt and cinnamon and drizzle over sweet potatoes. Cover and bake for 60 minutes or until tender. Serves 8.

# Sweet Potato Casserole with Pecans

*This is a beautiful Thanksgiving dish and perfect for Christmas dinner too.*
*Even people who are "lukewarm" about sweet potatoes like this casserole.*

1 (29 ounce) can sweet potatoes, drained
⅓ cup evaporated milk
¾ cup sugar
¼ cup packed brown sugar
2 eggs, beaten
¼ cup (½ stick) butter, melted
1 teaspoon vanilla

- Preheat oven to 350°.

- Place sweet potatoes in bowl and mash slightly with fork. Add evaporated milk, sugar, brown sugar, eggs, butter and vanilla and mix well. Pour into sprayed 7 x 11-inch or 2-quart baking dish.

## Topping:

1 cup packed light brown sugar
¼ cup (½ stick) butter, melted
½ cup flour
1 cup chopped pecans

- Combine brown sugar, butter and flour in bowl and mix well. Stir in pecans and sprinkle topping over casserole. Bake for 35 minutes or until crusty on top. Serves 6 to 8.

# Whipped Sweet Potatoes

1 (28 ounce) can sweet potatoes
1 cup (2 sticks) butter, melted, divided
1 cup packed light brown sugar
1½ cups crushed corn flakes

- Preheat oven to 350°.

- Drain most of liquid from sweet potatoes. Place sweet potatoes in bowl and cut large pieces of potatoes into several pieces. Beat sweet potatoes until creamy and fold in ¾ cup melted butter and brown sugar.

- Beat until butter and brown sugar thoroughly combine with sweet potatoes and pour into sprayed 2-quart baking dish. Combine crushed corn flakes and remaining 2 tablespoons melted butter and sprinkle over sweet potato casserole. Bake for 40 minutes. Serves 10 to 12.

# CREAMY SPINACH CASSEROLE FOR 20

*2 (16 ounce) packages frozen chopped spinach*
*2 (8 ounce) packages cream cheese and chives, softened*
*1 (8 ounce) package shredded cheddar cheese*
*1 (10 ounce) can cream of celery soup*
*1 cup milk*
*2 eggs, beaten*
*2 cups cheese cracker crumbs*

- Preheat oven to 350°.

- Cook spinach in saucepan according to package directions and drain well. Add cream cheese and cheddar cheese to hot spinach, stir until cheese melts and mixes well.

- Stir in soup, milk and eggs and mix well. Pour into 2 sprayed (2-quart) baking dishes or 1 (10 x 15-inch) baking dish. Top with cheese cracker crumbs.

- Bake small casserole uncovered for 35 minutes and larger casserole for 45 minutes. Serves 20.

# SUPER SPINACH BAKE

*¼ cup (½ stick) butter*
*⅔ cup cracker crumbs*
*2 (10 ounce) packages frozen chopped spinach, thawed, drained*
*1 (8 ounce) package shredded cheddar cheese, divided*
*1 (8 ounce) carton sour cream*
*1 tablespoon dry onion soup mix*

- Preheat oven to 325°.

- Melt butter in skillet over medium heat and add cracker crumbs. Cook, stirring often, for 5 minutes or until crumbs are light brown; set aside.

- In medium bowl, combine spinach, 1 cup cheese, sour cream and soup mix. Spoon into sprayed 7 x 11-inch baking dish. Top with browned crumbs.

- Bake uncovered for 30 minutes. Remove from oven, sprinkle remaining cheese over top and return to oven for 5 minutes. Serves 8.

*Remember that limp vegetables like carrots and potatoes regain much of their crispness if soaked in ice water for at least 1 hour.*

# CHEESE-PLEASE SPINACH

1 (16 ounce) package frozen chopped spinach
3 eggs
½ cup flour
1 (16 ounce) carton small curd cottage cheese, drained
1 (8 ounce) package shredded cheddar cheese

- Preheat oven to 350°.

- Cook spinach in saucepan according to package directions, drain* and set aside. Beat eggs in bowl and add flour, cottage cheese and a little salt and pepper.

- Stir in spinach and cheddar cheese and pour into 1½-quart baking dish. Bake for 35 minutes. Serves 8.

*TIP: Squeeze spinach between paper towels to completely remove any excess moisture.*

# CREAMED SPINACH BAKE

2 (10 ounce) packages frozen chopped spinach
2 (3 ounce) packages cream cheese, softened
3 tablespoons butter
1 cup seasoned breadcrumbs

- Preheat oven to 350° (175°C).

- Cook spinach in saucepan according to package directions and drain*. Combine cream cheese and butter with spinach. Heat until cream cheese and butter melt and mix well with spinach.

- Pour into sprayed baking dish and sprinkle a little salt over spinach. Cover with breadcrumbs and bake for 15 to 20 minutes. Serves 8.

*TIP: Squeeze spinach between paper towels to completely remove excess moisture.*

## BIRDS EYE FROZEN FOODS

When Clarence Birdseye went on an expedition to northern Canada in 1912, he saw Eskimos storing their catch in ice. For ten years Birdseye worked to perfect the process for freezing and delivering frozen foods to stores. Once frozen foods arrived in stores, our lives and eating habits were changed forever. Today, more than half the American population eat some kind of frozen food each week.

# EASY CREAMY SPINACH

2 (10 ounce) packages frozen chopped spinach
1 (8 ounce) package cream cheese and chives, softened
⅔ cup shredded cheddar cheese
1 (10 ounce) can cream of celery soup
½ cup milk
1 egg, beaten
1 cup cheese cracker crumbs

- Preheat oven to 350°.

- Cook spinach in saucepan according to package directions and drain well. Squeeze spinach between paper towels to completely remove excess moisture.

- Add cream cheese and cheddar cheese to hot spinach, stir until both cheeses melt and mix well. Stir in soup, milk and egg and mix well.

- Pour into sprayed 2-quart baking dish. Top with cheese cracker crumbs. Bake for about 35 minutes. Serves 4 to 6.

# SPINACH ENCHILADAS

*Wow, are these good and this recipe freezes well.*

2 (10 ounce) packages frozen chopped spinach, thawed, drained
1 (1 ounce) packet onion soup mix
3 cups shredded cheddar cheese, divided
3 cups shredded Monterey Jack cheese or mozzarella, divided
12 flour tortillas
1 (1 pint) carton whipping cream

- Preheat oven to 350°.

- Squeeze spinach between paper towels to completely remove excess moisture. Combine spinach and onion soup mix in medium bowl. Blend in half cheddar and half Jack cheese.

- Spread out 12 tortillas and place about 3 heaping tablespoons spinach mixture down middle of each tortilla and roll. Place each filled tortilla, seam-side down into sprayed 10 x 15-inch baking dish.

- Pour whipping cream over enchiladas and sprinkle with remaining cheeses. Cover and bake for 20 minutes. Uncover and bake for additional 10 minutes. Serves 10 to 12.

TIP: *To make ahead of time, freeze before adding whipping cream and remaining cheeses. Thaw in refrigerator before cooking. These enchiladas are great and so much fun to make and serve! Eat them all up because the tortillas get a little tough if reheated.*

# SPINACH CASSEROLE

*1 (16 ounce) package frozen chopped spinach*
*1 (8 ounce) package cream cheese and chives*
*1 (10 ounce) can cream of mushroom soup*
*1 egg, beaten*
*Cracker crumbs*

- Preheat oven to 350°.

- Cook spinach in saucepan according to directions and drain. Blend cream cheese and soup in saucepan on medium heat. Add egg.

- Mix with spinach and pour into sprayed 1-quart baking dish. Top with cracker crumbs. Bake for 35 minutes. Serves 8.

# SPINACH SPECIAL

*3 (10 ounce) packages frozen chopped spinach*
*1 onion, chopped*
*½ cup (1 stick) butter*
*1 (8 ounce) package cream cheese, cubed*
*1 (14 ounce) can artichokes, drained, chopped*
*⅔ cup grated parmesan cheese*

- Preheat oven to 350°. Cook spinach according to package directions and drain. Squeeze spinach between paper towels to completely remove excess moisture.

- Saute onion in butter in skillet, stir and cook until onion is clear but not brown. Add cream cheese and stir constantly on low heat until cheese melts. Stir in spinach, artichokes, and ½ teaspoon each of salt and pepper.

- Pour into sprayed 2-quart baking dish. Sprinkle parmesan cheese over top of casserole. Cover and bake for 30 minutes. Serves 4 to 6.

*Iceberg lettuce has little nutritional value. Choose romaine, butter lettuce, Boston bibb, spinach, kale, chard or any the leafy greens you see in the produce section.*

# SPINACH-CHEESE MANICOTTI

*This does take a little extra time to fill the shells, but it is
really a special dish and well worth the time it takes!*

1 onion, minced
2 teaspoons minced garlic
Canola oil
1 (15 ounce) carton ricotta cheese
1 (3 ounce) package cream cheese, softened
1 (8 ounce) package shredded mozzarella cheese, divided
1 (3 ounce) package grated parmesan cheese, divided
2 teaspoons Italian seasoning
1 (10 ounce) box frozen chopped spinach, thawed, drained
9 manicotti shells, cooked
1 (26 ounce) jar spaghetti sauce

- Preheat oven to 350°. Saute onion and garlic in a little oil in skillet and set aside. Combine ricotta, cream cheese, half mozzarella, half parmesan cheese, Italian seasoning, and ½ teaspoon each of salt and pepper in bowl and beat until they mix well.

- Squeeze spinach between paper towels to complete remove excess moisture. Add spinach and onion-garlic mixture to cheese mixture and mix well.

- Spoon mixture into manicotti shells. (Be careful not to tear shells.) Pour half of spaghetti sauce in sprayed 9 x 13-inch baking dish.

- Arrange shells over sauce and top with remaining sauce. Cover and bake for 30 minutes. Sprinkle remaining cheeses over top. Bake uncovered until cheese melts. Serves 8 to 10.

# BAKED TOMATOES

2 (16 ounce) cans diced tomatoes, drained
1½ cups toasted breadcrumbs, divided
Scant ¼ cup sugar
½ onion, chopped
¼ cup (½ stick) butter, melted

- Preheat oven to 325°. Combine tomatoes, 1 cup breadcrumbs, sugar, onion and butter in bowl. Pour into sprayed baking dish and cover with remaining breadcrumbs. Bake for 25 to 30 minutes or until crumbs are light brown. Serves 8.

# Okra-Tomato Gumbo

1 large onion, chopped
1 pound fresh okra, sliced
¼ cup (½ stick) butter
2 (15 ounce) cans tomatoes
1 potato, chopped

• Brown onion and okra in butter in skillet. Add tomatoes and potato and bring to a boil. Simmer until potatoes are tender about 30 minutes. Serves 6.

# Summer Pie

3 large tomatoes, peeled, sliced
1 (9 inch) deep-dish frozen piecrust, thawed
1 tablespoon bacon drippings
3 yellow onions, halved, thinly sliced
1 cup shredded cheddar cheese
1 cup mayonnaise
1 (3 ounce) package grated parmesan cheese
2 tablespoons seasoned breadcrumbs
4 bacon slices, cooked, drained, crumbled

• Preheat oven to 400°. Place tomatoes on paper towels and sprinkle with ½ teaspoon salt. Let stand for 30 minutes. Bake piecrust for about 10 minutes or until light brown.

• Saute onion in bacon drippings in large skillet. Spoon onion over prepared piecrust and top with tomato slices. Combine cheddar cheese, mayonnaise and a little pepper in bowl. Spread mixture over tomato slices.

• In separate bowl, combine parmesan cheese and breadcrumbs and sprinkle over top. Reduce oven to 350° and bake for 30 minutes or until light brown. Sprinkle crumbled bacon over top of pie. Let stand for 5 minutes before serving. Serves 6 to 8.

# Tasty Turnips

5 medium turnips
2 teaspoons sugar
¼ cup (½ stick) butter, melted

• Peel and dice turnips. Boil turnips in a little water with sugar and 1½ teaspoons salt in saucepan until tender and drain. Add butter to turnips and mash. Serve hot. Serves 4.

# YELLOW SQUASH DELUXE

*8 - 9 cups sliced yellow squash*
*1 large onion, chopped*
*1 (8 ounce) package cream cheese, softened, cubed*
*1 (4 ounce) jar chopped pimentos, drained*
*1 (8 ounce) carton sour cream*
*1 (16 ounce) carton small curd cottage cheese, drained*
*1 (8 ounce) package shredded Monterey Jack cheese*
*½ cup (1 stick) butter, melted, divided*
*1 (6 ounce) package chicken-flavor stuffing mix, divided*

- Preheat oven to 350°.

- Cook squash and onion in a little salted water in large saucepan until tender-crisp.
  Drain. While mixture is still hot, fold in cream cheese and stir until it melts.

- Add pimentos, sour cream, cottage cheese, Monterey Jack cheese and about ¼ cup
  (½ stick) melted butter and mix well.

- Stir in half stuffing mix and all of seasoning package included with mix; fold into
  squash mixture. Spoon into lightly sprayed 10 x 15-inch baking dish.

- Sprinkle remaining stuffing over top and drizzle remaining melted butter over top.
  Bake uncovered for 45 minutes. Serves 20.

# CREAMY-CHEESY ZUCCHINI

*3 pounds zucchini, sliced*
*1 sweet red bell pepper, finely diced*
*¼ cup (½ stick) plus 3 tablespoons butter, melted, divided*
*1 (10 ounce) can cream of celery soup*
*1 (8 ounce) package cubed Velveeta® cheese*
*1 teaspoon seasoned salt*
*2½ cups crushed buttery cheese crackers*
*⅓ cup slivered almonds*

- Preheat oven to 325°.

- In saucepan, boil zucchini and bell pepper just until barely tender and drain well.
  Do not overcook!

- Combine ¼ cup (½ stick) melted butter, soup, cheese, ¼ cup water and salt. Gently
  stir in zucchini mixture and spoon into 3-quart baking dish.

- Sprinkle crushed crackers and almonds over top and drizzle 3 tablespoons melted
  butter over crackers. Bake uncovered for 35 minutes or until hot and bubbly.
  Serves 8 to 10.

# ZUCCHINI AU GRATIN

6 medium zucchini, sliced
1 onion, chopped
1 (8 ounce) carton sour cream
1¼ cups shredded cheddar cheese
2 teaspoons sesame seeds, toasted

- Preheat oven to 350°.
- Cook zucchini and onion in a little salted water in saucepan but do not overcook. Drain well. Place half zucchini mixture in sprayed 2-quart baking dish and sprinkle with a little salt and pepper.
- Spread with half sour cream and half cheese. Repeat layer. Top with sesame seeds. Bake for 35 minutes. Serves 6.

# ZUCCHINI BAKE

3 cups zucchini, grated
1½ cups shredded Monterey Jack cheese
4 eggs, beaten
¼ teaspoon garlic powder
2 cups cheese cracker crumbs

- Preheat oven to 350°.
- Combine zucchini, cheese, eggs, garlic powder, and ½ teaspoon each of salt and pepper and mix well. Spoon into sprayed 2-quart baking dish. Sprinkle cracker crumbs over top. Bake for 35 to 40 minutes. Serves 4 to 6.

# ZUCCHINI PATTIES

1½ cups grated zucchini
1 egg, beaten
2 tablespoons flour
⅓ cup finely minced onion
½ teaspoon seasoned salt

- Mix all ingredients in bowl. Heat skillet with about 3 tablespoons oil. Drop tablespoonfuls of zucchini mixture into skillet on medium-high heat. Turn and brown both sides. Remove and drain on paper towels. Serves 4.

# SPEEDY ZUCCHINI AND FETTUCCINE

*1 (9 ounce) package refrigerated fresh fettuccine*
*⅓ cup extra-virgin olive oil, divided*
*1 tablespoon minced garlic*
*4 small zucchini, grated*
*½ cup pine nuts, toasted*
*⅓ cup grated parmesan cheese*

- Cook fettuccine according to package directions, drain and place in serving bowl.

- Heat large skillet over high heat and add 2 tablespoons oil, garlic and zucchini. Saute for 1 minute. Add zucchini mixture to pasta with pine nuts and a little salt and pepper.

- Stir in remaining olive oil and toss to combine. Sprinkle parmesan cheese over top of dish to serve. Serves 8 to 10.

# GARDEN CASSEROLE

*1 pound yellow squash, sliced*
*1 pound zucchini, sliced*
*1 green bell pepper, seeded, chopped*
*1 red bell pepper, seeded, chopped*
*1 (15 ounce) can sliced carrots, drained*
*1 (10 ounce) can cream of chicken soup*
*1 (8 ounce) carton sour cream*
*½ cup (1 stick) plus 3 tablespoons butter, melted, divided*
*1 (6 ounce) box herb stuffing mix*

- Preheat oven to 325°.

- Cook squash, zucchini and bell peppers in salted water for 8 to 10 minutes or until just tender-crisp and drain well. (Do not over cook.) Stir in carrots, chicken soup and sour cream; mix well.

- Melt ½ cup (1 stick) butter in large saucepan and add stuffing mix, mix well and reserve 1 cup for topping. Add vegetable-soup mixture and mix gently, but well.

- Spoon into sprayed 9 x 13-inch baking dish and sprinkle reserved stuffing mix over top.

- Drizzle remaining 3 tablespoons melted butter over top and bake uncovered for 35 minutes. Serves 10.

# SQUASH DRESSING

*2 (6 ounce) packages Mexican cornbread mix*
*2 eggs*
*1⅓ cups milk*
*2 pounds yellow squash, sliced*
*½ cup (1 stick) butter*
*1 cup chopped onion*
*1 cup chopped celery*
*½ cup green bell pepper, seeded, chopped*
*1 (10 ounce) can cream of chicken soup*
*2 teaspoons chicken bouillon granules*

- Preheat oven to 350°.

- Prepare cornbread according to package directions with eggs and milk. Cool and crumble into large bowl. Combine squash and 1 cup water in saucepan and bring to a boil. Cook for about 10 minutes until squash is tender. Drain and mash.

- Melt butter in skillet over medium heat and saute onion, celery and bell pepper. Combine crumbled cornbread, squash, onion mixture, soup and chicken bouillon in large bowl.

- Mix well and spoon into sprayed 9 x 13-inch baking dish. Bake for 45 minutes. Serves 8 to 10.

# FILLED SUMMER SQUASH

*5 large yellow squash*
*1 (16 ounce) package frozen chopped spinach*
*1 (8 ounce) package cream cheese, cubed*
*1 (1 ounce) packet dry onion soup mix*
*¾ cup shredded cheddar cheese*

- Steam squash whole until tender. Slit squash lengthwise and remove seeds with spoon.

- Cook spinach according to package directions in saucepan and drain. When spinach is done, remove pan from heat, add cream cheese and stir until cream cheese melts. Stir in soup mix and blend well.

- Preheat oven to 325°.

- Place squash shells on large, sprayed baking pan. Fill shells with spinach mixture and top with heaping tablespoon of cheddar cheese. Bake for 10 to 15 minutes or until squash is thoroughly hot. Serves 5.

# Chile-Cheese Squash

*1 pound yellow squash, sliced*
*⅔ cup mayonnaise*
*1 (4 ounce) can diced green chilies, drained*
*⅔ cup shredded longhorn cheese*
*⅔ cup breadcrumbs*

- Cook squash in salted water in saucepan just until tender-crisp and drain. Return squash to saucepan and stir in mayonnaise, green chilies, cheese and breadcrumbs. Serve hot. Serves 6.

# Seasoned Squash and Onion

*8 yellow squash, sliced*
*2 onions, chopped*
*¼ cup (½ stick) butter*
*1 cup shredded American cheese*

- Cook squash and onion in small amount of water in saucepan over medium heat until tender and drain. Add butter and cheese, toss and serve hot. Serves 6 to 8.

# Sunny Yellow Squash

*6 - 8 medium yellow squash, sliced*
*1 (8 ounce) package cream cheese, cubed, softened*
*2 tablespoons butter*
*1 teaspoon sugar*

- Place squash and add a little water in saucepan and boil until tender. Drain. Add cream cheese, butter, sugar and a little salt and pepper. Cook over low heat, stirring until cream cheese melts. Serves 6.

*An excellent health tip: Try to Make Someone Smile at Least Once a Day.*

# AWESOME BUTTERNUT CASSEROLE WITH PECAN CRUST

*2½ cups cooked, mashed butternut squash\**
*½ cup (1 stick) butter, melted*
*¾ cup sugar*
*3 tablespoons brown sugar*
*3 eggs, beaten*
*1 (5 ounce) can evaporated milk*
*1 teaspoon vanilla*
*½ teaspoon ground cinnamon*

- Preheat oven to 350°.

- Place squash in bowl and beat until fairly smooth. Add butter, sugar, brown sugar, eggs, evaporated milk, vanilla and cinnamon and mix well. (Mixture will be thin.)

- Pour into sprayed 3-quart baking dish. Bake for 45 minutes or until almost set.

## PECAN CRUST:

*1 cup crushed corn flakes*
*½ cup packed light brown sugar*
*½ cup chopped pecans*

- Combine topping ingredients in bowl, sprinkle over hot casserole and return to oven for 10 to 15 minutes or until top is crunchy. Serves 6 to 8.

*\*TIP: The quickest way to cook a butternut squash is to cut the squash in half, scoop out seeds and membranes and place cut-side down on plate and microwave on HIGH for 2 to 5 minutes. Let stand in microwave for several minutes. If it is not soft enough, microwave for additional 1 minute.*

# HERB-SEASONED VEGETABLES

*1 (14 ounce) can seasoned chicken broth with Italian herbs*
*½ teaspoon garlic powder*
*1 (16 ounce) package frozen vegetables*
*¼ cup grated parmesan cheese*

- Heat broth, garlic powder and vegetables in saucepan to a boil. Cover and cook over low heat for 5 minutes or until tender-crisp and drain. Place in serving dish and sprinkle cheese over vegetables. Serves 6.

# CREAMY VEGETABLE CASSEROLE

*This is a vegetable dish at its best!*

1 (16 ounce) package frozen broccoli, carrots and cauliflower
1 (10 ounce) box frozen green peas
1 (10 ounce) can cream of mushroom soup
½ cup milk
1 (8 ounce) carton spreadable garden-vegetable cream cheese
1 cup seasoned croutons, crushed

- Preheat oven to 350°.

- Cook all vegetables according to package directions, but don't overcook! Drain and place in large bowl. Combine soup, milk and cream cheese in saucepan and heat just enough to mix easily.

- Pour into vegetable mixture and stir well. Spoon into 2-quart baking dish. Sprinkle with crushed croutons. Bake for 25 minutes or until bubbly. Serves 4 to 6.

# MIXED VEGETABLE-CHEESE CASSEROLE

1 (16 ounce) package frozen mixed vegetables
1¾ cups shredded American cheese
¾ cup mayonnaise
1 tube round, buttery crackers, crushed
6 tablespoons (¾ stick) butter, melted

- Preheat oven to 350°.

- Cook vegetables in saucepan according to package directions, drain and place in sprayed 2-quart baking dish. Mix cheese and mayonnaise in bowl and spread over vegetables.

- In separate bowl, combine cracker crumbs and butter and sprinkle on top. Bake for 35 minutes. Serves 8.

*According to* National Geographic, *scientists have settled the old dispute over which came first – the chicken or the egg. They say that reptiles were laying eggs thousands of years before chickens appeared, and the first chicken came from an egg laid by a bird that was not quite a chicken. Clearly, the egg came first.*

# ABSOLUTELY DELICIOUS VEGETABLES

*Amazingly, you don't realize that this dish is loaded with vegetables. The crispy*
*top just sets it off and it couldn't be easier! This is really, really delicious.*

2 (15 ounce) cans mixed vegetables, drained
1 cup chopped celery
½ onion, chopped
1 (8 ounce) can sliced water chestnuts, drained
1 cup shredded sharp cheddar cheese
¾ cup mayonnaise
1½ cups round buttery crackers, crushed
6 tablespoons (¾ stick) butter, melted

- Preheat oven to 350°.

- Combine mixed vegetables, celery, onion, water chestnuts, cheese and mayonnaise in bowl and mix well. Spoon into sprayed 9 x 13-inch baking dish.

- Combine crushed crackers and butter in bowl and sprinkle over vegetable mixture. Bake for 30 minutes or until crackers are light brown. Serves 8 to 10.

# FESTIVE CRANBERRIES

*What a great dish for Thanksgiving or Christmas!*

2 (20 ounce) cans pie apples*
1 (16 ounce) can whole cranberries
¾ cup sugar
½ cup packed brown sugar

- Preheat oven to 325°.

- Combine pie apples, cranberries, sugar and brown sugar in bowl and mix well. Spoon into sprayed 2-quart baking dish.

## TOPPING:

¼ cup (½ stick) butter
1½ cups crushed corn flakes
⅔ cup sugar
½ teaspoon ground cinnamon
1 cup chopped pecans

- Melt butter in saucepan and mix in corn flakes, sugar, cinnamon and pecans. Sprinkle over apples and cranberries. Bake for 1 hour. This can be served hot or at room temperature. Serves 4 to 6.

*TIP: Look for pie apples, not apple pie filling.*

# FESTIVE CRANBERRY STUFFING

*1 (14 ounce) can chicken broth*
*1 rib celery, chopped*
*½ cup fresh or frozen cranberries*
*1 small onion, chopped*
*4 cups herb-seasoned stuffing*

- Preheat oven to 325°.

- Mix broth, dash of pepper, celery, cranberries and onion in saucepan and heat to a boil. Cover and cook over low heat for 5 minutes. Add stuffing, mix lightly and spoon into baking dish. Bake until thoroughly hot. Serves 8.

# PECAN-MUSHROOM RICE

*1 cup whole pecans*
*1½ cups instant rice*
*2 cups chicken broth*
*2 tablespoons butter*
*2 (8 ounce) cans whole mushrooms, drained*
*2 teaspoons minced garlic*
*3 cups baby spinach leaves without stems*
*½ cup grated parmesan cheese*

- Cook and stir pecans in large saucepan over medium heat for 5 minutes. Remove from pan and cool slightly.

- Cook rice in chicken broth and butter according to package directions. Gently stir in mushrooms, garlic, spinach, parmesan cheese and pecans. Serves 8.

# GREEN CHILE-RICE

*1 cup instant rice, cooked*
*1 (12 ounce) package shredded Monterey Jack cheese*
*1 (7 ounce) can diced green chilies*
*2 (8 ounce) cartons sour cream*
*½ teaspoon garlic powder*

- Preheat oven to 350°. Combine all ingredients in large bowl and add a little salt, if you like. Spoon into sprayed 9 x 13-inch baking dish and bake for 30 minutes. Serves 8.

# CREAMY RICE BAKE

*1 cup finely chopped green onions with tops*
*¼ cup (½ stick) butter*
*3 cups cooked instant rice*
*1 (8 ounce) carton sour cream*
*¾ cup small curd cottage cheese*
*1¼ cups shredded Monterey Jack cheese*

- Preheat oven to 350°.  Saute onion in butter in large skillet.  Remove from heat and add rice, sour cream, cottage cheese, ½ teaspoon each of salt and pepper and Monterey Jack cheese.

- Toss lightly to mix and spoon into sprayed 2-quart baking dish.  Cover and bake for 35 minutes.  Serves 4 to 6.

# CHEESY RICE, CORN AND CARROTS CASSEROLE

*This is absolutely the prettiest casserole you will*
*place on your table… and delicious and elegant.*

*4 cups finely shredded carrots*
*3 cups cooked instant rice*
*3 eggs, beaten*
*1 (12 ounce) package cubed Velveeta® cheese*
*2 (15 ounce) can cream-style corn*
*1 (8 ounce) carton whipping cream*
*¼ cup (½ stick) butter, melted*
*3 tablespoons dried minced onion*

- Preheat oven to 350°.  In large bowl, combine all ingredients with 1½ teaspoons salt and ½ teaspoon pepper.  Spoon into sprayed 1 (10 x 15-inch) or 2 (2-quart) baking dishes.

- Bake uncovered for 45 minutes or until set.  Serves 20.

# GREEN RICE AND SPINACH

*1 cup instant rice*
*1 (10 ounce) package frozen chopped spinach*
*1 onion, finely chopped*
*3 tablespoons butter*
*¾ cup shredded cheddar cheese*

- Preheat oven to 350°. Cook rice in large saucepan according to package directions. Punch holes in box of spinach and cook in microwave for about 3 minutes.

- Add spinach, onion, butter, cheese, rice and ¼ teaspoon salt. If it seems a little dry, add several tablespoons water. Pour into sprayed 2-quart baking dish. Bake for 25 minutes. Serves 6.

# RED AND GREEN WILD RICE

*You have rice and vegetables all in one delicious dish –*
*and beside that, you have color and character!*

*1 (6 ounce) package long grain-wild rice mix*
*1 red bell pepper, seeded, julienned*
*2 small zucchini, julienned*
*2 stalks fresh broccoli cut into bite-size pieces*
*½ head cauliflower, cut into bite-size pieces*
*½ cup (1 stick) butter, melted*
*1 teaspoon dried sweet basil*
*½ cup slivered almonds*
*1 (8 ounce) package shredded cheddar cheese*

- Preheat oven to 350°.

- Cook rice according to package directions and set aside.

- Combine bell pepper, zucchini, broccoli and cauliflower in large bowl. Cover with wax paper and microwave for 3 minutes. Turn bowl and stir vegetables. Microwave for additional 2 minutes.

- Add butter, 1 teaspoon each of salt and pepper, basil, almonds and rice and toss. Spoon into sprayed 9 x 13-inch baking dish.

- Cover and bake for about 20 minutes or until thoroughly hot. Sprinkle cheese over top and bake uncovered for 5 minutes. Serve 8 to 10.

# RED RICE

*1 (16 ounce) package smoked sausage, sliced*
*2 (10 ounce) cans diced tomatoes and green chilies*
*3 cups chicken broth*
*2 teaspoons Creole seasoning*
*1½ cups long grain rice*

- Saute sausage in large, heavy pan until brown. Stir in tomato and green chilies, broth and seasoning and bring to a boil. Stir in rice, cover and reduce heat. Simmer for 25 minutes, uncover and cook until liquid absorbs. Serves 8.

# CARNIVAL COUSCOUS

*1 (6 ounce) box herbed chicken couscous*
*¼ cup (½ stick) butter*
*1 red bell pepper, seeded, finely chopped*
*1 yellow squash, seeded, finely chopped*
*¾ cup fresh broccoli florets, finely chopped*

- Preheat oven to 325°. Cook couscous in saucepan according to package directions but do not use butter. With butter in saucepan, saute bell pepper, squash and broccoli and cook for about 10 minutes or until vegetables are tender.

- Combine couscous and vegetables in sprayed 2-quart baking dish and bake for about 20 minutes. Serves 8.

# CHEESY GRITS BAKE

*¼ cup (½ stick) butter*
*3½ cups milk, divided*
*1⅓ cups quick-cooking grits*
*1 (8 ounce) package shredded Monterey Jack cheese*
*5 large eggs, beaten*
*1 teaspoon hot sauce*

- Preheat oven to 325°. In large saucepan, bring butter, a little salt and 1½ cups milk, to a boil. Stir constantly and add grits. Reduce heat and simmer for 5 minutes. Stir in cheese.

- In large bowl, whisk eggs, hot sauce and remaining 2 cups milk until they blend well. Gradually stir in grits and pour into sprayed 3-quart baking dish.

- Bake uncovered for 45 minutes or until knife inserted in center comes out clean. Serves 10.

# Grits Souffle

*1½ cups grits*
*½ cup (1 stick) butter*
*1½ cups shredded cheddar cheese*
*5 eggs, beaten*

- Preheat oven to 350°.

- Boil grits in 6 cups water, and 1½ teaspoons salt in large saucepan and drain. Stir in butter and cheese until cheese melts. Cool until lukewarm and add eggs. Pour into sprayed 2-quart baking dish and bake for 45 minutes. Serves 8.

# Mushroom Pasta

*1 onion, chopped*
*1 cup celery, chopped*
*1 red bell pepper, seeded, chopped*
*6 tablespoons (¾ stick) butter*
*1⅓ cups orzo pasta*
*1 (14 ounce) can beef broth*
*1 (7 ounce) can sliced mushrooms, drained*
*1 tablespoon Worcestershire sauce*
*¾ cup chopped walnuts*
*Chopped green onions*

- Preheat oven to 325°.

- Saute onion, celery and bell pepper in butter in skillet. Cook orzo in beef broth and 1 cup water in saucepan for 10 to 11 minutes and drain.

- Combine onion-bell pepper mixture, orzo, mushrooms, Worcestershire, walnuts, and ½ teaspoon each of salt and pepper and mix well.

- Transfer to sprayed 2-quart baking dish. Cover and bake for 30 minutes. When ready to serve, sprinkle chopped green onions over top of casserole. Serves 4 to 6.

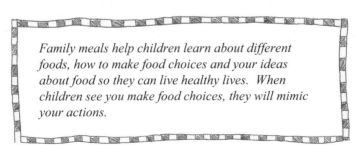

*Family meals help children learn about different foods, how to make food choices and your ideas about food so they can live healthy lives. When children see you make food choices, they will mimic your actions.*

# PARMESAN-GARLIC COUSCOUS

1 (10 ounce) box original plain couscous
3 teaspoons minced garlic
¼ cup olive oil
½ cup grated parmesan cheese
¼ cup milk
1 tablespoon dried parsley
1 (8 ounce) can green peas, drained

- Bring 2 cups water in large saucepan to a boil, stir in couscous and cover. Let stand for 5 minutes. Stir in garlic, oil, parmesan cheese, milk, parsley, peas and a little salt and pepper.

- Cook and stir until thoroughly hot. Serves 8.

# CREAMY MACARONI AND CHEESE

*It is well worth the time to make this macaroni and cheese.*

1 (12 ounce) package macaroni
6 tablespoons (¾ stick) butter
¼ cup flour
2 cups milk
1 (16 ounce) package cubed Velveeta® cheese

- Preheat oven to 350°.

- Cook macaroni according to package directions and drain. Melt butter in saucepan and stir in flour, and ½ teaspoon each of salt and pepper until they blend well.

- Slowly add milk, stirring constantly, and heat until it begins to thicken. Add cheese and stir until cheese melts. Pour cheese sauce over macaroni and mix well.

- Pour into sprayed 2½-quart baking dish. Cover and bake for 30 minutes or until it bubbles. Serves 4 to 6.

> *There is no dispute about the origin of macaroni and cheese in America. Thomas Jefferson served it in the White House at a State Dinner in 1802.*
>
> *Jefferson served as an envoy while in France before becoming president. When he returned to Monticello, he brought many ideas and machines to make his life better. One of the machines was a press used to make long strings of pasta. Jefferson improved the machine and introduced America to pasta.*

# MACARONI, CHEESE AND TOMATOES

*2 cups elbow macaroni*
*1 (14 ounce) can stewed tomatoes with liquid*
*1 (8 ounce) package shredded cheddar cheese*
*2 tablespoons sugar*
*1 (6 ounce) package cheese slices*

- Preheat oven to 350°. Cook macaroni in saucepan according to package directions and drain. Combine macaroni, tomatoes, shredded cheese, sugar, ¼ cup water and a little salt in large bowl and mix well.

- Pour into sprayed 9 x 13-inch baking dish and place cheese slices on top. Bake for 30 minutes or until bubbly. Serves 8 to 10.

# A DIFFERENT MACARONI

*1 (8 ounce) package shell macaroni*
*½ cup whipping cream*
*1 (8 ounce) carton shredded gorgonzola cheese*
*1 (10 ounce) package frozen green peas, thawed*
*2 cups cubed ham*

- Cook macaroni according to package directions and drain. Add cream and gorgonzola cheese and stir until cheese melts.

- Fold in peas and ham and cook on low heat, stirring constantly, 5 minutes or until mixture is thoroughly hot. Spoon into serving bowl and serve hot. Serves 10.

# MACARONI AND CHEESE DELUXE

*1 (8 ounce) package small shell macaroni*
*3 tablespoons butter, melted*
*1 (15 ounce) can stewed tomatoes*
*1 (8 ounce) package shredded Velveeta® cheese*
*1 cup crushed potato chips, optional*

- Preheat oven to 350°. Cook macaroni according to package directions, drain and place in bowl. While macaroni is still hot, stir in butter, tomatoes, cheese and a little salt and pepper and mix well.

- Pour into sprayed 2-quart baking dish, cover and bake for 25 minutes. Remove from oven, uncover and sprinkle with crushed potato chips. Bake an additional 10 minutes or until potato chips are light brown. Serves 8.

# Spice Up the Macaroni

## Macaroni:

*1 (8 ounce) package spiral pasta*
*⅓ cup (5½ tablespoons) butter*

- Cook macaroni according to package directions, drain and add butter, stir until butter melts. Cover, set aside and keep warm.

## Spicy Tomatoes:

*1 (8 ounce) package shredded Mexican Velveeta® cheese*
*1 (10 ounce) can tomatoes and green chilies with liquid*
*½ yellow onion, finely diced*
*1 (8 ounce) carton sour cream*

- Preheat oven to 325°.
- In large saucepan, combine cheese, tomatoes and green chilies and diced onion. Stir in macaroni, heat on low for 5 minutes and stir occasionally.
- Fold in sour cream and pour into 2-quart baking dish. Cover and bake for 20 minutes. Serves 8.

# Worth-It Macaroni

*2 cups macaroni*
*2 cups milk*
*¼ cup flour*
*1 (12 ounce) package shredded sharp cheddar cheese*
*¼ cup (½ stick) butter, melted*
*1 cup soft breadcrumbs*

- Preheat oven to 350°.
- Cook macaroni according to package directions, drain and set aside. Combine milk, flour and an ample amount of seasoned salt in jar with lid; shake to mix well.
- Combine macaroni, flour-milk mixture and cheese in large bowl. Pour into sprayed 9 x 13-inch baking dish. Stir melted butter over breadcrumbs, toss and sprinkle over top.
- Cover and bake for 35 minutes, remove cover and return to oven for 10 minutes. Serves 8.

# CHEESY NOODLE CASSEROLE

*1 (8 ounce) package egg noodles*
*1 (16 ounce) package frozen broccoli florets, thawed*
*1 sweet red bell pepper, seeded, chopped*
*1 (8 ounce) package shredded Velveeta® cheese*
*1 cup milk*
*¾ cup coarsely crushed bite-size cheese crackers*

- Preheat oven to 350°.

- Cook noodles in large saucepan according to package directions. Add broccoli and bell pepper for last 2 minutes of cooking time. Drain in colander.

- In same saucepan, combine cheese and milk over low heat and stir until cheese melts. Stir in noodle-broccoli mixture and spoon into sprayed 3-quart baking dish.

- Sprinkle with crushed crackers and bake uncovered for 25 to 30 minutes or until top is golden brown. Serves 10.

# CREAMY SEASONED NOODLES

*1 (8 ounce) package wide egg noodles*
*¼ cup (½ stick) butter*
*1 (.04 ounce) packet Italian salad dressing mix*
*½ cup whipping cream*
*¼ cup grated parmesan cheese*

- Cook noodles in saucepan according to package directions and drain. Cut butter in chunks so it will melt easier. Add remaining ingredients and toss lightly to blend thoroughly. Serve hot. Serves 6.

# FAVORITE PASTA

*4 ounces spinach linguine*
*1 cup whipping cream*
*1 cup chicken broth*
*½ cup freshly grated parmesan cheese*
*½ cup frozen English peas*

- Cook linguine in medium saucepan according to package directions, drain and keep warm. In separate saucepan, combine whipping cream and chicken broth and bring to a boil.

- Reduce heat and simmer for 25 minutes or until it thickens and reduces to 1 cup. Remove from heat, add cheese and peas and stir until cheese melts. Toss with linguine and serve immediately. Serves 6.

# Pasta with Basil

2½ cups small tube pasta
1 small onion, chopped
2 tablespoons olive oil
2½ tablespoons dried basil
1 cup shredded mozzarella cheese

- Cook pasta in saucepan according to package directions. Saute onion in oil in skillet. Stir in basil, 1 teaspoon salt and ¼ teaspoon pepper. Cook and stir for 1 minute.

- Drain pasta leaving about ½ cup water so pasta won't be too dry and add to basil mixture. Remove from heat and stir in cheese just until it begins to melt. Serve immediately. Serves 8.

# Sensational Spaghetti

*Forget the tomato sauce. This is spaghetti to love!*

1 (12 ounce) package thin spaghetti
½ cup (1 stick) butter
1½ teaspoons minced garlic
1 cup grated parmesan cheese
1 (1 pint) carton whipping cream
1 teaspoon dried parsley flakes
10 - 12 strips bacon, fried crisp, crumbled

- Preheat oven to 325°.

- Cook spaghetti according to package directions and drain. Melt butter in large skillet and saute garlic until slightly brown.

- Add spaghetti, parmesan cheese, cream, parsley flakes, and ½ teaspoon each of salt and pepper and mix well.

- Spoon into sprayed 2-quart baking dish. Cover and bake just until warm, about 15 minutes. Uncover and sprinkle crumbled bacon over casserole. Serves 4 to 6.

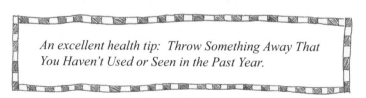

*An excellent health tip: Throw Something Away That You Haven't Used or Seen in the Past Year.*

# RANCH SPAGHETTI

*1 (12 ounce) package spaghetti*
*¼ cup (½ stick) butter, cut in 3 pieces*
*¾ cup sour cream*
*¾ cup bottled ranch dressing*
*½ cup grated parmesan cheese*

- Cook spaghetti according to package directions, drain and return to saucepan. Stir in butter, sour cream and ranch dressing and toss. Spoon into serving bowl and sprinkle with grated parmesan cheese. Serves 8.

*TIP: You can make a main dish with this recipe just by adding 1 or 2 cups cubed ham or turkey.*

# EASY VEGETABLE LASAGNA

*1 (14 ounce) can Italian stewed tomatoes*
*1½ cups pasta sauce*
*2 cups cottage cheese, drained*
*1 cup grated parmesan cheese*
*9 lasagna noodles, divided*
*4 zucchinis, shredded, divided*
*7 (1 ounce) provolone cheese slices, cut into strips, divided*

- Combine stewed tomatoes and pasta sauce in bowl and set aside. In separate bowl, combine cottage cheese, parmesan cheese, and ¼ teaspoon each of salt and pepper.

- Place following layers in sprayed 9 x 13-inch baking dish: one-third tomato mixture, 3 lasagna noodles, one-third zucchini, one-third cheese mixture and one-third provolone cheese strips. Repeat layering procedure twice more.

- Cover and refrigerate for at least 8 hours. Remove from refrigerator and let stand for 30 minutes. When ready to bake, preheat oven to 350°.

- Cover and bake for 45 minutes. Uncover and bake for additional 20 minutes. Let stand for 15 minutes before serving. Serves 8 to 10.

*An excellent health tip: Spend time with people over the age of 70 and under the age of 6.*

## BAKED APPLESAUCE

*5 pounds tart green apples, peeled, cored, sliced*
*1 (8 ounce) jar plum jelly*
*½ cup sugar*
*⅓ cup lemon juice*
*¼ teaspoon ground nutmeg*

- Preheat oven to 350°.

- Place apples in 2-quart baking dish. Combine jelly, sugar and ⅔ cup water in saucepan. Heat until jelly melts. Remove from heat, stir in lemon juice and nutmeg and pour over apples.

- Cover and bake for 1 hour 15 minutes or until apples are soft. Delicious served with pork. Serves 8.

# BEEF MAIN DISHES

## BEEFY POTATO BAKE

*1½ pounds lean ground beef*
*1 onion, chopped*
*4 medium potatoes, peeled, sliced*
*1 (10 ounce) can golden mushroom soup*
*1 (10 ounce) can condensed vegetable-beef soup*
*1 (3 ounce) can french-fried onions*

- Preheat oven to 350°. In skillet, brown and cook beef and onion about 10 minutes and drain. In large bowl, combine beef mixture, sliced potatoes and both soups and mix well.

- Transfer to greased 3-quart baking dish. Cover and bake 1 hour 10 minutes. Uncover and spread fried onions over top of casserole and return to oven for 15 minutes. Serves 4 to 6.

# CABBAGE ROLLS

*This is a wonderful family recipe and a super way to get the kids to eat cabbage.*

1 large head cabbage, cored
1½ pounds lean ground beef
1 egg, beaten
3 tablespoons ketchup
⅓ cup seasoned breadcrumbs
2 tablespoons dried minced onion flakes
2 (15 ounce) cans Italian stewed tomatoes
¼ cup cornstarch
3 tablespoons brown sugar
2 tablespoons Worcestershire sauce

- Place head of cabbage in large kettle of boiling water for 10 minutes or until outer leaves are tender. Drain well. Rinse in cold water and remove 10 large outer leaves*. Set aside.

- Slice or grate remaining cabbage. Place in bottom of greased 9 x 13-inch baking dish. In large bowl combine ground beef, egg, ketchup, breadcrumbs, onion flakes and 1 teaspoon salt and mix well.

- Pack together about ½ cup meat mixture and put on each cabbage leaf. Fold in sides and roll up leaf to completely enclose filling. (You may have to remove thick vein from cabbage leaves for easier rolling.) Place each rolled-up leaf over grated cabbage.

- Place stewed tomatoes in large saucepan. Combine cornstarch, brown sugar and Worcestershire sauce in bowl and spoon mixture into tomatoes. Cook on high heat, stirring constantly, until stewed tomatoes and juices thicken. Pour over cabbage rolls. Cover and bake at 325° for 1 hour. Serves 6 to 8.

*\*TIP: To get that many large leaves, you may have to put 2 smaller leaves together to make one roll.*

# CASSEROLE SUPPER

1 pound lean ground beef
¼ cup uncooked white rice
1 (10 ounce) can French-onion soup
1 (6 ounce) can french-fried onions

- Preheat oven to 325°. Brown ground beef, drain and place in sprayed 7 x 11-inch baking dish. Add rice, onion soup and ½ cup water and mix.

- Cover and bake for 40 minutes. Uncover, sprinkle fried onions over top and return to oven for 10 minutes. Serves 4.

# CHEESEBURGER PIE

*1 pound lean ground beef*
*1 onion, chopped*
*1 cup chili sauce*
*1 (10 - inch) deep-dish piecrust*
*1 egg, beaten*
*1 teaspoon Worcestershire sauce*
*¼ cup milk*
*1 (8 ounce) package shredded American cheese*

- Preheat oven to 350°. In large skillet with little oil, brown beef and onion with salt and pepper to taste; drain. Stir in chili sauce and simmer for 5 minutes. Pour into piecrust.

- For cheese topping, combine egg, Worcestershire, milk and cheese and mix well. Spoon over meat mixture and cook 30 minutes or until center of cheese layer is firm. Serves 4 to 6.

# COWBOY CASSEROLE

*1½ pounds lean ground beef*
*2 onions, coarsely chopped*
*5 medium potatoes, peeled, sliced*
*1 (15 ounce) can kidney beans, rinsed, drained*
*1 (15 ounce) can pinto beans, drained*
*1 (15 ounce) can Mexican stewed tomatoes*
*1 (10 ounce) can tomato soup*
*½ teaspoon basil*
*½ teaspoon oregano*
*2 teaspoons minced garlic*

- Sprinkle beef with some salt and pepper in skillet, brown meat and drain. Place onions in bottom of slow cooker and spoon beef over onions. On top of beef, layer potatoes, kidney beans and pinto beans.

- Mix stewed tomatoes and tomato soup in small saucepan over low heat just long enough to mix well. Pour over beans and potatoes and sprinkle with basil, oregano and garlic. Cover and cook on LOW for 7 to 8 hours. Serves 6 to 8.

# CHEESY BEEFY GNOCCHI

1 pound lean ground beef
1 (10 ounce) can cheddar cheese soup
1 (10 ounce) can tomato bisque soup
2 cups uncooked gnocchi or shell pasta

- In skillet, cook beef until no longer pink and drain. Add soups, 1½ cups water and pasta. Bring mixture to boil and mix well.

- Cover and cook over medium heat for 10 to 12 minutes or until pasta is done; stir often. Serves 4.

# CHEESY STUFFED BELL PEPPERS

6 green bell peppers
1½ pounds lean ground beef
½ cup chopped onion
¾ cup cooked rice
1 egg
2 (15 ounce) cans Italian stewed tomatoes, divided
½ teaspoon garlic powder
1 tablespoon Worcestershire sauce
1 (8 ounce) package shredded cheddar cheese, divided

- Preheat oven to 350°. Cut off tops of bell pepper and remove seeds and membranes. Place in roasting pan with salted water and boil. Cook for 10 minutes so they will be only partially done. Drain and set aside to cool.

- Brown ground beef and onion in skillet and drain. Add rice, egg, 1 can tomatoes, garlic powder, Worcestershire, and 1 teaspoon each of salt and pepper. Simmer for 5 minutes. Remove from heat, add half cheese and mix well.

- Stuff peppers with mixture and set upright in sprayed round baking dish. (You may have to trim little slivers off bottoms of peppers so they will sit upright.)

- Pour remaining can of tomatoes over top and around peppers. Bake for 25 minutes. Sprinkle remaining cheese on top and bake for 10 minutes. Serves 6.

*If no one sees you eat it, do you still have to count the calories?*

# DELICIOUS MEATLOAF

*1½ pounds lean ground beef*
*⅔ cup Italian-seasoned breadcrumbs*
*1 (10 ounce) can golden mushroom soup, divided*
*2 eggs, beaten*
*2 tablespoons butter*

- Preheat oven to 350°. Mix beef, breadcrumbs, half mushroom soup and eggs thoroughly in bowl. Shape firmly into 8 x 4-inch loaf baking pan. Bake for 45 minutes.

- Mix butter, remaining soup and ¼ cup water in small saucepan. Heat thoroughly. Serve with meat loaf. Serves 6 to 8.

# MEATLOAF TONIGHT

*1½ pounds lean ground beef*
*1 (10 ounce) can golden cream of mushroom soup*
*1 (10 ounce) can cream of celery soup*
*1 (1 ounce) packet savory herb-garlic soup mix*
*1 cup cooked instant rice*

- Preheat oven to 350°. Combine ground beef, both soups, dry onion soup mix and cooked rice. Place on sprayed 9 x 13-inch baking pan and form into loaf.

- Bake for 45 to 50 minutes or until loaf is golden brown. Serves 8.

# HASH BROWN DINNER

*1½ pounds lean ground chuck, browned*
*1 (1 ounce) package dry brown gravy mix*
*1 (15 ounce) can cream corn*
*1 (15 ounce) can whole kernel corn*
*1 (8 ounce) package shredded cheddar cheese, divided*
*1 (16 ounce) package frozen hash browns, partially thawed*
*1 (10 ounce) can golden mushroom soup*
*1 (5 ounce) can evaporated milk*

- Place browned beef in skillet and toss with brown gravy mix. Add cream corn and whole kernel corn and cover with half cheddar cheese. Pour into 5-quart, sprayed slow cooker. Top with hash browns and remaining cheese.

- In saucepan, combine mushroom soup and evaporated milk and heat over medium heat to mix well. Pour over hash browns and cheese. Cover and cook on LOW for 6 to 8 hours. Serves 6 to 8.

# Mac and Cheese Supper

*This is an easy slow cooker recipe!*

*1½ pounds lean ground beef*
*2 (7 ounce) packages macaroni and cheese dinners*
*1 (15 ounce) can whole kernel corn, drained*
*1½ cups shredded Monterey Jack cheese*

- Sprinkle ground beef with 1 teaspoon salt in large skillet, brown until no longer pink and drain. Prepare macaroni and cheese in saucepan according to package directions.

- Spoon beef, macaroni and corn into sprayed 5-quart slow cooker and mix well. Cover and cook on LOW for 4 to 5 hours.

- When ready to serve, sprinkle Jack cheese over top and leave in cooker until cheese melts. Serves 6 to 8.

# Pinto Bean Pie

*1 pound lean ground beef*
*1 onion, chopped*
*2 (16 ounce) cans pinto beans with liquid*
*1 (10 ounce) can tomatoes and green chilies with liquid*
*1 (6 ounce) can french-fried onions*

- Preheat oven to 350°.

- In skillet, brown beef and onion and drain. In 2-quart casserole dish, layer 1 can beans, beef-onion mixture and ½ can tomatoes and green chilies.

- Repeat layer, top with fried onions and bake uncovered for 30 minutes. Serves 4.

# Potato-Beef Casserole

*4 medium potatoes, peeled, sliced*
*1¼ pounds lean ground beef, browned, drained*
*1 (10 ounce) can cream of mushroom soup*
*1 (10 ounce) can condensed vegetable beef soup*

- In large bowl, combine all ingredients. Add a little salt and pepper to taste. Transfer to greased 3-quart baking dish. Bake covered at 350° for 1 hour 30 minutes or until potatoes are tender. Serves 4.

# POTATO-BEEF BAKE

*1 pound ground beef*
*1 (10 ounce) can sloppy Joe sauce*
*1 (10 ounce) can fiesta nacho cheese soup*
*1 (32 ounce) package frozen hash browned potatoes, thawed*

- Brown beef in skillet over medium heat and drain. Add sloppy Joe sauce and fiesta nacho cheese soup to beef and mix well.

- Place hash browns in greased 9 x 13-inch baking dish and top with beef mixture. Cover and bake at 400° for 25 minutes. Uncover and bake 10 minutes longer. Serves 6 to 8.

*TIP: This is really good sprinkled with 1 cup grated cheddar cheese.*

# QUICK BEEF-BEAN FIX

*1 pound lean ground beef*
*1 onion, chopped*
*⅔ cup chili sauce*
*1 (15 ounce) can baked beans with liquid*
*1 (11 ounce) can Mexicorn®*
*2 cups crushed garlic-flavored croutons*

- Preheat oven to 350°. In skillet, brown beef, onion and salt and pepper to taste. Stir in chili sauce and simmer, covered, on medium heat for 10 minutes.

- Stir in beans and corn and spoon into greased 3-quart baking dish. Cover with croutons and bake 30 minutes. Serves 4.

# SKILLET BEEF AND PASTA

*1 (8 ounce) package spiral pasta*
*1 (14 ounce) can beef broth*
*1 pound lean ground beef*
*2 (11 ounce) cans Mexicorn®, drained*
*1 (12 ounce) package cubed Mexican processed cheese*

- Cook pasta according to package directions, except instead of 6 cups water in directions, use 4¼ cups water and 1¾ cups beef broth.

- While pasta cooks, brown beef in large skillet, stir and drain. Stir in corn and cheese and cook on low heat until cheese melts.

- Gently stir cooked pasta into beef mixture until it coats pasta. Spoon mixture into serving bowl and garnish with few springs parsley, if desired. Serves 4.

# Classic Beefy Noodles

1½ pounds lean ground beef
2 (10 ounce) cans tomatoes and green chilies
2 teaspoons minced garlic
1 (8 ounce) package noodles
1 (3 ounce) package cream cheese
1 (8 ounce) carton sour cream
1 (8 ounce) package shredded cheddar cheese

- Preheat oven to 350°. In large skillet, brown beef. Drain and stir in tomatoes and green chilies, garlic and salt and pepper to taste. Bring to boil, reduce heat and simmer 25 minutes.

- While beef mixture cooks, place noodles in large pan and cook according to package directions. Drain, stir in cream cheese and stir until it melts. Fold in sour cream and stir in beef mixture.

- Spoon into greased 9 x 13-inch baking dish. Cover and bake 30 minutes. Remove from oven, sprinkle cheese over top and return to oven for 5 minutes. Serves 4 to 6.

# Summer Cabbage Deluxe

1½ pounds lean ground beef
1 (16 ounce) package frozen broccoli florets, thawed
1 medium head cabbage, cored, coarsely chopped
½ teaspoon sugar
1 (8 ounce) carton sour cream
½ cup mayonnaise
2 cups shredded white cheddar cheese
1½ cups fresh breadcrumbs
2 tablespoons butter, melted

- Preheat oven to 350°. Cook beef in large skillet until meat is no longer pink. Lay broccoli florets out on cutting board and cut off most of stems.

- Place broccoli florets, cabbage, 1 teaspoon salt, sugar and ¾ cup water in large saucepan. Cook over medium heat for about 10 minutes, stirring occasionally, until vegetables are tender-crisp. Drain well.

- Combine beef, broccoli-cabbage mixture, sour cream, mayonnaise, cheese and 1 teaspoon each of salt and pepper in large bowl. Transfer to sprayed 3-quart baking dish.

- Combine breadcrumbs and butter in bowl and sprinkle over casserole. Bake for 25 minutes or until breadcrumbs are light brown. Serves 6.

# Supper Casserole

*1 pound lean ground beef*
*1 cup onion, chopped*
*1 cup bell pepper, chopped*
*2 (10 ounce) cans golden mushroom soup*
*⅔ cup uncooked rice*
*3 tablespoons soy sauce*
*1 (8 ounce) can green peas*
*1 (3 ounce) can french-fried onions*

- Preheat oven to 350°. In large skillet, brown ground beef. Drain. Add onion, bell pepper, soup, rice, soy sauce, peas and 2 cups water and mix well.

- Spoon into greased 9 x 13-inch baking dish. Cover and bake 50 minutes. Remove from oven, sprinkle fried onions over casserole and return to oven for 10 minutes. Serves 4 to 6.

# Good Night Casserole Supper

*1 pound lean ground beef*
*1 onion, chopped*
*1 red bell pepper, seeded, chopped*
*1 green bell pepper, seeded, chopped*
*2 (10 ounce) cans golden cream of mushroom soup*
*⅔ cup white rice*
*¼ cup soy sauce*
*1 (2.8 ounce) can french-fried onions*

- Preheat oven to 350°.

- Brown ground beef and onions in large skillet and drain off fat. Pour into sprayed 9 x 13-inch baking dish.

- Stir in bell peppers, both cans soup, rice, soy sauce, ¾ cup water and a little salt and pepper.

- With paper towel, clean edges of baking dish and cover with foil. Bake for 30 minutes, remove dish from oven and sprinkle fried onions over top. Return to oven and bake for additional 15 minutes. Serves 6.

> *The secret of staying young is to live honestly, eat slowly and lie about your age.*
> —*Lucille Ball*

# CREAMY BEEF CASSEROLE

1½ pounds lean ground beef
1 onion, chopped
1 (15 ounce) can tomato sauce
1 (7 ounce) can chopped green chilies
1 (12 ounce) package medium noodles
1 (16 ounce) carton small curd cottage cheese
¾ cup mayonnaise
1 cup shredded 4-cheese blend

- Preheat oven to 350°.

- In large skillet over medium-high heat, brown beef and onion. Stir in tomato sauce, green chilies and a little salt and pepper. Reduce heat, stir well and simmer for 20 minutes.

- Cook noodles according to package directions and drain well.

- In bowl, combine cottage cheese and mayonnaise and fold into noodles. Spoon noodle mixture into sprayed 9 x 13-inch baking dish.

- Pour beef mixture over noodle mixture. Cover and bake 30 minutes. Remove cover, sprinkle cheese on top and return to oven for additional 5 minutes. Serves 6.

# BEEF PATTIES IN ONION SAUCE

2½ pounds lean ground beef
1 (1 ounce) packet savory herb-garlic soup mix
1 egg, beaten
2 (10 ounce) cans French onion soup

- Preheat oven to 350°.

- Combine beef, soup mix, egg and ¼ cup water and shape into patties about ¾-inch thick. Brown on both sides in large skillet over high heat.

- Place patties in sprayed 9 x 13-inch baking pan and pour onion soup and ¾ cup water over patties. Cover and bake for 35 minutes. Serves 8.

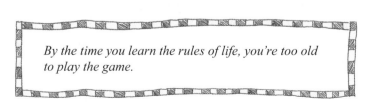

*By the time you learn the rules of life, you're too old to play the game.*

# BEEFY-RICE CASSEROLE

1 pound lean ground beef
¾ cup white rice
1 (10 ounce) package frozen corn, thawed
1 (10 ounce) can French onion soup
1 (2.8 ounce) can french-fried onions

- Preheat oven to 325°.

- Brown ground beef, drain and place in sprayed 3-quart baking dish.

- Stir in rice, corn, onion soup and ½ cup water. Cover and bake for 30 minutes. Uncover and sprinkle fried onions over top of casserole and return to oven for 15 minutes. Serves 5 to 6.

# SAVORY BEEF PATTIES

1½ pounds lean ground beef
½ cup chili sauce
½ cup buttery cracker crumbs
1 (10 ounce) can beef broth
1 (6.8 ounce) packet beef-flavored rice

- Combine beef, chili sauce and cracker crumbs and form into 5 or 6 patties. In skillet, brown patties and pour beef broth over patties. Bring to a boil, reduce heat to low and simmer for 35 minutes.

- Prepare rice according to package directions and place on serving plate. Cover rice with patties and serve. Serves 6.

# BUENO TACO CASSEROLE

2 pounds ground beef
1½ cups taco sauce
2 (15 ounce) cans Spanish rice
1 (8 ounce) package shredded Mexican 4-cheese blend, divided

- Brown ground beef in skillet and drain. Add taco sauce, rice and half cheese. Spoon mixture into buttered 3-quart baking dish.

- Cover and bake at 350° for 35 minutes. Uncover and sprinkle remaining cheese on top and return to oven for 5 minutes. Serves 6 to 8.

# BEEF AND NOODLES GRANDE

*This is an ideal casserole to make ahead of time for a quick and easy supper.*
*These blended flavors create a delicious dish that people always remember.*

*1½ - 2 pounds lean ground beef*
*1 onion, chopped*
*1 green bell pepper, seeded, chopped*
*1 (16 ounce) package cubed Mexican Velveeta® cheese*
*1 (10 ounce) can fiesta nacho cheese soup*
*1 (15 ounce) can stewed tomatoes*
*1 (10 ounce) can tomatoes and green chilies*
*1 (8 ounce) can whole kernel corn, drained*
*½ teaspoon chili powder*
*1 (8 ounce) package medium egg noodles*
*¼ cup (½ stick) butter, cut into 4 - 5 slices*
*1 cup shredded cheddar cheese*

- Preheat oven to 350°. Cook beef, onion and bell pepper in skillet until beef is no longer pink and vegetables are tender. Drain. Remove from heat, add Velveeta® cheese and stir until cheese melts.

- Combine soup, stewed tomatoes, tomatoes and green chilies, corn, chili powder, 1½ teaspoons salt and ½ teaspoon pepper in large bowl. Add beef mixture and mix well.

- Cook egg noodles according to package directions and drain well. While noodles are still very hot, add butter and stir until it melts.

- Stir noodles in with tomato-beef mixture. Transfer to sprayed 10 x 15-inch baking dish. Cover and bake for 45 minutes. Sprinkle cheese over casserole and bake uncovered for 4 to 10 minutes. Serves 10 to 12.

# BEEF PICANTE SKILLET

*1 pound lean ground beef*
*1 (10 ounce) can tomato soup*
*1 cup chunky salsa or picante sauce*
*6 (6 inch) flour tortillas, cut into 1-inch pieces*
*1¼ cups shredded cheddar cheese, divided*

- Cook beef in skillet until no longer pink and drain. Add soup, salsa, ¾ cup water, tortillas, ½ teaspoon salt and half cheese.

- Heat to a boil. Cover and cook over low heat for 10 minutes. Top with remaining cheese. Serve right from skillet. Serves 4 to 6.

# Enchilada Casserole Grande

*1½ pounds lean ground beef*
*½ teaspoon minced garlic*
*1 (8 ounce) package shredded colby-Jack cheese blend*
*1 onion, chopped*
*1 (10 ounce) can cream of chicken soup*
*1 (5 ounce) can evaporated milk*
*1 (8 ounce) package Velveeta® cheese, cubed*
*1 (1 ounce) packet ranch dip mix*
*1 (7 ounce) can diced green chilies*
*1 (2 ounce) jar chopped pimento, drained*
*12 (8-inch) corn tortillas*

- Preheat oven to 350°. Cook beef and garlic in skillet until beef crumbles and is no longer pink. Drain well. Stir in shredded colby-Jack cheese and onion and set aside.

- Combine soup, evaporated milk and cheese in saucepan over medium heat and stir until cheese melts. Add dip mix, green chilies and pimento.

- Pour water to depth of 1 inch in skillet and heat on high. (Keep heat on medium so water will stay hot.) Dip tortillas, 1 at a time, into hot water using tongs. Soak 2 to 3 seconds, remove and drain.

- Spoon about ⅓ cup meat mixture onto 1 side of each tortilla. Roll tightly and place seam-side down in sprayed 9 x 13-inch baking dish. Spoon cheese sauce over enchiladas.

- Cover and bake for 30 minutes. Uncover and bake for additional 10 minutes. Serves 6 to 8.

# Mexican Casserole

*1 (13 ounce) bag tortilla chips, divided*
*2 pounds lean ground beef*
*1 (15 ounce) can Mexican stewed tomatoes*
*1 (8 ounce) package shredded Mexican 4-cheese blend*

- Preheat over to 350°.

- Partially crush half bag chips and place in bottom of buttered 9 x 13-inch baking dish. Brown ground beef and drain.

- Add stewed tomatoes and cheese and mix well. Sprinkle finely crushed chips over casserole. Bake uncovered for 40 minutes. Serves 6 to 8.

# CHILI RELLENO CASSEROLE

*1 pound lean ground beef*
*1 onion, chopped*
*1 bell pepper, chopped*
*1 teaspoon oregano*
*1 teaspoon minced garlic*
*1 cup whole green chilies*
*1 (12 ounce) package shredded Monterey Jack cheese*
*3 large eggs, beaten*
*1 cup half-and-half cream*

- Preheat oven to 350°. In skillet with little oil, brown beef, onion, bell pepper and salt and pepper to taste. Stir in oregano and garlic.

- Spread green chilies in greased 9 x 13-inch baking dish. Cover with meat-onion mixture and sprinkle with cheese.

- Combine beaten eggs and cream and pour over top of meat mixture. Bake uncovered for 35 minutes or until top is slightly brown. Serves 4 to 6.

# SAVORY BEEF AND BEAN PIE

*1 pound lean ground beef*
*1 onion, chopped*
*3 ribs celery, sliced*
*2 (15 ounce) cans pinto beans, drained*
*2 (10 ounce) cans tomatoes and green chilies*
*1½ cups crushed tortilla chips*
*1 (3 ounce) can french-fried onions*

- Preheat oven to 350°.

- In skillet, brown beef, onion and celery. Drain. In greased 3-quart baking dish, layer 1 can beans, beef-onion mixture and 1 can tomatoes and green chilies. Repeat layers and sprinkle tortilla chips over top.

- Bake 20 minutes, remove from oven and spread fried onions over chips and return to oven for 15 minutes. Serves 4.

# ENCHILADA CASSEROLE

*1½ pounds lean ground beef*
*1 package taco seasoning mix*
*Oil*
*8 flour or corn tortillas*
*1 cup shredded cheddar cheese*
*1 onion, chopped*
*1 (10 ounce) can enchilada sauce*
*1 (7 ounce) can green chilies*
*1½ cups grated Monterey Jack cheese*
*1 (8 ounce) carton sour cream*

- Preheat over to 350°.

- Brown beef in skillet with a little salt and pepper until it crumbles and is no longer pink. Drain well. Add taco seasoning mix and 1¼ cups water to beef and simmer for 5 minutes.

- In another skillet pour just enough oil to cover bottom of skillet and heat until oil is hot. Cook tortillas one at a time, until soft and limp, about 5 to 10 seconds on each side. Drain on paper towels.

- As you cook tortillas, spoon ⅓ cup meat mixture into center of each tortilla. Sprinkle with small amount of cheddar cheese and 1 spoonful of chopped onion. Roll up and place seam-side down in sprayed 9 x 13-inch baking dish.

- After filling all tortillas, add enchilada sauce and green chilies to remaining meat mixture. Spoon over tortillas. Cover and bake for about 30 minutes.

- Uncover and sprinkle remaining cheddar cheese and Monterey Jack cheese over casserole. Return to oven and bake just until cheese melts. Place dabs of sour cream over enchiladas to serve. Serves 4 to 6.

# SHEPHERD'S PIE

*1 pound lean ground beef*
*1 (1 ounce) envelope taco seasoning mix*
*1 cup shredded cheddar cheese*
*1 (11 ounce) can whole kernel corn, drained*
*2 cups cooked instant mashed potatoes*

- Preheat oven to 350°. In skillet, brown beef, cook about 10 minutes and drain. Add taco seasoning and ¾ cup water and cook another 5 minutes.

- Spoon beef mixture into 8-inch baking pan, sprinkle cheese on top. Sprinkle with corn and spread mashed potatoes over top. Bake for 25 minutes or until top is golden. Serves 4.

# SPANISH MEATLOAF

*1½ pounds lean ground beef*
*1 (16 ounce) can Spanish rice*
*1 egg, beaten*
*¾ cup round, buttery cracker crumbs*
*Chunky salsa*

- Preheat oven to 350°. Combine beef, rice, egg and crumbs in bowl. Shape into loaf in sprayed pan. Bake for 1 hour. Serve with salsa on top of meat loaf. Serves 6 to 8.

# SPICED BEEF

*1 pound lean ground beef*
*1 (1 ounce) packet taco seasoning mix*
*1 (15 ounce) can Mexican stewed tomatoes with liquid*
*1 (15 ounce) can kidney beans with liquid*
*1 (1 pound) package egg noodles*

- Cook beef in skillet and drain. Add taco seasoning and ½ cup water and simmer for 15 minutes. Add stewed tomatoes and kidney beans. (You may need to add ¼ teaspoon salt.)

- Cook egg noodles according to package directions and serve beef over noodles. Serves 4 to 6.

*TIP: For a change, use white rice or Spanish rice instead of egg noodles*

# TASTY TACO CASSEROLE

*2 pounds lean ground beef*
*1 (10 ounce) can taco sauce*
*2 (15 ounce) cans Spanish rice*
*1 (8 ounce) can whole kernel corn, drained*
*1 (8 ounce) package shredded Mexican 4-cheese blend, divided*
*1 cup crushed tortilla chips*

- Preheat oven to 350°.

- In skillet, brown beef and cook and stir until beef is crumbly. Add taco sauce, rice, corn and half cheese and mix well. Spoon into sprayed 9 x 13-inch baking pan, cover and bake for 35 minutes.

- Remove from oven, sprinkle remaining cheese and chips over top of casserole and continue baking for 5 minutes. Serves 8.

# TACO PIE

1½ pounds lean ground beef
½ green bell pepper, seeded, chopped
1 teaspoon canola oil
1 (15 ounce) can Mexican stewed tomatoes
1 tablespoon chili powder
¼ teaspoon garlic powder
1½ cups shredded cheddar cheese
1 (6 ounce) package corn muffin mix
1 egg
⅔ cup milk

- Preheat oven to 375°. Brown ground beef and bell pepper in oil in large skillet and drain well. Add ½ teaspoon salt, tomatoes, 1 cup water, chili powder and garlic powder.
- Cook on medium heat for about 10 minutes or until most of liquid evaporates. Pour into sprayed 9 x 13-inch baking dish. Sprinkle cheese on top.
- Combine corn muffin mix, egg and milk in bowl and beat well. Pour over cheese. Bake for 25 minutes or until corn muffin mix is light brown. Remove from oven and let stand for about 10 minutes before serving. Serves 6 to 8.

# IMPOSSIBLE TACO PIE

1 pound ground beef
½ cup chopped onion
1 (1 ounce) packet taco seasoning
1 (4 ounce) can chopped green chilies, drained
1½ cups milk
¾ cup biscuit mix
3 eggs

- Preheat oven to 400°. Brown ground beef and onion in large skillet and drain. Stir in taco seasoning and green chilies. Spread in sprayed 10-inch quiche dish or 10-inch pie pan.
- Combine milk, biscuit mix and eggs in bowl and beat for 1 minute until smooth. Pour mixture into pie pan with beef and bake for 25 minutes.

## TOPPING:

1½ cups shredded cheddar cheese
Sour cream
Picante sauce

- Remove from oven and sprinkle with cheese. Return to oven and bake for additional 5 to 8 minutes. Cool for 5 minutes before slicing. Serve with dab of sour cream and picante sauce. Serves 8.

# TEX-MEX SUPPER

*1 pound lean ground beef*
*1 large onion, chopped*
*1 (15 ounce) can pinto beans, drained*
*2 teaspoons cumin*
*½ head lettuce, torn*
*2 large tomatoes, chopped, drained*
*2 avocados, peeled, diced*
*1 (8 ounce) package shredded cheddar cheese*
*2 cups original corn chips*
*1 (8 ounce) bottle Catalina salad dressing*

- Saute beef and onion in skillet. Drain grease and add beans, cumin, a little salt and pepper and ½ cup water and simmer until liquid cooks out.

- In large serving bowl, combine lettuce, tomatoes and avocados and toss.

- When ready to serve, toss salad with warm beef mixture, cheese, chips and dressing. Serves 8.

*TIP: Have your beef-bean mixture cooked and remaining ingredients "ready" to take to a potluck supper. Toss all together just before time to eat.*

# BLACK BEAN CHILI CASSEROLE

*1 pound lean ground beef*
*1 onion, finely chopped*
*2 (15 ounce) cans black beans, drained*
*1 teaspoon cumin*
*1 teaspoon chili powder*
*1½ cups thick-and-chunky salsa*
*1 (6.5 ounce) package corn muffin mix*
*1 egg*
*¼ cup milk*

- Preheat oven to 375°.

- In large skillet with a little oil, cook beef and onion on medium-high heat for 8 to 10 minutes. Stir in black beans (or pinto beans if you prefer), cumin, chili powder, salsa and a little salt. Bring to a boil and reduce heat to medium. Cook 5 minutes and stir occasionally. Spoon into sprayed 3-quart round baking dish.

- In small bowl, prepare muffin mix according to package directions with egg and milk. Drop 8 spoonfuls batter around edge of baking dish, onto bean-beef mixture. Bake uncovered for 20 to 25 minutes or until topping is golden brown. Serves 6 to 8.

# CHILI PIE

*2 cups small corn chips*
*1 onion, chopped*
*1 (19 ounce) can chili without beans*
*1½ cups shredded cheddar cheese*

- Preheat oven to 350°.

- Place corn chips in 7 x 11-inch baking dish. Top with onion, chili and cheese. Bake for about 15 minutes. Serves 4.

# QUICK CHILI CASSEROLE

*1 (40 ounce) can chili with beans*
*1 (4 ounce) can diced green chilies*
*1 (11 ounce) can Mexicorn®*
*1 (2 ounce) can sliced ripe olives*
*1 (8 ounce) package shredded cheddar cheese*
*2 cups crushed ranch-flavored tortilla chips*

- Preheat oven to 350°.

- In large bowl, combine all ingredients and mix well. Transfer to greased 3-quart baking dish. Bake uncovered for 35 minutes or until bubbly. Serves 4.

# QUICK FIESTA SUPPER

*2 (15 ounce) cans chili without beans*
*2 (15 ounce) cans pinto beans with liquid*
*2 (15 ounce) cans beef tamales, shucked*
*1 (8 ounce) package shredded Mexican 4-cheese blend, divided*

- Preheat oven to 350°. In greased 9 x 13-inch baking pan, spoon both cans chili in pan and spread out with back of large spoon.

- Spread beans with liquid over chili. Spread tamales over beans. Sprinkle about ½ cup cheese over top, cover and bake for 30 minutes.

- Remove from oven and sprinkle remaining cheese over top of casserole. Return to oven for just 5 minutes. Serve with lots of tortilla chips. Serves 4 to 6.

# CHINESE-CASHEW BEEF

*This is great! It takes very little time to prepare and*
*you will love serving it to your family and friends.*

*1½ pounds lean ground beef*
*1 onion, chopped*
*1 green bell pepper, seeded, chopped*
*2 cups chopped celery*
*1 cup rice*
*¼ cup soy sauce*
*½ teaspoon hot sauce*
*1 (15 ounce) can Chinese vegetables, drained*
*1 (4 ounce) can sliced mushrooms, drained*
*1¼ cups cashews*
*1 (10 ounce) can golden mushroom soup*
*1½ teaspoon beef bouillon granules*
*1½ cups chow mein noodles*

- Preheat oven to 350°.

- Brown beef in skillet and stir well to break up meat. Combine onion, bell pepper, celery, rice, soy sauce, hot sauce, Chinese vegetables, mushrooms, cashews and ½ teaspoon salt in large bowl.

- Combine soup, 2 cups water and beef bouillon granules in saucepan and heat just enough to mix well. Combine beef and soup mixture with onion-vegetable mixture.

- Pour into sprayed 9 x 13-inch baking dish. Cover and bake for 50 minutes. Sprinkle with noodles and bake uncovered for additional 20 minutes. Serves 6 to 8.

# ASIAN BEEF AND NOODLES

*1¼ pounds ground beef*
*2 (3 ounce) packages oriental-flavored ramen noodles*
*1 (16 ounce) package frozen oriental stir-fry mixture*
*½ teaspoon ground ginger*
*3 tablespoons thinly sliced green onions*

- Brown ground beef in large skillet and drain. Add ½ cup water, salt and pepper to taste, simmer for 10 minutes and transfer to separate bowl.

- In same skillet, combine 2 cups water, noodles (broken up), vegetables, ginger and both seasoning packets. Bring to boil and reduce heat.

- Cover, simmer 3 minutes or until noodles are tender and stir once. Return beef to skillet and stir in green onions. Serve right from skillet. Serves 4 to 6.

# SPAGHETTI PIE SPECIAL

*6 ounces spaghetti, cooked, drained*
*⅓ cup grated parmesan cheese*
*1 egg, beaten*
*1 cup small curd cottage cheese, drained*
*1 pound lean ground beef*
*½ cup chopped onion*
*1 (15 ounce) can tomato sauce*
*1 teaspoon minced garlic*
*1 teaspoon dried oregano*
*1 tablespoon sugar*
*½ cup mozzarella cheese*

- Preheat oven to 350°. Mix spaghetti while still warm with parmesan and egg in large bowl.

- Spoon onto well greased 10-inch pie plate (or pizza pan) and pat mixture up and around sides with spoon to form crust. Spoon cottage cheese over spaghetti layer.

- In skillet, brown meat and onion. Drain and add tomato sauce, seasonings and salt and pepper to taste. Simmer for 15 minutes.

- Spoon meat mixture over cottage cheese and bake 30 minutes. Sprinkle mozzarella on top and return to oven for 5 minutes or just until cheese melts. To serve, cut into wedges. Serves 4 to 6.

# SIMPLE SPAGHETTI BAKE

8 ounces spaghetti
1 pound lean ground beef
1 green bell pepper, seeded, finely chopped
1 onion, chopped
1 (10 ounce) can tomato bisque soup
1 (15 ounce) can tomato sauce
2 teaspoons Italian seasoning
1 (4 ounce) can black sliced olives, drained
1 (12 ounce) package shredded cheddar cheese

- Cook spaghetti according to package directions, drain and set aside. Cook beef, bell pepper and onion in skillet and drain.

- Add remaining ingredients, ⅓ cup water, ½ teaspoon salt and spaghetti and stir well. Pour into sprayed 9 x 13-inch baking dish. Refrigerate 2 to 3 hours.

- When ready to bake, preheat oven to 350°. Cover and bake for 45 minutes. Serves 6 to 8.

# RAVIOLI AND MORE

1 pound lean ground beef
1 teaspoon garlic powder
1 large onion, chopped
2 grated zucchini squash
¼ cup (¼ stick) butter
1 (28 ounce) jar spaghetti sauce
1 (25 ounce) package ravioli with portobello mushrooms, cooked
1 (12 ounce) package shredded mozzarella cheese

- Brown ground beef in large skillet until no longer pink and drain. Add garlic powder and ½ teaspoon each of salt and pepper.

- Cook onion and zucchini with butter in saucepan just until tender-crisp and stir in spaghetti sauce. Spread ½ cup sauce in buttered 9 x 13-inch baking dish.

- Layer half ravioli, half spaghetti sauce, half beef and half cheese. Repeat layers, but save remaining cheese for topping.

- Cover and bake at 350° for 35 minutes. Uncover and sprinkle remaining cheese on top. Let stand 10 minutes before serving. Serves 6 to 8.

194

# Easy Winter Warmer

*This is such a good spaghetti sauce on noodles
and is a great substitute for cream sauce.*

1 (12 ounce) package medium egg noodles
Canola oil
3 tablespoons butter
1½ pounds lean ground round beef
1 (10 ounce) package frozen seasoning blend (chopped onions and peppers), thawed
1 (28 ounce) jar spaghetti sauce, divided
1 (12 ounce) package shredded mozzarella cheese

- Preheat oven to 350°. Cook noodles according to package directions in pot of boiling water with a dab of oil and salt. Drain thoroughly, add butter and stir until butter melts.

- Brown beef and onions and peppers in skillet and drain thoroughly. Pour half spaghetti sauce in sprayed 9 x 13-inch baking dish. Layer half noodles, half beef and half cheese. Repeat for second layer.

- Cover and bake for about 30 minutes or until dish is hot. Serves 6 to 8.

# Beef Tips with Mushrooms

2 (10 ounce) cans golden mushroom soup
1 (14 ounce) can beef broth
1 tablespoon beef seasoning
2 (4 ounce) cans sliced mushrooms, drained
2 pounds round steak
Hot buttered noodles
1 (8 ounce) carton sour cream

- Combine both cans of mushroom soup, beef broth, beef seasoning and sliced mushrooms. Place in slow cooker and stir to blend. Add slices of beef and stir well. Cover and cook on LOW for 4 to 5 hours.

- When ready to serve, cook noodles, drain, add salt and a little butter. Stir sour cream into sauce in slow cooker. Spoon sauce and beef over noodles. Serves 4 to 6.

# Skillet Steak and Veggies

*1 pound boneless sirloin steak, cut in strips*
*2 (15 ounce) cans Italian stewed tomatoes with liquid*
*1 (16 ounce) package frozen Italian green beans, thawed*
*1 (8 ounce) carton sour cream*
*Egg noodles, cooked*

- Place sirloin strips in large skillet with a little oil. Cook on high heat about 3 minutes.

- Add stewed tomatoes and green beans, bring to boiling, lower heat and cook for 5 minutes. Just before serving, fold in sour cream. Serve over hot, cooked egg noodles. Serves 4 to 6.

# Round Steak Supper

*1½ pounds lean round steak, tenderized*
*1 onion, chopped*
*1 green bell pepper, seeded, julienned*
*1 red bell pepper, seeded, julienned*
*1½ cups rice*
*2 (10 ounce) cans beef broth*
*1 (7 ounce) can green chilies*

- Trim edges of steak and cut into serving-size pieces. In large skillet with little oil, brown each piece of steak on both sides.

- Add onion, bell peppers, rice, beef broth and green chilies. Bring to boil. Reduce heat and simmer for 50 minutes. Serves 4 to 6.

# Slow Cooker Round Steak

*1 pound round steak, cubed*
*2 cups fresh mushroom halves*
*1 (15 ounce) can Italian stewed tomatoes*
*1 (10 ounce) can beef broth*
*½ cup red wine*
*2 teaspoons Italian seasoning*
*3 tablespoons quick-cooking tapioca*

- Place beef in sprayed 4 to 5-quart slow cooker. Combine mushrooms, tomatoes, beef broth, wine, Italian seasoning, tapioca and a little salt and pepper. Pour over steak.

- Cover and cook on LOW for 8 to 10 hours. Serve over hot, buttered linguine. Serves 4.

# ROUND STEAK CASSEROLE

*This is definitely not a luncheon dish. The men are*
*going to call for this beef over and over again.*

2 pounds lean round steak, tenderized
3 tablespoons canola oil
1 onion, chopped
1 cup rice
1 (14 ounce) can beef broth
1 tablespoon dried parsley flakes
½ teaspoon garlic powder
2 tablespoons Worcestershire sauce
2 green bell peppers, seeded, sliced

- Preheat oven to 350°. Trim fat from steak and cut into serving-size pieces. Season with a little salt and pepper.

- Pour oil in large skillet and brown steak on both sides. Remove to sprayed 9 x 13-inch baking dish.

- Combine onion, rice, broth, 1 soup can plus ⅓ cup water, parsley flakes, garlic powder, a little salt, Worcestershire and bell peppers in bowl. Spoon over steak. Cover and bake for 45 minutes. Serves 6 to 8.

# TOMATO-TOPPED ROUND STEAK

*Slow cooker favorite!*

1½ pounds boneless, beef round steak
2 small onions
2 tablespoons quick-cooking tapioca
1 teaspoon dried thyme
2 (15 ounce) cans Mexican stewed tomatoes
1 (8 ounce) package fettuccini or medium egg noodles, cooked

- Trim fat from steak and cut into 4 serving-size pieces. Brown steak in skillet. Drain and place in sprayed 4 to 5-quart slow cooker.

- Slice onions and separate into rings. Cover meat with onions and sprinkle with tapioca, thyme, a little salt and pepper. Pour stewed tomatoes over onion and seasonings. Cover and cook on LOW for 5 to 8 hours. Serve over noodles. Serves 4 to 6.

# STEAK AND POTATOES

2 pounds round steak
⅓ cup flour
⅓ cup oil
5 peeled potatoes, diced
¼ cup chopped onions
1 (10 ounce) cream of mushroom soup

- Preheat oven to 350°. Dice steak, sprinkle with salt and pepper and coat in flour. Brown in heavy skillet with a little oil and drain. Place steak in 9-inch baking dish.

- Season potatoes with a little salt and pepper, place over steak and cover with mushroom soup diluted with ½ cup water. Bake 1 hour 30 minutes. Serves 4 to 6.

# SMOTHERED STEAK

1½ pounds (¾ inch) thick beef round or sirloin steak
⅓ cup flour
3 tablespoons canola oil
3 medium onions, sliced
1 (10 ounce) can beef broth
1 tablespoon lemon juice
1 teaspoon garlic powder
¼ teaspoon dried thyme
½ teaspoon summer savory

- Cut meat into serving-size pieces. Salt and pepper steak pieces and dip in flour. Pound flour into steak with meat tenderizer.

- Brown steak in oil in large skillet and top with onion slices.

- Combine remaining ingredients in bowl. Pour over steak, bring to a boil and reduce heat to simmer. Cover and cook slowly for 1 hour. Check steak while cooking and add a little water if needed. Serves 6 to 8.

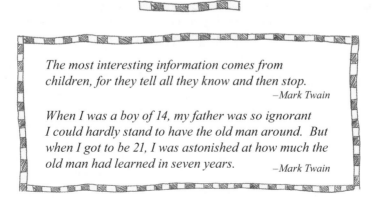

*The most interesting information comes from children, for they tell all they know and then stop.*
—Mark Twain

*When I was a boy of 14, my father was so ignorant I could hardly stand to have the old man around. But when I got to be 21, I was astonished at how much the old man had learned in seven years.*
—Mark Twain

# SWISS STEAK

*1 - 1½ pounds boneless, round steak*
*½ teaspoon seasoned salt*
*½ teaspoon seasoned pepper*
*8 - 10 medium new (red) potatoes with peel, halved*
*1 cup baby carrots*
*1 onion, sliced*
*1 (15 ounce) can stewed tomatoes*
*1 (12 ounce) jar beef gravy*

- Cut steak in 6 to 8 serving-size pieces, season with seasoned salt and pepper and brown in non-stick skillet. Layer steak pieces, potatoes, carrots and onion in slow cooker.

- Combine tomatoes and beef gravy in saucepan over heat to mix. Spoon over vegetables. Cover and cook on LOW for 7 to 8 hours. Serves 4 to 6.

# STEAK AND GRAVY

*1 - 1½ pounds round steak, tenderized*
*Flour*
*Canola oil*
*1 (10 ounce) can golden cream of mushroom soup*
*1½ cans milk*
*1 (1 ounce) packet onion soup mix*
*1 (4 ounce) can mushrooms with liquid*

- Preheat oven to 350°.

- Trim off fat from steak and season with ample amount of pepper. Cut steak in serving-size pieces, dip each piece in flour and coat well. Brown in a little oil in large skillet.

- Place steak pieces in sprayed 9 x 13-inch glass baking dish.

- In same skillet, combine mushroom soup, milk, onion soup mix and mushrooms. Blend and pour over steak pieces. Cover and bake for 1 hour. Serves 4 to 6.

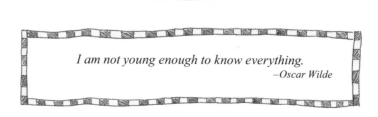

*I am not young enough to know everything.*
*—Oscar Wilde*

# Classy Beef and Noodles

*2 pounds lean round steak, cut in strips*
*Oil*
*2 (10 ounce) cans golden mushroom soup*
*½ cup cooking sherry*
*1 (1 ounce) packet dry onion-mushroom soup mix*
*1 (12 ounce) package medium egg noodles*
*¼ cup (½ stick) butter*

- Preheat oven to 325°.

- Brown steak strips in skillet with a little oil and drain off fat. Stir in mushroom soup, sherry, dry onion-mushroom soup mix and ¾ cup water. Spoon into sprayed 3-quart baking dish, cover and bake for 1 hour or until steak is tender.

- Cook noodles according to package directions, drain and stir in butter. Spoon onto serving platter and spoon steak mixture over noodles. Serves 8 to 10.

# Smothered Steak and Potatoes

*1 (1½ pound) round steak*
*2 (15 ounce) cans whole new potatoes, drained*
*1 (10 ounce) can golden mushroom soup*
*1 (1 ounce) packet dry onion soup mix*
*1½ cups milk*

- Preheat oven to 325°. Cut steak into serving-size pieces and brown in skillet with a little oil on high heat. Transfer to sprayed 9 x 13-inch baking pan and place potatoes over steak.

- In saucepan, combine mushroom soup, dry onion soup mix and milk and heat just enough to be able to mix well. Pour over steak and potatoes. Cover and bake for 50 minutes. Serves 6.

*No matter how old a mother is, she watches her middle-aged children for signs of improvement.*
*—Florida Scott-Maxwell*

# SPICY TOMATO STEAK

*1½ pounds tenderized round steak*
*Flour*
*1 (15 ounce) can Mexican stewed tomatoes*
*¾ cup picante sauce*
*1 (14 ounce) can beef broth*
*1 (6.4 ounce) package Mexican-style rice*

- Cut round steak into serving-size pieces and dredge in flour. Brown steak in skillet with a little oil and stir in tomatoes, picante and beef broth. Bring to a boil, reduce heat to low, cover and simmer for 50 to 60 minutes.

- Prepare rice according to package directions and spoon onto serving platter. Spoon steak and sauce over rice. Serves 8.

# BEEF STEW CASSEROLE

*1 (2 - 3 pounds) chuck roast, cut in bite-size pieces*
*2 tablespoons canola oil*
*1 cup sliced carrots*
*2 onions, chopped*
*4 potatoes, peeled, cubed*
*1 cup chopped celery*
*1 (10 ounce) can golden cream of mushroom soup*
*½ cup burgundy wine*

- Preheat oven to 300°. Brown pieces of roast in oil in skillet. Place in large sprayed roasting pan. Add all remaining ingredients with 2 teaspoons salt, 1 teaspoon pepper and ½ cup water. Cover and bake for 5 hours. Serves 6 to 8.

# O'BRIAN'S HASH

*3 cups cooked, cubed beef roast*
*1 (28 ounce) package frozen hash browns with onions and peppers, thawed*
*1 (16 ounce) jar salsa*
*1 tablespoon beef seasoning*
*1 cup shredded cheddar-jack cheese*

- Place cubed beef in 5 to 6-quart, sprayed slow cooker. Brown potatoes in little oil in large skillet and transfer to slow cooker.

- Stir in salsa and beef seasoning. Cover and cook on HIGH for 4 to 5 hours. When ready to serve, sprinkle cheese over hash. Serves 4 to 6.

# BEST POT ROAST DINNER

*Everybody loves pot roast and this is always a winner.*

1 (4 pound) boneless rump or chuck roast
Garlic powder
6 potatoes, peeled, quartered
8 carrots, peeled, quartered
3 onions, peeled, quartered
3 tablespoons cornstarch

- Preheat oven to 375°. Set roast in roasting pan with lid and sprinkle liberally with salt, pepper and garlic powder. Add 1½ cups water. Cover and bake for about 30 minutes.

- Turn heat down to 325° and bake for about 2 to 2 hours 30 minutes or until roast is fork tender. (Add water if needed.) Add potatoes, carrots and onions. Cook for additional 35 to 40 minutes.

- Lift roast out of roasting pan and place on serving platter. Place potatoes, carrots and onions around roast. Combine cornstarch and ¾ cup water in bowl and add to juices left in roasting pan. Add ½ teaspoon each of salt and pepper and stir to make gravy.

- Cook on high on top of stove until gravy thickens, stirring constantly. Serve in gravy boat with roast and vegetables. Serves 8 to 10.

# LEMON-HERB POT ROAST

1 teaspoon garlic powder
2 teaspoons lemon-pepper seasoning
1 teaspoon dried basil
1 (3 - 3½ pound) boneless beef chuck roast
1 tablespoon canola oil

- Combine garlic powder, lemon pepper and basil in bowl and press evenly into surface of beef.

- Heat oil in large, heavy pan over medium-high heat and brown roast.

- Add 1 cup water, bring to a boil and reduce heat to low. Cover tightly and simmer for 3 hours. (Add water if necessary.) Vegetables may be added to roast the last hour of cooking. Serves 4.

*An excellent health tip: Drink Plenty of Water.*

# Old-Time Pot Roast

*1 (2 - 2½) pound boneless rump roast*
*5 medium potatoes, peeled, quartered*
*1 (16 ounce) package peeled baby carrots*
*2 medium onions, quartered*
*1 (10 ounce) can golden mushroom soup*
*½ teaspoon dried basil*
*½ teaspoon seasoned salt*

- In skillet, brown roast on all sides. Place potatoes, carrots and onions in sprayed 4 to 5-quart slow cooker. Place browned roast on top of vegetables.

- In saucepan, heat soup, basil and seasoned salt just enough to mix and pour mixture over meat and vegetables. Cover and cook on LOW for 9 to 11 hours.

- Transfer roast and vegetables to serving plate. Stir juices remaining in slow cooker and spoon over roast and vegetables. Serves 4 to 6.

# Savory Rib Roast

*1 tablespoon dried thyme*
*1 teaspoon dried rosemary, crushed*
*1 teaspoon rubbed sage*
*1 teaspoon pepper*
*1 (6 pound) beef rib roast*

- Preheat oven to 350°. Combine thyme, rosemary, sage and pepper in small bowl and rub over roast. Place roast, fat-side up, on rack in large roasting pan.

- Bake for 2 hours to 2 hours 30 minutes or until meat reaches desired doneness (rare is 140°; medium is 160°; and well done is 170°). Remove roast to a warm serving platter and let stand for 10 minutes before slicing. Serves 6 to 8.

> *Make the most of leftover foods. One of the very best ways to use all kinds of leftovers is with delicious soups and stews. Save even small amounts of meats, vegetables, gravies and sauces together or in separate containers. Freeze containers until you have enough for a dish.*

# PRIME RIB OF BEEF

⅓ cup chopped onion
⅓ cup chopped celery
½ teaspoon garlic powder
1 (6 - 8 pound) beef rib roast
1 (14 ounce) can beef broth

- Preheat oven to 350°. Combine onion and celery and place in sprayed roasting pan.

- Combine 1 teaspoon salt, garlic powder and a little black pepper and rub over roast. Place roast over vegetables with fat-side up.

- Bake for 2 hours 30 minutes to 3 hours 30 minutes or until meat reaches desired doneness. (Medium-rare is 145°; medium is 160°; well-done is 170°.)

- Let stand for about 15 minutes before carving. Skim fat from pan drippings and add beef broth. Stir to remove browned bits and heat. Strain and discard vegetables. Serve au jus with roast. Serves 10 to 12.

# DUTCH-OVEN ROAST

1 (3 pound) rump roast
1 onion, sliced
1 (10 ounce) can golden mushroom soup
1 (1 ounce) packet brown gravy mix
2 teaspoons minced garlic

- Preheat oven to 325°.

- Place roast in sprayed Dutch ovens or large, heavy pot and place onion slices on top of roast.

- Combine soup, gravy mix, garlic and ⅔ cup water in saucepan and heat just enough for mixture to blend well. Pour mixture over roast.

- Place lid on Dutch oven or pot and bake for 3 hours 30 minutes or until roast is tender. Serves 8 to 10.

*If a dish is too salty, add several slices of potato to absorb the salt. Remove them before serving.*

# REUBEN CASSEROLE

1 (20 ounce) package frozen hash brown potatoes, thawed
2 pounds deli corned beef, sliced ¼-inch thick
1 (8 ounce) bottle Russian salad dressing, divided
1 (15 ounce) can sauerkraut, drained
8 slices Swiss cheese

- Preheat oven to 425°. Place hash brown potatoes in sprayed 9 x 13-inch baking dish and season with a little salt and pepper. Bake uncovered for 25 minutes.

- Place overlapping corned beef slices on top of potatoes. Spoon half bottle of dressing over top of beef and arrange sauerkraut over beef. Cover with slices of cheese.

- Reduce oven to 375° and bake for 20 minutes. Serve remaining Russian dressing on the side. Serves 6 to 8.

# CORNED BEEF SUPPER

1 (4 - 5 pound) corned beef brisket
4 large potatoes, peeled, quartered
6 carrots, peeled, halved
4 onions
1 head cabbage

- Place corned beef in roasting pan, cover with water and bring to boil. Turn heat down and simmer 3 hours. (Add water if necessary.)

- Add potatoes, carrots and onions. Cut cabbage into eighths and lay over top of other vegetables. Bring to boil, turn heat down and cook another 30 to 40 minutes until vegetables are done.

- When slightly cool, slice corned beef across grain and serve. Serves 6 to 8.

# EASY BREEZY BRISKET

1 (4 - 5 pound) brisket
1 (1 ounce) package dry onion soup mix
2 tablespoons Worcestershire sauce
1 cup red wine

- Preheat oven to 325°.

- Place brisket in shallow baking pan. Sprinkle onion soup mix over brisket. Pour Worcestershire and red wine in pan.

- Cover and bake for 5 to 6 hours. Serves 8 to 10.

# Next-Day Brisket

1 (5 - 6 pound) trimmed beef brisket
1 (1 ounce) package dry onion soup mix
1 (10 ounce) bottle steak sauce
1 (12 ounce) bottle barbecue sauce

- Preheat oven to 325°.
- Place brisket, cut side up, in roasting pan.
- In bowl, combine onion soup mix, steak sauce and barbecue sauce. Pour over brisket.
- Cover and bake for 4 to 5 hours or until tender. Remove brisket from pan and pour off drippings. Refrigerate both, separately, overnight.
- The next day, trim all fat from meat, slice and reheat. Skim fat off drippings and reheat. Serve sauce over brisket. Serves 10 to 12.

# Great Brisket

2 onions, sliced
Paprika
Seasoned salt
1 (5 - 6 pound) trimmed brisket
1 (12 ounce) can cola

- Preheat oven to 450°. Place onions in roasting pan. Sprinkle with paprika and seasoned salt. Lay brisket on top of onions and sprinkle more seasoned salt.
- Bake for 30 minutes. Pour cola over roast and reduce oven to 325°. Cover and bake for about 4 hours. Baste occasionally with cola and juices from brisket. Serves 8 to 10.

# Slow Cookin', Good Tastin' Brisket

½ cup liquid hickory-flavored smoke
1 (4 - 5 pound) beef brisket
1 (5 ounce) bottle Worcestershire sauce
¾ cup barbecue sauce

- Pour liquid smoke over brisket. Cover and refrigerate overnight. Drain and pour Worcestershire sauce over brisket.
- Cover and bake at 275° for 6 to 7 hours. Cover with barbecue sauce. Bake uncovered for another 30 minutes. Slice very thin across grain. Serves 6 to 8.

# Heavenly Smoked Brisket

*½ cup packed dark brown sugar*
*2 tablespoons Cajun seasoning*
*1 tablespoon lemon pepper*
*1 tablespoon Worcestershire sauce*
*1 (5 - 6 pound) beef brisket*

- Combine brown sugar, Cajun seasoning, lemon pepper and Worcestershire sauce in shallow dish. Add brisket and turn to coat both sides. Cover and refrigerate for 8 hours.

- Soak hickory wood chunks in water for 1 hour. Prepare charcoal fire in smoker and burn about 20 minutes. Drain chunks and place on coals. Place water pan in smoker and add water to depth of fill line.

- Place brisket on lower food rack and cover with smoker lid. Cook for 5 hours or until meat thermometer inserted in thickest portion registers 170°. Serves 8 to 10.

# Oven-Smoked Brisket

*1 (5 - 6 pound) trimmed brisket*
*1 (6 ounce) bottle liquid smoke*
*Garlic salt*
*Celery salt*
*1 onion, chopped*
*Worcestershire sauce*
*1 (6 ounce) bottle barbecue sauce*

- Place brisket in roasting pan. Pour liquid smoke over brisket. Sprinkle with garlic and celery salts and top with onion. Cover and refrigerate overnight.

- Before cooking, pour off liquid smoke and douse with Worcestershire sauce. When ready to bake, preheat oven to 300°.

- Cover and bake for 5 hours. Uncover and pour barbecue sauce over brisket and bake for additional 1 hour. Serves 8 to 10.

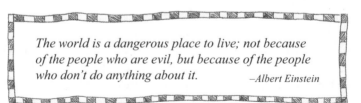

*The world is a dangerous place to live; not because of the people who are evil, but because of the people who don't do anything about it.*   *—Albert Einstein*

# Sweet and Savory Brisket

*1 (3 - 4 pound) trimmed beef brisket, halved*
*⅓ cup grape or plum jelly*
*1 cup ketchup*
*1 (1 ounce) packet onion soup mix*

- Place half brisket in sprayed slow cooker. Combine jelly, ketchup, soup mix and ¾ teaspoon pepper in bowl. Spread half over meat.

- Top with remaining brisket and ketchup mixture. Cover and cook on LOW for 8 to 10 hours or until meat is tender. Slice brisket and serve with cooking juices. Serves 6 to 8.

# Chuck Wagon Barbecue

*1 (5 - 7 pound) trimmed beef brisket*
*1 (4 ounce) bottle liquid smoke*
*½ teaspoon garlic salt*
*½ teaspoon onion salt*
*½ teaspoon celery salt*
*½ teaspoon seasoned pepper*

- Preheat oven to 350°.

- Place brisket in large baking pan and coat generously with liquid smoke. Sprinkle spices over brisket, cover with foil and refrigerate overnight. Next day, pour off about three-fourths liquid smoke.

## Barbecue Sauce:

*1 (16 ounce) bottle ketchup*
*½ cup packed brown sugar*
*1 teaspoon mustard*
*1½ teaspoons garlic powder*
*2 tablespoons Worcestershire sauce*
*⅛ teaspoon cayenne pepper*
*¼ cup vinegar*

- Combine barbecue sauce ingredients in bowl and pour over brisket. Bake for 1 hour, lower heat to 275° and bake for 5 more hours. Let brisket stand for at least 2 hours before slicing.

- Barbecue sauce will be thin so pour it in saucepan, boil for 15 minutes and it will be thick enough to serve over brisket. (Makes about 2 cups sauce.) Serves 8 to 10.

# CHEESY MEATBALL PIE

2 cups shredded hash brown potatoes, thawed
1 (10 ounce) box frozen green peas, thawed
18 frozen Italian meatballs, thawed, halved
¾ cup shredded cheddar cheese
½ cup biscuit mix
1 cup milk
2 large eggs

- Preheat oven to 375°. In bowl, toss hash brown potatoes with a little salt and pepper and spread in sprayed deep-dish pie plate. Layer peas, meatballs and cheese over potatoes in pie plate.

- In bowl, whisk biscuit mix, milk and eggs until ingredients blend well. Pour over layers of potato-cheese mixture and bake uncovered for 35 minutes or until center sets and top is golden brown. Let stand 10 minutes before cutting in wedges to serve. Serves 8 to 10.

# REUBEN DOGS

1 (27 ounce) can sauerkraut, rinsed, drained
2 teaspoons caraway seeds ˙
8 all-beef wieners, halved lengthwise
1 cup shredded Swiss cheese
Thousand Island salad dressing

- Preheat oven to 350°. Place sauerkraut in greased 2-quart baking dish. Sprinkle caraway seeds over top and add wieners.

- Bake uncovered for 20 minutes or until they are hot. Sprinkle with cheese. Bake 3 to 5 minutes longer or until cheese melts. Serve with salad dressing. Serves 4 to 6.

*You cannot help the poor by destroying the rich. You cannot strengthen the weak by weakening the strong. You cannot bring about prosperity by discouraging thrift. You cannot lift the wage earner up by pulling the wage payer down. You cannot further the brotherhood of man by inciting class hatred. You cannot build character and courage by taking away people's initiative and independence. You cannot help people permanently by doing for them, what they could and should do for themselves.*

*—William J. H. Boetcker*

# CHICKEN MAIN DISHES

## SPICY ORANGE CHICKEN OVER NOODLES

*1 pound boneless skinless chicken tenders*
*2 tablespoons oil*
*2 tablespoons soy sauce*
*1 (16 ounce) package frozen stir-fry vegetables, thawed*

### SAUCE:

*⅔ cup orange marmalade*
*1 tablespoon oil*
*1 tablespoon soy sauce*
*1½ teaspoons lime juice*
*½ teaspoon minced ginger*
*½ teaspoon cayenne pepper*

- Lightly brown chicken tenders in oil in large skillet over medium to high heat. Add 2 tablespoons soy sauce and cook another 3 minutes or until chicken cooks through.

- Add stir-fry vegetables and cook about 5 minutes or until vegetables are tender-crisp. In saucepan, combine marmalade, oil, soy sauce, lime juice, minced ginger and cayenne pepper and mix well.

- Heat and pour over stir-fry chicken and vegetables. Serve over chow mein noodles. Serves 4.

## SUNDAY CHICKEN

*5 - 6 boneless, skinless chicken breast halves*
*½ cup sour cream*
*¼ cup soy sauce*
*1 (10 ounce) can French onion soup*

- Preheat oven to 350°. Place chicken in sprayed 9 x 13-inch baking dish. In saucepan, combine sour cream, soy sauce and soup and heat just enough to mix well. Pour over chicken breasts. Bake covered for 55 minutes. Serves 4 to 6.

# Stir-Fry Chicken Spaghetti

*1 pound boneless, skinless chicken breast halves*
*1½ cups sliced mushrooms*
*1½ cups seeded, sliced bell pepper strips*
*1 cup sweet-and-sour stir-fry sauce*
*1 (16 ounce) package spaghetti, cooked*
*¼ cup (½ stick) butter*

- Season chicken with salt and pepper and cut into thin slices. Brown chicken slices in large skillet with a little oil and cook for 5 minutes (or until juices are clear) on low to medium heat. Transfer to plate and set aside.

- In same skillet with a little more oil, stir-fry mushrooms and bell pepper strips for 5 minutes. Add chicken strips and sweet-and-sour sauce and stir until ingredients are hot.

- While spaghetti is still hot, drain well, add butter and stir until butter melts. Place in large bowl and toss with chicken mixture. Serve hot. Serves 4.

# Sunny Chicken Supper

*1½ teaspoons curry powder*
*4 boneless, skinless chicken breast halves*
*1½ cups orange juice*
*1 tablespoon brown sugar*
*1 cup uncooked rice*
*1 teaspoon mustard*

- Rub chicken breasts with curry powder and a little salt and pepper. Combine orange juice, brown sugar, rice and mustard in large skillet and mix well.

- Place chicken breasts on top of rice mixture and bring to boil. Reduce heat, cover and simmer for 30 minutes or until chicken cooks through.

- Remove from heat and let stand, covered, about 10 minutes until all liquid absorbs into rice. Serves 4.

# Sweet-and-Sour Chicken

*8 boneless, skinless chicken breast halves*
*Canola oil*
*1 (1 ounce) packet onion soup mix*
*1 (6 ounce) can frozen orange juice concentrate, thawed*

- Preheat oven to 350°. Brown chicken in a little oil in skillet and place in sprayed 10 x 15-inch baking dish.

- Combine onion soup mix, orange juice and ⅔ cup water in small bowl. Mix well and pour over chicken. Bake for 45 to 50 minutes. Serves 8.

# TASTY CHICKEN–RICE WITH VEGGIES

*4 boneless, skinless chicken breast halves*
*2 (10 ounce) jars sweet and sour sauce*
*1 (16 ounce) package frozen broccoli, cauliflower and carrots, thawed*
*1 (10 ounce) package frozen baby peas, thawed*
*2 cups sliced celery*
*1 (6 ounce) package parmesan-butter rice mix*
*⅓ cup toasted, slivered almonds*

- Cut chicken in 1-inch strips. Combine chicken, sweet and sour sauce and all vegetables in 6-quart slow cooker sprayed with vegetable cooking spray. Cover and cook on LOW for 4 to 6 hours.

- When ready to serve, cook parmesan-butter rice according to package directions and fold in almonds. Serve chicken and vegetables over hot cooked rice. Serves 4.

# ONE–DISH CHICKEN BAKE

*1 (6 ounce) package chicken stuffing mix*
*4 boneless, skinless chicken breast halves*
*1 (10 ounce) can cream of mushroom soup*
*⅓ cup sour cream*

- Preheat oven to 375°.

- Toss contents of seasoning packet, stuffing mix and 1⅔ cups water in bowl and set aside. Place chicken in sprayed 9 x 13-inch baking dish.

- Mix soup and sour cream in saucepan over low heat just enough to pour over chicken. Spoon stuffing evenly over top. Bake for 40 minutes. Serves 4.

# OVEN–FRIED CHICKEN

*⅔ cup fine dry breadcrumbs*
*⅓ cup grated parmesan cheese*
*½ teaspoon garlic salt*
*6 boneless, skinless chicken breast halves*
*½ cup Italian salad dressing*

- Preheat oven to 350°. Combine breadcrumbs, parmesan cheese and garlic salt in small bowl. Dip chicken in salad dressing and dredge in crumb mixture.

- Place chicken in sprayed 9 x 13-inch baking pan. Bake for 50 minutes or until juices are clear. Serves 6.

# ORANGE-SPICED CHICKEN

⅔ cup flour
½ teaspoon dried basil
¼ teaspoon dried oregano
¼ teaspoon marjoram
3 tablespoons canola oil
6 boneless, skinless chicken breast halves
1 (6 ounce) can frozen orange juice concentrate, thawed
½ cup white wine vinegar
⅔ cup packed brown sugar
1 (6 ounce) box long grain-wild rice mix

- Preheat oven to 325°.

- Mix flour, basil, oregano, marjoram and ½ teaspoon each of salt and pepper in resealable plastic bag.

- Pour oil into large skillet and heat. Coat chicken in flour mixture, 1 or 2 pieces at a time. Brown both sides of chicken breasts in skillet.

- Place browned chicken breasts in sprayed 9 x 13-inch baking dish. Combine orange juice concentrate, ½ cup water, vinegar and brown sugar in bowl and mix well.

- Spoon about one-half of orange juice mixture over chicken breasts and bake for 30 minutes. While chicken cooks, prepare rice according to package directions and spoon onto large serving platter.

- Place cooked chicken breasts over rice and pour remaining orange juice sauce over top of chicken. Serves 6 to 8.

# PARTY CHICKEN BREASTS

8 boneless, skinless chicken breast halves
8 strips bacon
1 (2.5 ounce) jar dried beef
1 (10 ounce) can cream of chicken soup
1 (8 ounce) carton sour cream

- Preheat oven to 325°. Wrap each chicken breast with 1 strip bacon and secure with toothpicks. Place dried beef in bottom of large, shallow baking pan and top with chicken.

- Heat soup and sour cream in saucepan just enough to pour over chicken. Bake for 1 hour. Serves 8.

# PICANTE CHICKEN

*4 boneless, skinless chicken breast halves*
*1 (16 ounce) jar salsa*
*¼ cup packed brown sugar*
*1 tablespoon mustard*
*Rice, cooked*

- Preheat oven to 375°. Place chicken in sprayed, shallow baking dish. Combine salsa, brown sugar and mustard in small bowl and pour over chicken.

- Bake for 45 minutes or until chicken juices run clear and serve over rice. Serves 4.

# TERIYAKI-PINEAPPLE CHICKEN

*6 boneless, skinless chicken breast halves*
*½ red onion, sliced*
*1 green bell pepper, seeded, sliced*
*1 cup teriyaki marinade*
*1 (15 ounce) can pineapple slices with juice*

- Preheat oven to 350°.

- Place chicken in sprayed 9 x 13-inch baking dish and arrange vegetables over chicken. Mix teriyaki with juice from pineapple in bowl. Pour over vegetables and chicken.

- Bake for 45 minutes. Spoon juices over chicken once during baking. About 10 minutes before chicken is done, place pineapple slices over chicken and return to oven for remaining 10 minutes. Serves 6.

# SKILLET CHICKEN AND PEAS

*4 - 5 boneless, skinless chicken breast halves*
*2 (10 ounce) can cream of chicken soup*
*2 cups uncooked instant rice*
*1 (10 ounce) package frozen green peas*

- Heat a little oil in very large skillet. Add chicken and cook until it browns well. Transfer chicken to plate and keep warm.

- To skillet, add soup, 1¾ cups water and about ½ teaspoon pepper and paprika if you have it. Heat to boiling, stir in rice and peas and reduce heat. Place chicken on top and cook on low heat for 15 minutes. Serves 4 to 6.

# SASSY CHICKEN OVER TEX-MEX CORN

*2 teaspoons garlic powder*
*1 teaspoon ground cumin*
*⅔ cup flour*
*4 boneless, skinless chicken breast halves*

## TEX-MEX CORN:

*1 (10 ounce) can chicken broth*
*1½ cups hot salsa*
*1 (11 ounce) can Mexicorn®*
*1 cup instant rice*

- Combine garlic powder, cumin, flour and ample salt in shallow bowl. Dip chicken in flour mixture and coat each side of chicken.

- Place a little oil in heavy skillet over medium to high heat. Cut each chicken breast in half lengthwise. Brown each piece of chicken on both sides, reduce heat and add 2 tablespoons water to skillet.

- Cover and simmer for 15 minutes. Transfer chicken to foil-lined baking pan and place in oven at 250° until Tex-Mex Corn is ready to serve.

- Use same unwashed skillet, combine broth, salsa and corn and cook about 10 minutes. Stir in rice and let stand 10 minutes or until rice is tender. To serve, spoon Tex-Mex Corn on platter and place chicken breasts over corn. Serves 4.

# SAUCY CHICKEN

*5 - 6 boneless, skinless chicken breast halves*
*2 cups thick, chunky salsa*
*⅓ cup packed light brown sugar*
*1½ tablespoons dijon-style mustard*

- Preheat oven to 350°. Place chicken breasts in sprayed 9 x 13-inch baking dish. Combine salsa, sugar and mustard and pour over chicken. Cover and bake for 45 minutes. Serve over rice. Serves 4 to 6.

*A jumper cable walks into a bar and orders a drink. The bartender says, "Okay, I'll serve you, but don't start anything."*

# SKILLET CHICKEN AND STUFFING

*1 (16 ounce) box stuffing mix for chicken*
*1 (16 ounce) package frozen whole kernel corn*
*¼ cup (½ stick) butter*
*4 boneless, skinless chicken breast halves, cooked*

- Combine corn, 1⅔ cups water and butter in large skillet and bring to a boil. Reduce heat, cover and simmer for 5 minutes. Stir in stuffing mix just until moist. Cut chicken into thin slices and mix with stuffing-corn mixture. Cook on low heat just until mixture heats well. Serves 4.

# FIESTA CHICKEN

*This is another dish that is great for leftover turkey.*

*1 (16 ounce) bag tortilla chips, divided*
*4 cups cooked, chopped chicken breasts*
*1 large onion, chopped*
*1 green bell pepper, seeded, chopped*
*1 red bell pepper, seeded, chopped*
*1 (12 ounce) package shredded Mexican 4-cheese blend*
*1 teaspoon chili powder*
*1 teaspoon ground cumin*
*2 (10 ounce) cans cream of chicken soup*
*1 (15 ounce) can Mexican stewed tomatoes*

- Preheat oven to 325°. Pour about two-thirds of tortilla chips into sprayed 10 x 15-inch baking dish and crush slightly with palm of your hand.

- In large bowl, combine chicken, onion, bell peppers, cheese, chili powder, 1 teaspoon pepper, cumin, soup and tomatoes and mix well. Spoon mixture over crushed tortilla chips.

- Crush remaining tortilla chips in plastic bag and spread over casserole. Bake uncovered for 45 to 50 minutes or until chips are light brown. Serves 20.

---

*Four cities in the United States have the word "chicken" in their names:* **Chicken,** *Alaska;* **Chicken Bristle,** *Illinois;* **Chicken Bristle,** *Kentucky; and* **Chicken Town,** *Pennsylvania. According to lore, Chicken, Alaska got its name because the locals wanted to honor the state bird, the ptarmigan, by naming their town Ptarmigan, Alaska. But they couldn't spell ptarmigan. However, they could spell chicken. Chicken, Alaska currently has a population of about 170 and an average household income of around $65,000.*

# SOUTH-OF-THE-BORDER CHICKEN

*This is really a delicious chicken dish, but it is spicy.  A tossed*
*green salad garnished with avocado slices is a nice combination.*

8 boneless, skinless chicken breast halves
1 cup shredded Monterey Jack cheese
½ cup shredded cheddar cheese
1 (4 ounce) can diced green chilies
3 tablespoons dried onions
½ cup (1 stick) butter
2 teaspoons cumin
1 teaspoon chili powder
Tortilla chips, crushed

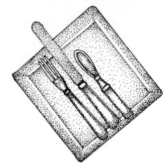

• Preheat oven to 350°.

• Pound chicken breasts flat.  Mix cheeses, green chilies and onions in bowl.  Place
  2 tablespoons cheese mixture on each chicken breast, roll and place seam-side down
  in sprayed 9 x 13-inch baking dish.

• Melt butter in saucepan, add cumin and chili powder and mix well.  Pour over
  chicken.  Cover and bake for 40 minutes.

• Top with crushed tortilla chips and bake uncovered for additional 5 minutes.  Serve
  over rice.  Serves 6 to 8.

# IMPERIAL CHICKEN

1 (6 ounce) box long grain and wild rice
1 (16 ounce) jar cheesy roasted garlic parmesan sauce
6 boneless, skinless chicken breast halves
1 (16 ounce) box frozen French-style green beans, thawed
½ cup slivered almonds, toasted

• Spray oblong slow cooker with vegetable cooking spray and pour in 2½ cups water,
  rice and seasoning packet and stir well.

• Spoon in jar of cheese and mix well.  Place chicken breasts in slow cooker and cover
  with green beans.  Cover and cook on LOW for 3 to 5 hours.  When ready to serve,
  sprinkle with slivered almonds.  Serves 4 to 6.

# CHICKEN BAKE SPECIAL

*This is a great basic dish that everyone loves.*

¼ cup (½ stick) butter
1 (16 ounce) package frozen bell peppers and onions
3 ribs celery, chopped
1 (16 ounce) carton sour cream
1 (7 ounce) can diced green chilies, drained
1 (14 ounce) can chicken broth
4 - 5 cups cooked, cubed chicken
1 (16 ounce) package shredded cheddar cheese, divided
1 (2 pound) package frozen hash brown potatoes, thawed

- Preheat oven to 350°. In saucepan, melt butter and saute peppers and onions and celery.

- In large bowl, combine sour cream, green chilies, 1½ teaspoons pepper and 1 teaspoon salt. Stir in pepper-onion mixture, chicken broth, chicken and half the cheese.

- Fold in hash brown potatoes and spoon into sprayed 10 x 15-inch baking dish. Bake uncovered for 45 minutes or until casserole bubbles.

- Remove from oven and sprinkle remaining cheese over top of casserole. Return to oven for about 5 minutes. Serves 20.

# JOLLY OL' CHICKEN

*With this casserole you have the chicken and cranberry sauce all in one dish.*

1 (6 ounce) package long grain-wild rice with seasonings
1 (16 ounce) can whole berry cranberry sauce
⅓ cup orange juice
3 tablespoons butter, melted
½ teaspoon curry powder
6 - 8 boneless, skinless chicken breast halves
⅔ cup slivered almonds

- Preheat oven to 325°. Cook rice according to package directions and pour into sprayed 9 x 13-inch baking dish.

- Combine cranberry sauce, orange juice, butter and curry powder in saucepan and heat just enough to mix ingredients well.

- Place chicken breasts over rice and pour cranberry-orange juice mixture over chicken. Cover and bake for about 15 minutes or until chicken cooks through.

- Uncover and sprinkle almonds over casserole and return to oven for about 10 to 15 minutes, just until chicken browns lightly. Serves 8.

# LEMONADE CHICKEN

*6 boneless, skinless chicken breast halves*
*1 (6 ounce) can frozen lemonade, thawed*
*⅓ cup soy sauce*
*1 teaspoon garlic powder*

- Place chicken in sprayed 9 x 13-inch baking dish. Combine lemonade, soy sauce and garlic powder and pour over chicken.

- Cover with foil and bake at 350° for 45 minutes. Uncover, baste chicken with juices and cook another 10 minutes uncovered. Serves 4 to 6.

# APRICOT CHICKEN

*1 cup apricot preserves*
*1 (8 ounce) bottle Catalina dressing*
*1 (1 ounce) packet onion soup mix*
*6 boneless, skinless chicken breast halves*
*Rice, cooked*

- Preheat oven to 325°. Combine apricot preserves, dressing and soup mix in bowl. Place chicken breasts in large, sprayed baking dish and pour apricot mixture over chicken. Bake for 1 hour 20 minutes. Serve over hot rice. Serves 6.

*TIP: For a change of pace, use Russian dressing instead of Catalina.*

# ALFREDO CHICKEN

*5 - 6 boneless, skinless chicken breast halves*
*1 (16 ounce) package frozen broccoli florets, thawed*
*1 red bell pepper, seeded, chopped*
*1 (16 ounce) jar alfredo sauce*

- Preheat oven to 325°. Brown and cook chicken breasts in large skillet with a little oil until juices run clear. Transfer to greased 9 x 13-inch baking dish.

- Microwave broccoli according to package directions and drain. (If broccoli stems are extra long, trim and discard.) Spoon broccoli and bell pepper over chicken.

- In small saucepan, heat alfredo sauce with ¼ cup water. Pour over chicken and vegetables. Cover and cook 15 to 20 minutes. Serves 4 to 6.

*TIP: This chicken-broccoli dish can be "dressed up" a bit by sprinkling a little shredded parmesan cheese over the top after casserole comes out of the oven.*

# CHEESY SPAGHETTI CHICKEN FOR 20

*This recipe is a little different twist on the popular chicken spaghetti and it's a winner.*

*1 bunch fresh green onions with tops, chopped*
*1 cup chopped celery*
*1 yellow bell pepper, seeded, chopped*
*1 red bell pepper, seeded, chopped*
*¼ cup (½ stick) butter*
*2 teaspoons Italian seasoning*
*1 (12 ounce) package angel-hair spaghetti, cooked, drained*
*4 cups cooked, chopped chicken or turkey*
*1 (8 ounce) carton sour cream*
*1 (16 ounce) jar creamy alfredo sauce*
*1 (10 ounce) box frozen green peas, thawed*
*1 (16 ounce) package shredded mozzarella cheese, divided*

- Preheat oven to 350°. Saute onions, celery and bell peppers in large skillet with butter. In large bowl combine onion-pepper mixture, seasoning, a little salt and pepper, spaghetti, chicken, sour cream and alfredo sauce; mix well.

- Fold in peas and half the mozzarella cheese and spoon into sprayed 10 x 15-inch deep baking dish. Cover and bake for 50 minutes.

- Remove from oven and sprinkle remaining cheese over casserole. Return to oven for about 5 minutes. Serves 20.

# ASPARAGUS-CHEESE CHICKEN

*1 tablespoon butter*
*4 boneless, skinless chicken breast halves*
*1 (10 ounce) can broccoli-cheese soup*
*1 (10 ounce) package frozen cut asparagus*
*⅓ cup milk*

- Heat butter in skillet and cook chicken for 10 to 15 minutes or until brown on both sides. Remove chicken and set aside.

- In same skillet, combine soup, asparagus and milk and heat to a boil.

- Return chicken to skillet, reduce heat to low, cover and cook for additional 25 minutes until chicken is no longer pink and asparagus is tender. Serves 4.

# BACON-WRAPPED CHICKEN

*6 boneless, skinless chicken breast halves*
*1 (8 ounce) carton whipped cream cheese with onion and chives, softened*
*Butter*
*6 bacon strips*

- Preheat oven to 375°.  Flatten chicken to ½-inch thickness.  Spread 3 tablespoons cream cheese over each piece.  Dot with butter and a little salt and roll.

- Wrap each with 1 bacon strip and place seam-side down in sprayed 9 x 13-inch baking dish.  Bake for 40 to 45 minutes or until juices run clear.

- To brown, broil 6 inches from heat for about 3 minutes or until bacon is crisp.  Serves 6.

# BAKED CHICKEN DIJON

*2 tablespoons dijon-style mustard*
*2 tablespoons canola oil*
*1 teaspoon garlic powder*
*½ teaspoon Italian seasoning*
*4 boneless, skinless chicken breast halves*

- Preheat oven to 375°.

- Mix mustard, oil, garlic powder and seasoning in plastic bag, add chicken breasts and let stand for 15 minutes.  Place chicken in sprayed shallow baking pan.  Bake for 35 minutes.  Serves 4.

# BROCCOLI-CHEESE CHICKEN

*1 tablespoon butter*
*4 boneless, skinless chicken breast halves*
*1 (10 ounce) can condensed broccoli-cheese soup*
*1 (10 ounce) package frozen broccoli spears*
*⅓ cup milk*

- Heat butter in skillet, cook chicken 15 minutes or until brown on both sides, remove and set aside.

- In same skillet, combine soup, broccoli, milk and a little black pepper and heat to boiling, return chicken to skillet and reduce heat to low.

- Cover and cook another 25 minutes until chicken is no longer pink and broccoli is tender and serve over rice.  Serves 4.

# CHEESY CHICKEN WITH BROCCOLI AND CAULIFLOWER

¾ cup (1½ sticks) butter, divided
¼ cup flour
1 (1 pint) carton half-and-half cream
1 (10 ounce) can chicken broth
2 (10 ounce) cans cream of chicken soup
1 (16 ounce) package frozen broccoli spears, thawed
1 (10 ounce) package frozen cauliflower, thawed
2 red bell peppers, seeded, thinly sliced
1 cup chopped celery
2 cups cooked brown rice
4 cups cooked, cubed chicken or turkey
1 (12 ounce) package shredded cheddar cheese
2 cups soft breadcrumbs

- Preheat oven to 350°.

- In saucepan, melt ½ cup (1 stick) butter in saucepan, add flour and stir until mixture is smooth.

- Slowly stir in cream and chicken broth. Cook and stir constantly until mixture is thick. Stir in soup until mixture blends well; set aside.

- Place broccoli, cauliflower, bell pepper and celery in sprayed 10 x 15-inch baking dish. Cover with rice, half the cream sauce and top with chicken. Stir shredded cheese into remaining sauce and pour over chicken.

- Melt remaining ¼ cup butter. Combine breadcrumbs and melted butter. Sprinkle over casserole. Bake uncovered for about 45 to 50 minutes or until casserole is thoroughly hot. Serves 20.

# CHICKEN OREGANO

¼ cup (½ stick) butter, melted
1 (.04 ounce) packet Italian salad dressing mix
2 tablespoons lemon juice
4 boneless, skinless chicken breast halves
2 tablespoons dried oregano

- Preheat oven to 350°. Combine butter, salad dressing mix and lemon juice in bowl. Place chicken in 9 x 13-inch baking pan. Spoon butter mixture over chicken. Cover and bake for 45 minutes.

- Uncover and baste with pan drippings and sprinkle with oregano. Bake for additional 15 minutes or until chicken juices are clear. Serves 4.

# ALMOND-CRUSTED CHICKEN

1 egg
¼ cup seasoned breadcrumbs
1 cup sliced almonds
4 boneless, skinless chicken breast halves
1 (5 ounce) package grated parmesan cheese

- Preheat oven to 350°. Place egg and 1 tablespoon water in shallow bowl and beat. In separate shallow bowl, combine breadcrumbs and almonds.

- Dip each chicken breast in egg, then in almond mixture and place in sprayed 9 x 13-inch baking pan.

- Bake for 20 minutes. Remove from oven and sprinkle parmesan cheese over top and bake for an additional 15 minutes or until almonds and cheese are golden brown.

## SAUCE:

1 teaspoon minced garlic
⅓ cup finely chopped onion
2 tablespoons oil
1 cup white wine
¼ cup teriyaki sauce

- Saute garlic and onion in oil in saucepan. Add wine and teriyaki sauce, bring to a boil and reduce heat. Simmer about 10 minutes or until mixture reduces by half. Serve sauce over chicken. Serves 4.

# SWEET 'N SPICY CHICKEN

1 pound boneless, skinless chicken breast halves
1 (1 ounce) packet taco seasoning
½ cup seasoned breadcrumbs
1 (16 ounce) jar chunky salsa
1½ cups peach preserves
2 cups cooked rice

- Cut chicken into ½-inch cubes and place in large, plastic bag. Add taco seasoning, breadcrumbs and toss to coat.

- In skillet, brown chicken in a little oil. Combine salsa and preserves, stir into skillet and bring mixture to a boil.

- Reduce heat, cover and simmer until juices run clear, about 15 minutes. Serve over hot, cooked rice. Serves 10.

# WALNUT CHICKEN

*Walnuts give this dish a special touch.  It gets rave reviews.*

2 (6 ounce) boxes long grain and wild rice
2 red bell peppers, seeded, chopped
2 cups chopped celery
1 large onion, chopped
2 cups coarsely chopped walnuts
½ cup (1 stick) butter
2 cups mayonnaise
1 (1 pint) carton sour cream
2 tablespoons lemon juice
4 cups cooked, cubed chicken
2 cups crushed potato chips

- Preheat oven to 325°.

- Cook rice according to package directions.

- In skillet, lightly saute bell peppers, celery, onion and walnuts in butter.  Stir in mayonnaise, sour cream, lemon juice, 2 teaspoons salt and chicken; mix well.

- Fold in cooked rice and transfer to sprayed 10 x 15-inch baking dish.  Sprinkle potato chips over top of casserole.

- Bake uncovered for 35 to 40 minutes or until potato chips are light brown.  Serves 20.

# CHICKEN ORANGE

2 green bell peppers, cored, seeded, sliced
2 red bell peppers, cored, seeded, sliced
1 onion, sliced thinly
6 - 8 boneless, skinless chicken breast halves
2 cups orange juice
½ cup chili sauce

- Place bell peppers and onion in sprayed slow cooker.  Season chicken with a little salt and pepper.  Sear outside of chicken in large skillet with a little hot oil.  Place on top of vegetables in slow cooker.

- Mix orange juice and chili sauce in separate bowl.  Pour over chicken.  Cover and cook on LOW for 6 to 8 hours or until chicken juices are clear.  Serves 6 to 8.

# TACO CHICKEN OVER SPANISH RICE

*1¼ cups flour*
*2 (1 ounce) packets taco seasoning*
*2 large eggs, beaten*
*8 boneless, skinless chicken breast halves*
*2 (15 ounce) cans Spanish rice*
*1 cup shredded Mexican 4-cheese blend*

- Preheat oven to 350°.

- Place flour and taco seasoning in large shallow bowl. Place eggs and 3 tablespoons water in another shallow bowl and beat together. Dip each chicken breast in egg mixture, dredge in flour-taco mixture and coat heavily with flour mixture.

- Place in sprayed 10 x 15-inch baking pan and arrange so chicken pieces do not touch. Bake for 55 to 60 minutes or until chicken is cooked through.

- About 10 minutes before chicken is done, place Spanish rice in saucepan and stir in cheese. Stir constantly over medium meat, just until cheese melts. Spoon onto serving platter and place chicken pieces over hot rice. Serves 8.

# PIMENTO CHEESE STUFFED FRIED CHICKEN

*4 skinless, boneless chicken breast halves*
*½ cup milk*
*1 large egg, beaten*
*2 cups seasoned breadcrumbs*
*Oil*
*1 (16 ounce) carton pimento cheese*

- Preheat oven to 350°.

- Dry chicken breasts with paper towels and sprinkle well with salt and pepper.

- Combine milk and beaten egg in shallow bowl and mix well. Place breadcrumbs in second shallow bowl. Dip chicken in milk mixture and dredge in breadcrumbs.

- In large skillet over medium-high heat, pour in a little oil to ⅛-inch depth and cook chicken about 10 to 12 minutes on each side. Transfer to baking sheet.

- Hold chicken with tongs and cut slit in 1 side of each chicken breast to form a pocket. Spoon about ¼ cup pimento cheese into each pocket and secure chicken pocket with toothpick. Bake about 3 minutes or until cheese melts. Serves 4.

# CRUNCHY BAKED CHICKEN

*¼ pound (1 stick) butter, melted*
*2 tablespoons mayonnaise*
*2 tablespoons marinade for chicken*
*1 (6 ounce) can french-fried onions, crushed*
*6 boneless, skinless chicken breasts halves*

- Preheat oven to 350°.
- Combine butter, mayonnaise and marinade for chicken in shallow bowl. In separate shallow bowl, place crushed onions.
- Dry chicken breasts with paper towels, dip first into butter mixture and dredge each chicken breast in crushed onions. Place in large baking pan and arrange so pieces do not touch. Bake for 30 minutes or until chicken is cooked through. Serves 6.

# MARINATED SALSA CHICKEN

## CHICKEN:

*6 boneless, skinless chicken breast halves*
*1 tablespoon cornstarch*

## MARINADE:

*1 (16 ounce) jar salsa*
*¾ cup honey*
*½ cup light soy sauce*
*2 tablespoons oil*
*½ teaspoon dried ginger*

- Dry each chicken piece with paper towels. In bowl, combine all marinade ingredients and mix well. Pour 1½ cups into sealable plastic bag, add chicken and refrigerate 2 to 3 hours. Cover and refrigerate remaining marinade.
- Preheat oven to 350°.
- Drain chicken, discard marinade. Place chicken in sprayed 9 x 13-inch baking dish. Top with remaining refrigerated marinade and bake, uncovered, for 25 to 30 minutes or until juices run clear. Remove chicken and keep warm.
- In small saucepan, combine cornstarch with 2 tablespoons water and stir in pan juices. Bring to a boil and cook about 2 minutes, stirring constantly, until it thickens. Pour sauce over chicken to serve. Serves 6.

# CHICKEN A LA ORANGE

*1 (11 ounce) can mandarin oranges, drained*
*1 (6 ounce) can frozen orange juice concentrate*
*1 tablespoon lemon juice*
*1 tablespoon cornstarch*
*6 boneless, skinless chicken breast halves*
*2 tablespoons garlic-and-herb seasoning*
*2 tablespoons butter*
*Rice, cooked*

- Combine oranges, orange juice concentrate, lemon juice, ⅔ cup water and cornstarch in saucepan. Stir constantly over medium heat until mixture thickens. Set aside.

- Sprinkle chicken breasts with herb seasoning and place in skillet with butter. Cook about 7 minutes on each side until brown.

- Lower heat and spoon orange juice mixture over chicken, cover and simmer about 20 minutes. Add a little water if sauce gets too thick.

- Serve over hot, cooked rice. Serves 6.

# QUICK AND EASY CHICKEN BAKE

*1 (10 ounce) can cream of chicken soup*
*1 cup regular brown rice*
*4 - 6 boneless, skinless chicken breast halves*
*1 (8 ounce) package shredded Colby-Jack cheese*

- Preheat oven to 350°. Combine soup, rice, 1½ cups water and salt and pepper to taste. Place in 9 x 13-inch baking dish.

- Sprinkle chicken with additional black pepper and place in baking dish with rice-soup mixture. Cover and bake for 50 minutes. Uncover, sprinkle cheese over chicken and rice and serve. Serves 4 to 6.

*A boneless chicken breast will cook in approximately 10 minutes in a steamer. After you remove the chicken, let it sit uncut for 2 to 3 minutes and any slight pinkness on the interior will gently finish cooking in the chicken's own steam. Chicken is thoroughly cooked when internal temperature is at least 165°.*

# CHICKEN TACO PIE

*1 pound boneless, skinless chicken breast halves*
*1 (1 ounce) packet taco seasoning mix*
*1 green bell pepper, seeded, finely chopped*
*1 red bell pepper, seeded, finely chopped*
*1 (8 ounce) package shredded Mexican 4-cheese blend*
*1 (8 ounce) package corn muffin mix*
*1 egg*
*⅓ cup milk*

- Preheat oven to 400°. Cut chicken into 1-inch chunks and cook on medium-high heat in large skillet with a little oil. Cook about 10 minutes and drain.

- Stir in taco seasoning, bell peppers and ¾ cup water. Reduce heat, cook another 10 minutes and stir several times. Spoon into sprayed 9-inch deep-dish pan and sprinkle with cheese.

- Prepare corn muffin mix with egg and milk and mix well. Spoon over top of pie and bake for 20 minutes or until top is golden brown. Let stand about 5 minutes before serving. Serves 8 to 10.

# CHICKEN LINGUINE

*1 pound boneless, skinless chicken breast halves, cut into strips*
*Oil*
*1 (28 ounce) can garlic-onion spaghetti sauce*
*1 (16 ounce) package frozen broccoli, carrots and cauliflower, thawed*
*1 bell pepper, seeded, chopped*
*⅓ cup grated parmesan cheese*
*1 (12 ounce) package dry linguine, cooked, drained*

- In large skillet over medium heat, cook half chicken strips in a little oil until light brown. Remove and set aside. Repeat with remaining chicken and set aside.

- In same skillet combine spaghetti sauce, vegetables and cheese and bring to a boil. Reduce heat to medium-low, cover and cook 10 minutes or until vegetables are tender. Stir occasionally.

- Return chicken to skillet and heat thoroughly.

- Place cooked linguine on serving platter and spoon chicken mixture over linguine. Serves 12.

*TIP: Break linguine into thirds before cooking to make serving a little easier.*

# CHICKEN AND PASTA

*How could anything be easier?*

4 chicken breast halves, cooked, cubed
2 (8 ounce) cartons sour cream
1 (7 ounce) box ready-cut spaghetti, uncooked
2 (10 ounce) cans cream of chicken soup
1 (4 ounce) can mushrooms, drained
½ cup (1 stick) butter, melted
1 cup grated parmesan cheese

- Preheat oven to 325°.

- In large bowl, combine chicken, sour cream, spaghetti, chicken soup, mushrooms, butter and ¼ teaspoon white pepper.

- Pour into greased 9 x 13-inch baking dish. Sprinkle cheese on top of casserole. Bake covered for 50 minutes. Serves 4 to 6.

# CHICKEN AND BROWN RICE SUPPER

3 cups instant brown rice
¼ cup (½ stick) butter
3 cups cooked chicken breasts, finely cubed
½ cup golden raisins
½ cup chopped red bell pepper

- Cook brown rice according to package directions. Add butter and salt and pepper to taste. While rice is still hot, stir in cubed chicken, raisins and chopped bell pepper. Transfer to serving bowl.

## DRESSING:

2 tablespoons lemon juice
1 tablespoon dijon-style mustard
2 tablespoons honey
1 teaspoon white wine vinegar
¼ cup slivered almonds, toasted

- Combine lemon juice, mustard, honey and wine vinegar in jar and shake until ingredients blend well. Drizzle over rice-chicken mixture and sprinkle with almonds. Serves 4 to 6.

# CHICKEN AND NOODLES

*1 (3 ounce) package chicken-flavored, instant ramen noodles*
*1 (16 ounce) package frozen broccoli, cauliflower and carrots*
*⅔ cup sweet and sour sauce*
*3 boneless, skinless chicken breast halves, cooked*

- Cook noodles and vegetables in saucepan with 2 cups boiling water for 3 minutes, stir occasionally and drain.

- Combine noodle-vegetable mixture with seasoning packet, sweet and sour sauce and a little salt and pepper. Cut chicken in strips, add chicken to noodle mixture and heat thoroughly. Serves 4.

# CHICKEN-TORTILLA DUMPLINGS

*This recipe is actually easy. It just takes a little time to add tortilla strips, one at a time.*
*Using tortillas is certainly a lot easier than making up biscuit dough for the dumplings!*

*6 large boneless, skinless chicken breasts*
*2 celery ribs, chopped*
*1 onion, chopped*
*2 tablespoons chicken bouillon*
*1 (10 ounce) can cream of chicken soup*
*10-11 (8 inch) flour tortillas*

- Place chicken breasts, 10 cups water, celery and onion in very large pan. Bring to boil, reduce heat and cook about 30 minutes or until chicken is tender. Remove chicken and set aside to cool.

- Save broth in roasting pan. (You should have about 9 cups.) Add chicken bouillon and taste to make sure it is rich and tasty. (Add more bouillon if needed and more water if you don't have 9 cups of broth.)

- When chicken is cool enough, cut into bite-size pieces and set aside. Add chicken soup to broth and bring to boil.

- Cut tortillas into 2 x 1-inch strips. Add strips, one at a time, to briskly boiling broth mixture and stir constantly.

- When all strips are in saucepan, pour in chicken, reduce heat to low and simmer for 5 to 10 minutes, stir well, but gently to prevent dumplings from sticking. Serves about 8 to 10.

# SESAME CHICKEN

*½ cup (1 stick) butter, melted*
*2¼ teaspoons chili powder*
*4 boneless, skinless chicken breast halves*
*1 cup sesame seeds, lightly toasted*

- Preheat oven to 325°. Combine butter and chili powder in bowl. Dip chicken in butter mixture then roll in sesame seeds.

- Place in sprayed 9 x 13- inch baking dish. Bake for 1 hour; turn after 30 minutes. Serves 4.

# CHICKEN AND RICE

*6 boneless, skinless chicken breast halves*
*2 (10 ounce) cans cream of chicken soup*
*2 cups uncooked, instant white rice*
*1 (10 ounce) package frozen green peas, thawed*

- Sprinkle chicken with black pepper and paprika and brown in large, 12-inch skillet with a little oil. Reduce heat, cover and simmer about 15 minutes. Transfer chicken to plate and keep warm.

- Add soup, 2 cups water and mix well. Heat to boiling and stir in rice and green peas. Top with chicken breasts, cover and simmer over low heat about 10 minutes. Serves 4 to 6.

# CHICKEN AND SAUERKRAUT

*6 large, boneless, skinless chicken breast halves*
*1 (16 ounce) can sliced potatoes, drained*
*1 (16 ounce) can sauerkraut, drained*
*¼ cup pine nuts or ½ teaspoon caraway seeds*

- Season chicken in prepared large skillet with a little black pepper and cook over medium heat for 15 minutes or until chicken browns on both sides.

- Add potatoes to skillet and spoon sauerkraut over potatoes. Cover and cook over low heat for 35 minutes or until chicken is done.

- Toast pine nuts in dry skillet on medium heat until golden brown. Stir constantly. Sprinkle chicken and sauerkraut with toasted pine nuts or caraway seeds. Serves 4 to 6.

*TIP: This is good served with sour cream.*

# CHICKEN CRUNCH

*4 boneless, skinless chicken breast halves*
*½ cup Italian salad dressing*
*½ cup sour cream*
*2½ cups corn flakes, crushed*

- Place chicken in resealable plastic bag and add dressing and sour cream. Seal and refrigerate for 1 hour. When ready to bake, preheat oven to 375°.

- Remove chicken from marinade and discard marinade. Dredge chicken in corn flakes and place in sprayed 9 x 13-inch sprayed baking dish. Bake for 45 minutes. Serves 4.

# CHICKEN CUTLETS

*6 boneless, skinless chicken breast halves*
*1½ cups dry breadcrumbs*
*½ cup grated parmesan cheese*
*1 teaspoon dried basil*
*½ teaspoon garlic powder*
*1 (8 ounce) carton sour cream*

- Preheat oven to 325°. Flatten chicken to ½-inch thickness. Combine breadcrumbs, parmesan cheese, basil and garlic powder in shallow dish.

- Dip chicken in sour cream, coat with crumb mixture and place (so chicken breasts do not touch) in sprayed 10 x 15-inch baking dish. Bake for 50 to 60 minutes or until golden brown. Serves 4 to 6.

# CHICKEN MARSEILLES

*3 tablespoons butter*
*5 - 6 boneless, skinless chicken breast halves*
*1 (1 ounce) packet vegetable soup mix*
*½ teaspoon dill weed*
*½ cup sour cream*
*Brown rice, cooked*

- Melt butter in skillet, brown chicken for about 10 to 15 minutes and turn occasionally. Stir 2 cups water, soup mix and dill weed into skillet and bring to a boil. Reduce heat, cover and simmer, stirring occasionally for 25 to 30 minutes or until juices are clear.

- Remove chicken to heated plate, add sour cream to skillet and stir until creamy. Place chicken on hot brown rice and spoon sauce over chicken. Serves 5 to 6.

# CHICKEN SUPPER READY

*4 - 5 carrots*
*6 medium new potatoes with peels, quartered*
*4 - 5 boneless, skinless chicken breast halves*
*1 tablespoon chicken seasoning*
*2 (10 ounce) cans cream of chicken soup*
*⅓ cup white wine or cooking wine*

- Cut carrots into ½-inch pieces. Place potatoes and carrots in slow cooker. Sprinkle chicken breasts with chicken seasoning and place over vegetables.

- Combine soups and wine with ¼ cup water over chicken and vegetables. Cover and cook on LOW for 5 to 6 hours. Serves 4 to 6.

*TIP: For a tasty change, use 1 (10 ounce) can chicken soup and 1 (10 ounce) can mushroom soup instead of cream of chicken soup.*

# CHICKEN-ORZO FLORENTINE

*4 boneless, skinless chicken breast halves*
*¾ cup orzo*
*1 (8 ounce) package fresh mushrooms, sliced*
*1 (10 ounce) package frozen spinach, thawed, well drained\**
*1 (10 ounce) can golden mushroom soup*
*½ cup mayonnaise*
*1 tablespoon lemon juice*
*1 (8 ounce) package shredded Monterey Jack cheese, divided*
*½ cup seasoned Italian breadcrumbs*

- Preheat oven to 350°.

- Cook chicken in boiling water in large saucepan for about 15 minutes and set aside broth. Cut chicken in bite-size pieces and set aside. Pour broth through strainer and cook orzo in strained broth.

- Saute mushrooms in large sprayed skillet until tender. Remove from heat and stir in chicken, orzo, spinach, soup, mayonnaise, lemon juice and ½ teaspoon pepper. Fold in half cheese and mix well.

- Pour into sprayed 9 x 13-inch baking dish and sprinkle with remaining cheese and breadcrumbs. Bake for 35 minutes. Serves 6 to 8.

*\*TIP: Squeeze spinach between paper towels to completely remove excess moisture.*

# CREAMY CHICKEN AND VEGETABLES

*4 large boneless, skinless chicken breast halves*
*1 (10 ounce) can cream of chicken soup*
*1 (16 ounce) package frozen peas and carrots, thawed*
*1 (12 ounce) jar chicken gravy*

- Cut chicken in thin slices. Spray 6-quart slow cooker with vegetable cooking spray. Pour soup and ½ cup water into slow cooker, mix and add chicken slices.

- Sprinkle a little salt and lots of pepper over chicken and soup. Cover and cook on LOW for 4 to 5 hours.

- Add peas, carrots, chicken gravy and another ½ cup water. Increase heat to HIGH and cook for about 1 hour or until peas and carrots are tender. Serves 4.

*TIP: Serve over large, refrigerated buttermilk biscuits or over thick Texas toast.*

# DELIGHTFUL CHICKEN SOUFFLE

*This is such a fabulous dish for any occasion. It is really*
*easy to make, you may make it the day before you need it.*

*16 slices white bread, crusts removed*
*5 boneless, skinless, chicken breast halves, cooked, thinly sliced diagonally*
*½ cup mayonnaise*
*1 cup shredded cheddar cheese, divided*
*5 large eggs*
*2 cups milk*
*1 (10 ounce) can cream of mushroom soup*

- Butter 9 x 13-inch baking dish. Butter 8 slices of bread on 1 side and line bottom of baking dish. Cover with sliced chicken.

- Spread chicken slices with mayonnaise and sprinkle with ½ cup shredded cheese. Top with remaining 8 slices bread. Beat eggs, milk, and about ½ teaspoon each of salt and pepper to taste and pour over entire casserole. Refrigerate 8 hours or overnight.

- When ready to bake, preheat oven to 350°. Spread mushroom soup with back of large spoon over top of casserole. Bake covered at for 45 minutes. Uncover, sprinkle with remaining ½ cup cheddar cheese and bake for another 15 minutes. Serves 6 to 8.

# CREAMY BROCCOLI CHICKEN

*5 large chicken breast halves, thawed*
*2 (10 ounce) cans cream of chicken soup*
*½ cup milk*
*1 (16 ounce) package frozen broccoli florets, thawed*

- Sprinkle chicken with salt and pepper as desired and brown breasts with a little oil in very large skillet with lid. On medium to high heat in saucepan, pour in both cans chicken soup and milk and stir to mix.

- Ladle soup mixture over top of chicken breasts. When mixture mixes and is hot, reduce heat to low, cover and simmer for 20 minutes.

- Place broccoli florets around chicken in creamy sauce. Return heat to high until broccoli is hot. Reduce heat and simmer about 10 minutes or until broccoli is tender-crisp. Serve chicken and sauce over whole-grain brown rice. Serves 4 to 6.

*TIP: Uncle Ben's (8.8 ounce) package ready-rice can be made in the microwave in*
*90 seconds and it's great, not to mention fast!*

# CHICKEN AND POTATOES

*5 boneless, skinless chicken breast halves*
*5 slices onion*
*5 new, red potatoes, quartered*
*1 (10 ounce) can cream of celery soup*
*1 (10 ounce) can cream of chicken soup*

- Preheat oven to 325°. Place chicken breasts in sprayed 9 x 13-inch baking dish. Top chicken with onion slices and place potatoes around chicken.

- Combine both soups and ½ cup water and heat slightly. Pour mixture over chicken and vegetables. Cover and bake for 1 hour. Serves 5.

# CURRY-GLAZED CHICKEN

*3 tablespoons butter*
*⅓ cup honey*
*2 tablespoons dijon-style mustard*
*1½ teaspoons curry powder*
*4 boneless, skinless chicken breast halves*
*Rice, cooked*

- Preheat oven to 375°. Melt butter in 9 x 13-inch baking pan. Mix honey, mustard and curry powder in pan with butter. Add chicken to pan and turn mixture until chicken is coated. Bake for 50 minutes and baste twice. Serve over rice. Serves 4.

# DIJON CHICKEN IN A SKILLET

¼ *cup ranch salad dressing*
*1 tablespoon dijon-style mustard*
*4 boneless, skinless chicken breast halves*
*2 tablespoons butter*
*3 tablespoons white wine or chicken broth*
*Rice, cooked*

- Combine salad dressing and mustard in bowl and set aside. Cook chicken in butter in skillet and simmer for 10 to 15 minutes. Add wine or broth and simmer for additional 20 minutes.

- Whisk in mustard mixture, cook and stir until it blends and heats through. Serve over rice. Serves 4.

# FAVORITE CHICKEN BREASTS

*6 - 8 boneless, skinless chicken breast halves*
*1 (10 ounce) can golden mushroom soup*
*1 cup white wine or white cooking wine*
*1 (8 ounce) carton sour cream*
*Rice, cooked*

- Preheat oven to 350°.

- Place chicken breasts in large, sprayed, shallow baking pan, sprinkle with a little salt and pepper and bake for 30 minutes.

- Combine soup, wine and sour cream in saucepan and heat enough to mix well. Remove chicken from oven and cover with sour cream mixture.

- Reduce heat to 300° and return to oven for additional 30 minutes. Baste twice. Serve over rice. Serves 6 to 8.

*A group of chess players were checking into a hotel and talked to each other in the lobby about a tournament. After some time, the hotel manager asked them to leave the lobby. "Why?" asked one of the players. "Because", he replied, "I don't like a bunch of chess nuts boasting in an open foyer."*

# GARDEN CHICKEN

*This colorful, delicious casserole is not only flavor packed, it is also a
sight to behold! You can't beat this bountiful dish for family or company.*

4 boneless, skinless chicken breast halves, cut into strips
1 teaspoon minced garlic
5 tablespoons butter, divided
1 small yellow squash, thinly sliced
1 small zucchini, thinly sliced
1 red bell pepper, seeded, thinly sliced
¼ cup flour
2 teaspoons pesto seasoning
1 (14 ounce) can chicken broth
1 cup half-and-half cream
1 (8 ounce) package angel hair pasta, cooked al dente, drained
⅓ cup shredded parmesan cheese

- Preheat oven to 350°. Saute chicken and garlic in 2 tablespoons butter in large skillet over medium heat for about 15 minutes. Remove chicken and set aside.

- With butter in skillet, saute squash, zucchini and bell pepper and cook just until tender-crisp. Melt remaining butter in separate saucepan and add flour, pesto seasoning and ½ teaspoon each of salt and pepper. Stir to form smooth paste.

- Gradually add broth, stirring constantly, over medium-high heat until thick. Stir in half-and-half cream and heat thoroughly.

- Combine chicken, vegetables, broth-cream mixture and pasta in large bowl. Transfer to sprayed 9 x 13-inch baking dish. Cover and bake for 30 minutes.

- Sprinkle parmesan cheese over top of casserole and bake uncovered for additional 5 minutes. Serves 6 to 8.

# FRUITED CHICKEN

6 boneless, skinless chicken breast halves
½ cup (1 stick) butter, melted
⅔ cup flour
Paprika
1 (15 ounce) can chunky fruit cocktail with juice

- Preheat oven to 350°. Dip chicken in butter and flour. Place in sprayed 9 x 13-inch shallow baking dish. Sprinkle with a little salt, pepper and paprika. Bake for 45 minutes.

- Pour fruit and half juice over chicken. Bake for additional 20 minutes. Serves 6.

# GLAZED CHICKEN AND RICE

*4 boneless, skinless chicken breast halves, cubed*
*1 (20 ounce) can pineapple chunks with juice*
*½ cup honey mustard grill-and-glaze sauce*
*1 red bell pepper, chopped*
*2 cups cooked rice*

- Brown chicken in skillet with a little oil and cook on low heat for 15 minutes. Add pineapple, honey mustard and bell pepper and bring to a boil.

- Reduce heat to low and simmer for 10 to 15 minutes or until sauce thickens slightly and chicken cooks through. Serve over hot cooked rice. Serves 4.

# GOLDEN CHICKEN DINNER

*6 medium new potatoes, unpeeled, cubed*
*6 medium carrots*
*5 boneless, skinless chicken breast halves*
*1 tablespoon dried parsley flakes*
*1 teaspoon seasoned salt*
*1 (10 ounce) can golden mushroom soup*
*1 (10 ounce) can cream of chicken soup*
*¼ cup dried mashed potato flakes*

- Cut chicken into ½-inch pieces. Place potatoes and carrots in slow cooker and top with chicken breasts. Sprinkle parsley flakes, seasoned salt and a little pepper over chicken.

- Combine soups in saucepan and heat just to mix; spread over chicken. Cover and slow cook on LOW for 6 to 7 hours. Stir in potato flakes and a little water or milk if necessary to make gravy and cook another 30 minutes. Serves 4 to 6.

# RANCH CHICKEN

*½ cup parmesan cheese*
*1½ cups corn flakes*
*1 (.04 ounce) packet dry ranch salad dressing mix*
*2 pounds chicken drumsticks*
*½ cup (1 stick) butter, melted*

- Preheat oven to 350°.

- Combine cheese, corn flakes and dressing mix in bowl. Dip washed, dried chicken in melted butter and dredge in corn flake mixture. Bake for 50 minutes or until golden brown. Serves 4 to 6.

# TEMPTING CHICKEN AND VEGGIES

*1½ pounds chicken breast tenderloins*
*½ cup (1 stick) butter, divided*
*1 (6.2 ounce) box fried rice with seasoning packet*
*⅛ teaspoon cayenne pepper*
*¼ cup chopped sweet red bell pepper*
*1 (10 ounce) package frozen broccoli spears, thawed*
*1 (10 ounce) package frozen corn, thawed*

- Preheat oven to 350°. In skillet, brown chicken tenderloins in about 3 tablespoons butter. Remove chicken to large mixing bowl.

- Saute rice until light brown in same skillet with remaining butter and spoon into bowl with chicken. Add 2½ cups water, about ⅛ teaspoon cayenne pepper (if desired), bell pepper, broccoli spears and corn and mix well.

- Spoon into sprayed 9 x 13-inch baking dish. Cover and cook for 25 minutes or until rice and vegetables are tender. Serves 4 to 6.

# SOUTHERN CHICKEN

*1 cup half-and-half cream*
*1 tablespoon flour*
*1 (1 ounce) package chicken gravy mix*
*1 pound boneless, skinless chicken thighs*
*1 (16 ounce) package frozen stew vegetables, thawed*
*1 (4 ounce) jar sliced mushrooms, drained*
*1 (10 ounce) package frozen green peas, thawed*
*1½ cups biscuit baking mix*
*1 bunch fresh green onions, chopped*
*½ cup milk*

- Combine cream, flour, gravy mix and 1 cup water, stir until smooth and pour in large slow cooker. Cut chicken into 1-inch pieces and stir in vegetables, mushrooms and peas.

- Cover and cook on LOW for 4 to 6 hours or until chicken is tender and sauce thickens.

- Combine baking mix, onions and milk in bowl and mix well. Drop dough by tablespoonfuls onto chicken mixture. Change heat to HIGH, cover and cook another 50 to 60 minutes. Serves 4 to 6.

# ORANGE CHICKEN OVER RICE

*2 pounds boneless, skinless chicken thighs*
*2 bell peppers, seeded, cut in strips*
*1 (1 ounce) packet dry onion soup mix*
*1 (6 ounce) can frozen orange juice concentrate, thawed*
*1 (6 ounce) box long grain and wild rice mix*

- Preheat oven to 350°. In large skillet, brown chicken in a little oil and place in sprayed 9 x 13-inch baking pan. Place bell pepper strips over chicken.

- In bowl, combine dry onion soup mix, orange juice concentrate and 1½ cups water and mix well. Pour over chicken, cover and bake for 50 minutes

- Prepare rice mix according to package directions and place on serving plate. Spoon chicken mixture over rice and serve hot. Serves 10 to 12.

# SAVORY CHICKEN FETTUCCINE

*2 pounds boneless, skinless chicken thighs, cubed*
*½ teaspoon garlic powder*
*1 red bell pepper, chopped*
*2 ribs celery, chopped*
*1 (10 ounce) can cream of celery soup*
*1 (10 ounce) can cream of chicken soup*
*1 (8 ounce) package cubed processed cheese*
*1 (4 ounce) jar diced pimentos*
*1 (16 ounce) package spinach fettuccine*

- Place chicken in slow cooker. Sprinkle with garlic powder, ½ teaspoon black pepper, bell pepper and celery. Top with undiluted soups.

- Cover and cook on HIGH for 4 to 6 hours or until chicken juices are clear. Stir in cheese and pimentos. Cover and cook until cheese melts.

- Cook fettuccine according to package directions and drain. Place fettuccine in serving bowl and spoon chicken over fettuccine. Serve hot. Serves 4 to 6.

*An excellent health tip: Smile and Laugh More.*

# BUFFALO WINGS

*This is very similar to the original recipe from the Anchor Bar
in Buffalo, New York where buffalo wings were created.*

4 - 5 pounds chicken wings
4 cups oil
½ cup (1 stick) butter, melted
½ cup Frank's® RedHot® Original Cayenne Pepper Sauce
2 teaspoons wine vinegar

• Season wings with a little salt and freshly ground black pepper. Heat half oil in
  large saucepan. When oil starts to pop and bubble, carefully drop wings into hot oil.
  (No breading.)

• Cook 3 to 5 minutes or until juices run clear. Drain on paper towel and stack on platter.
  Combine butter, hot sauce and vinegar and pour over wings. Serves 8 to 10.

# TANGY CHICKEN

1 (2 pound) broiler-fryer chicken, cut up
3 tablespoons butter
½ cup steak sauce

• Preheat oven to 350°. Brown chicken pieces in skillet with butter and place in
  sprayed shallow pan. Combine sauce and ½ cup water and pour over chicken.

• Cover and bake for 45 minutes. Uncover last 10 minutes of cooking time so chicken
  browns. Serves 4 to 6.

# ROASTED CHICKEN AND VEGETABLES

3 pounds chicken pieces
1 cup lemon pepper marinade, divided
1 (16 ounce) package frozen mixed vegetables, thawed
¼ cup olive oil
1 tablespoon seasoned salt

• Preheat oven to 375°.

• Spray baking pan with non-stick vegetable spray. Arrange chicken skin-side down in
  pan. Pour ⅔ cup marinade over chicken.

• Bake uncovered for 30 minutes. Turn chicken over and baste with remaining
  ⅓ cup marinade.

• Toss vegetables with oil and 1 tablespoon salt. Arrange vegetables around chicken
  and cover with foil. Return pan to oven and bake another 30 minutes. Serves 4 to 6.

# SPICED SPANISH CHICKEN

*2 cups instant rice*
*4 boneless, skinless, cooked chicken breast halves,*
*cut into strips*
*1 (15 ounce) can Mexican stewed tomatoes with liquid*
*1 (8 ounce) can tomato sauce*
*1 (15 ounce) can whole kernel corn, drained*
*1 teaspoon chili powder*
*1 teaspoon ground cumin*

- Preheat oven to 350°.

- Spread rice evenly in sprayed 3-quart baking dish.  Place chicken strips over top of rice.

- Combine stewed tomatoes, tomato sauce, corn, pimentos, chili powder, cumin, ½ teaspoon each of salt and pepper or cayenne pepper in bowl and mix well.

- Slowly and gently pour mixture over chicken and rice.  Cover and bake for 1 hour. Serves 6.

*TIP: The first time you try this with cayenne pepper, you might want to use only*
*¼ teaspoon, unless you know for sure you are prepared for "hot".*

# CREAMY CHICKEN BAKE

*1 (8 ounce) package egg noodles*
*1 (16 ounce) package frozen broccoli florets, thawed*
*¼ cup (½ stick) butter, melted*
*1 (8 ounce) package shredded cheddar cheese*
*1 (10 ounce) can cream of chicken soup*
*1 cup half-and-half cream*
*¼ teaspoon ground mustard*
*3 cups cooked, cubed chicken breasts*
*⅔ cup slivered almonds, toasted*

- Preheat oven to 350°.  Cook noodles according to package directions and drain.  Cut some stems off broccoli and discard.  In large bowl, combine noodles and broccoli.

- Combine butter and cheese in saucepan and stir until cheese melts.  Stir in chicken soup, cream, mustard, chicken and about 1 teaspoon each of salt and pepper. Combine with noodles-broccoli mixture in buttered 2½-quart baking dish.

- Bake covered for about 25 minutes and cook for 15 minutes longer.  Remove from oven, sprinkle with slivered almonds and cool for 15 minutes longer.  Serves 6 to 8.

# CREAMY CHICKEN CASSEROLE

*3 cups cooked, chopped chicken or turkey*
*1 (16 ounce) package frozen broccoli florets, thawed*
*1 (10 ounce) can cream of chicken soup*
*⅔ cup mayonnaise*
*1 cup shredded cheddar cheese*
*1½ cups crushed cheese crackers*

- Preheat oven to 350°. Combine chicken and broccoli in large bowl. Dilute cream of chicken soup with ¼ cup water in saucepan, heat on medium-low and stir to mix well. Pour over chicken and stir well.

- Add mayonnaise and cheese and mix well. Pour into buttered 3-quart baking dish and spread cheese crackers over top. Bake, uncovered, for 40 minutes. Serves 4.

# COMFORT CHICKEN PLUS

*1 (6 ounce) box chicken stuffing mix*
*1 bunch fresh broccoli florets*
*1 cup chopped red bell pepper*
*2 tablespoons butter*
*1 (8 ounce) can whole kernel corn, drained*
*2½ cups finely chopped chicken or left-over turkey*
*1 envelope hollandaise sauce mix*
*1 (2.8 ounce) can french-fried onions*

- Preheat oven to 325°. Prepare chicken stuffing mix according to package directions. Place broccoli, bell pepper, butter and ¼ cup water in microwave-safe bowl. Cover with wax paper and microwave on HIGH for 1½ minutes.

- Add broccoli-celery mixture, corn and chicken to stuffing and mix well. Spoon into sprayed 8 x 12-inch baking dish.

- Prepare hollandaise sauce according to package directions, but use 1¼ cups water instead of 1 cup water stated. Pour hollandaise sauce over casserole and sprinkle top with onions. Bake uncovered for 25 minutes or until juices are clear. Serves 4 to 6.

# CHICKEN MEDLEY

2 (10 ounce) cans cream of chicken soup
⅓ cup (⅔ stick) butter, melted
3 cups cooked, cubed chicken
1 (16 ounce) package frozen broccoli, corn, red peppers)
1 (10 ounce) package frozen green peas
1 (8 ounce) package cornbread stuffing mix

• Spray large slow cooker with vegetable spray. In mixing bowl, combine soup, melted butter and ⅓ cup water and mix well.

• Add chicken, vegetables and stuffing mix and stir well. Spoon mixture into slow cooker. Cover and cook on LOW for 5 to 6 hours or on HIGH for 2½ to 3 hours. Serves 4 to 6.

# CHICKEN-MUSHROOM CASSEROLE

1 (6.9 ounce) box chicken-flavored rice and macaroni
3 cups cooked, chopped chicken or turkey
1 (10 ounce) can cream of mushroom soup
1 (10 ounce) can cream of celery soup
1 (10 ounce) package frozen peas, thawed
1 cup shredded cheddar cheese

• Preheat oven to 350°.

• Cook rice and macaroni according to package directions. Combine chicken, cooked rice and macaroni, soups, peas, cheese and ½ cup water and mix well.

• Pour into buttered 3-quart casserole dish, cover and bake for 40 minutes. Serves 4 to 6.

*When you shop at the grocery store, you are paying the farmer, processor, packager, distributor and the grocer for goods. Locate locally grown produce and visit farmers' markets. Also, check out "pick your own" farms and make an event out of buying food.*

# CHOP SUEY VEGGIES AND CHICKEN

*3 cups cooked, cubed chicken*
*2 (10 ounce) cans cream of chicken soup*
*2 (15 ounce) cans chop suey vegetables, drained*
*1 (8 ounce) can sliced water chestnuts, drained*
*1 (16 ounce) package frozen seasoning blend (onions and bell peppers)*
*½ teaspoon hot sauce*
*½ - 1 teaspoon curry powder*
*2 cups chow mein noodles*

- Preheat oven to 350°. In large bowl, combine chicken, soup, vegetables, water chestnuts, onions and bell peppers, hot sauce, curry powder and a little salt and pepper and mix well.

- Spoon into sprayed 9 x 13-inch baking dish. Sprinkle chow mein noodles over top and bake for 40 minutes. Serves 10 to 12.

# CONFETTI SQUASH AND CHICKEN

*1 pound yellow squash, sliced*
*1 pound zucchini, sliced*
*2 cups cooked, cubed chicken*
*1 (10 ounce) can cream of chicken soup*
*1 (8 ounce) carton sour cream*
*1 (4 ounce) can chopped pimento, drained*
*½ cup (1 stick) butter, melted*
*1 (6 ounce) box herb stuffing mix*

- Preheat oven to 350°. In large saucepan, cook squash and zucchini in salted water about 10 minutes. Drain, stir in chicken, soup, sour cream and pimentos and mix well.

- Combine melted butter and stuffing mix, add to vegetable-chicken mixture and mix well. Spoon into sprayed 9 x 13-inch baking dish. Cover and bake for 35 minutes. Serves 10.

# CHICKEN-GREEN BEAN BAKE

*2 cups instant rice*
*1 (16 ounce) package shredded Velveeta® cheese*
*1 (16 ounce) package frozen cut green beans, thawed*
*3 cups cooked, cubed chicken*
*2 cups coarsely crushed potato chips*

- Preheat oven to 325°.

- Cook rice in large saucepan according to package directions and stir in cheese and extra ¼ cup water. Stir and mix until cheese melts.

- Cook green beans according to package directions and drain. Stir in rice-cheese mixture, add cubed chicken and mix well.

- Spoon into sprayed 9 x 13-inch baking dish. Top with crushed potato chips and bake for 20 minutes or until chips are light brown. Serves 10.

# CHICKEN SQUARES

*2 (12 ounce) cans chicken breast chunks with liquid*
*1 (8 ounce) carton cream cheese, softened*
*¼ cup finely chopped onion*
*2 tablespoons sesame seeds*
*1 (8 count) package refrigerated crescent rolls*

- Preheat oven to 350°.

- Pour chicken with liquid in mixing bowl. Add cream cheese and beat until creamy. Add onion, sesame seeds and a little salt and pepper. Mix well.

- Open package of crescent rolls, but do not divide into triangles. Form 4 squares using 2 triangles for each. Pinch seam in middle of each square together and pat into larger square.

- Spoon about ½ cup chicken mixture into center of each square. Fold corners up into center and lay like flower petals so roll seals. Repeat for all squares.

- Place each roll on sprayed baking sheet and bake about 15 minutes or until golden brown. Serves 4.

# CHICKEN-SPAGHETTI BAKE

*1 (12 ounce) package spaghetti*
*1 (16 ounce) package frozen seasoning blend onion and bell peppers*
*3 ribs celery, sliced*
*1 (15 ounce) can Mexican stewed tomatoes*
*1 (10 ounce) can chicken broth*
*4 cups cooked, cubed chicken*
*1 (12 ounce) package shredded Velveeta® cheese, divided*

- Preheat oven to 350°.

- Cook spaghetti according to package directions and drain.

- In large saucepan with a little oil, saute onion, bell peppers and celery. Add tomatoes, broth, chicken and a little salt and pepper. Stir in half cheese and spoon into sprayed 9 x 13-inch baking dish.

- Cover and bake for 40 minutes. Remove from oven and sprinkle remaining cheese over top of casserole. Return to oven for 5 minutes. Serves 12.

# CHICKEN-BROCCOLI BAKE

*1 (10 ounce) can cream of chicken soup*
*⅔ cup milk*
*2 cups cubed rotisserie chicken*
*1 (16 ounce) package broccoli florets, thawed*
*1 (4 ounce) can chopped pimentos, drained*
*1 (7.7 ounce) pouch cheese-garlic biscuit mix*
*1 teaspoon dried parsley*

- Preheat oven to 400°.

- Combine soup and milk in large bowl and blend well. Stir in chicken, broccoli and pimentos. Spoon into sprayed 3-quart round baking dish and bake for 20 minutes.

- About 5 minutes before removing dish from oven, prepare biscuit mix according to package directions and use ½ cup water and dried parsley.

- Drop 8 large spoonfuls of dough around edges of casserole onto chicken mixture. Continue baking for 15 minutes or until bubbly and biscuits are golden brown. Serves 8.

# CHICKEN-NOODLE DELIGHT

*This recipe is a hearty main dish and the bell peppers
make it colorful as well. It's a great family supper.*

*2 ribs celery, chopped*
*½ onion, chopped*
*½ green bell pepper, seeded, chopped*
*½ red bell pepper, seeded, chopped*
*¼ cup (½ stick) butter*
*3 cups cooked, cubed chicken breasts*
*1 (4 ounce) can sliced mushrooms, drained*
*1 (16 ounce) jar sun-dried tomato-alfredo sauce*
*½ cup half-and-half cream*
*1½ teaspoons chicken bouillon granules*
*1 (8 ounce) package medium egg noodles, cooked, drained*

- Preheat oven to 325°.

- Combine celery, onion, bell peppers and butter in skillet or large saucepan and saute
  for about 5 minutes.

- Remove from heat and add chicken, mushrooms, alfredo sauce, half-and-half cream,
  bouillon granules and noodles and mix well.  Pour into sprayed 3-quart baking dish.

## TOPPING:

*1 cup corn flake crumbs*
*½ cup shredded cheddar cheese*
*2 tablespoons butter, melted*

- Combine topping ingredients in bowl and sprinkle over casserole.  Bake for
  20 minutes or until casserole bubbles around edges.  Serves 6.

# CHICKEN COUSCOUS

*1 (5.6 ounce) package toasted pine nut couscous, cooked*
*1 rotisserie chicken, boned, cubed*
*1 (15 ounce) can baby green peas, drained*
*⅓ cup golden raisins*

- Combine couscous, chicken, peas and raisins in microwave-safe dish.  Heat on
  medium about 2 minutes or until mixture is warm and stir once.  Serves 4 to 6.

# CHICKEN SUPREME

*It is really delicious and "so-o-o-o" easy.  It is a "meal in itself"!*

1 onion, chopped
3 tablespoons butter
4 cups diced, cooked chicken breasts
1 (6 ounce) package long grain, wild rice with seasoning packet, cooked
1 (10 ounce) can cream of celery soup
1 (10 ounce) can cream of chicken soup
2 (15 ounce) cans French-style green beans, drained
1 cup slivered almonds
1 cup mayonnaise
2½ cups crushed potato chips

• Preheat oven to 350°.  Saute onion in butter.  In very large saucepan, combine onion-celery mixture, diced chicken, cooked rice, both soups, green beans, almonds, mayonnaise, ½ teaspoon salt and pepper and mix well.

• Spoon into sprayed 10 x 14-inch deep baking dish.  Sprinkle crushed potato chips over top of casserole.  Bake uncovered for 40 minutes or until potato chips are light brown.  Serves 8 to 10.

TIP:  *This recipe is a great way to serve a lot of people.  It may also be made with green peas instead of green beans.  If you want to make it in advance and freeze or just refrigerate for the next day, just wait until you are ready to cook casserole before adding potato chips.*

# EASY CHICKEN AND DUMPLINGS

3 teaspoons chicken bouillon granules
3 cups cooked, chopped chicken
2 (10 ounce) cans cream of chicken soup
1 (8 ounce) can refrigerated buttermilk biscuits

• Combine chicken bouillon granules and 4½ cups water in large pot and bring to a boil; stir to dissolve granules.  Add chopped chicken and both cans of soup and stir well.

• Separate biscuits and cut in half, cut again making 4 pieces out of each biscuit.  Drop biscuit pieces, 1 at a time, into boiling chicken  mixture and stir gently.

• When biscuits drop, reduce heat to low and simmer, stirring occasionally, for about 15 minutes.  Serves 4.

TIP:  *Deli turkey will work just fine in this recipe.  It's a great time-saver!*

# CHICKEN WOW!

1 (10 ounce) can cream of chicken soup
1 (10 ounce) can fiesta nacho cheese soup
1 (5 ounce) can evaporated milk
2 (15 ounce) cans French-style green beans, drained
1 teaspoon chicken bouillon granules
4 cups cooked, cubed chicken breasts
1 red bell pepper, seeded, chopped
2 ribs celery, sliced
¼ cup chopped onion
1 cup chow mein noodles
½ cup slivered almonds
1 (3 ounce) can french-fried onions

- Preheat oven to 350°. Combine soups and evaporated milk in large bowl and mix well.

- Fold in green beans, chicken bouillon granules, chicken, bell pepper, celery, onion, noodles, almonds, and ½ teaspoon each of salt and pepper.

- Spoon into sprayed 9 x 13-inch baking dish. Cover and bake for 35 minutes. Sprinkle fried onions over casserole. Bake uncovered for additional 10 minutes. Serves 6 to 8.

*TIP: This casserole may easily be made ahead of time and baked the next day. Just wait until you are ready to put it in the oven to add the fried onions.*

# CHICKEN-BROCCOLI SKILLET

3 cups cubed, cooked chicken
1 (16 ounce) package frozen broccoli florets
1 (8 ounce) package cubed processed cheese
⅔ cup mayonnaise

- Combine chicken, broccoli, cheese and ¼ cup water in skillet. Cover and cook over medium heat until broccoli is crisp-tender and cheese melts. Stir in mayonnaise and heat through, but do not boil. Serves 4.

*TIP: This is great served over hot cooked rice.*

# CHICKEN QUESADILLAS

*2 cups cooked, shredded chicken*
*¾ cup salsa*
*3 green onions, chopped*
*½ teaspoon ground cumin*
*4 (8 inch) flour tortillas*
*Butter, softened*
*1 cup shredded Mexican 4-cheese blend*

- Preheat oven to 400°.

- Combine and cook chicken, salsa, onions, cumin and a little salt in skillet over medium-high heat for about 5 minutes or just until it is hot.

- Brush 1 side of each tortilla with butter. Place half of chicken mixture on 1 tortilla, other half on second tortilla.

- Sprinkle cheese equally over 2 tortillas and place other 2 tortillas, buttered-side down, over cheese.

- Place on sprayed baking sheet and bake for about 10 minutes or until crisp. To serve cut into wedges. Serve with guacamole. Serves 2.

# CHICKEN POT PIE

*1 (15 ounce) package refrigerated piecrust*
*1 (10 ounce) can cream of chicken soup*
*2 cups cooked, diced chicken breast*
*1 (10 ounce) package frozen mixed vegetables, thawed*

- Preheat oven to 325°. Line 1 layer piecrust in 9-inch pie pan. Fill with chicken soup, chicken and mixed vegetables.

- Cover with second layer of piecrust; fold edges under and crimp. With knife, cut 4 slits in center of piecrust. Bake uncovered for 1 hour 15 minutes or until crust is golden. Serves 4.

*TIP: When you're too busy to cook a chicken, get the rotisserie chickens from the grocery store. They are great.*

# Spicy Chicken and Rice

3 cups cooked, sliced chicken
2 cups cooked brown rice
1 (10 ounce) can fiesta nacho cheese soup
1 (10 ounce) can diced tomatoes and green chilies

- Preheat oven to 375°. Combine chicken, rice, cheese soup, tomatoes and green chilies and mix well. Spoon mixture into buttered 3-quart baking dish. Bake covered for 45 minutes. Serves 4.

# Speedy Chicken Pie

1 (12 ounce) package shredded cheddar cheese, divided
1 (10 ounce) package frozen chopped broccoli, thawed, drained
2 cups cooked, finely diced chicken breasts
½ cup finely chopped onion
½ cup finely chopped red bell pepper
1⅓ cups half-and-half cream
3 eggs
¾ cup biscuit mix

- Preheat oven to 375°. Combine 2 cups cheddar cheese, broccoli, chicken, onion and bell pepper in bowl. Spread into sprayed 10-inch deep-dish pie pan.

- Beat half-and-half cream, eggs, biscuit mix, 1 teaspoon salt and ½ teaspoon pepper in bowl and mix well. Slowly pour cream-egg mixture over broccoli-chicken mixture, but do not stir.

- Cover and bake for 35 minutes or until center of pie is firm. Sprinkle remaining cheese over top. Bake uncovered for about 5 minutes or just until cheese melts. Serves 4 to 6.

# Mac Cheese and Chicken

1½ cups small elbow macaroni
1 (12 ounce) can evaporated milk
½ - ⅔ cup hot chipotle salsa
2 cups skinned, cut-up rotisserie chicken
1 (8 ounce) package cubed Velveeta® cheese

- Cook macaroni in 2 cups water according to package directions and drain well. Add evaporated milk and chipotle salsa, cook over medium heat about 10 minutes and stir frequently. (There will still be liquid in mixture.)

- Stir in rotisserie chicken and heat until chicken heats thoroughly. Fold in cheddar cheese, stir constantly and cook 1 minute. Serve immediately. Serves 4 to 6.

# NOT JUST CHICKEN

*This is a great recipe for leftover ham, chicken or turkey.*

3 cups cooked, cubed chicken
3 cups cooked, cubed ham
1 (8 ounce) package shredded cheddar cheese
1 (15 ounce) can English peas, drained
1 onion, chopped
3 ribs celery, chopped
¼ cup (½ stick) butter
⅓ cup plus 1 tablespoon flour
1 (1 pint) carton half-and-half cream
½ cup milk
1 teaspoon dill weed
Instant brown rice, cooked

- Preheat oven to 350°. Combine chicken, ham, cheese and English peas in large bowl. Saute onion and celery in butter in large saucepan until tender. Add flour and stir to make a paste.

- Gradually add half-and-half cream, milk, dill weed and 1 teaspoon salt. Heat, stirring constantly, until mixture thickens.

- Add thickened cream mixture to chicken-ham mixture and mix well. Spoon into sprayed 2½-quart baking dish. Cover and bake for 20 minutes. Spoon casserole over brown rice. Serves 6 to 8.

# HURRY-UP CHICKEN ENCHILADAS

2½ - 3 cups cooked, cubed chicken breasts
1 (10 ounce) can cream of chicken soup
1½ cups chunky salsa, divided
8 (6 inch) flour tortillas
1 (10 ounce) can fiesta nacho cheese soup

- Combine chicken, soup and ½ cup salsa in saucepan and heat. Spoon about ⅓ cup chicken mixture down center of each tortilla and roll up tortilla. Place seam-side down in sprayed 9 x 13-inch baking dish.

- Mix nacho cheese, soup, remaining salsa and ¼ cup water in bowl and pour over enchiladas.

- Cover with wax paper and microwave on HIGH, turning several times, for 5 minutes or until bubbly. Serves 6 to 8.

# TACO CASSEROLE

2 (10 ounce) cans fiesta nacho cheese soup
½ cup milk
1 (15 ounce) can whole kernel corn, drained
1 (1 ounce) packet taco seasoning
1 red bell pepper, seeded, chopped
1 onion, chopped
1 teaspoon ground cumin
1 (13 ounce) package corn Tostitos®, slightly crushed
3 - 4 cups cooked, diced chicken breasts or turkey
1 (12 ounce) package shredded cheddar-Jack cheese
1 (4 ounce) can sliced black olives, drained

- Preheat oven to 325°.

- Combine soup, milk, corn, taco seasoning, bell pepper, onion, cumin and ½ teaspoon salt in large bowl and mix well.

- Place layer of half crushed Tostitos®, half chicken, half soup mixture and half cheese in sprayed 9 x 13-inch baking dish. Repeat layers ending with cheese on top.

- Cover and bake for 40 minutes or until casserole bubbles around edges. When ready to serve, sprinkle black olives over top. Serves 6 to 8.

# TORTELLINI SUPPER

1 (9 ounce) package refrigerated cheese tortellini
1 (10 ounce) package frozen green peas, thawed
1 (8 ounce) carton cream cheese with chives and onion
½ cup sour cream
1 (9 ounce) package frozen cooked chicken breasts

- Cook cheese tortellini in saucepan according to package directions. Place peas in colander and pour hot pasta water over green peas. Return tortellini and peas to saucepan.

- Combine cream cheese and sour cream in smaller saucepan and heat on low, stirring well, until cheese melts. Spoon mixture over tortellini and peas and toss with heat on low.

- Heat cooked chicken in microwave according to package directions. Spoon tortellini and peas in serving bowl and place chicken on top. Serves 4.

# CHICKEN AND ORZO SUPPER

*1 (5 ounce) box chicken-flavored orzo*
*1 (7 ounce) package prepared cooked chicken strips*
*1 (10 ounce) frozen corn*
*1 (10 ounce) can cut green beans, drained*
*¼ cup extra-virgin olive oil*
*1 teaspoon minced garlic*

- Cook orzo according to package directions. Add chicken strips, corn, green beans, olive oil, garlic, ¼ cup water and a little salt and pepper and mix well.

- Cook on low heat, stirring several times, until mixture is hot, about 10 to 15 minutes. Serves 4.

# SPAGHETTI TOSS

*1 (10 ounce) package thin spaghetti*
*1 (10 ounce) package frozen sugar snap peas*
*2 tablespoons butter*
*3 cups rotisserie cooked chicken strips*
*1 (11 ounce) can mandarin oranges, drained*
*⅔ cup stir-fry sauce*

- Cook spaghetti according to package directions; stir in sugar snap peas and cook 1 additional minute. Drain and stir in butter. Spoon into serving bowl.

- Add chicken strips, oranges and stir-fry sauce and toss to coat. Serves 10.

# CHICKEN-PARMESAN SPAGHETTI

*1 (14 ounce) package frozen, cooked, breaded chicken cutlets, thawed*
*1 (28 ounce) jar spaghetti sauce*
*2 (5 ounce) packages grated parmesan cheese, divided*
*1 (8 ounce) package thin spaghetti, cooked*

- Preheat oven to 400°. Place cutlets in buttered 9 x 13-inch baking dish and top each with about ¼ cup spaghetti sauce and 1 heaping tablespoon parmesan. Bake for 15 minutes.

- Place cooked spaghetti on serving platter and top with cutlets. Sprinkle remaining cheese over cutlets. Heat remaining spaghetti sauce and serve with chicken and spaghetti. Serves 4.

# ITALIAN CHICKEN OVER POLENTA

1 pound frozen chicken tenders, each cut in half
1 onion, chopped
1 (15 ounce) can Italian stewed tomatoes
⅔ cup pitted kalamata olives

## POLENTA:

¾ cup cornmeal
⅔ cup grated parmesan cheese

- Season chicken with a little salt and pepper. Place in large skillet with a little oil over medium to high heat.

- Add onion chicken, cook about 8 minutes, covered, and turn once. Add tomatoes and olives, cover and cook another 8 minutes or until chicken is done.

- For polenta, place 2½ cups water in saucepan and bring to boiling. Stir in cornmeal and ½ teaspoon salt and cook, stirring occasionally, until mixture starts to thicken.

- Stir in cheese. Spoon polenta onto serving plates and top with chicken and sauce. Serves 4.

# STIR-FRY CASHEW CHICKEN

1 pound chicken tenders, cut into strips
1 (16 ounce) package frozen broccoli, cauliflower and carrots
1 (8 ounce) jar stir-fry sauce
⅓ cup cashew halves
1 (12 ounce) package chow mein noodles

- Place a little oil and stir-fry chicken strips in 12-inch wok or skillet over high heat for about 4 minutes.

- Add vegetables and stir-fry another 4 minutes or until vegetables are tender. Stir in stir-fry sauce and cashews; cook just until mixture is hot. Serve over chow mein noodles. Serves 4.

*Making sandwich spreads from leftover meats is far cheaper than buying these at the grocery store. Use a food processor, blender or food chopper to chop meats into small bits and add mayonnaise, sweet relish or chopped pickles, celery, onion or cheese, and a little salt and pepper. You'll be surprised how good it is and no one thinks of it as a "leftover".*

# TASTY CHICKEN AND VEGGIES

*1 (2½-3 pound) whole chicken, quartered*
*1 (16 ounce) package baby carrots*
*4 potatoes, peeled, sliced*
*3 ribs celery, sliced*
*1 onion, peeled, sliced*
*1 cup Italian salad dressing*
*⅔ cup chicken broth*

- Rinse, dry and place chicken quarters in sprayed 6-quart slow cooker with carrots, potatoes, celery and onion.

- Pour salad dressing and chicken broth over chicken and vegetables. Cover and cook on LOW for 6 to 8 hours. Serves 4.

# CHICKEN CACCIATORE

*1 (2½ pound) whole chicken*
*2 onions, sliced*

- Quarter chicken and sprinkle with plenty of salt and black pepper. Place in large skillet on medium to high heat with a little oil. Add sliced onions and cook until chicken is tender and juices are no longer pink, about 15 minutes.

## SAUCE:

*1 (15 ounce) can stewed tomatoes*
*1 (8 ounce) can tomato sauce*
*1 teaspoon dried oregano*
*1 teaspoon celery seed*

- Combine stewed tomatoes, tomato sauce, oregano and celery seed and add to chicken. Bring mixture to boil, reduce heat and simmer uncovered for about 20 minutes. Serves 4 to 6.

*TIP: This is great over hot cooked noodles or spaghetti.*

Q: Why did the chicken cross the basketball court?

A: He heard the referee calling fowls.

# ✝HAWAIIAN CHICKEN

*2 small whole chickens, quartered*
*Flour*
*Oil*
*1 (20 ounce) can sliced pineapple with juice*
*2 bell peppers, seeded, julienned*

- Pat chicken dry with paper towels. Shake a little salt, pepper and flour on chicken. Brown chicken in oil and place in shallow pan.

- Drain pineapple juice into 2-cup measure. Add water (or orange juice if you have it) to make 1½ cups liquid for sauce.

## SAUCE FOR ✝HAWAIIAN CHICKEN:

*1 cup sugar*
*3 tablespoons corn starch*
*¾ cup vinegar*
*1 tablespoon lemon juice*
*1 tablespoon soy sauce*
*2 teaspoons chicken bouillon*

- Preheat oven to 350°. Combine the 1½ cups pineapple juice mixture, sugar, cornstarch, vinegar, lemon juice, soy sauce and chicken bouillon in medium saucepan,.

- Bring to boil, stir constantly until thick and clear and pour over chicken. Bake covered for 40 minutes.

- Place pineapple slices and bell pepper on top of chicken and bake another 10 minutes. Serve on fluffy white rice. Serves 6 to 8.

# ✝HONEY-BAKED CHICKEN

*2 whole chickens, quartered*
*½ cup (1 stick) butter, melted*
*⅔ cup honey*
*¼ cup dijon-style mustard*
*1 teaspoon curry powder*

- Preheat oven to 350°. Place chicken pieces skin-side up in sprayed 10 x 15-inch baking dish and sprinkle with a little salt.

- Combine butter, honey, mustard and curry powder in bowl and pour over chicken. Bake for 1 hour 5 minutes; baste every 20 minutes. Serves 8.

# TURKEY TENDERLOIN DINNER

*1 (2 pound) lemon-garlic seasoned, turkey tenderloin*
*Seasoned black pepper*

## VEGETABLES AND GRAVY:

*12 - 14 medium new potatoes, halved*
*2 (14 ounce) cans chicken broth, divided*
*½ cup (1 stick butter), divided*
*5 - 6 medium yellow squash, sliced*
*¼ cup cornstarch*

- Preheat oven to 325°. Place turkey tenderloin in 9 x 13-inch baking dish lined with foil. Sprinkle lots of seasoned black pepper over turkey and bake uncovered for 1 hour 30 minutes.

- After tenderloin cooks 1 hour 10 minutes, place new potatoes in large saucepan and add 1 can chicken broth and ¼ cup butter. Cook 15 to 20 minutes or until tender.

- While potatoes cook, place squash in second saucepan and add remaining can broth and remaining ¼ cup butter. Cook about 10 minutes or until squash is just barely tender. Place tenderloin on large platter and use slotted spoon to place potatoes and squash around sliced tenderloin.

- Combine cornstarch and about ½ cup cooking broth and mix well. Combine broth into 1 saucepan, bring to boil and stir in cornstarch mixture.

- Add about 1 teaspoon pepper (and salt if you like) and cook, stirring constantly, until liquid thickens. Serve in gravy boat with tenderloin and vegetables. Serves 6 to 8.

# TURKEY AND RICE OLÉ

*1 pound ground turkey*
*1 (5.5 ounce) package Mexican rice mix*
*1 (15 ounce) can black beans, rinsed, drained*
*1 cup thick and chunky salsa*

- Brown turkey in large skillet and break up large pieces with fork. Add rice mix and 2 cups water, bring to boil, reduce heat and simmer about 8 minutes or until rice is tender.

- Stir in beans and salsa and cook just until mixture heats thoroughly. Serves 4 to 6.

*TIP: This can be served as a main course or as a sandwich wrap in flour tortillas.*

# HERB-ROASTED TURKEY

## RUB:

2 tablespoons poultry seasoning
2 tablespoons seasoned salt
2 teaspoons paprika
2 teaspoons garlic powder
½ teaspoon ground nutmeg

## TURKEY:

1 (12 pound) turkey, if frozen, thawed
1 large onion, cut into wedges
2 tablespoons oil

- Preheat oven to 325°. Combine poultry seasoning, seasoned salt, paprika, garlic powder, nutmeg and 1 teaspoon pepper in small bowl.

- Rinse turkey under cold water and pat dry. Place onion wedges in turkey cavity and rub about half of rub ingredients inside.

- Place turkey, breast side up on shallow roasting pan lined with heavy foil and spread oil over outside of turkey. Sprinkle remaining rub mixture over outside and add ½ cup water to roaster.

- Cover loosely with heavy foil and bake about 3½ hours or until meat thermometer inserted in breast reaches 175°. Let stand about 15 minutes before carving. Save pan juices for gravy.

## TURKEY GRAVY:

1 package dry turkey gravy mix
3 tablespoons flour
1 cup pan drippings or canned turkey broth
½ cup cooked chopped turkey giblets, optional

- Combine dry gravy mix and flour in saucepan. Stir constantly and gradually stir in pan drippings and 1 cup water.

- Bring to boil, reduce heat and stir constantly until mixture thickens. Add turkey giblets if desired. Serves 8 to 10.

*Family meals teach basic manners and social skills that children must learn to be successful in life. What they learn will help them in new situations and give them more confidence because they will know how to act and what to say and do.*

# TURKEY CASSEROLE

1 (6 ounce) package herb-seasoned stuffing mix
1 cup canned whole cranberry sauce
6 (¼-inch thick) slices deli turkey
1 (15 ounce) jar turkey gravy

- Preheat oven to 375°. Prepare stuffing according to package directions. In medium bowl, combine prepared stuffing and cranberry sauce and set aside.

- In buttered 9 x 13-inch baking dish, place slices of turkey and pour gravy over turkey. Spoon stuffing mixture over casserole. Bake about 15 minutes or until hot and bubbly. Serves 4.

# CREAMY TURKEY ENCHILADAS

*Forget about calories with this recipe. You'll get rave reviews.*

2 tablespoons butter
1 onion, finely chopped
3 green onions with tops, finely chopped
½ teaspoon garlic powder
1 (7 ounce) can diced green chilies
2 (8 ounce) packages cream cheese, softened
3 cups cooked, diced turkey
8 (8 inch) flour tortillas
2 (8 ounce) cartons whipping cream
1 (16 ounce) package shredded Mexican 4-cheese blend

- Preheat oven to 350°. Melt butter in skillet and saute onion and green onions. Add garlic powder, green chilies, and ½ teaspoon each of salt and pepper. Stir in cream cheese. Heat and stir just until cream cheese melts. Add turkey.

- Spread out 8 tortillas and spoon about 3 heaping tablespoons turkey-cream cheese mixture on each tortilla. Use all turkey mixture.

- Roll tortillas and place seam-side down in sprayed 10 x 15-inch baking dish. Pour whipping cream over enchiladas and sprinkle with cheese.

- Bake for 30 minutes or just until cream and cheese bubble but do not brown. Serves 6 to 8.

*TIP: Use a long, wide spatula to serve these enchiladas. (If you happen to have a couple enchiladas left over, heat them in the microwave and pour hot salsa over them. You'll love these leftovers.)*

# TURKEY-BROCCOLI BAKE

*1 (16 ounce) package frozen broccoli spears, thawed*
*2 cups cooked, diced (left-over) turkey*

- Preheat oven to 350°. Arrange broccoli spears in greased 9 x 13-inch baking dish and sprinkle with diced turkey.

## CREAM SAUCE:

*1 (10 ounce) can cream of chicken soup*
*½ cup mayonnaise*
*2 tablespoons lemon juice*
*⅓ cup grated parmesan cheese*

- Combine chicken soup, mayonnaise, lemon juice, cheese and ¼ cup water in saucepan. Heat just enough to mix well.

- Spoon over broccoli and turkey. Cover and bake for 20 minutes, uncover and continue baking for another 15 minutes. Serves 4.

# TURKEY-STUFFING CASSEROLE

*3 - 4 cups cooked, chopped turkey*
*1 (16 ounce) package frozen broccoli florets, thawed*
*1 (10 ounce) can cream of chicken soup*
*⅔ cup sour cream*
*1 (8 ounce) package shredded Swiss cheese*
*1 (6 ounce) package turkey stuffing mix*
*½ cup chopped walnuts*

- Preheat oven to 325°.

- Spread chopped turkey in 9 x 13-inch baking dish and top with broccoli florets.

- Combine soup, sour cream and cheese in bowl and spread over broccoli. In separate bowl, combine stuffing mix, walnuts and ¾ cup water and spread evenly over broccoli. Bake for 40 minutes or until hot and bubbly. Serves 12.

# Turkey and Noodles Plus

1 (12 ounce) package medium egg noodles
3 cups cooked, diced turkey
1 (16 ounce) package frozen peas and carrots, thawed
2 (12 ounce) jars turkey gravy
2 cups slightly crushed potato chips

- Preheat oven to 350°.

- Cook noodles according to package directions and drain. Arrange alternate layers of noodles, turkey, peas, carrots and gravy in sprayed 9 x 13-inch baking dish. Cover and bake for 20 minutes.

- Remove from oven, sprinkle potato chips over casserole and return to oven for 15 minutes or until chips are light brown. Serves 12.

# Ginger-Orange Glazed Cornish Hens

1 cup fresh orange juice
2 tablespoons peeled, minced fresh ginger
1 tablespoon soy sauce
3 tablespoons honey
2 (1½ pounds) Cornish hens, halved
½ teaspoon ground ginger

- Preheat oven to 450°. Combine orange juice, minced ginger, soy sauce and honey in saucepan and cook on high heat, stirring constantly, for 3 minutes or until thick and glossy.

- Place hens in greased baking pan and sprinkle ground ginger and ½ teaspoon each of salt and pepper over birds. Spoon glaze mixture over hens and bake 25 minutes. Brush glaze over hens several times during cooking. Serves 2 to 4.

*Family meals teach basic manners and social skills that children must learn to be successful in life. What they learn will help them in new situations and give them more confidence because they will know how to act and what to say and do.*

# PORK MAIN DISHES

## SAUCY HAM LOAF

*1 pound ham, ground*
*½ pound ground beef*
*½ pound ground pork*
*2 eggs*
*1 cup bread or cracker crumbs*
*2 teaspoons Worcestershire sauce*
*1 (5 ounce) can evaporated milk*
*3 tablespoons chili sauce*

- Preheat oven to 350°.
- Combine all ingredients plus 1 teaspoon each salt and pepper. Form into loaf in 9 x 13-inch baking pan and bake 1 hour.

### SWEET-AND-HOT MUSTARD:

*4 ounces dry mustard*
*1 cup vinegar*
*3 eggs, beaten*
*1 cup sugar*

- Combine mustard and vinegar in bowl until smooth and set aside overnight. Add eggs and sugar and cook in double boiler. Stir for 8 to 10 minutes or until mixture coats spoon. Cool and store in covered jars in refrigerator. Serve with ham loaf. Serves 6 to 8.

*TIP: The hot mustard recipe also goes well on sandwiches.*

*Children who eat at home almost every night during the week are more likely to make better grades and perform better in school than those who do not. In 1994 in a* Reader's Digest *national poll of high school seniors, Lou Harris reported higher school scores among seniors who ate with their families. He also found that high school seniors were happier with themselves and prospects for the future than seniors who did not eat at home regularly.*

# OLD-FASHIONED HAM LOAF WITH SASSY HORSERADISH SAUCE

*3 eggs*
*3 pounds lean ground ham*
*3 cups fresh fine breadcrumbs*
*2 teaspoons brown sugar*
*3 teaspoons horseradish, divided*
*½ pint whipping cream*

- Preheat oven to 350°.

- Slightly beat eggs in large bowl. Stir in ground ham and mix thoroughly. Add breadcrumbs, brown sugar and 2 teaspoons horseradish and stir to mix well. Shape into loaf and put in sprayed baking dish. Bake for 1 hour 30 minutes.

- Mix 1 teaspoon horseradish, whipping cream and a dash of salt in bowl and refrigerate. Allow sauce to reach room temperature before serving (about 20 minutes).

- Remove loaf from oven, let stand for about 5 minutes before slicing. Serve with sauce. Serves 6 to 8.

# HAM QUESADILLAS

*2 cups shredded ham*
*½ cup chunky salsa*
*2 teaspoons chili powder*
*¾ cup whole kernel corn*
*8 large whole-wheat tortillas*
*1 (8 ounce) package shredded Mexican 4-cheese blend*

- In large bowl, combine shredded ham, salsa, chili powder and corn. Spread mixture over 4 tortillas to within ½-inch of edge. Then sprinkle cheese on top.

- Top with remaining tortillas and cook (1 quesadilla at a time) on medium-high heat, in large non-stick skillet about 5 minutes. Turn after 2 minutes or until light golden brown. Cut in wedges to serve and serve with pinto beans and guacamole. Serves 4 to 6.

# HAM AND SWEET POTATOES

*3 tablespoons dijon-style mustard, divided*
*1 (3 - 4 pound) boneless smoked ham*
*½ cup honey or packed brown sugar*
*1 (29 ounce) can sweet potatoes, drained*

- Preheat oven to 325°. Spread mustard on ham. Place ham in sprayed, shallow baking pan and bake for 20 minutes per pound.

- Combine remaining mustard with brown sugar or honey and spread over ham. Add sweet potatoes, baste with sauce and bake for 20 minutes per pound. Serves 6 to 8.

# PEACH-PINEAPPLE BAKED HAM

*1 (3 - 4) pound boneless smoked ham*
*4 tablespoons dijon-style mustard, divided*
*1 cup peach preserves*
*1 cup pineapple preserves*

- Preheat oven to 325°. Spread 2 tablespoons mustard on ham. Place ham in sprayed, shallow baking pan and bake for 20 minutes.

- Combine remaining 2 tablespoons mustard and both preserves and heat in microwave oven for 20 seconds (or in small saucepan at low heat for 2 to 3 minutes). Pour over ham and bake for about 15 minutes. Serves 8 to 10.

# PEACHY GLAZED HAM

*1 (15 ounce) can sliced peaches in light syrup with juice*
*2 tablespoons dark brown sugar*
*2 teaspoons dijon-style mustard*
*1 (1 pound) center-cut ham slice*
*⅓ cup sliced green onions*

- Drain peaches and set aside ½ cup syrup in large skillet. Set peaches aside. Add brown sugar and mustard to skillet and bring to a boil over medium-high heat. Cook for 2 minutes or until it reduces slightly.

- Add ham and cook for 2 minutes on each side. Add peaches and green onions, cover and cook over low heat for 3 minutes or until peaches are thoroughly hot. Serves 4.

# SWEET POTATO HAM

*1 (16 ounce/½-inch thick) fully cooked ham slice*
*1 (18 ounce) can sweet potatoes, drained*
*½ cup packed brown sugar*
*⅓ cup chopped pecans*

- Cut outer edge of ham fat at 1-inch intervals to prevent curling, but do not cut into ham. Place on ovenproof plate or baking dish and broil with top 5 inches from heat for 5 minutes.

- Mash each piece of sweet potatoes in bowl with fork just once (not totally mashed) and add brown sugar, a little salt and chopped pecans and mix well.

- Spoon mixture over ham slice and cook at 350° for about 15 minutes. Serve right from ovenproof plate. Serves 4.

# PRALINE HAM

*2 (½ inch) thick ham slices, cooked*
*½ cup maple syrup*
*3 tablespoons brown sugar*
*1 tablespoon butter*
*⅓ cup chopped pecans*

- Preheat oven to 325°.

- Bake ham slices in shallow pan for 10 minutes. Bring syrup, brown sugar and butter in small saucepan to a boil and stir often. Stir in pecans and spoon over ham. Bake for additional 20 minutes. Serves 8.

# SANDWICH SOUFFLE

*A fun lunch!*

*Butter, softened*
*8 slices white bread, crusts removed*
*4 slices ham*
*4 slices American cheese*
*2 cups milk*
*2 eggs, beaten*

- Butter bread on both sides, make 4 sandwiches with ham and cheese. Place sandwiches in sprayed 8-inch square baking pan.

- Beat milk, eggs and a little salt and pepper in bowl. Pour over sandwiches and soak for 1 to 2 hours. When ready to bake, preheat oven to 375°. Bake for 45 to 50 minutes. Serves 4.

# HAM WITH ORANGE SAUCE

*1 (½ inch) thick slice fully cooked ham*
*1 cup orange juice*
*2 tablespoons brown sugar*
*1½ tablespoons cornstarch*
*⅓ cup white raisins*

- Preheat oven to 350°.

- Place ham slice in shallow baking dish. Combine orange juice, brown sugar, cornstarch and raisins in saucepan.

- Bring to a boil, stirring constantly, until mixture thickens and pour over ham slice. Warm in oven for about 20 minutes. Serves 4.

# HAM WITH PINEAPPLE SAUCE

*2 cooked honey-baked ham slices*
*1 (15 ounce) can pineapple chunks with juice*
*1 cup apricot preserves*
*1¼ cups packed brown sugar*
*¼ teaspoon ground cinnamon*

- Preheat oven to 325°.

- Place ham slices in shallow baking pan and heat for 10 minutes. Combine pineapple, preserves, brown sugar and cinnamon in saucepan and heat.

- Pour sauce over ham slices and bake for 15 to 20 minutes. Serves 4 to 6.

# HAM AND PASTA BAKE

*1 (10 ounce) can broccoli-cheese soup*
*½ cup grated parmesan cheese*
*1 cup milk*
*1 tablespoon spicy brown mustard*
*1 (16 ounce) package frozen broccoli florets, thawed*
*2 cups shell macaroni, cooked*
*8 ounces (deli) cooked ham, cut in bite-size chunks*

- In large skillet, combine soup, parmesan cheese, milk and mustard and mix well. Add broccoli and stir over medium heat. Reduce heat to low, cover and cook 5 minutes or until broccoli is tender-crisp.

- Stir in macaroni and ham and heat thoroughly. Transfer to sprayed 2-quart microwave dish, so it can be reheated, if needed. Serves 8 to 10.

# TORTELLINI-HAM SUPPER

*This is another great recipe for leftover ham.*

2 (9 ounce) packages fresh tortellini
1 (10 ounce) package frozen green peas, thawed
1 (16 ounce) jar alfredo sauce
2 - 3 cups cubed ham

- Cook tortellini according to package directions. Add green peas about 5 minutes before tortellini is done and drain.

- In saucepan, combine alfredo sauce and ham and heat until thoroughly hot. Toss with tortellini and peas. Serve immediately. Serves 6 to 8.

# STOVETOP HAM SUPPER

1 (12 ounce) package spiral pasta
3 tablespoons butter, sliced
2 - 3 cups cooked, cubed ham
1 teaspoon minced garlic
1 (16 ounce) package frozen broccoli, cauliflower and carrots
½ cup sour cream
1 (8 ounce) package shredded cheddar cheese, divided

- Preheat oven to 375°.

- Cook pasta in large saucepan, according to package directions; drain. While still hot, stir in butter. Add ham, garlic and 1 teaspoon salt.

- Cook vegetables in microwave according to package directions and stir, undrained, into pasta-ham mixture. Stir in sour cream and half cheese and mix until they blend well.

- Spoon into sprayed 3-quart baking dish. Bake 15 minutes or just until bubbly around edges. Sprinkle remaining cheese on top and let stand just until cheese melts. Serves 4 to 6.

*When selecting pork, look for meat that is pale pink with a small amount of marbling and white fat (not yellow). The darker pink the flesh appears, the older the animal.*

# Bow-Tie Pasta with Ham and Veggies

*This is great for leftover ham.*

1 (8 ounce) package (bow-tie) farfalle pasta
1 (10 ounce) package frozen broccoli florets, thawed
1 (10 ounce) package frozen green peas, thawed
1 (16 ounce) jar alfredo sauce
1 pound cubed, cooked ham or deli ham

- In large saucepan, cook pasta according to package directions. Add broccoli and peas during last 3 minutes of cooking time. Drain well.

- Add alfredo sauce and ham. Cook and stir gently over very low heat to keep ingredients from sticking to pan. Pour into serving bowl. Serves 4.

# Fettuccine Supreme

1 (8 ounce) package fettuccine
½ cup whipping cream
½ cup (1 stick) butter, sliced
½ teaspoon dried basil
1 cup diced ham
1 tablespoon dried parsley
1 cup grated parmesan cheese

- Cook fettuccine according to package directions and drain. Immediately place fettuccine back into saucepan.

- Add whipping cream, butter, basil, diced ham, parsley and ¼ teaspoon salt and toss until butter melts. Fold in parmesan cheese, pour into serving bowl and serve hot. Serves 8.

*Two ounces dry pasta will make about 1 cup cooked pasta. Spaghetti and macaroni products usually double in volume when cooked. Egg noodles don't expand quite as much.*

# HAM, NOODLES AND THE WORKS

1 (8 ounce) package small egg noodles
2 (10 ounce) cans cream of broccoli soup
1 (8 ounce) carton whipping cream
1 (8 ounce) can whole kernel corn, drained
1 (16 ounce) package frozen broccoli, cauliflower and carrots, thawed
3 cups cooked, cubed ham
1 (8 ounce) package shredded cheddar-jack cheese, divided

- Preheat oven to 325°.

- Cook noodles according to package directions. In large bowl, combine broccoli soup, cream, corn, broccoli-carrot mixture, ham and salt and pepper to taste. Fold in noodles and half of cheese.

- Spoon into sprayed 9 x 13-inch baking dish. Cover and bake for 45 minutes. Remove from oven, sprinkle remaining cheese over top and return to oven for 5 minutes. Serves 4.

# MAC 'N CHEESE CASSEROLE

4 eggs
1½ cups milk
1 (12 ounce) package macaroni, cooked
1 (8 ounce) package shredded cheddar cheese
2 cups cubed ham
¾ cup seasoned breadcrumbs
¼ cup (½ stick) butter, cubed

- Preheat oven to 350°.

- Lightly beat eggs and milk with a little salt and pepper in large bowl. Stir in macaroni, cheese and ham.

- Spoon into sprayed 7 x 11-inch baking dish and bake uncovered for 20 minutes. Remove from oven, sprinkle with breadcrumbs and dot with butter. Continue baking an additional 15 minutes. Serves 8.

# HAM-VEGETABLE SUPPER

*1½ cups dry corkscrew pasta*
*1 (16 ounce) package frozen broccoli, cauliflower and carrots*
*1 (10 ounce) can broccoli-cheese soup*
*1 (3 ounce) package cream cheese with chives, softened*
*¾ cup milk*
*1 (8 ounce) package cubed Velveeta® cheese*
*1 tablespoon dijon-style mustard*
*2 cups cooked, cubed ham*

- In large saucepan, cook macaroni according to package directions. For last 5 minutes of cooking time, bring back to boiling, add vegetables and cook remaining 5 minutes. Drain in colander.

- In same saucepan, combine soup, cream cheese, milk, cheese and mustard over low heat and stir until cream cheese melts.

- Gently stir in ham, macaroni-vegetable mixture and a little salt and pepper. Heat thoroughly and stir often. Transfer to 3-quart serving dish. Serves 8.

# BROCCOLI-RICE AND HAM SUPPER

*1 (14 ounce) can chicken broth*
*1 (10 ounce) package frozen broccoli florets, thawed*
*1 carrot, shredded*
*1¼ cups instant rice*
*2 teaspoons lemon juice*
*1½ cups cooked ham, cut in strips*

- In large saucepan over high heat, bring broth to a boil. Add broccoli, carrots and rice and return to a boil. Reduce heat to low, cover and cook 5 minutes.

- Remove from heat, stir in rice, lemon juice and ham. Cover and let stand 5 minutes or until liquid absorbs. Fluff rice with fork and add a little salt and pepper. Serves 6.

Superfoods, said to have the most nutrients, include berries, chicken, garlic, grains, nuts, oats and soy, raisins, yogurt, apples, spinach, to name a few. These superfoods help to fight disease, boost the immune system, slow aging and increase energy.

# SUPER HAM FRITTATA

*2 cups cooked white rice*
*1 (10 ounce) box frozen green peas, thawed*
*1 cup cooked, cubed ham*
*8 large eggs, beaten*
*1 cup shredded pepper-jack cheese, divided*
*1 teaspoon dried thyme*
*1 teaspoon sage*

- Cook rice, peas and ham 3 to 4 minutes or until mixture is thoroughly hot in large heavy ovenproof skillet with a little oil.

- In separate bowl, whisk eggs, three-fourths of cheese, thyme, sage and 1 teaspoon salt. Add to mixture in skillet and shake pan gently to distribute evenly.

- On medium heat, cover and cook, without stirring, until set on bottom and sides. (Eggs will still be runny in center.) Sprinkle remaining cheese over top. Place skillet in oven and broil about 5 minutes or until frittata is firm in center. Serves 6.

# HAM AND RICE WITH PEAS

*1 (7 ounce) box brown and wild rice, mushroom recipe*
*3 - 4 cups chopped or cubed, cooked ham*
*1 (4 ounce) can sliced mushrooms, drained*
*1 (10 ounce) package frozen green peas*
*2 cups chopped celery*

- In 4 to 5-quart slow cooker, combine rice, seasoning packet, ham, mushrooms, peas, celery plus 2⅔ cups water. Stir to mix well. Cover and cook in slow cooker on LOW for 2 to 4 hours. Serves 4 to 6.

# HAM SUPPER QUICK

*1 (4.6 ounce) box boil-in-bag broccoli and cheese rice*
*2 cups cooked, cubed ham*
*1 (10 ounce) can cream of chicken soup*
*1 (10 ounce) package frozen green peas, thawed*
*1 cup shredded cheddar cheese*

- Preheat oven to 325°. Prepare rice according to package directions, but omit butter. In large bowl, combine cooked rice, ham, soup and peas. Stir well.

- Spoon into sprayed 3-quart baking dish, cover and bake for 20 minutes. Remove from oven, sprinkle cheese over top of casserole and return to oven for 5 minutes. Serves 6 to 8.

# HAM AND WILD RICE BAKE

1 (6 ounce) box long grain and wild rice mix
1 (10 ounce) package frozen broccoli florets, thawed
1 (11 ounce) can Mexicorn®
3 cups cooked, cubed ham
1 (10 ounce) can cream of mushroom soup
1 cup mayonnaise
1 cup shredded cheddar cheese
1 (3 ounce) can french-fried onions

- Preheat oven to 350°. Cook rice according to package directions and spread into sprayed 3-quart baking dish. Top with broccoli, corn and ham.

- In large bowl, combine soup, mayonnaise, cheese and salt to taste. Spread over broccoli-ham mixture.

- Cover and bake 25 minutes. Remove from oven and sprinkle fried onions on top. Return to oven and bake another 15 minutes. Serves 4 to 6.

# BAKED HAM-AND-POTATO SUPPER

1 (24 ounce) package frozen hash browns with onions and peppers, thawed
3 cups cooked, cubed ham
1 (10 ounce) can cream of chicken soup
1 (10 ounce) can cream of celery soup
1 (10 ounce) package frozen green peas, thawed
1 (8 ounce) package shredded Swiss cheese

- Preheat oven to 350°. In large bowl, combine hash browns, ham, both soups and peas and mix well.

- Spoon into sprayed 9 x 13-inch baking dish and bake 40 minutes. Remove from oven, uncover, sprinkle cheese over casserole and return to oven for another 5 minutes. Serves 4 to 6.

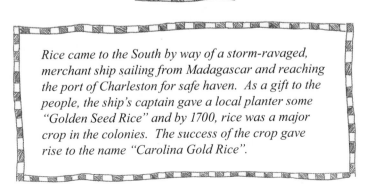

*Rice came to the South by way of a storm-ravaged, merchant ship sailing from Madagascar and reaching the port of Charleston for safe haven. As a gift to the people, the ship's captain gave a local planter some "Golden Seed Rice" and by 1700, rice was a major crop in the colonies. The success of the crop gave rise to the name "Carolina Gold Rice".*

# CREAMY POTATOES AND HAM

5 medium potatoes, peeled, sliced, divided
1 teaspoon seasoned salt, divided
1 onion, chopped, divided
2 cups cooked, cubed ham, divided
1 (8 ounce) package cubed processed cheese, divided
1 (10 ounce) can broccoli cheese soup
¼ cup milk

- In slow cooker, layer half each of potatoes, seasoned salt, onion, ham and cheese and repeat layer.
- In bowl, combine soup and milk until fairly smooth and pour over potato mixture. Cover and cook on HIGH for 1 hour. Reduce heat to LOW and cook for 6 to 7 hours. Serves 4.

# HAM AND POTATOES OLÉ!

1 (24 ounce) package frozen hash browns with onion and peppers, thawed
3 cups cubed, cooked ham
1 (10 ounce) can cream of chicken soup
1 (10 ounce) can fiesta nacho cheese soup
1 cup hot salsa
1 (8 ounce) package shredded cheddar-jack cheese

- Preheat oven to 350°. In large bowl, combine potatoes, ham, both soups and salsa and mix well. Spoon into buttered 9 x 13-inch baking dish.
- Cover and cook for 40 minutes. Remove from oven, sprinkle cheese over casserole and bake uncovered another 5 minutes. Serves 6 to 8.

# HAM-STUFFED TOMATOES

6 large tomatoes
1 (10 ounce) package frozen chopped broccoli
1½ cups cooked, shredded ham
1 (8 ounce) package shredded Mexican 3-cheese blend

- Preheat oven to 375°. Cut tops off tomatoes and scoop out pulp. Cook broccoli according to package directions. Drain.
- In bowl, combine broccoli, ham, 1 teaspoon salt and about three-fourths of cheese.
- Stuff broccoli mixture into tomatoes, place on baking sheet and bake 10 minutes. When serving, sprinkle remaining cheese over tops of stuffed tomatoes. Serves 4 to 6.

# HAM-CHEESE BARS

*2 cups biscuit mix*
*1 cup cooked, finely chopped ham*
*1 cup shredded cheddar cheese*
*½ onion, finely chopped*
*½ cup grated parmesan cheese*
*¼ cup sour cream*
*1 teaspoon garlic powder*
*1 cup milk*
*1 egg*

- Preheat oven to 350°.
- Combine all ingredients plus ½ teaspoon of salt in bowl and mix with spoon. Spread in sprayed 9 x 13-inch baking dish.
- Bake for 30 minutes or until light brown. Cut in rectangles, about 2 x 1 inch. Serve hot or room temperature. Serves 6 to 8.

*TIP: This can be served at brunch or lunch and can be kept in the refrigerator (cooked) and reheated. To reheat, bake at 325° for about 15 minutes. The bars will be good and crispy when reheated.*

# QUICK QUICHE

*½ cup (1 stick) butter, melted*
*1½ cups half-and-half cream*
*3 green onions with tops, chopped*
*½ cup biscuit mix*
*1 cup shredded Swiss cheese*
*¾ cup chopped ham*
*4 eggs, beaten*

- Preheat oven to 350°.
- Combine butter, half-and-half cream, green onions, biscuit mix, and ¼ teaspoon each of salt and pepper in bowl. Blend well with mixer and pour into sprayed 10-inch deep-dish pie pan.
- Sprinkle batter with cheese and ham. Push meat below surface with back of spoon. In same bowl, beat eggs and pour over ham and cheese. Bake for 35 minutes or until center sets. Let stand at room temperature for about 10 minutes before slicing. Serves 6 to 8.

# HAM AND CORN CASSEROLE

2 cups biscuit mix
2 cups finely chopped, cooked ham
1 cup shredded cheddar cheese
¼ cup (½ stick) butter, melted
1 small onion, chopped
1 bell pepper, seeded, finely chopped
3 large eggs, slightly beaten
1 (15 ounce) can cream-style corn
1 (11 ounce) can Mexicorn®
3 fresh green onions, finely chopped

- Preheat oven to 350°. In large bowl, combine all ingredients except green onions. Pour into sprayed 7 x 11-inch baking dish and bake uncovered for 50 minutes or until golden brown and set. Cut into squares to serve. Garnish with chopped green onions. Serves 8 to 10.

# PICNIC, SHANK OR BUTT HAM

- Buy picnic, shank or butt ham (half or whole), unwrap and place it in roaster. Cover and bake at 350° for about 3 hours. Check it after two hours to make sure there is juice in the pan. If it is drying out, add 1 to 2 inches of water. This will fall off the bone. Serves 6 to 8.

*TIP: All shank, butt and picnic hams are similar enough to be cooked the same way. All have bones and can be purchased as a half or whole. Usual cooking time is 2 hours to 3 hours 30 minutes and internal temperature should reach 160°. This may sound vague, but it works – and it's great!*

# BAKED HAM AND PINEAPPLE

1 (6 - 8 pound) fully cooked, bone-in ham
Whole cloves
½ cup packed brown sugar
1 (8 ounce) can sliced pineapple with juice
5 maraschino cherries

- Preheat oven to 325°. Place ham in roasting pan. Score surface with shallow diagonal cuts making diamond shapes and insert cloves into diamonds. Cover and bake for 1 hour 30 minutes.

- Combine brown sugar and juice from pineapple in bowl and pour over ham. Arrange pineapple slices and cherries on ham. Bake uncovered for additional 40 minutes. Serves 8 to 10.

# APRICOT BAKED HAM

*This is the ham you will want for Easter dinner!*

1 (12 - 20 pound) whole ham, fully cooked
Whole cloves
2 tablespoons dry mustard
1¼ cups apricot jam
1¼ cups packed light brown sugar

- Preheat oven to 450°. Place ham on rack in large roasting pan and insert cloves in ham every inch or so. Combine dry mustard and jam in bowl. Spread over entire surface of ham.

- Pat brown sugar over jam mixture. Reduce heat to 325°. Bake for 15 minutes per pound. Serves 10 to 18.

# ORANGE SAUCE FOR HAM

⅔ cup orange juice concentrate
1 tablespoon dijon-style mustard
2 tablespoons brown sugar
2 tablespoons cornstarch
⅓ cup light raisins

- Mix all ingredients with ⅔ cup water in saucepan. Heat and cook, stirring constantly, until sauce thickens and is clear and bubbly. Serve warm with pre-cooked ham. Makes 1½ cups.

# CHOICE TENDERLOIN SLICES

2 (1 pound) pork tenderloins
1 (12 ounce) jar apricot preserves
⅓ cup lemon juice
⅓ cup ketchup
1 tablespoon light soy sauce
2 cups cooked instant rice

- Preheat oven to 325°. Place tenderloins in sprayed 7 x 11-inch baking pan. Combine preserves, lemon juice, ketchup and soy sauce in saucepan and heat just until mixture blends well.

- Spoon sauce over tenderloins, cover and bake for 1 hour. Baste twice during cooking. Let tenderloins stand about 15 minutes before slicing. Place slices and sauce over hot, cooked rice. Serves 6 to 8.

# Spicy Glazed Pork Tenderloin

*½ cup orange juice*
*¼ cup lime juice*
*½ cup packed brown sugar*
*1 teaspoon ground cumin*
*2 (1 pound) pork tenderloins*

- In small bowl, combine orange juice, lime juice, brown sugar and cumin.

- Pat tenderloins dry with paper towels and season with a little salt and pepper. Place a little oil in large skillet over medium-high heat. Brown tenderloins on all sides, about 9 to 10 minutes total. Reduce heat to medium, add orange juice mixture and cook until mixture is thick and syrupy, about 10 minutes.

- Transfer to cutting board, cover tenderloins with foil and let rest 10 minutes before slicing crosswise into ½-inch slices. Arrange on serving plate and pour glaze over slices. Serves 8.

# Garlic-Roasted Pork Tenderloin

*2 (1 pound) pork tenderloins*

## Rub:

*4 teaspoons minced garlic*
*1 tablespoon dijon-style mustard*
*1 tablespoon ketchup*
*1 tablespoon soy sauce*
*1 tablespoon honey*

- Preheat oven to 350°. Place tenderloins on foil-lined roasting pan. Combine garlic, mustard, ketchup, soy sauce and honey and rub evenly over pork.

- Roast for 30 minutes or until thermometer inserted into thickest portion registers 155°. Remove from oven, cover with foil and let stand for 10 minutes.

## Sauce:

*2 teaspoons rice vinegar*
*2 teaspoons sesame oil*
*1 tablespoon soy sauce*
*¼ cup honey*

- Combine all sauce ingredients. Slice pork diagonally and place on serving platter. Drizzle sauce over pork slices. Serves 8.

# Nutty Pork Loin

*1 (3 - 4 pound) boneless pork loin roast*
*1 teaspoon Creole seasoning*
*⅔ cup orange juice*
*⅔ cup orange marmalade*
*⅓ cup smooth peanut butter*

- Preheat oven to 350°.

- Place pork loin in roasting pan and season well with Creole seasoning. Cover and bake for 1 hour or until thermometer registers 160°.

- In saucepan, combine orange juice, marmalade and peanut butter. Heat just enough to mix well.

- Reduce oven heat to 325° and pour orange sauce over roast, cover and cook for additional 1 hour 30 minutes. Brush occasionally with sauce during last hour of cooking time. To serve, slice roast, place in serving dish and cover with orange sauce. Serves 8 to 10.

# Pork Tenderloin with Cranberry Sauce

*2 (1 pound) pork tenderloins*
*½ cup chopped fresh cilantro*
*½ teaspoon ground cumin*
*2 teaspoons minced garlic*

- Preheat oven to 375°. Season tenderloin with a little salt and pepper, cilantro, cumin and garlic.

- Place in foil-lined baking pan and bake 15 minutes. Reduce heat to 325° and bake another 35 minutes. Slice to serve.

## Cranberry Sauce:

*1 (16 ounce) can whole cranberries*
*1 cup orange marmalade*
*1 (8 ounce) can crushed pineapple, drained*
*¾ cup chopped pecans*

- Combine cranberries, marmalade, pineapple and pecans and serve with tenderloin. Sauce may be served room temperature or warmed. Serves 6 to 8.

# Sweet-and-Sour Pork Loin Roast

*4 - 5 pound pork loin roast*
*1 (12 ounce) bottle chili sauce*
*1 (12 ounce) jar apricot preserves*
*1 (20 ounce) can chunk pineapple, drained*
*2 bell peppers, seeded, sliced*

- Preheat oven to 325°.

- Season roast with salt and pepper and brown in a little oil in large heavy roasting pan. Add ½ cup water to pan, cover and bake for 1 hour.

- Mix chili sauce and apricot preserves and pour over roast. Reduce heat to 275° and cook additional 2 hours.

- Add pineapple and bell pepper and cook for 15 minutes. Serves 10 to 12.

# Pork Picante

*1 pound pork tenderloin, cubed*
*2 tablespoons taco seasoning*
*1 cup chunky salsa*
*⅓ cup peach preserves*

- Toss pork with taco seasoning and brown with a little oil in skillet. Stir in salsa and preserves. Bring to boil. Lower heat and simmer 30 minutes. Pour over hot cooked rice. Serves 4.

# Apple Pork Chops

*4 butterflied pork chops*
*2 apples, peeled, cored*
*2 tablespoons butter*
*2 tablespoons brown sugar*

- Place pork chops in non-stick sprayed shallow baking dish. Season with salt and pepper. Cover and bake at 350° for 30 minutes.

- Uncover and place apple halves on top of pork chops. Add a little butter and a little brown sugar on each apple. Bake for another 15 minutes. Serves 4.

# BAKED PORK CHOPS

¾ cup ketchup
¾ cup packed brown sugar
¼ cup lemon juice
4 butterflied pork chops

- Preheat oven to 325°.

- Combine ketchup, ½ cup water, brown sugar and lemon juice. Place pork chops in sprayed 7 x 11-inch baking dish and pour sauce over pork chops. Bake covered for 50 minutes. Serves 4.

# ITALIAN-STYLE PORK CHOPS

6 (¾ inch thick) bone-in pork chops
2 green bell peppers, seeded
1 (15 ounce) can tomato sauce
1 (15 ounce) can Italian stewed tomatoes with liquid
½ onion, chopped
1 teaspoon Italian seasoning
1 clove garlic, minced
1 tablespoon Worcestershire sauce
½ cup brown rice

- Preheat oven to 350°.

- Sprinkle pork chops with a little salt and pepper. Brown chops on both sides in a little oil in skillet. Remove chops from skillet, drain and set aside. Cut 1 bell pepper into 6 (¼ inch thick) rings and set aside. Seed and chop remaining bell pepper.

- Combine chopped bell pepper, tomato sauce, stewed tomatoes, 1 cup water, onion, Italian seasoning, garlic, Worcestershire and ½ teaspoon each of salt and pepper in bowl and mix well.

- Spread rice evenly in lightly sprayed 9 x 13-inch baking dish. Slowly pour tomato mixture over rice. Arrange pork chops over rice mixture and top each pork chop with bell pepper ring. Cover and bake for 1 hour or until rice is tender. Serves 6.

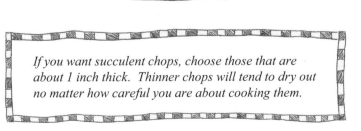

*If you want succulent chops, choose those that are about 1 inch thick. Thinner chops will tend to dry out no matter how careful you are about cooking them.*

# MEXICALI PORK CHOPS

*1 (1 ounce) packet taco seasoning*
*4 (½ inch thick) boneless pork loin chops*
*1 tablespoon canola oil*
*Salsa*

- Rub taco seasoning over pork chops. Brown pork chops in oil in skillet over medium heat.

- Add 2 tablespoons water, turn heat to low and simmer pork chops for about 40 minutes. (Add more water if needed.) Spoon salsa over pork chops to serve. Serves 4.

# ORANGE PORK CHOPS

*6 - 8 medium thick pork chops*
*Flour*
*3 tablespoons butter*
*2 cups orange juice*

- Preheat oven to 325°.

- Dip pork chops in flour and brown in skillet with a little butter. Place chops in 9 x 13-inch baking pan and pour remaining butter over top of pork chops.

- Pour orange juice over chops. Cover and bake for 40 minutes. Uncover and bake additional 15 minutes. Serves 6 to 8.

# ONION-SMOTHERED PORK CHOPS

*1 tablespoon canola oil*
*6 (½ inch thick) pork chops*
*2 tablespoons butter*
*1 onion, chopped*
*1 (10 ounce) can cream of onion soup*
*Brown rice, cooked*

- Preheat oven to 325°.

- Brown pork chops in oil in skillet, simmer for about 10 minutes and place pork chops in sprayed shallow baking pan.

- In same skillet, add butter and saute onion. (Pan juices are brown from pork chops so onions will be brown from juices already in skillet.)

- Add onion soup and ½ cup water and stir well. (Sauce will be light brown.) Pour onion soup mixture over pork chops. Cover and bake for 40 minutes and serve over brown rice. Serves 6.

# OVEN PORK CHOPS

*6 - 8 medium-thick pork chops*
*Canola oil*
*1 (10 ounce) can cream of chicken soup*
*3 tablespoons ketchup*
*1 tablespoon Worcestershire sauce*
*1 medium onion, chopped*

- Preheat oven to 350°. Brown pork chops in a little oil and season with a little salt and pepper. Drain and place in shallow baking dish.

- Combine soup, ketchup, Worcestershire sauce and onion in small saucepan. Heat just enough to mix and pour over pork chops. Cover and bake for 50 minutes. Uncover the last 15 minutes. Serves 6 to 8.

# PINEAPPLE-PORK CHOPS

*6 - 8 thick boneless pork chops*
*Canola oil*
*1 (6 ounce) can frozen pineapple juice concentrate, thawed*
*3 tablespoons brown sugar*
*⅓ cup wine or tarragon vinegar*
*⅓ cup honey*
*Rice, cooked*

- Preheat oven to 325°. Place pork chops in a little oil in skillet and brown. Remove to shallow baking dish. Combine pineapple juice, brown sugar, vinegar and honey in bowl.

- Pour over pork chops. Cover and cook for about 50 minutes. Serve over hot rice. Serves 6 to 8.

# PORK CHOP SUPPER

*1 (18 ounce) package smoked pork chops*
*1 (12 ounce) jar pork gravy*
*¼ cup milk*
*1 (12 ounce) package very small new potatoes*

- Brown pork chops in large skillet with a little oil. Pour gravy and milk or water into skillet and stir mixture around chops until they mix well.

- Add new potatoes around chops and gravy. Place lid on skillet and simmer on low to medium heat for about 15 minutes or until potatoes are tender. Serves 4 to 6.

# Pork Chops and Gravy

*6 (½-inch thick) pork chops*
*8 - 10 new potatoes with peel, quartered*
*1 (16 ounce) package baby carrots*
*2 (10 ounce) cans cream of mushroom soup with roasted garlic*

- Sprinkle a little salt and pepper on pork chops. In skillet, brown pork chops and place in 5 to 6-quart slow cooker. Place potatoes and carrots around pork chops.

- In saucepan, heat mushroom soup with ½ cup water and pour over chops and vegetables. Cover and cook in slow cooker on LOW for 6 to 7 hours. Serves 4 to 6.

# Pork Chop-Cheddar Bake

*8 boneless pork chops*
*1 (10 ounce) can cream of mushroom soup*
*1 cup rice*
*1½ cups shredded cheddar cheese, divided*
*½ cup minced onion*
*⅓ cup chopped bell pepper*
*1 (4 ounce) can sliced mushrooms, drained*
*1 (6 ounce) can french-fried onions*

- Preheat oven to 325°.

- Brown pork chops lightly in large skillet. Drain and place in sprayed 9 x 13-inch baking dish.

- In same skillet, combine soup, 1¼ cups water, rice, ½ cup cheese, onion, bell pepper and mushrooms and mix well. Pour over pork chops.

- Cover and bake for 1 hour 10 minutes. Uncover and top with remaining cheese and french-fried onions. Return to oven just until cheese melts. Serves 8.

# PORK CHOPS AND APPLES

6 (¾ inch thick) bone-in pork chops
¼ cup (½ stick) butter, divided
6 cups plain croutons
1 cup green apples, peeled, chopped
½ cup chopped celery
½ cup chopped pecans
2 teaspoons rubbed sage
1 tablespoon dijon-style mustard

- Preheat oven to 325°.

- Brown pork chops on both sides in 2 tablespoons butter in large skillet and set aside. In same skillet, melt remaining butter, stir in croutons, apples, celery, pecans, ½ cup water, sage and 1 teaspoon salt and mix well.

- Place crouton mixture into sprayed 7 x 11-inch baking dish. Top with pork chops. Spread thin layer of mustard over each pork chop. Cover and bake for 40 minutes. Uncover and bake for additional 10 minutes. Serves 6.

# PORK CHOPS WITH BLACK BEAN SALSA

2 teaspoons chili powder
½ teaspoon seasoned salt
2 tablespoons vegetable oil
6 boneless thin-cut pork chops

- Combine chili powder and salt. Rub oil over pork chops and rub chili powder mixture over chops.

- Place in skillet over medium heat and cook pork chops about 5 minutes on both sides or until it cooks through.

## BLACK BEAN SALSA:

1 (15 ounce) can black beans, rinsed, drained
1 (24 ounce) refrigerated citrus fruit, drained
1 ripe avocado, sliced
⅔ cup Italian salad dressing

- Combine beans, fruit and avocado and toss with salad dressing. Serve with pork chops. Serves 4 to 6.

# PORK CHOPS IN CREAM GRAVY

4 (¼ inch thick) pork chops
¼ cup flour
Canola oil
2¼ cups milk
Rice, cooked

- Trim all fat off pork chops. Dip chops in flour with a little salt and pepper. Brown pork chops on both sides in a little oil in skillet. Remove chops from skillet.

- Add about 2 tablespoons flour to skillet, brown lightly and stir in a little salt and pepper. Slowly stir in milk to make gravy.

- Return chops to skillet with gravy. Cover and simmer on low burner for about 40 minutes. Serve over rice. Serves 4.

# PORK CHOPS, POTATOES AND GREEN BEANS

6 - 8 boneless or loin pork chops
2 (1 ounce) packets gravy mix or 2 (12 ounce) jars prepared gravy
2 (15 ounce) cans white potatoes, drained
2 (15 ounce) cans cut green beans, drained

- Season pork chops with salt and pepper if desired and brown pork chops over medium heat in large, sprayed roasting pan.

- Mix gravy with water according to package directions or pour prepared gravy over pork chops. Cover and simmer for 30 minutes.

- Add potatoes and green beans and simmer about 10 minutes or until pork chops are tender and green beans and potatoes are hot. Serves 6 to 8.

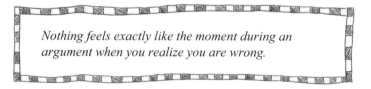

*Nothing feels exactly like the moment during an argument when you realize you are wrong.*

# Savory Pork Chop Bake

*8 lean pork chops*
*1 onion, chopped*
*1 red bell pepper, seeded, chopped*
*1 (10 ounce) can cream of mushroom soup*
*1 cup uncooked rice*
*1 cup shredded processed cheese*
*1 (8 ounce) can green peas, drained*
*1 (4 ounce) can sliced mushrooms, drained*
*1 (3 ounce) can french-fried onions*

- Preheat oven to 325°.

- Brown pork chops in large skillet with a little oil. Add onion and bell pepper and cook 10 minutes. Drain and place in greased 9 x 13-inch baking dish.

- In same skillet, combine mushroom soup, rice, cheese, green peas, mushrooms and 1¼ cups water and mix well. Spoon mixture over pork chops, onion and bell pepper.

- Cover and bake 50 minutes. Uncover and top with french-fried onions and bake another 15 minutes or until fried onions are light brown. Serves 6 to 8.

# Pork Chops Deluxe

*1 cup rice*
*¼ cup flour*
*1 teaspoon seasoned salt*
*6 pork chops with bone*
*3 tablespoons oil, divided*
*1 onion, chopped*
*1 green bell pepper, seeded, chopped*
*1 (15 ounce) can Mexican stewed tomatoes*
*1 (10 ounce) can chicken broth*

- Preheat oven to 325°.

- Place rice in sprayed 9 x 13-inch baking dish. Combine flour and seasoned salt in shallow bowl and dredge pork chops in flour mixture. Brown pork chops in large skillet with half oil and place on top of rice.

- With remaining oil, saute onion and bell pepper about 4 minutes. Add stewed tomatoes and chicken broth and mix well. Pour over pork chops in baking dish. Cover and bake for 1 hour. Serves 6.

# PORK CHOPS AND POTATOES

6 - 8 bone-in pork chops
2 (15 ounce) cans whole new potatoes, drained
2 (1 ounce) packets dry onion gravy mix
1 (14 ounce) can chicken broth

- Preheat oven to 325°.

- Brown pork chops in large skillet and place in sprayed 9 x 13-inch baking pan. Add potatoes to pork chops in baking pan.

- Place dry gravy mix in bowl, stir in about one-fourth of broth and mix well. Stir in remaining broth and pour over pork chops and potatoes. Cover and bake for 45 minutes. Serves 6 to 8.

# STUFFED PORK CHOPS

4 (¾ inch thick) boneless center-cut pork chops
Oil

## STUFFING:

2 slices rye bread, diced
⅓ cup chopped onion
⅓ cup chopped celery
⅓ cup dried apples, diced
⅓ cup chicken broth
½ teaspoon dried thyme

- Preheat oven to 400°.

- Make 1-inch wide slit on side of each chop and insert knife blade to other side, but not through pork chop. Sweep knife back and forth and carefully cut pocket opening larger.

- In bowl, combine rye bread pieces, onion, celery, apples, broth and thyme and mix well. Stuff chops with stuffing mixture and press to use all stuffing mixture in pork chops.

- Place chops in heavy skillet with a little oil and saute each chop about 3 minutes on each side. Transfer to non-stick baking dish and bake uncovered for 15 minutes. Serves 4.

# CRUNCHY PORK CHOPS

*1 cup crushed saltine crackers*
*¼ cup biscuit mix*
*¾ teaspoon seasoned salt*
*1 egg, beaten*
*5 - 6 (½ inch thick) boneless pork chops*
*Oil*

• Combine crushed crackers, biscuit mix and seasoned salt in shallow bowl. In separate shallow bowl, combine beaten egg and 2 tablespoons water.

• Dip pork chops into egg mixture and dredge in cracker mixture.

• Cook pork chops with a little oil in heavy skillet for about 15 minutes and turn once. Serves 5 to 6.

# TANGY APRICOT RIBS

*3 - 4 pounds baby back pork loin ribs*
*1 (16 ounce) jar apricot preserves*
*⅓ cup soy sauce*
*¼ cup packed light brown sugar*
*2 teaspoons garlic powder*

• Place ribs in large roasting pan. Whisk preserves, soy sauce, brown sugar and garlic powder in bowl until they blend and pour over ribs. Cover and refrigerate overnight.

• When ready to bake, preheat oven to 325°.

• Remove ribs from marinade and reserve marinade in small saucepan. Line baking pan with foil, add ribs and sprinkle with a little salt and pepper.

• Bring marinade to a boil, cover, reduce heat and simmer for 5 minutes. Bake ribs for 1 hour 30 minutes or until tender and baste frequently with marinade. Serves 4 to 6.

# DIJON BABY BACK RIBS

*4 pounds baby back pork ribs*
*1 (12 ounce) bottle dijon-honey marinade with lemon juice, divided*

• Place ribs in bag and add ¾ cup marinade. Seal bag and shake to coat. Marinate in refrigerator overnight. (If needed, cut ribs to fit in large, resealable plastic bag.)

• When ready to bake, preheat oven to 300°.

• Discard used marinade and place ribs on sprayed broiler pan. Bake for about 2 hours. Finish browning and cooking on grill and baste often with remaining marinade. Serves 3 to 4.

# SUNSHINE SPARERIBS

*5 - 6 pounds spareribs*
*1 (6 ounce) can frozen orange juice concentrate*
*2 teaspoons Worcestershire sauce*
*½ teaspoon garlic powder*

- Preheat oven to 375°.

- Place spareribs in shallow baking pan, meat-side down. Sprinkle with a little salt and pepper. Roast for 30 minutes. Turn ribs and roast for additional 15 minutes and drain off fat.

- Combine remaining ingredients in bowl and brush mixture on ribs. Reduce heat to 300°. Cover ribs and roast for 2 hours or until tender and baste occasionally. Serves 6.

# SWEET-AND-SOUR SPARERIBS

*3 - 4 pounds spareribs*
*3 tablespoons soy sauce*
*⅓ cup mustard*
*1 cup packed brown sugar*
*½ teaspoon garlic salt*

- Preheat oven to 325°.

- Place spareribs in roasting pan and bake for 45 minutes and drain. Make sauce in bowl with remaining ingredients and brush on ribs.

- Return to oven, reduce heat to 300° and bake for 1 hour or until tender. Baste several times while cooking. Serves 4 to 6.

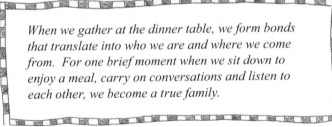

*When we gather at the dinner table, we form bonds that translate into who we are and where we come from. For one brief moment when we sit down to enjoy a meal, carry on conversations and listen to each other, we become a true family.*

# Zesty Ziti

*1 pound Italian sausage links, cut into ½ inch chunks*
*1 onion, cut into strips*
*1 green bell pepper, seeded, julienned*
*1 tablespoon oil*
*1 (15 ounce) can diced tomatoes*
*1 (15 ounce) can Italian stewed tomatoes*
*2 tablespoons ketchup*
*1 (16 ounce) package ziti pasta*
*1 cup shredded mozzarella cheese*

- Preheat oven to 350°.

- Cook sausage, onion and bell pepper in oil over medium heat in large skillet and drain. In separate bowl combine diced tomatoes, stewed tomatoes and ketchup and mix well.

- Cook ziti according to package directions and drain. In large bowl, combine sausage-onion mixture and tomato mixture and toss with pasta and cheese. Spoon into greased 3-quart baking dish. Cover and bake from 20 minutes. Serves 4 to 6.

# Pizza Pies

*½ pound bulk pork sausage*
*⅔ cup prepared pizza sauce*
*1 (10 ounce) package refrigerated pizza dough*
*1 cup shredded mozzarella cheese*

- Preheat oven to 400°.

- Brown sausage in skillet and stir to break up pieces of meat. Drain fat, add pizza sauce and heat until bubbly.

- Unroll pizza dough, place on flat surface and pat into 8 x 12-inch rectangle. Cut into 6 squares.

- Divide sausage mixture evenly among squares and sprinkle with cheese. Lift one corner of each square and fold over filling to make triangle.

- Press edges together with tines of fork to seal. Bake about 12 minutes or until light golden brown. Serve immediately. Serves 2 to 4.

# SAUSAGE AND BEANS

*1 (1 pound) fully cooked smoked, link sausage*
*2 (15 ounce) cans baked beans*
*1 (15 ounce) can great northern beans, drained*
*1 (15 ounce) can pinto beans, drained*
*½ cup chili sauce*
*⅔ cup packed brown sugar*
*1 tablespoon Worcestershire sauce*

- Cut link sausage into 1-inch slices. Layer sausage and beans in slow cooker. Combine chili sauce, brown sugar, a little black pepper and Worcestershire sauce and pour over beans and sausage.

- Cover and cook in slow cooker on LOW for 4 hours. Stir before serving. Serves 4 to 6.

# ITALIAN SAUSAGE AND RAVIOLI

*1 pound sweet Italian pork sausage, casing removed*
*1 (26 ounce) jar extra chunky mushroom and green pepper spaghetti sauce*
*1 (24 ounce) package frozen cheese-filled ravioli, cooked, drained*
*Grated parmesan cheese*

- Cook sausage in very large skillet over medium heat until brown and no longer pink. Stir to separate sausage or slice sausage; drain.

- Stir in spaghetti sauce and heat to boiling. Cook ravioli according to package directions and add to spaghetti and sausage. Sprinkle with parmesan cheese. Pour into serving dish. Serves 4 to 6.

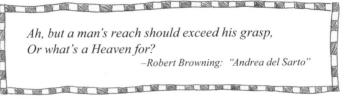

*Ah, but a man's reach should exceed his grasp,*
*Or what's a Heaven for?*
*                    —Robert Browning: "Andrea del Sarto"*

# COLORFUL SAUSAGE SUPPER

*1 pound cooked Polish sausage, sliced thin*
*1 red bell pepper, seeded, julienned*
*3 small zucchini, sliced*
*3 small yellow squash, sliced*
*4 tablespoons olive oil, divided*
*1 (16 ounce) package penne pasta*
*1 (26 ounce) jar spaghetti sauce, heated*

- Saute sausage, bell pepper, zucchini and squash until vegetables are tender-crisp in large skillet with 2 tablespoons oil. Keep warm.

- Cook pasta according to package directions, drain and stir in remaining oil. Add salt and pepper to taste. Spoon into large serving bowl and spread hot spaghetti sauce over pasta.

- Use slotted spoon to top with sausage-vegetable mixture and serve immediately. Serve with hot, buttered garlic bread. Serves 6.

# SAUSAGE-POTATO BAKE

*1 (10 ounce) can cream of celery soup*
*½ cup sour cream*
*1 teaspoon freeze-dried chives*
*1 cup shredded cheddar cheese*
*2 (15 ounce) cans whole new potatoes, halved, drained*
*1 (10 ounce) package frozen cut green beans, thawed*
*1 pound cooked Polish sausage, sliced*
*1 (2.8 ounce) can french-fried onions*

- Preheat oven to 350°.

- Combine soup, sour cream, chives and cheese in large bowl. Stir in potatoes, green beans and sausage and spoon into sprayed 7 x 11-inch baking dish. Cover and bake for 30 minutes.

- Remove from oven and sprinkle fried onions over casserole. Bake for an additional 15 minutes or until onions are golden brown. Serves 8 to 10.

# SAUSAGE-BEAN CASSEROLE

1 pound pork sausage
2 (15 ounce) cans pork and beans with liquid
1 (15 ounce) can Mexican stewed tomatoes
1 (8 ounce) package muffin mix
1 egg
⅓ cup milk

- Preheat oven to 350°.

- Brown sausage in large skillet and drain. Add beans and stewed tomatoes, stir and bring to a boil. Pour into sprayed 3-quart baking dish.

- Prepare muffin mix with egg and milk according to package directions. Drop by teaspoonfuls over meat-bean mixture and bake for 30 minutes or until top is light brown. Serves 8.

# EGG-BISCUIT SUPPER

12 - 14 eggs, slightly beaten
1 pound sausage, cooked, crumbled
2 cups milk
1 (8 ounce) package shredded cheddar cheese
1 (5.5 ounce) box seasoned croutons
Hot biscuits

- Preheat oven to 350°. In large bowl, combine all ingredients except biscuits and pour into greased 9 x 13-inch baking dish. Cover and bake for 45 minutes or until center is firm.

- Let stand about 10 minutes before slicing to serve. Serve with biscuits. Serves 8 to 14.

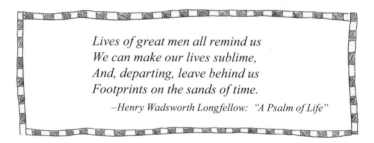

*Lives of great men all remind us*
*We can make our lives sublime,*
*And, departing, leave behind us*
*Footprints on the sands of time.*

*–Henry Wadsworth Longfellow: "A Psalm of Life"*

# QUESADILLA PIE

*1 (4 ounce) can diced green chilies*
*½ pound sausage, cooked, crumbled*
*2 cups shredded cheddar cheese*
*3 eggs, well beaten*
*1½ cups milk*
*¾ cup biscuit mix*
*Hot salsa*

- Preheat oven to 350°.

- Sprinkle green chilies in sprayed 9-inch pie pan. Add layer of cooked sausage and layer of cheese. Combine eggs, milk and biscuit mix in bowl and mix well.

- Slowly pour over green chilies, sausage and cheese. Bake for 35 minutes or until center sets. Serve with salsa on top of each slice. Serves 4 to 6.

*TIP: To give this "pie" a little more zip, use hot sausage and a few drops of hot sauce!*

# BREAKFAST BAKE

*1 pound hot sausage, cooked, crumbled, drained*
*2 tablespoons dried onion flakes*
*1 cup shredded cheddar cheese*
*1 cup biscuit mix*
*5 eggs*
*2 cups milk*

- Preheat oven to 350°. Place cooked sausage in sprayed 9 x 13-inch baking dish. Sprinkle with onion flakes and cheese.

- Combine biscuit mix, eggs and a little salt and pepper in bowl. Beat well with fork (not mixer). Add milk, stir until fairly smooth and pour over sausage mixture. Cover and bake for 35 minutes. Serves 8 to 10.

*Breakfast is the most important meal of the day because it sets your metabolism in motion. You need quick, high-energy foods to sustain you. Fruit and yogurt, whole grain hot cereal, eggs and high protein drinks are all great.*

## SAUSAGE AND CHILIES QUICHE

*1 (9 inch) refrigerated piecrust*
*1 (7 ounce) can whole green chilies, drained*
*1 pound hot sausage, cooked, crumbled, drained*
*4 eggs, slightly beaten*
*2 cups half-and-half cream*
*½ cup grated parmesan cheese*
*¾ cup shredded Swiss cheese*

- Preheat oven to 350°.

- Line bottom of piecrust with green chilies. Sprinkle sausage over chilies.

- Combine eggs, half-and-half cream, cheeses, ½ teaspoon salt and ¼ teaspoon pepper in bowl and pour over sausage.

- Cover edge of pastry with foil to prevent excessive browning. Bake for 35 minutes or until top is golden brown. Let quiche stand for about 5 minutes before serving. Serves 4 to 6.

# SEAFOOD
# MAIN DISHES

## ALFREDO SALMON AND NOODLES

*3 cups uncooked medium egg noodles*
*1 (16 ounce) package frozen broccoli florets, thawed*
*1 cup prepared alfredo sauce*
*1 (15 ounce) can salmon, drained, boned*

- Cook noodles in large saucepan according to package directions. Add broccoli last 5 minutes of cooking time and drain.

- Stir in alfredo sauce and salmon and cook on low heat, stirring occasionally, until mixture heats through. Pour into serving bowl. Serves 4 to 6.

# SALMON AND GREEN BEANS

*4 (6 ounce) salmon steaks*
*¼ cup lite soy sauce*
*2 tablespoons lemon juice*
*1 (10 ounce) package frozen whole green beans*

- Place a little oil in skillet over medium to high heat and add salmon steaks. Combine soy sauce and lemon juice and pour over steaks. Cover and cook about 5 minutes.

- Turn salmon and place green beans over salmon with 2 tablespoons water. Cover and steam 5 minutes or until beans are tender-crisp. Season green beans with a little salt and pepper and serve over hot buttered rice. Serves 4.

# EVER-READY TUNA CASSEROLE

*1 (7 ounce) package elbow macaroni*
*1 (8 ounce) package shredded processed cheese*
*2 (6 ounce) cans tuna, drained*
*1 (10 ounce) can cream of celery soup*
*1 cup milk*

- Preheat oven to 350°. Cook macaroni according to package directions. Drain well, add cheese and stir until cheese melts.

- Add tuna, celery soup and milk and continue stirring. Spoon into sprayed 7 x 11-inch baking dish. Cover and bake 35 minutes or until bubbly. Serves 4 to 6.

# TUNA-STUFFED TOMATOES

*4 large tomatoes*
*2 (6 ounce) cans white meat tuna, drained*
*2 cups chopped celery*
*½ cup chopped cashews*
*1 small zucchini with peel, finely chopped*
*½ cup mayonnaise*

- Cut thin slice off top of each tomato, scoop out pulp and discard. Turn tomatoes, top down, on paper towels to drain.

- Combine tuna, celery, cashews, zucchini, mayonnaise and a little salt and pepper to taste and mix well. Spoon mixture into hollowed-out tomatoes. Refrigerate. Serves 4.

# TUNA CASSEROLE WITH BASIL SAUCE

*1 tablespoon olive oil*
*2 teaspoons minced garlic*
*2 teaspoons sugar*
*¼ teaspoon cayenne pepper*
*2 teaspoons dried basil*
*1 (18 ounce) can stewed tomatoes*
*1 (12 ounce) can water-packed tuna, drained*
*¾ cup pitted, green olives, sliced*
*¼ cup drained capers*
*1 cup pasta, cooked*

- Heat olive oil in saucepan and add garlic, sugar, pepper and basil. Cook on low heat for 2 minutes. Add stewed tomatoes, bring to boil, reduce heat and simmer for 20 minutes.

- In serving bowl, combine tuna, olives, capers and pasta. Stir in basil-tomato sauce and toss. Serves 4 to 6.

# TUNA-IN-THE-STRAW

*1 (8 ounce) package egg noodles*
*2 (10 ounce) cans cream of chicken soup*
*1 (8 ounce) carton sour cream*
*1 teaspoon Creole seasoning*
*½ cup milk*
*2 (6 ounce) cans white meat tuna, drained*
*1 cup shredded Velveeta® cheese*
*1 (10 ounce) package green peas, thawed*
*1 (2 ounce) jar diced pimento*
*1 (2 ounce) can shoe-string potatoes*

- Preheat oven to 350°.

- Cook noodles according to package directions and drain. Combine soup, sour cream, Creole seasoning and milk in bowl and mix well. Add noodles, tuna, cheese, peas and pimento.

- Pour into sprayed 9 x 13-inch baking dish. Sprinkle top with shoe-string potatoes. Bake for about 35 minutes or until shoe-string potatoes are light brown. Serves 8 to 10.

# TUNA-ASPARAGUS POT PIE

*1 (8 ounce) package crescent rolls, divided*
*1 (6 ounce) can solid white tuna in water, drained*
*1 (15 ounce) can cut asparagus, drained*
*1 cup shredded cheddar cheese*

- Preheat oven to 375°. Form 7-inch square using 4 crescent rolls, pinch edges together to seal and place in 8 x 8-inch square, sprayed baking pan.

- Spread dough with tuna, then asparagus and shredded cheese. Form remaining 4 crescent rolls into 1 square and place on top of cheese.

- Bake for 20 minutes or until top browns and cheese bubbles. Serves 4.

# THAI PEANUT SHRIMP AND NOODLES

*1 (5.5 ounce) box Thai stir-fry rice noodles with seasoning packet*
*1 pound peeled, veined shrimp*
*1 (10 ounce) package frozen broccoli florets, thawed*
*½ cup peanuts*

- Boil 3 cups water in saucepan and stir in noodles. Turn heat off and soak noodles about 5 minutes. Drain and rinse in cold water.

- Saute shrimp and broccoli in skillet with a little oil for about 8 minutes or just until shrimp turns pink.

- Add softened noodles, seasoning packet and peanuts. (There are chopped peanuts in seasoning, but this dish is better, if you add more peanuts.) Serves 4 to 6.

*TIP: If noodles are still too firm after they soak, add 1 tablespoon water and stir-fry until noodles are tender.*

# SHRIMP AND CHICKEN CURRY

*2 (10 ounce) cans cream of chicken soup*
*⅓ cup milk*
*1½ teaspoons curry powder*
*1 (12 ounce) can chicken breast, drained*
*2 (6 ounce) cans shrimp, drained*
*1 cup cooked rice*

- In saucepan, heat soup, milk and curry powder. Stir in chicken pieces and shrimp. Heat, stirring constantly, until mixture is thoroughly hot. Serve over hot, cooked rice. Serves 6.

# Speedy Jambalaya

*¼ pound bacon*
*1 pound fresh okra, sliced*
*2 onions, chopped*
*2 (15 ounce) cans stewed tomatoes*
*1 (15 ounce) can whole kernel corn*
*1 (16 ounce) package frozen salad shrimp, thawed*
*1 (6 ounce) box long grain and wild rice*

- In large skillet, fry bacon until crisp. Remove bacon with slotted spoon; leave bacon drippings in skillet. Crumble bacon and set aside.

- In same skillet, saute okra and onion, but do not brown. Add tomatoes and corn. Bring to boil, reduce heat to medium and simmer about 10 minutes or until most liquid absorbs. Stir in well-drained shrimp and heat just until mixture is thoroughly hot.

- Cook rice according to package directions and serve jambalaya over rice. Sprinkle crumbled bacon over top. Serves 6 to 8.

# Gulf Coast Casserole

*2 (10 ounce) cans cream of chicken soup*
*⅔ cup mayonnaise*
*⅓ cup milk*
*3 ribs celery, sliced*
*2 tablespoons marinade for chicken*
*1 (16 ounce) package frozen salad shrimp, thawed*
*1 (6 ounce) can crabmeat, drained*
*2 tablespoons dried parsley flakes*
*Hot, buttered rice*

- Preheat oven to 350°. In large bowl, combine soup, mayonnaise, milk, celery and marinade for chicken and mix well. Stir in well-drained shrimp, crabmeat and parsley.

- Spoon into greased 3-quart baking dish, cover and bake for 45 minutes. Serve with hot, buttered white rice. Serves 4 to 6.

# CRAB-STUFFED BAKED POTATOES

*This potato is truly a meal in itself!*

4 large baking potatoes
½ cup (1 stick) butter
½ cup whipping cream
1 bunch fresh green onions, chopped
2 (6 ounce) cans crabmeat, drained, flaked
¾ cup shredded cheddar cheese
2 tablespoons fresh minced parsley

- Preheat oven to 375°.

- Bake potatoes for 1 hour or until well done. Halve each potato lengthwise and scoop out pulp, but leave skins intact. Decrease heat to 350°.

- In large bowl, mash potatoes with butter. Add whipping cream, ¾ teaspoon salt, ½ teaspoon pepper and green onions. Stir in crabmeat.

- Fill reserved potato skins with potato mixture. Sprinkle with cheese. Bake at 350° for about 15 minutes. To serve, sprinkle fresh parsley over cheese. Serves 4.

# NO-PANIC CRAB CASSEROLE

2 (6 ounce) cans crabmeat, drained, flaked
1 cup half-and-half cream
1½ cups mayonnaise
6 eggs, hard-boiled, finely chopped
1 cup seasoned breadcrumbs, divided
1 tablespoon dried parsley flakes
½ teaspoon dried basil
1 (8 ounce) can sliced water chestnuts, drained
2 tablespoons butter, melted

- Preheat oven to 350°.

- Combine crabmeat, half-and-half cream, mayonnaise, hard-boiled eggs, ½ cup seasoned breadcrumbs, parsley, basil, water chestnuts and a little salt and pepper in bowl and mix well.

- Pour into sprayed 2-quart baking dish. Combine remaining breadcrumbs and butter in bowl and sprinkle over top of casserole. Bake for 40 minutes. Serves 6.

# SWEET TREATS CAKES & CUPCAKES

## EASY POUND CAKE

*1 cup (2 sticks) butter, softened*
*2 cups sugar*
*5 eggs*
*2 cups flour*
*1 tablespoon almond flavoring*

- Preheat oven to 325°. Combine all ingredients in bowl and beat for 10 minutes at medium speed. Pour into sprayed, floured tube pan. (Batter will be very thick.)

- Bake for 1 hour. Cake is done when toothpick inserted in center comes out clean. Serves 12 to 16.

## EASY LEMON POUND CAKE

*1 cup butter, softened*
*½ cup shortening*
*2¾ cups sugar*
*5 large eggs, beaten*
*1 teaspoon lemon extract*
*¾ cup lemon-lime soda*
*3 cups flour*
*Powdered sugar*

- Preheat oven to 325°.

- In mixing bowl, beat butter, shortening and sugar about 4 minutes until light and fluffy. Add eggs, one at a time, and beat well after each addition. Add lemon extract and lemon-lime soda alternately with flour.

- Pour into sprayed, floured bundt pan and bake for 1 hour 15 minutes or until toothpick inserted near center comes out clean. Cool about 10 minutes before removing from pan. When cake is completely cool, dust with powdered sugar. Serves 20.

# BLUEBERRY POUND CAKE

*1 (18 ounce) box yellow cake mix*
*1 (8 ounce) package cream cheese, softened*
*½ cup canola oil*
*4 eggs*
*1 (15 ounce) can whole blueberries, drained*
*Powdered sugar*

- Preheat oven to 350°. Combine all ingredients in bowl except blueberries and beat for 3 minutes. Gently fold in blueberries. Pour into sprayed, floured bundt or tube pan. Bake for 50 minutes.

- Cake is done when toothpick inserted in center comes out clean. Sprinkle sifted powdered sugar over top of cake. Serves 12 to 16.

# POUND CAKE DELUXE

*1 (10 inch) bakery pound cake*
*1 (20 ounce) can crushed pineapple with juice*
*1 (3.5 ounce) package instant coconut pudding mix*
*1 (8 ounce) carton frozen whipped topping, thawed*
*½ cup flaked coconut*

- Slice cake horizontally to make 3 layers. Mix pineapple, pudding and whipped topping in bowl and blend well. Spread on each layer and over top. Sprinkle top of cake with coconut and refrigerate. Serves 12 to 16.

# STRAWBERRY POUND CAKE

*1 (18 ounce) box strawberry cake mix*
*1 (3.4 ounce) package instant vanilla pudding mix*
*⅓ cup canola oil*
*4 eggs*
*1 (3 ounce) package strawberry gelatin*

- Preheat oven to 350°. Mix all ingredients plus 1 cup water in bowl and beat for 2 minutes at medium speed. Pour into sprayed, floured bundt pan. Bake for 55 to 60 minutes.

- Cake is done when toothpick inserted in center comes out clean. Cool for 20 minutes before removing cake from pan. If you would like an icing, use prepared vanilla icing. Serves 12 to 16.

*TIP: If you like coconut better than pineapple, use coconut cream pudding mix.*

# REALLY GREAT POUND CAKE

*½ cup shortening*
*1 cup (2 sticks) butter*
*3 cups sugar*
*5 eggs*
*3½ cups flour*
*½ teaspoon baking powder*
*1 cup milk*
*1 teaspoon rum flavoring*
*1 teaspoon coconut flavoring*

- Preheat oven to 325°.

- Cream shortening, butter and sugar in mixing bowl. Add eggs and beat for 4 minutes. Combine flour and baking powder.

- Add dry ingredients and milk alternately to butter mixture; begin and end with flour. Add rum and coconut flavorings.

- Pour into large greased, floured tube pan and bake for 1 hour 35 minutes. Test with toothpick to check for doneness. (Do not open door during baking.)

## GLAZE:

*1 cup sugar*
*½ teaspoon almond extract*

- Right before cake is done, bring sugar and ⅓ cup water to rolling boil. Remove from heat and add almond extract. While cake is still in pan, pour glaze over cake and set aside for 30 minutes before removing from pan. Serves 12 to 16.

# HOLIDAY RED VELVET CAKE

*1 (18 ounce) package German chocolate cake mix*
*1 (1 ounce) bottle red food coloring*
*⅓ cup oil*
*3 eggs, slightly beaten*
*1 (16 ounce) can white frosting*
*Small decorative candies and sprinkles*

- Preheat oven to 350°. Before you measure water for cake mix, place red food coloring in cup first, then add enough water to make 1⅓ cups.

- Prepare cake mix according to package directions with water, oil and eggs. Pour into sprayed, floured 2 (8 or 9-inch) cake pans.

- Bake for 25 to 30 minutes. Cake is done when toothpick inserted in center comes out clean. Frost each layer with white frosting and decorate top layer with tiny red candies. Serves 20.

# RED VELVET POUND CAKE

*3 cups sugar*
*¾ cup shortening*
*6 eggs*
*1 teaspoon vanilla*
*3 cups flour*
*1 cup milk*
*2 (1 ounce) bottles red food coloring*

- Preheat oven to 325°.

- Cream sugar and shortening, add eggs, one at a time, and beat after each addition. Add vanilla and mix.

- Add ¼ teaspoon salt, flour and milk and alternate each beginning and ending with flour. Add food coloring and beat until smooth.

- Bake in greased, floured tube pan for 1 hour 30 minutes or until cake tests done. Set aside in pan for 10 minutes. Remove cake from pan, cool completely and frost.

## ICING:

*1 (1 pound) box powdered sugar*
*1 (3 ounce) package cream cheese, softened*
*¼ cup (½ stick) butter, softened*
*3 tablespoons milk*
*Red sprinkles*

- To make icing, blend powdered sugar, cream cheese, butter and milk and mix well. Frost cake and top with few red sprinkles. Serves 12 to 16.

# POPPY SEED BUNDT CAKE

*1 (18 ounce) box yellow cake mix*
*1 (3.4 ounce) package instant coconut cream pudding mix*
*½ cup canola oil*
*3 eggs*
*2 tablespoons poppy seeds*
*Powdered sugar*

- Preheat oven to 350°.

- Combine cake mix and pudding mix, 1 cup water, oil and eggs in bowl. Beat on low speed until moist. Beat on medium speed for 2 minutes. Stir in poppy seeds. Pour into sprayed, floured bundt pan.

- Bake for 50 minutes or until toothpick inserted in center comes out clean. Cool for 10 minutes and remove from pan. Dust with sifted powdered sugar. Serves 12 to 16.

# ANGEL-CREAM CAKE

*1 large angel food cake*
*1 (18 ounce) jar chocolate ice cream topping*
*½ gallon vanilla ice cream, softened*
*1 (12 ounce) carton frozen whipped topping, thawed*
*½ cup slivered almonds, toasted*

- Tear cake into large pieces. Stir in chocolate topping to coat pieces of cake and mix in softened ice cream. Work fast! Stir into tube pan and freeze overnight.

- Turn out onto large cake plate and frost with whipped topping. Decorate with almonds and freeze. Serves 12 to 16.

# CHERRY-NUT CAKE

*1 (18 ounce) box French vanilla cake mix*
*½ cup (1 stick) butter, melted*
*2 eggs*
*1 (20 ounce) can cherry pie filling*
*1 cup chopped pecans*
*Powdered sugar*

- Preheat oven to 350°.

- Mix all ingredients, except powdered sugar, in large bowl with spoon. Pour into sprayed, floured bundt or tube pan. Bake for 1 hour. Sprinkle sifted powdered sugar on top of cake, if you like. Serves 12 to 16.

# SPECIAL CHERRY DUMP CAKE

*1 (20 ounce) can crushed pineapple with juice*
*1 (20 ounce) can cherry pie filling or flavor of your choice*
*1 (18 ounce) box yellow cake mix*
*¾ cup (1½ sticks) butter, melted*
*¾ cup flaked coconut*
*1 cup chopped pecans*

- Preheat oven to 350°. Spoon pineapple evenly over bottom of unsprayed 9 x 13-inch baking pan; cover evenly with pie filling.

- Sprinkle cake mix evenly over filling and drizzle with melted butter; do not stir. Sprinkle coconut and pecans evenly over cake mix. Bake for 55 minutes to 1 hour or until top browns. Serves 20.

# GOLDEN RUM CAKE

*1 (18 ounce) box yellow cake mix with pudding*
*3 eggs*
*⅓ cup canola oil*
*½ cup rum*
*1 cup chopped pecans*

- Preheat oven to 325°. Blend cake mix, eggs, 1 cup water, oil and rum in bowl. Stir in pecans. Pour into sprayed, floured 10-inch tube or bundt pan.

- Bake for 1 hour. (If you like, sprinkle sifted powdered sugar over cooled cake.) Serves 12 to 16.

# LEMON-POPPY SEED CAKE

*1 (18 ounce) box lemon cake mix with pudding*
*1 (8 ounce) carton sour cream*
*3 eggs*
*⅓ cup oil*
*⅓ cup poppy seeds*

- Preheat oven to 350°. Prepare 12-cup bundt pan with non-stick spray (Baker's non-stick spray with flour works best). In mixing bowl, combine dry cake mix, sour cream, eggs, oil and ¼ cup water and beat on medium speed until ingredients mix well.

- Stir in poppy seeds and mix until seeds are evenly distributed. Pour batter into prepared bundt pan. Bake for 45 minutes and test for doneness with toothpick. Cool. Serves 12 to 16.

*TIP: For a sweeter taste, dust cake with powdered sugar or spread prepared vanilla icing on top of cake.*

# CHERRY-PINEAPPLE CAKE

*1 (20 ounce) can crushed pineapple, drained*
*1 (20 ounce) can cherry pie filling*
*1 (18 ounce) box yellow cake mix*
*1 cup (2 sticks) butter, softened*
*1¼ cups chopped pecans*

- Preheat oven to 350°. Place all ingredients in bowl and mix with spoon. Pour into sprayed, floured 9 x 13-inch baking dish. Bake for 1 hour 10 minutes. Serves 16 to 20.

# The Best Fresh Apple Cake

*1½ cups oil*
*2 cups sugar*
*3 eggs*
*2½ cups sifted flour*
*1 teaspoon baking soda*
*2 teaspoons baking powder*
*½ teaspoon cinnamon*
*1 teaspoon vanilla*
*3 cups peeled, grated apples*
*1 cup chopped pecans*

- Preheat oven to 350°.

- Mix oil, sugar and eggs and beat well. In separate bowl, sift flour, ½ teaspoon salt, baking soda, baking powder and cinnamon. Gradually add flour mixture to sugar mixture.

- Add vanilla, fold in apples and pecans and pour into sprayed tube pan. Bake for 1 hour. Remove from oven, cool and invert onto serving plate.

## Glaze:

*2 tablespoons (¼ stick) butter, melted*
*2 tablespoons milk*
*1 cup powdered sugar*
*1 teaspoon vanilla*
*¼ teaspoon lemon extract*

- For glaze, mix all ingredients and drizzle over cake. Serves 12 to 16.

# Chess Cake

*1 (18 ounce) box yellow cake mix*
*2 eggs*
*½ cup (1 stick) butter, softened*

- Beat cake mix, eggs and butter. Press into sprayed 9 x 13-inch baking pan.

## Topping:

*2 eggs*
*1 (8 ounce) package cream cheese, softened*
*1 (16 ounce) box powdered sugar*

- Beat 2 eggs, cream cheese and powdered sugar. Pour topping mixture over cake batter. Bake at 350° for 35 minutes. Serves 16 to 20.

## WHITE CAKE WITH SPECIAL CHOCOLATE TOPPING

*1 (18 ounce) package white cake mix*
*1 cup graham cracker crumbs*
*⅓ cup oil*
*3 eggs*
*½ cup chopped pecans*
*1 (16 ounce) jar chocolate ice cream topping, divided*
*1 (7 ounce) jar marshmallow creme*

- Preheat oven to 350°.

- In mixing bowl, beat cake mix, cracker crumbs, 1¼ cups water, oil and eggs with mixer on medium speed for 2 minutes.

- Stir in chopped pecans and pour into sprayed, floured 9 x 13-inch baking pan. Reserve ¼ cup chocolate topping and drop remaining topping by generous tablespoonfuls randomly in 12 to 14 mounds onto batter in pan. Bake for 40 to 45 minutes. Cool 15 minutes.

- Spoon teaspoonfuls of marshmallow creme onto warm cake and carefully spread with knife dipped in hot water. Drop small dollops of reserved chocolate topping randomly over marshmallow creme.

- Swirl topping through marshmallow creme with knife for marbled design. Cool for 2 hours before cutting.

- To cut cake easily, use serrated knife and dip in hot water before cutting each piece to keep frosting from sticking. Serves 20.

## WHITE CHOCOLATE-ALMOND CAKE

*1 (18 ounce) box white cake mix*
*4 egg whites*
*¼ cup oil*
*1 teaspoon almond extract*
*1 cup slivered almonds, chopped*
*6 (1 ounce) squares white chocolate, melted*
*1 (16 ounce) container caramel icing*

- Preheat oven to 350°. In mixing bowl, combine cake mix, egg whites, oil, almond extract and 1½ cups water; beat until mixture blends well. Stir in almonds and melted white chocolate and pour into 2 sprayed, floured (9-inch) round cake pans.

- Bake for 30 to 35 minutes or until toothpick inserted in center comes out clean. Spread each layer with half of caramel icing. Place second layer on top of first layer. Serves 20.

# CHOCOLATE–CHERRY CAKE

*This is a chocolate lover's dream.*

1 (18 ounce) box milk chocolate cake mix
1 (20 ounce) can cherry pie filling
3 eggs

- Preheat oven to 350°. Combine cake mix, pie filling and eggs in bowl and mix with spoon. Pour into sprayed, floured 9 x 13-inch baking dish. Bake for 35 to 40 minutes.

- Cake is done when toothpick inserted in center comes out clean. Spread Chocolate-Cherry Cake Frosting over hot cake.

## CHOCOLATE–CHERRY CAKE FROSTING:

5 tablespoons butter
1¼ cups sugar
½ cup milk
1 (6 ounce) package chocolate chips

- When cake is done, combine butter, sugar and milk in medium saucepan. Boil 1 minute, stirring constantly. Add chocolate chips and stir until chips melt. Pour over hot cake. Serves 16 to 20.

# CHOCOLATE HURRICANE CAKE

*This is easy and very, very yummy.*

1 cup chopped pecans
1 (3 ounce) can sweetened flaked coconut
1 (18 ounce) box German chocolate cake mix
1¼ cups water
⅓ cup oil
3 eggs
½ cup (1 stick) butter, melted
1 (8 ounce) package cream cheese, softened
1 (16 ounce) box powdered sugar

- Preheat oven to 350°. Spray 9 x 13-inch baking pan. Cover bottom of pan with pecans and coconut. In mixing bowl, combine cake mix, water, oil and eggs and beat well. Carefully pour batter over pecans and coconut.

- Combine butter, cream cheese and powdered sugar in mixing bowl and whip to blend. Spoon mixture over unbaked batter and bake for 40 to 42 minutes. Serves 10 to 12.

*TIP: You cannot test for doneness with cake tester because cake will appear sticky even when it is done. The icing sinks into bottom as it bakes and forms white ribbon inside.*

# COCONUT CAKE DELUXE

*This is a fabulous cake!*

1 (18 ounce) box yellow cake mix
1 (14 ounce) can sweetened condensed milk
1 (15 ounce) can coconut cream
1 (3 ounce) can flaked coconut
1 (8 ounce) carton frozen whipped topping, thawed

- Preheat oven to 350°.

- Mix cake mix according to package directions. Pour batter into sprayed, floured 9 x 13-inch baking pan and bake for 30 to 35 minutes or until toothpick inserted in center comes out clean.

- While cake is warm, punch holes in cake about 2 inches apart. Pour sweetened condensed milk over cake and spread until all milk soaks into cake.

- Pour coconut cream over cake and sprinkle with coconut. Cool, frost with whipped topping and refrigerate. Serves 16 to 20.

# CRANBERRY COFFEE CAKE

2 eggs
1 cup mayonnaise
1 (18 ounce) box spice cake mix
1 (16 ounce) can whole berry cranberry sauce
Powdered sugar

- Preheat oven to 325°.

- Beat eggs, mayonnaise and cake mix in bowl. Fold in cranberry sauce. Pour into sprayed, floured 9 x 13-inch baking pan. Bake for 45 minutes.

- Cake is done when toothpick inserted in center comes out clean. When cake is cool, dust with sifted powdered sugar. (If you would rather have icing than powdered sugar, use prepared icing.) Serves 16 to 20.

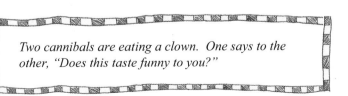

*Two cannibals are eating a clown. One says to the other, "Does this taste funny to you?"*

# Shortcut Blueberry Coffee Cake

*1 (16 ounce) package blueberry muffin mix*
*⅓ cup sour cream*
*1 egg*
*⅔ cup powdered sugar*

- Preheat oven to 400°.
- Combine muffin mix, sour cream, egg and ½ cup water in bowl. Rinse blueberries from muffin mix and gently fold into batter. Pour into sprayed, floured 7 x 11-inch baking dish.
- Bake for about 25 minutes and cool. Mix powdered sugar and 1 tablespoon water in bowl and drizzle over coffee cake. Serves 12.

# Easy Pineapple Cake

*2 cups sugar*
*2 cups flour*
*1 (20 ounce) can crushed pineapple with juice*
*1 teaspoon baking soda*
*1 teaspoon vanilla*

- Preheat oven to 350°.
- Combine all cake ingredients in bowl and mix with spoon. Pour into sprayed, floured 9 x 13-inch baking pan. Bake for 30 to 35 minutes.

### Easy Pineapple Cake Icing:

*1 (8 ounce) package cream cheese, softened*
*½ cup (1 stick) butter, melted*
*1 cup powdered sugar*
*1 cup chopped pecans*

- Beat cream cheese, butter and powdered sugar in bowl. Add chopped pecans and pour over hot cake. Serves 16 to 20.

*In the 1800's the first bakery was started on the yeast coast.*

# DEATH BY CHOCOLATE

*What a way to go!*

2 cups flour
2 cups sugar
½ cup (1 stick) butter
½ cup shortening
¼ cup cocoa
½ cup buttermilk*
2 eggs
1 teaspoon baking soda
1 teaspoon cinnamon
1 teaspoon vanilla

- Preheat oven to 375°.

- Combine flour and sugar in large mixing bowl. In saucepan, combine butter, shortening, cocoa and 1 cup water and bring to a boil. Pour mixture into flour-sugar mixture and beat.

- Add buttermilk, eggs, baking soda, cinnamon and vanilla and beat well. Pour into sprayed baking dish and bake for 25 minutes.

## ICING:

½ cup (1 stick) butter, melted
¼ cup cocoa
6 tablespoons milk
1 (16 ounce) box powdered sugar
1 teaspoon vanilla
1 cup chopped pecans

- Combine melted butter, cocoa, milk, powdered sugar and vanilla and mix well. Add pecans. Pour icing over hot cake. Serves 16 to 20.

*TIP: If you don't want to buy buttermilk, make your own by adding 1 tablespoon lemon juice or vinegar to 1 cup milk and let milk stand for 10 minutes.*

*Two antennas met on a roof, fell in love and got married. The ceremony wasn't much, but the reception was excellent.*

# GOOEY BUTTER CAKE

*4 eggs, divided*
*1 (18 ounce) box butter cake mix*
*½ cup (1 stick) butter, melted*
*4 eggs, divided*
*1 (16 ounce) box powdered sugar*
*1 (8 ounce) package cream cheese, softened*

- Preheat oven to 350°.

- Beat 2 eggs with cake mix and butter in bowl. Spread mixture into sprayed, floured 9 x 13-inch baking pan. Reserve ¾ cup powdered sugar for topping.

- Mix remaining powdered sugar, 2 remaining eggs and cream cheese in bowl and beat until smooth. Spread mixture on top of dough. Sprinkle remaining sugar on top. Bake for 40 minutes. Cake will puff up and then go down when it cools. Serves 16 to 20.

# HAWAIIAN DREAM CAKE

*1 (20 ounce) can crushed pineapple with juice, divided*
*1 (18 ounce) yellow cake mix*
*4 eggs*
*¾ cup canola oil*

- Preheat oven to 350°.

- Drain pineapple and save one-half for icing. Beat all ingredients and half pineapple juice in bowl for 4 minutes. Pour into sprayed, floured 9 x 13-inch baking pan.

- Bake for 30 to 35 minutes or until toothpick inserted in center comes out clean. Cool and spread coconut-pineapple icing over cake.

## COCONUT-PINEAPPLE ICING:

*½ cup (1 stick) butter*
*1 (16 ounce) box powdered sugar*
*1 (6 ounce) can flaked coconut*

- Heat remaining pineapple and butter in saucepan and boil for 2 minutes. Add powdered sugar and coconut. Punch holes in cake with knife and pour hot icing over cake. Serves 16 to 20.

# PINEAPPLE-ANGEL CAKE

*1 (1-step) angel food cake mix*
*1 (20 ounce) can crushed pineapple with juice*

- Preheat oven to 350°. Place angel food cake mix in bowl and add in pineapple. Beat according to directions on cake mix box. Pour into unsprayed 9 x 13-inch baking pan. (Do not spray pan.)

- Bake for 30 minutes. (This is a good low-calorie cake, but if you want it iced, just use a prepared vanilla icing.) Serves 16 to 20.

# OLD-FASHIONED APPLESAUCE-SPICE CAKE

*1 (18 ounce) box spice cake mix*
*3 eggs*
*1¼ cups applesauce*
*⅓ cup canola oil*
*1 cup chopped pecans*

- Preheat oven to 350°.

- Combine cake mix, eggs, applesauce and oil in bowl. Beat at medium speed for 2 minutes. Stir in pecans. Pour into sprayed, floured 9 x 13-inch baking pan. Bake for 40 minutes.

- Cake is done when toothpick inserted in center comes out clean. Cool. Serves 16 to 20.

*TIP: For frosting, use prepared vanilla frosting and add ½ teaspoon ground cinnamon.*

# PINA COLADA CAKE

*1 (18 ounce) box orange cake mix*
*3 eggs*
*⅓ cup oil*
*1 (14 ounce) can sweetened, condensed milk*
*1 (15 ounce) can coconut cream*
*1 cup flaked coconut*
*1 (8 ounce) can crushed pineapple, drained*
*1 (8 ounce) carton frozen whipped topping, thawed*

- Preheat oven to 350°. Combine cake mix, eggs, 1¼ cups water and oil in mixing bowl. Beat for 3 or 4 minutes and pour into deep, greased, floured 10 x 14-inch baking pan. Bake for 35 minutes.

- When cake is done, punch holes in cake with fork so frosting will soak into cake. Mix condensed milk, coconut cream, coconut and pineapple. While cake is warm, pour mixture over cake. Refrigerate until cake is cold, spread layer whipped topping over cake and return to refrigerator. Serves 16 to 20.

# STRAWBERRY-ANGEL DELIGHT CAKE

*1 cup sweetened condensed milk*
*¼ cup lemon juice*
*1 pint fresh strawberries, halved*
*1 angel food cake*
*1 (1 pint) carton whipping cream, whipped*
*Extra strawberries for topping*

- Combine sweetened condensed milk and lemon juice in bowl. Fold in strawberries. Slice cake in half.

- Spread strawberry filling on bottom layer and place top layer of cake over filling. Cover with whipped cream and top with extra strawberries. Serves 12 to 16.

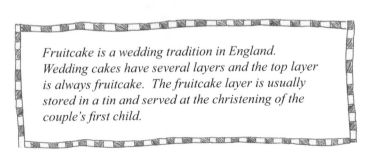

*Fruitcake is a wedding tradition in England. Wedding cakes have several layers and the top layer is always fruitcake. The fruitcake layer is usually stored in a tin and served at the christening of the couple's first child.*

# TURTLE CAKE

*1 (18 ounce) box German chocolate cake mix*
*½ cup (1 stick) butter, softened*
*½ cup oil*
*1 (14 ounce) can sweetened, condensed milk, divided*
*1 (1 pound) bag caramels*
*1 cup chopped pecans*

- Preheat oven to 350°.
- Combine cake mix, butter, 1½ cups water, oil and half condensed milk. Pour half batter into sprayed 9 x 13-inch pan and bake for 20 minutes.
- Melt caramels and blend with remaining condensed milk. Spread evenly over baked cake layer and sprinkle with pecans. Cover with remaining batter and bake additional 20 to 25 minutes.

## ICING:

*½ cup (1 stick) butter*
*3 tablespoons cocoa*
*6 tablespoons evaporated milk*
*1 (16 ounce) box powdered sugar*
*1 teaspoon vanilla*

- For icing, melt butter in saucepan and mix in cocoa and milk. Add powdered sugar and vanilla to mixture and blend well. Spread over cake. Serves 24.

# TWO-SURPRISE CAKE

*The first surprise is how easy this recipe is and the second*
*surprise is how good it is! You'll make this more than once.*

*1 bakery orange-chiffon cake*
*1 (15 ounce) can crushed pineapple with juice*
*1 (3.4 ounce) package vanilla instant pudding*
*1 (8 ounce) carton frozen whipped topping, thawed*
*½ cup slivered almonds, toasted*

- Slice cake horizontally to make 3 layers. Mix pineapple, pudding and whipped topping in bowl and blend well. Spread on each layer and cover top of cake. Sprinkle almonds on top and refrigerate. Serves 12 to 16.

# OREO CAKE

*1 (18 ounce) box white cake mix*
*⅓ cup oil*
*4 egg whites*
*1¼ cups coarsely crushed Oreo® cookies*

- Preheat oven to 350°.
- Spray 2 (8 or 9-inch) round cake pans. Combine cake mix, 1¼ cups water, oil and egg whites in large mixing bowl. Blend on low speed until moist. Beat for 2 minutes at high speed and gently fold in coarsely crushed cookies.
- Pour batter into prepared pans and bake for 25 to 30 minutes or until toothpick inserted in center comes out clean. Cool for 10 minutes, remove from pan and cool.

## ICING:

*4¼ cups powdered sugar*
*1 cup (2 sticks) butter, softened*
*1 cup shortening (not butter flavored)*
*1 teaspoon almond flavoring*
*¼ cup crushed Oreo® cookies*
*¼ cup chopped pecans*

- Beat all ingredients except crushed cookie pieces and pecans. Frost first layer, place second layer on top and frost top and sides. Sprinkle crushed Oreo® cookies and pecans on top. Serves 12 to 16.

# CHOCOLATE-ORANGE CAKE

*1 (16 ounce) loaf frozen pound cake, thawed*
*1 (12 ounce) jar orange marmalade*
*1 (16 ounce) can ready-to-spread chocolate-fudge frosting*

- Cut cake horizontally to make 3 layers. Place 1 layer on cake platter and spread with half marmalade. Place second layer over first and spread on remaining marmalade.
- Top with third cake layer and spread frosting liberally on top and sides of cake. Refrigerate. Serves 10 to 12.

# Banana Layer Cake with Butter Pecan Frosting

*1 (18 ounce) box yellow cake mix*
*3 eggs*
*⅓ cup vegetable oil*
*½ cup packed light brown sugar*
*1 cup milk*
*1 cup mashed ripe bananas*

- Preheat oven to 350°. In large bowl, combine cake mix, eggs, oil, brown sugar and milk. Beat on low speed to blend, then beat on medium for 2 minutes.

- Add bananas and beat for 1 additional minute on medium speed for 2 minutes. Divide batter between 2 sprayed, floured round cake pans. Bake for 30 to 35 minutes or until toothpick inserted in center comes out clean.

- Cool and frost with Butter Pecan Frosting or a prepared icing.

## Butter Pecan Frosting:

*½ cup (1 stick) butter*
*6 cups powdered sugar, divided*
*¼ cup light cream*
*1 teaspoon vanilla*
*½ teaspoon butter flavoring*
*1 cup chopped pecans, toasted\**

- In large bowl, cream butter, 2 cups powdered sugar, cream, vanilla and butter flavoring until smooth. Add remaining powdered sugar in several additions, mixing well after each addition. Stir in pecans and frost cake. Serves 10 to 12.

*\*TIP: Toast pecans by placing them on a cookie sheet and baking them at 300° for 8 to 10 minutes. Remove them when they become light brown. (Watch closely to be sure they don't burn.)*

You can buy a bus load of cheap bananas if you get them when they are overripe at the grocery store. Bring them home, peel them and cut them in half. Put them in sealable plastic bags and freeze them for quick and easy smoothies, muffins, breads and cakes.

# QUICK FRUITCAKE

*1 (15.6 ounce) package cranberry or blueberry quick-bread mix*
*½ cup chopped pecans*
*½ cup chopped dates*
*¼ cup chopped maraschino cherries*
*¼ cup crushed pineapple, drained*

- Preheat oven to 350°.

- Prepare quick-bread batter according to package directions. Stir in remaining ingredients. Pour into sprayed 9 x 5-inch loaf pan.

- Bake for 60 minutes or until toothpick inserted in center comes out clean. Cool for 10 minutes before removing from pan. Serves 16 to 20.

# QUICK AND EASY CHEESECAKE

*2 (8 ounce) packages cream cheese, softened*
*½ cup sugar*
*½ teaspoon vanilla*
*2 eggs*
*1 (9 ounce) ready graham cracker piecrust*

- Preheat oven to 350°.

- Beat cream cheese, sugar, vanilla and eggs in bowl. Pour into piecrust. Bake for 40 minutes. Cool and serve with any pie filling. Serves 6 to 8.

# EASY BASIC CUPCAKES

*½ cup shortening*
*1 cup sugar*
*3 eggs*
*½ cup milk*
*1¾ cups flour*
*2 teaspoons baking powder*
*1 teaspoon vanilla*
*1 (12 ounce) ready-to-serve frosting*

- Preheat oven to 350°. Cream shortening, sugar and eggs together until light and fluffy. Sift flour, baking powder and ½ teaspoon salt and add alternately with milk to creamed mixture.

- Add vanilla. Beat thoroughly. Pour into paper liners in cupcake pans. Bake for 15 to 20 minutes. Cool and frost. Makes 18 cupcakes.

# SOUR CREAM CUPCAKES

*1 tablespoon shortening*
*1 cup sugar*
*2 eggs*
*½ teaspoon baking soda*
*½ cup sour cream*
*1½ cups flour*
*½ teaspoon cream of tartar*
*⅛ teaspoon mace*

* Cream shortening, sugar and eggs together until light and fluffy. Dissolve baking soda in sour cream. Sift flour, 1½ teaspoons salt, cream of tartar and mace together and add alternately with cream to first mixture. Beat thoroughly. Bake in sprayed cupcake pans at 350° for 18 to 22 minutes. Makes 18 cupcakes.

# WHITE VELVET DAZZLE

*1 (18 ounce) box white cake mix*
*⅓ cup canola oil*
*1 teaspoon almond extract*
*3 large egg whites*
*1 cup white chocolate chips*

* Preheat oven to 350°. Place blue paper baking cups in 24 muffin cups. Beat cake mix, 1¼ cups water, oil, almond extract and egg whites in bowl on low speed for 30 seconds.

* Increase speed to medium and beat for 2 minutes. Stir in white chocolate chips. Divide batter among muffin cups.

* Bake for 19 to 22 minutes or until toothpick inserted in center comes out clean. Cool for 10 minutes before removing from pan. Cool for 30 minutes before frosting. Makes 24 cupcakes.

> *Cooking with love means never having to feel chained to your stove, never feeling that getting dinner on the table is a teeth-gritting experience rather a charming interlude.*
> *–Francis Anthony*

# DOUBLE BUTTERSCOTCH CUPCAKES

*2 cups flour*
*1¼ cups sugar*
*1 (3.4 ounce) package instant butterscotch pudding mix*
*1 (3.4 ounce) package instant vanilla pudding mix*
*2 teaspoons baking powder*
*4 eggs, lightly beaten*
*¾ cup canola oil*
*1 teaspoon vanilla*
*1 (12 ounce) package butterscotch chips, divided*
*1 (12 ounce) ready-to-serve buttercream frosting*

- Preheat oven to 350°. Place paper baking cups in 24 muffin cups. Combine flour, sugar, both pudding mixes, baking soda and ½ teaspoon salt in bowl.

- In separate bowl, combine 1 cup water, eggs, oil and vanilla; stir this mixture into dry ingredients and mix just until moist. Stir in 1 cup butterscotch chips and mix well.

- Spoon batter into muffin cups about two-thirds full. Bake for 16 to 20 minutes or until toothpick comes out clean. Cool for 5 minutes before removing from pan. Cool completely before frosting. Makes 24 cupcakes.

# WHITE AND DARK CHOCOLATE CUPCAKES

*1 (18 ounce) box French vanilla cake mix*
*⅓ cup canola oil*
*3 eggs*
*1 teaspoon vanilla*
*1 cup white chocolate chips or 1 cup dark chocolate chips or ½ cup white chocolate and*
*    ½ cup dark chocolate chips*
*1 (16 ounce) ready-to-serve white frosting*

- Preheat oven to 350°.

- Place paper baking cups in 24 muffin cups. Combine cake mix, 1¼ cups water, oil, eggs and vanilla in bowl and beat on low for 30 seconds.

- Increase speed to medium and beat for 2 minutes. Stir in white chocolate chips. Spoon into muffin cups.

- Bake for 18 to 23 minutes or until toothpick inserted in center comes out clean.

- Cool for 5 minutes before removing from pan. Cool for 30 minutes before frosting. Makes 24 cupcakes.

# CHOCOLATE CHIP CUPCAKES

*1 (18 ounce) box yellow cake mix*
*3 eggs*
*⅓ cup canola oil*
*1 teaspoon vanilla*
*1 (12 ounce) package chocolate chips*

- Preheat oven to 350°.

- Place paper baking cups in 24 muffin cups. Combine cake mix, 1¼ cups water, eggs, oil and butter flavoring in bowl.

- Beat on low speed for 30 seconds, increase speed to medium and beat for 2 minutes. Fold in chocolate chips and pecans and spoon into all muffin cups.

- Bake for 19 to 22 minutes or until toothpick inserted in center comes out clean. Cool for 5 to 10 minutes in pan. Remove from pan and place cupcakes on wire rack to cool completely before frosting. Makes 24 cupcakes.

# SURPRISE CUPCAKES

*These cupcakes are great and you don't have to frost them.*

*1 (8 ounce) package cream cheese, softened*
*2 cups sugar, divided*
*1 egg, slightly beaten*
*1 cup white chocolate chips*
*2 cups flour*
*1 teaspoon baking soda*
*⅓ cup canola oil*

- Preheat oven to 350°.

- Place paper baking cups in 18 muffin cups. Combine cream cheese, ½ cup sugar and egg in bowl and beat until mixture is smooth; stir in white chocolate chips.

- In separate bowl, combine remaining 1½ cups sugar, flour, baking soda, oil and 1 cup water and mix well, but not too vigorously.

- Fill muffin cups one-half full with batter and place 1 heaping tablespoon cream cheese mixture over each cupcake.

- Bake for 25 to 27 minutes or until toothpick inserted in batter comes out clean. Cool on wire rack. Remove cupcakes from pan and cool completely before decorating or storing. These cupcakes need to be refrigerated. Makes 18 cupcakes.

# COCONUT CUPCAKES

*2 cups flaked coconut*
*½ cup sweetened condensed milk*
*1 (18 ounce) package yellow cake mix*
*⅓ cup oil*
*3 eggs*
*1 (16 ounce) can vanilla frosting*
*1 cup flaked coconut, toasted*

- Preheat oven to 375°. Place paper baking cups in 24 regular-size muffin cups. In medium bowl, combine coconut and sweetened condensed milk and set aside.

- In mixing bowl, beat cake mix, 1¼ cups water, oil and eggs with electric mixer on low speed for 30 seconds. Beat 2 minutes on medium speed. Divide batter evenly among muffin cups and top each cupcake with 1 tablespoon coconut mixture.

- Bake for 18 to 22 minutes or until top springs back when lightly touched. Cool completely. Ice each cupcake with frosting and dip tops in toasted coconut. Serves 20 to 24.

*TIP: Toast coconut on baking sheet at 325° for about 5 minutes.*

# HARVEST PUMPKIN CUPCAKES

*1 (15 ounce) can pumpkin*
*3 eggs, slightly beaten*
*½ cup oil*
*1½ teaspoons ground cinnamon*
*1 teaspoon baking soda*
*1 (18 ounce) box yellow cake mix*
*½ cup chopped walnuts*

- Preheat oven to 350°. Place paper baking cups in 24 muffin cups. Combine pumpkin, eggs, oil, cinnamon and baking soda in bowl and mix well.

- Add cake mix, ¼ cup water and beat for 1 minute on low speed. Increase speed to high and beat for 2 minutes. Fold in walnuts.

- Fill muffin cups two-thirds full and bake for 19 to 22 minutes or until toothpick inserted in center comes out clean. Cool for 10 minutes in pan; remove from pan and cool completely before frosting. Makes 24 cupcakes.

# PUMPKIN CUPCAKES

*1 (18 ounce) box spice cake mix*
*1 (15 ounce) can pumpkin*
*3 eggs*
*⅓ cup canola oil*

- Preheat oven to 350°. Blend cake mix, pumpkin, eggs, oil and ⅓ cup water in bowl. Beat for 2 minutes. Pour batter into 24 paper-lined muffin cups and fill three-fourths full.

- Bake for 18 to 20 minutes or until toothpick inserted in center comes out clean. (After cooling completely, you might want to spread with prepared icing.) Makes 24 cupcakes.

# BANANA-NUT CUPCAKES

*1 (16 ounce) box banana nut cake mix*
*⅔ cup milk*
*2 tablespoons canola oil*
*1 egg*
*1 (12 ounce) ready-to-serve buttercream frosting*

- Preheat oven to 350°. Place paper baking cups in 12 muffin cups. Combine cake mix, milk, oil and egg in medium bowl. Stir mixture just until they blend well. (Batter will be slightly lumpy.) Divide batter among muffin cups and sprinkle walnuts from cake mix evenly over batter.

- Bake for about 20 minutes or until golden brown and tops spring back when touched. Cool in pan for 10 minutes; cool completely before frosting. Makes 12 cupcakes.

# LEMON CUPCAKES

*1 (18 ounce) box lemon cake mix*
*⅓ cup canola oil*
*3 eggs*
*1 (8 ounce) can crushed pineapple, drained*
*1 (16 ounce) ready-to-serve lemon frosting*

- Preheat oven to 350°. Place paper baking cups in 24 muffin cups. Combine cake mix, 1¼ cups water, oil and eggs in bowl and beat on low speed for 30 seconds. Increase mixer speed to medium and beat for 2 minutes. Stir in pineapple and mix well.

- Spoon into muffin cups and bake for 18 to 22 minutes or until toothpick inserted in cupcakes comes out clean. Cool in pan for about 5 minutes. Cool to room temperature before frosting. Makes 24 cupcakes.

# STRAWBERRY DELIGHT CUPCAKES

*1 (18 ounce) box strawberry cake mix*
*3 eggs*
*⅓ cup canola oil*
*1 (6 ounce) package white chocolate chips*
*1 (16 ounce) ready-to-serve strawberry frosting*

- Preheat oven to 350°. Place paper baking cups in 24 muffin cups. Combine cake mix, eggs, oil and 1¼ cups water in bowl and beat on low speed for about 30 seconds.

- Increase speed to medium and beat for 2 minutes. Stir in white chocolate chips and spoon about ¼ cup batter into each muffin cup.

- Bake for 19 to 23 minutes or until toothpick inserted in center comes out clean. Cool in pan for 5 to 10 minutes. Cool completely before frosting. Makes 24 cupcakes.

# CARROT CAKE CUPCAKES

*1 (18 ounce) box carrot cake mix*
*3 eggs*
*½ cup canola oil*
*1 (8 ounce) can crushed pineapple with juice*
*¾ cup chopped pecans*

- Preheat oven to 350°. Place paper baking cups in 24 muffin cups. Mix cake mix, eggs, oil, pineapple and ½ cup water in bowl and beat on low speed for 1 minute.

- Increase speed to medium and beat for 2 minutes. Fold in pecans and spoon into muffin cups.

- Bake for 19 to 23 minutes or until toothpick inserted in center comes out clean. Cool in pan for 5 minutes. Remove cupcakes from pan and cool completely before frosting. Makes 24 cupcakes.

> *The origin and creator of cupcakes cannot be pinpointed in culinary history, but some believe the name "cupcake" derived from its measurements. The basic cupcake recipe started out with 1 cup butter, 1 cup sugar and 1 cup flour. This was similar to the traditional pound cake named for its measurements of 1 pound butter, 1 pound sugar, 1 pound flour and 1 pound eggs. Others attribute the name to the fact that early cupcakes were baked in cups.*

# ZUCCHINI CUPCAKES

*1½ cups self-rising flour*
*1 teaspoon baking soda*
*1½ teaspoons pumpkin pie spice*
*3 egg whites or ¾ cup egg substitute*
*¾ cup packed brown sugar*
*½ cup canola oil*
*2 cups peeled, grated zucchini*

- Preheat oven to 350°.

- Combine flour, baking soda and pumpkin pie spice in small bowl.

- Beat eggs, brown sugar and oil in mixing bowl for about 3 minutes. Add zucchini and stir until they blend well. Add flour mixture and stir until ingredients combine thoroughly.

- Fill sprayed non-stick muffin cups three-fourths full and bake for 20 to 25 minutes. Cool on wire rack 5 minutes. Makes 12 cupcakes.

# CHOCOLATE-STRAWBERRY CUPCAKES

*1 (18 ounce) box milk chocolate cake mix*
*⅓ cup canola oil*
*3 eggs*
*1 teaspoon almond extract*
*1 cup white chocolate chips*
*1 (16 ounce) ready-to-serve strawberry frosting*

- Preheat oven to 350°.

- Place paper baking cups in 24 muffin cups. Combine cake mix, 1¼ cups water, oil, eggs and almond extract in bowl.

- Beat on low speed for 30 seconds; increase speed to medium and beat for 2 minutes. Stir in white chocolate chips and spoon into 24 muffin cups.

- Bake for 18 to 22 minutes or until toothpick inserted in center comes out clean. Cool for 10 minutes; then let cool completely for 30 minutes before frosting. Makes 24 cupcakes.

# CHERRY-CHOCOLATE CUPCAKES

*1 (18 ounce) box devil's food chocolate cake mix*
*3 large eggs*
*⅓ cup oil*
*2 (6 ounce) bottle maraschino cherries, drained, divided*
*1 cup white chocolate chips*
*1 teaspoon almond extract*
*1 (16 ounce) ready-to-serve cherry frosting*

- Preheat oven to 350°.

- Place paper baking cups in 24 muffin cups. Combine cake mix, eggs, oil and 1¼ cups water in bowl and beat on low speed for about 30 seconds. Increase speed to medium and beat mixture for 2 minutes.

- Drain 1 bottle of maraschino cherries and chop. Stir in chopped cherries and white chocolate chips and mix well, but gently.

- Pour into muffin cups and bake for 19 to 23 minutes or until toothpick inserted in center comes out clean. Cool on wire rack for 5 to 10 minutes; cool completely before frosting. Makes 24 cupcakes.

# NUTTY RED VELVET CUPCAKES

*1 (18 ounce) box red velvet cake mix*
*3 eggs*
*⅓ cup canola oil*
*1 (6 ounce) package white chocolate chips*
*½ cup chopped walnuts*

- Preheat oven to 350°.

- Place paper baking cups in 24 muffin cups. Blend cake mix, 1¼ cups water, eggs and oil in bowl on low speed for 30 seconds.

- Beat on medium speed for 2 minutes. Stir in white chocolate chips and walnuts and pour into muffin cups.

- Bake for 19 to 23 minutes or until toothpick inserted in center in center comes out clean. Let stand on wire rack for 30 minutes. Remove each cupcake from pan and cool completely before frosting. Makes 24 cupcakes.

# CHOCOLATE CUPCAKES TOPPED WITH WHITE CHOCOLATE AND BRICKLE BITS

*1 (18 ounce) box devil's food cake mix*
*3 eggs*
*⅓ cup canola oil*
*1 cup chocolate chips*

- Preheat oven to 350°.

- Place paper baking cups in 24 muffin cups. Combine cake mix, 1¼ cups water, eggs and oil in bowl and beat on low speed for 30 seconds.

- Increase speed to medium and beat for 2 minutes. Stir in chocolate chips and pour batter into muffin cups.

- Bake for 21 to 25 minutes or until toothpick inserted in center comes out clean. Cool for 10 minutes before removing from pan. Cool for additional 30 minutes before frosting.

## TOPPING:

*1 cup white chocolate chips*
*1 (16 ounce) container ready-to-serve creamy chocolate frosting*
*1 cup brickle bits*

- Microwave white chocolate chips in microwave-safe bowl on MEDIUM for about 2½ minutes and stir after 1 or 2 minutes. Stir until smooth and cool for 5 minutes. Stir in frosting until mixture blends well. Immediately frost cupcakes. Sprinkle with brickle bits. Makes 24 cupcakes.

# TRIPLE-CHOCOLATE CONES

*1 (18 ounce) box triple chocolate fudge cake mix*
*½ cup canola oil*
*2 eggs*
*1 (3 ounce) box ice cream cones*
*1 (12 ounce) ready-to-serve frosting*

- Preheat oven to 350°. Place paper baking cups in 24 muffin cups. Combine cake mix, 1¼ cups water, oil and eggs in bowl. Beat on low speed for 30 seconds.

- Increase speed to medium and beat for 2 minutes. Stir in chocolate chips and spoon into cone within ½ inch of top. Place pieces of foil where needed to stabilize each cone.

- Bake for 19 to 23 minutes or until toothpick inserted in center comes out clean. Cool in pan for about 10 minutes. Cool completely before frosting. Makes 24 cupcakes.

# Sweet Treats
# Cookies

## Creamy Cheesecake Cookies

*1 cup (2 sticks) butter, softened*
*2 (3 ounce) packages cream cheese, softened*
*2 cups sugar*
*2 cups flour*

- Preheat oven to 325°.

- Beat butter and cream cheese in bowl. Add sugar and beat until light and fluffy. Add flour and beat well.

- Drop teaspoonfuls of dough onto cookie sheet and bake for 12 to 15 minutes or until edges are golden. Makes 3 dozen.

## Chocolate Kisses

*2 egg whites, room temperature*
*⅔ cup sugar*
*1 teaspoon vanilla*
*1¼ cups chopped pecans*
*1 (6 ounce) package chocolate chips*

- Preheat oven to 375°. Beat egg whites in bowl until very stiff. Blend in sugar, vanilla and dash of salt. Fold in pecans and chocolate chips. Drop on shiny side of foil on cookie sheet.

- Put cookies in oven, TURN OVEN OFF and leave overnight. If cookies are a little sticky, leave out in air to dry. Makes 3 dozen cookies.

# CHOCOLATE MACAROONS

*1 (4 ounce) package sweet baking chocolate*
*2 egg whites, room temperature*
*½ cup sugar*
*¼ teaspoon vanilla*
*1 (7 ounce) can flaked coconut*

- Preheat oven to 350°. Place chocolate in double boiler. Cook until chocolate melts and stir occasionally. Remove from heat and cool.

- Beat egg whites in bowl at high speed for 1 minute. Gradually add sugar, 1 tablespoon at a time and beat until stiff peaks form (about 3 minutes). Add chocolate and vanilla and beat well. Stir in coconut.

- Drop teaspoonfuls of dough onto cookie sheet lined with parchment paper. Bake for 12 to 15 minutes. Transfer cookies on parchment paper to cooling rack and cool. Carefully remove cookies. Makes about 3 dozen cookies.

# CHOCOLATE-COCONUT COOKIES

*1 cup sweetened condensed milk*
*4 cups flaked coconut*
*⅔ cup miniature semi-sweet chocolate bits*
*1 teaspoon vanilla*
*½ teaspoon almond extract*

- Preheat oven to 325°. Combine sweetened condensed milk and coconut in bowl. (Mixture will be gooey.) Add chocolate bits, vanilla and almond extract and stir until they blend well.

- Drop teaspoonfuls of dough onto sprayed cookie sheet. Bake for 12 minutes. Store in airtight container. Makes 2 to 3 dozen cookies.

# CHOCOLATE-CRUNCH COOKIES

*These cookies are incredibly easy.*

*1 (18 ounce) box German chocolate cake mix with pudding*
*1 egg, slightly beaten*
*½ cup (1 stick) butter, melted*
*1 cup rice crispy cereal*

- Preheat oven to 350°. Combine cake mix, egg and butter in bowl. Add cereal and stir until they blend. Shape dough into 1-inch balls. Place on sprayed cookie sheet.

- Dip fork in flour and flatten cookies in crisscross pattern. Bake for 10 to 12 minutes and cool. Makes 3 dozen cookies.

# Double-Chocolate Cookies

*6 egg whites*
*3 cups powdered sugar*
*¼ cup cocoa*
*3½ cups finely chopped pecans*

- Beat egg whites until light and frothy. Fold sugar and cocoa into egg whites and beat lightly. Fold in pecans. Drop by spoonfuls on lightly sprayed, floured cookie sheet.

- Bake at 325° for about 20 minutes. Do not over bake and cool completely before removing from cookie sheet. Makes about 2 to 3 dozen.

# Devil's Food Cookies

*1 (18 ounce) box devil's food cake mix*
*½ cup canola oil*
*2 eggs*
*¾ cup chopped pecans*

- Preheat oven to 350°.

- Combine cake mix, oil, eggs and pecans in bowl and mix well. Drop teaspoonfuls of dough onto non-stick cookie sheet.

- Bake for 10 to 12 minutes. Cool and remove to wire rack. Makes 3 dozen.

# Angel Macaroons

*1 (16 ounce) package 1-step angel food cake mix*
*1½ teaspoons almond extract*
*2 cups flaked coconut*

- Preheat oven to 350°.

- Beat cake mix, ½ cup water and almond extract in bowl on low speed for 30 seconds. Scrape bowl and beat on medium for 1 minute. Fold in coconut.

- Drop rounded teaspoonfuls of dough onto parchment paper-lined cookie sheet. Bake for 10 to 12 minutes or until set. Remove paper with cookies to wire rack to cool. Makes 3 dozen cookies.

# COCONUT MACAROONS

2 (7 ounce) packages flaked coconut
1 (14 ounce) can sweetened condensed milk
2 teaspoons vanilla
½ teaspoon almond extract

- In mixing bowl, combine coconut, condensed milk and extracts and mix well. Drop by rounded teaspoons onto foil-lined cookie sheet.

- Bake at 350° for 8 to 10 minutes or until light brown around edges. Immediately remove from foil. (Macaroons will stick if allowed to cool.) Store at room temperature. Makes about 2 dozen.

# COCONUT NIBBLES

2 cups flaky wheat cereal
1¼ cups shredded coconut
2 large egg whites
1¼ cups sugar
½ teaspoon vanilla

- Preheat oven to 350°.

- Combine cereal and coconut in large bowl and mix well. In separate bowl, beat egg whites on high speed until soft peaks form. Gradually add sugar and vanilla while mixing. Fold egg whites into cereal-coconut mixture and mix well.

- Drop spoonfuls of dough onto sprayed baking sheet about 2 inches apart and bake for about 8 to 10 minutes. Watch closely and remove from oven when golden brown. Do not let them get too brown on bottom. Store in airtight container. Makes 3 dozen cookies.

# COCONUT YUMMIES

1 (12 ounce) package white chocolate chips
¼ cup (½ stick) butter
16 large marshmallows
2 cups quick-cooking oats
1 cup flaked coconut

- Melt chocolate chips, butter and marshmallows in saucepan over low heat and stir until smooth. Stir in oats and coconut and mix well.

- Drop rounded spoonfuls of mixture onto wax paper-lined baking sheets. Refrigerate until set. Store in airtight container. Makes 3 dozen.

# MACADAMIA NUT COOKIES

*½ cup shortening*
*½ cup (1 stick) butter, softened*
*2½ cups flour, divided*
*1 cup packed brown sugar*
*½ cup sugar*
*2 eggs*
*1 teaspoon vanilla*
*½ teaspoon butter flavoring*
*½ teaspoon baking soda*
*2 cups white chocolate chips*
*1 (3 ounce) jar macadamia nuts, chopped*

- Preheat oven to 350°. Beat shortening and butter in mixing bowl. Add half flour and mix well.

- Add sugars, eggs, vanilla, butter flavoring and baking soda. Beat until mixture combines well.

- Add remaining flour, mix well and stir in chocolate chips and nuts. Drop dough by spoonfuls on baking sheet and bake for 8 minutes. Makes 2 to 3 dozen.

# COCONUT-OATMEAL TREATS

*3 cups quick-rolled oats*
*1 cup chocolate chips*
*½ cup flaked coconut*
*½ cup chopped pecans*
*2 cups sugar*
*¾ cup (1½ sticks) butter*
*½ cup evaporated milk*

- Combine oats, chocolate chips, coconut and pecans in large bowl. In saucepan, boil sugar, butter and milk for 1 to 2 minutes and stir constantly.

- Pour hot mixture over oat-chocolate mixture in bowl and stir until chocolate chips melt. Drop by spoonfuls on wax paper. Cool at room temperature and store in covered container. Makes 2 to 3 dozen.

*TIP: Use white chocolate chips and ¾ cup candied, cut-up cherries for a colorful variation.*

# Mom's Brown Sugar Cookies

¾ cup packed brown sugar
1 cup (2 sticks) butter, softened
1 egg yolk
2 cups flour

- Cream brown sugar and butter in bowl until light and fluffy. Mix in egg yolk. Blend in flour. Refrigerate dough for 1 hour.
- When ready to bake, preheat oven to 325°.
- Form dough into 1-inch balls, flatten and criss-cross with fork on lightly sprayed cookie sheet. Bake for 10 to 12 minutes or until golden brown. Makes 2 dozen.

# Yummy Cookies

3 egg whites
1¼ cups sugar
2 teaspoons vanilla
3½ cups frosted corn flakes
1 cup chopped pecans

- Preheat oven to 250°. Beat egg whites in bowl until stiff. Gradually add sugar and vanilla. Fold in frosted corn flakes and pecans. Drop spoonfuls of dough onto cookie sheet lined with parchment paper. Bake for 40 minutes. Makes 4 dozen cookies.

# Vanishing Butter Cookies

1 (18 ounce) box butter cake mix
1 (3.4 ounce) package butterscotch instant pudding mix
1 cup canola oil
1 egg, beaten
1¼ cups chopped pecans

- Preheat oven to 350°.
- Mix cake and pudding mixes in bowl with spoon and stir in oil. Add egg, mix thoroughly and stir in pecans.
- Place spoonfuls of dough onto cookie sheet about 2 inches apart. Bake for 8 or 9 minutes. Do not overcook. Makes 3 dozen cookies.

# Scotch Shortbread

*1 cup butter*
*2 cups flour*
*¾ cup cornstarch*
*⅔ cup sugar*
*Granulated sugar or colored-sugar sprinkles*

- Preheat oven to 325°.

- Melt butter in saucepan and stir in remaining ingredients. Press into 9-inch square pan. Bake for 45 minutes.

- Cut into squares immediately after removing from oven. Sprinkle with granulated sugar or colored-sugar sprinkles. Makes 2 dozen squares.

# Snappy Almond-Sugar Cookies

*1 cup (2 sticks) butter, softened*
*1 cup plus 2 tablespoons sugar, divided*
*½ teaspoon almond extract*
*2 cups flour*
*1 cup chopped almonds*

- Cream butter, 1 cup sugar and almond extract until light and fluffy. Slowly beat in flour and stir in almonds. Shape dough into roll, wrap and refrigerate for about 2 hours.

- Preheat oven to 325°.

- Slice roll into ¼-inch pieces and bake for 20 minutes. Sprinkle with remaining 2 tablespoons sugar while still hot. Makes 2 to 3 dozen.

# Lemon Drops

*½ (8 ounce) carton frozen whipped topping, thawed*
*1 (18 ounce) box lemon cake mix*
*1 egg*
*Powdered sugar*

- Preheat oven to 350°.

- Stir whipped topping into lemon cake mix in bowl with spoon. Add egg and mix thoroughly. Shape into balls and roll in sifted powdered sugar. Bake for 8 to 10 minutes. Do not overcook. Makes 3 dozen cookies.

# LEMON COOKIES

*½ cup (1 stick) butter, softened*
*1⅔ cups sugar*
*2 tablespoons lemon juice*
*2 cups flour*

- Cream butter, sugar and lemon juice and slowly stir in flour. Drop by spoonfuls onto unsprayed cookie sheet. Bake at 350° for 14 to 15 minutes. Makes about 2 to 3 dozen.

# HELLO DOLLIES

*1½ cups graham cracker crumbs*
*1 (6 ounce) package chocolate chips*
*1 cup flaked coconut*
*1¼ cups chopped pecans*
*1 (14 ounce) can sweetened condensed milk*

- Preheat oven to 350°.

- Sprinkle cracker crumbs in 9-inch square pan. Layer chocolate chips, coconut and pecans. Pour sweetened condensed milk over top of layered ingredients. Bake for 25 to 30 minutes. Cool and cut into squares. Makes 16 squares.

# LOADED PEANUT BUTTER COOKIES

*1 (18 ounce) package sugar cookie dough, softened*
*½ cup peanut butter*
*½ cup miniature chocolate chips*
*½ cup peanut butter chips*
*½ cup chopped peanuts*

- Preheat oven to 350°.

- Beat cookie dough and peanut butter in large bowl until they blend and mixture is smooth. Stir in remaining ingredients.

- Drop heaping spoonfuls of dough onto cookie sheet. Bake for 15 minutes. Cool on wire rack. Makes 3 dozen cookies.

# PEANUT BUTTER-DATE COOKIES

*1 egg, beaten*
*⅔ cup sugar*
*⅓ cup packed brown sugar*
*1 cup crunchy peanut butter*
*½ cup chopped dates*

- Preheat oven to 350°.

- Blend egg, sugar, brown sugar and peanut butter in bowl and mix thoroughly. Stir in dates and roll into 1-inch balls.

- Place on cookie sheet. Use fork to press ball down to about ½ inch. Bake for about 12 minutes. Cool before storing. Makes 2 dozen cookies.

# PEPPY PEANUT BUTTER CUPS

*1 (18 ounce) roll refrigerated peanut butter cookie dough*
*48 miniature peanut butter cup candies*

- Preheat oven to 350°.

- Slice cookie dough into ¾-inch slices. Cut each slice into quarters and place each quarter, pointed side up in sprayed miniature muffin cups.

- Bake for 10 minutes. Remove from oven and immediately press peanut butter cup candy gently and evenly into cookies. (Be sure to remove paper wrappers from peanut butter cups.)

- Cool and remove from pan and refrigerate until firm. Makes 48.

# CHINESE COOKIES

*1 (6 ounce) package butterscotch chips*
*1 (6 ounce) package chocolate chips*
*2 cups chow mein noodles*
*1¼ cups salted peanuts*

- Melt butterscotch and chocolate chips in saucepan over low heat. Pour over noodles and peanuts and mix well.

- Drop spoonfuls of dough onto wax paper. Refrigerate to harden. Store in airtight container. Makes 3 dozen cookies.

# BUTTERSCOTCH COOKIES

*1 (12 ounce) and 1 (6 ounce) package butterscotch chips*
*2¼ cups chow mein noodles*
*½ cup chopped walnuts*
*¼ cup flaked coconut*

- Melt butterscotch chips in double boiler. Add noodles, walnuts and coconut. Drop by spoonfuls onto waxed paper. Makes 2 to 3 dozen.

# BROWN SUGAR WAFERS

*1 cup (2 sticks) butter, softened*
*¾ cup packed dark brown sugar*
*1 egg yolk*
*1 tablespoon vanilla*
*1¼ cups flour*

- Beat butter in bowl and gradually add brown sugar. Add egg yolk and vanilla and beat well. Add flour and dash of salt and mix well. Shape dough into 1-inch balls and refrigerate for 2 hours.
- Preheat oven to 350°.
- Place on cookie sheet and flatten each cookie. Bake for 10 to 12 minutes. Makes 3 dozen cookies.

# EASY SAND TARTS

*1 cup (2 sticks) butter, softened*
*¾ cup powdered sugar*
*2 cups sifted flour*
*1 cup chopped pecans*
*1 teaspoon vanilla*

- Preheat oven to 325°.
- Cream butter and powdered sugar in bowl and add flour, pecans and vanilla. Roll into crescents and place on cookie sheet. Bake for 20 minutes. Roll in extra powdered sugar after tarts cool. Makes 3 dozen.

# ORANGE BALLS

*1 (12 ounce) box vanilla wafers, crushed*
*½ cup (1 stick) butter, melted*
*1 (16 ounce) box powdered sugar*
*1 (6 ounce) can frozen orange juice concentrate*
*1 cup finely chopped pecans*

- Combine wafers, butter, powdered sugar and orange juice in bowl and mix well. Form into balls and roll in chopped pecans. Store in airtight container. Makes 3 dozen balls.

*TIP: Make these in finger shapes for something different.*

# POTATO CHIP CRISPIES

*1 cup (2 sticks) butter, softened*
*⅔ cup sugar*
*1 teaspoon vanilla*
*1½ cups flour*
*½ cup crushed potato chips*

- Preheat oven to 350°. Cream butter, sugar and vanilla in bowl. Add flour and chips and mix well. Drop spoonfuls of dough onto cookie sheet. Bake for about 12 minutes or until light brown. Makes 3 dozen cookies.

# SEVEN-LAYER COOKIES

*½ cup (1 stick) butter*
*1 cup crushed graham crackers*
*1 (6 ounce) package semi-sweet chocolate bits*
*1 (6 ounce) package butterscotch bits*
*1 (3 ounce) can flaked coconut*
*1 (14 ounce) can sweetened, condensed milk*
*1 cup chopped pecans*

- Preheat oven to 350°. Melt butter in 9 x 13-inch baking pan. Sprinkle remaining ingredients in order listed. Do not stir or mix and bake for 30 minutes. Cool before cutting. Makes about 2 to 3 dozen.

# PRALINE GRAHAMS

⅓ *(16 ounce) box graham crackers (1 package)*
¾ *cup butter*
½ *cup sugar*
*1 cup chopped pecans*

- Preheat oven to 300°.

- Separate each graham cracker into 4 sections. Arrange in jellyroll pan with edges touching. Melt butter in saucepan and stir in sugar and pecans. Bring to a boil and cook for 3 minutes. Stir frequently.

- Spread mixture evenly over graham crackers. Bake for 10 to 12 minutes. Remove from pan and cool on wax paper. Break up to serve. Makes 20 to 24 pieces.

# GINGERBREAD COOKIES

¾ *cup (1½ sticks) butter, softened*
*2 egg yolks*
*1 (18 ounce) spice cake mix*
*1 teaspoon ginger*

- In large bowl combine butter and egg yolks. Gradually blend in cake mix and ginger and mix well. Roll out to ⅛-inch thickness on lightly floured surface.

- Use gingerbread cookie cutter to cut out cookies and place 2 inches apart on cookie sheet. Bake at 375° for about 8 minutes or until edges are slightly brown. Cool cookies before transferring to cookie bowl. Makes about 2 dozen.

*Ginger was introduced to Europe about 1000 AD and was used to flavor many dishes. The most popular ginger confection is gingerbread, a moist sweet bread made with ginger and molasses or honey.*

# Sweet Treats Bars & Squares

## Easy Blonde Brownies

*This is another one of those recipes that seems too easy
to be a recipe. These brownies are so good and chewy.*

1 (1 pound) box light brown sugar
4 eggs
2 cups biscuit mix
2 cups chopped pecans

- Preheat oven to 350°. Use mixer to beat brown sugar, eggs and biscuit mix. Stir in
  pecans. Pour into greased 9 x 13-inch baking pan. Bake for 35 minutes. Cool and
  cut into squares. Makes 3 dozen.

## Snickers Brownies

1 (18 ounce) German chocolate cake mix
¾ cup (1½ sticks) butter, melted
½ cup evaporated milk
4 (3 ounce) Snickers® candy bars, cut in ⅛-inch slices

- Preheat oven to 350°. In large bowl, combine cake mix, butter and evaporated milk.
  Beat on low speed until mixture blends well. Add half batter into greased, floured
  9 x 13-inch baking pan. Bake for 10 minutes.

- Remove from oven and place candy bar slices evenly over brownies. Drop remaining
  half of batter by spoonfuls over candy bars and spread as evenly as possible. Place
  back in oven and bake for 20 minutes longer. When cool, cut into bars. Makes
  about 3 dozen.

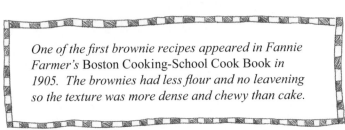

*One of the first brownie recipes appeared in Fannie
Farmer's* Boston Cooking-School Cook Book *in
1905. The brownies had less flour and no leavening
so the texture was more dense and chewy.*

# PECAN SQUARES

*2 cups flour*
*½ cup powdered sugar*
*1 cup (2 sticks) butter, cut up*
*1 (14 ounce) can sweetened, condensed milk*
*2 eggs*
*1 teaspoon vanilla*
*1 (7 ounce) package Bits 'O Brickle™ chips*
*1 cup chopped pecans*

- Preheat oven to 350°.

- Combine flour and powdered sugar in medium bowl and mix well. Cut in butter with pastry blender or fork until crumbly. Press mixture evenly into sprayed 9 x 13-inch baking pan and bake for 15 minutes.

- Combine condensed milk, eggs, vanilla, Bits 'O Brickle™ and chopped pecans and pour over prepared crust. Bake for 25 minutes or until golden brown. Cool and cut into squares. Makes 3 to 4 dozen.

# WALNUT BARS

*1⅔ cups graham cracker crumbs*
*1½ cups coarsely chopped walnuts*
*1 (14 ounce) can sweetened condensed milk*
*¼ cup coconut, optional*

- Preheat oven to 350°.

- Place cracker crumbs and walnuts in bowl. Slowly add condensed milk, coconut and a pinch of salt. (Mixture will be very thick.)

- Pack mixture into greased 9-inch square pan with back of spoon. Bake for 35 minutes. When cool, cut into squares. Makes 8 to 10.

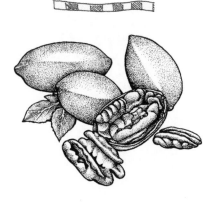

# ROCKY ROAD BARS

*1 (12 ounce) package semi-sweet chocolate chips*
*1 (14 ounce) can sweetened condensed milk*
*2 tablespoons butter*
*2 cups dry-roasted peanuts*
*1 (10 ounce) package miniature marshmallows*

- Place chocolate chips, sweetened condensed milk and butter in double boiler. Heat until chocolate and butter melt, stirring constantly. Remove from heat and stir in peanuts and marshmallows.

- Spread mixture quickly on wax paper-lined 9 x 13-inch pan. Refrigerate for at least 2 hours. Cut into bars and store in refrigerator. Makes 3½ dozen bars.

# CHOCOLATE CHIP CHEESE BARS

*1 (18 ounce) tube refrigerated chocolate chip cookie dough*
*1 (8 ounce) package cream cheese, softened*
*½ cup sugar*
*1 egg*

- Preheat oven to 350°. Cut cookie dough in half. For crust, press half dough onto bottom of sprayed 9-inch square baking pan or 7 x 11-inch baking pan.

- Beat cream cheese, sugar and egg in bowl until smooth. Spread over crust and crumble remaining dough over top.

- Bake for 35 to 40 minutes or until toothpick inserted in center comes out clean. Cool on wire rack. Cut into bars and refrigerate leftovers. Makes 3 dozen cookies.

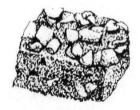

# GOOEY TURTLE BARS

*½ cup (1 stick) butter, melted*
*2 cups vanilla wafer crumbs*
*1 (12 ounce) semi-sweet chocolate chips*
*1 cup pecan pieces*
*1 (12 ounce) jar caramel topping*

- Preheat oven to 350°.

- Combine butter and wafer crumbs in 9 x 13-inch baking pan and press into bottom of pan. Sprinkle with chocolate chips and pecans.

- Remove lid from caramel topping and microwave on HIGH for 30 seconds or until hot. Drizzle over pecans.

- Bake for about 15 minutes or until chips melt. Cool in pan. Refrigerate for at least 30 minutes before cutting into squares. Makes 20 bars.

*TIP: Watch bars closely – you want the chips to melt, but you don't want the crumbs to burn.*

# LEMON-ANGEL BARS

*1 (1 pound) package 1-step angel food cake mix*
*1 (20 ounce) can lemon pie filling*
*⅓ cup (⅔ stick) butter, softened*
*2 cups powdered sugar*
*2 tablespoons lemon juice*

- Preheat oven to 350°. Combine cake mix and lemon pie filling in bowl and stir to mix well.

- Pour into sprayed 9 x 13-inch baking pan and bake for about 20 minutes. Remove cake from oven just before cake is done.

- Combine butter, powdered sugar and lemon juice and spread over hot cake. Cake will sink down a little in middle, so make sure icing is on edges of cake as well as in middle.

- When cool, cut into bars and store in refrigerator. Bars can be served at room temperature or cold. Makes 18 to 24.

# APRICOT BARS

*1¼ cups flour*
*¾ cup packed brown sugar*
*6 tablespoons (¾ stick) butter*
*¾ cup apricot preserves*

- In mixing bowl, combine flour, brown sugar and butter and mix well. Place half mixture in 9-inch square baking pan. Spread apricot preserves over top of mixture.
- Add remaining flour mixture over top of dessert. Bake at 350° for 30 minutes. Cut into squares. Makes about 1 dozen.

# CARAMEL-CHOCOLATE CHIP BARS

*1 (18 ounce) box caramel cake mix*
*2 eggs*
*⅓ cup firmly packed light brown sugar*
*¼ cup (½ stick) butter, softened*
*1 cup semi-sweet chocolate chips*

- Preheat oven to 350°.
- Combine cake mix, eggs, ¼ cup water, brown sugar and butter in large bowl. Stir until it blends thoroughly. (Mixture will be thick.)
- Stir in chocolate chips. Spread in sprayed, floured 9 x 13-inch baking pan. Bake for about 25 to 30 minutes or until toothpick inserted in center comes out clean. Cool. Makes 20 bars.

*TIP: These bars are especially good when frosted with a prepared caramel icing.*

# KIDS' BARS

*1 cup sugar*
*1 cup light corn syrup*
*1½ cups crunchy peanut butter*
*6 cups crispy rice cereal*
*1 (12 ounce) package chocolate chips*

- In saucepan, combine sugar and corn syrup. Bring to a boil, stirring constantly. Remove from heat and stir in peanut butter and crispy rice cereal. Spread into buttered 9 x 13-inch pan.
- In saucepan over low heat, melt chocolate chips. Spread over cereal layer. Refrigerate until set and cut into bars. Store in refrigerator. Makes 1 to 2 dozen.

# TOFFEE BARS

*1½ cups (3 sticks) butter, softened*
*1¾ cups packed light brown sugar*
*2 teaspoons vanilla*
*3 cups flour*
*1 (8 ounce) package chocolate chips*

- Preheat oven to 350°. In mixing bowl, combine butter, brown sugar and vanilla and beat on medium speed for 3 minutes. Add flour, mix until it blends completely and stir in chocolate chips.

- Place dough on greased 9 x 13-inch baking pan. Bake 25 minutes or until light brown. Cool slightly and cut into bars. Serves 12 to 16.

# BUTTERY WALNUT SQUARES

*These are great just as they are or with a scoop of ice cream.*

*1 cup (2 sticks) butter, softened*
*1¾ cups packed brown sugar*
*1¾ cups flour*

- Preheat oven to 350°. Combine butter and sugar and beat until smooth and creamy. Add flour and mix well. Pat mixture down evenly in sprayed 9 x 13-inch glass pan and bake for 15 minutes.

## TOPPING:

*1 cup packed brown sugar*
*4 eggs, lightly beaten*
*2 tablespoons flour*
*2 cups chopped walnuts*
*1 cup flaked coconut*

- Combine sugar and eggs in medium bowl. Add flour and mix well. Fold in walnuts and coconut and pour over crust. Bake for 20 to 25 minutes or until set in center. Cool in pan and cut into squares. Makes about 3 dozen.

*President James Monroe said of the most respected ethics courses taught in colleges that "The question to be asked at the end of an educational step is not 'What has the student learned?' but 'What has the student become?'"*

# CARMELITAS

## CRUST:

*1 cup flour*
*¾ cup packed brown sugar*
*1 cup quick-cooking oats*
*½ teaspoon baking soda*
*¾ cup (1½ sticks) butter, melted*

- Preheat oven to 350°.

- Use mixer to blend flour, brown sugar, ⅛ teaspoon salt, oats, baking soda and butter well enough to form crumbs. Pat down two-thirds crumb mixture into sprayed 9 x 13-inch baking pan and bake for 10 minutes.

## FILLING:

*1 (6 ounce) package chocolate chips*
*¾ cup chopped pecans*
*1 (12 ounce) jar caramel ice cream topping*
*3 tablespoons flour*

- Remove from oven and sprinkle with chocolate chips and pecans. Blend caramel topping with flour and spread over chips and pecans.

- Sprinkle with remaining crumb mixture and bake for 20 minutes or until golden brown.

- Refrigerate for 2 hours before cutting into squares. Makes 3 dozen.

# PECAN CREAM CHEESE SQUARES

*1 (18 ounce) box yellow cake mix*
*3 eggs, divided*
*½ cup (1 stick) butter, softened*
*2 cups chopped pecans*
*1 (8 ounce) package cream cheese, softened*
*3⅔ cups powdered sugar*

- Preheat oven to 350°.

- Combine cake mix, 1 egg and butter in bowl. Stir in pecans and mix well. Press into sprayed 9 x 13-inch baking pan.

- Beat cream cheese, sugar and remaining eggs in bowl until smooth. Pour over pecan mixture. Bake for 55 minutes or until golden brown. Cool and cut into squares. Makes 20 squares.

# RAINBOW COOKIE BARS

*½ cup (1 stick) butter*
*2 cups graham cracker crumbs*
*1 (14 ounce) can sweetened condensed milk*
*⅔ cup flaked coconut*
*1 cup chopped pecans*
*1 cup M&M's® plain chocolate candies*

- Preheat oven to 350°.

- Melt butter in 9 x 13-inch baking pan. Sprinkle crumbs over butter and pour sweetened condensed milk over crumbs.

- Top with remaining ingredients and press down firmly. Bake for 25 to 30 minutes or until light brown. Cool and cut into bars. Makes 20 bars.

*TIP: If you don't have M&M's®, white chocolate bits work but you won't have the "rainbow".*

# PEANUTTY MARSHMALLOW TREATS

*¼ cup (½ stick) butter*
*4 cups miniature marshmallows*
*½ cup crunchy peanut butter*
*5 cups rice crispy cereal*

- Melt butter in saucepan and add marshmallows. Stir until they melt and add peanut butter. Remove from heat. Add cereal and stir well. Press mixture into 9 x 13-inch pan. Cut in squares when cool. Makes 20 squares.

# CRISPY FUDGE TREATS

*6 cups rice crispy cereal*
*¾ cup powdered sugar*
*1¾ cups semi-sweet chocolate chips*
*½ cup light corn syrup*
*⅓ cup butter*
*2 teaspoons vanilla*

- Combine cereal and powdered sugar in large bowl and set aside.

- Place chocolate chips, corn syrup and butter in 1-quart microwave-safe dish. Microwave uncovered on HIGH for about 1 minute and stir until smooth.

- Pour over cereal mixture and mix well. Spoon into sprayed 9 x 13-inch pan. Refrigerate for 30 minutes and cut into squares. Makes 20 squares.

## CHOCOLATE CRISPIES

*1 (6 ounce) package milk chocolate chips*
*⅔ cup crunchy peanut butter*
*4¼ cups chocolate-flavored rice crispy cereal*

- Melt chocolate chips in double boiler and stir in peanut butter. Stir in cereal. Press into 9 x 9-inch square pan, cool and cut into bars. Makes 16 bars.

## PEANUT CLUSTERS

*1 (24 ounce) package almond bark*
*1 (12 ounce) package milk chocolate chips*
*5 cups salted peanuts*

- Melt almond bark and chocolate chips in double boiler. Stir in peanuts and drop teaspoonfuls of mixture onto wax paper. Store in airtight container. Makes 2 dozen.

# SWEET TREATS
# PIES & COBBLERS

## BLACK FOREST PIE

*This is a great party dessert.*

*4 (1 ounce) bars unsweetened baking chocolate*
*1 (14 ounce) can sweetened condensed milk*
*1 teaspoon almond extract*
*1½ cups whipping cream, whipped*
*1 (9 inch) baked piecrust*
*1 (20 ounce) can cherry pie filling, chilled*

- Melt chocolate with sweetened condensed milk in saucepan over medium-low heat and stir well to mix. Remove from heat and stir in almond extract. Set aside to cool.

- When mixture is about room temperature, pour chocolate into whipped cream and fold gently until both they blend.

- Pour into piecrust. To serve, spoon heaping spoonful of cherry filling over each piece of pie. Serves 6 to 8.

# CHEESECAKE PIE

*2 (8 ounce) packages cream cheese*
*3 eggs*
*1 cup sugar, divided*
*1½ teaspoons vanilla, divided*
*1 (8 ounce) carton sour cream*

• Preheat oven to 350°.

• Combine cream cheese, eggs, ¾ cup sugar and ½ teaspoon vanilla in bowl. Beat for 5 minutes. Pour into sprayed 9-inch pie pan and bake for 25 minutes. Cool for 20 minutes.

• Combine sour cream, remaining ¼ cup sugar and 1 teaspoon vanilla. Pour over cooled pie and bake for additional 10 minutes. Refrigerate for at least 4 hours. Serve with your favorite fruit topping. Serves 8.

# CHOCOLATE-CREAM CHEESE PIE

*1 (8 ounce) package cream cheese, softened*
*¾ cup powdered sugar*
*¼ cup cocoa*
*1 (8 ounce) container frozen whipped topping, thawed*
*1 (6 ounce) ready graham cracker piecrust*
*½ cup chopped pecans*

• Combine cream cheese, powdered sugar and cocoa in bowl and beat at medium speed until creamy. Add whipped topping and fold until smooth. Spread into piecrust, sprinkle pecans over top and refrigerate. Serves 6.

# COOL CHOCOLATE PIE

*22 large marshmallows*
*3 (5 ounce) milk chocolate-almond candy bars*
*1 (8 ounce) carton frozen whipped topping, thawed*
*1 (6 ounce) ready graham cracker piecrust*

• Melt marshmallows and chocolate bars in double boiler. Cool partially and fold in whipped topping.

• Pour into piecrust. Refrigerate for several hours before serving. Serves 6.

# OLD-FASHIONED CHESS PIE

*½ cup (1 stick) butter, softened*
*2 cups sugar*
*1 tablespoon cornstarch*
*4 eggs*
*1 (9 inch) refrigerated piecrust*

- Preheat oven to 325°.

- Cream butter, sugar and cornstarch in bowl. Add eggs one at a time and beat well after each addition. Pour mixture in piecrust.

- Cover piecrust edges with strips of foil to prevent excessive browning. Bake for 45 minutes or until center sets. Serves 6 to 8.

# OLD-FASHIONED BUTTERMILK PIE

*4 eggs*
*1 cup sugar*
*3 tablespoons flour*
*2 tablespoons butter, melted*
*3 tablespoons lemon juice*
*1¼ cups buttermilk\**
*½ teaspoon lemon extract*
*1 (9 inch) baked piecrust, chilled*

- Preheat oven to 350°.

- Beat eggs in large bowl until light and fluffy. Gradually add sugar and blend in flour, butter and lemon juice. Add buttermilk slowly and mix until it blends well. Stir in lemon extract.

- Pour into piecrust; bake for 45 minutes or until knife inserted in center comes out clean. Serve room temperature or chilled, but refrigerate any leftovers. Serves 8.

*\*TIP: To make buttermilk, mix 1 cup milk with 1 tablespoon lemon juice or vinegar and let stand for about 10 minutes.*

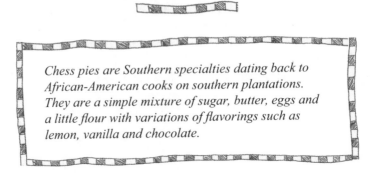

*Chess pies are Southern specialties dating back to African-American cooks on southern plantations. They are a simple mixture of sugar, butter, eggs and a little flour with variations of flavorings such as lemon, vanilla and chocolate.*

# CHERRY-PECAN PIE

*1 (14 ounce) can sweetened condensed milk*
*¼ cup lemon juice*
*1 (8 ounce) carton frozen whipped topping, thawed*
*1 cup chopped pecans*
*1 (20 ounce) can cherry pie filling*
*2 (9-inch) graham cracker piecrusts*

- Combine condensed milk and lemon juice, stir well and fold in whipped topping. Fold pecans and pie filling into mixture. Spoon into piecrusts. Refrigerate overnight. Two pies serve 12 to 14.

# CHOCOLATE-COCONUT PIE

*1½ cups flaked coconut*
*1½ cups chopped pecans*
*1 (12 ounce) package chocolate chips*
*1 (6 ounce) prepared graham cracker piecrust*
*1 (14 ounce) can sweetened condensed milk*

- Preheat oven to 350°.

- Combine coconut, pecans and chocolate chips. Sprinkle mixture over piecrust. Spoon sweetened condensed milk evenly over coconut mixture. Bake for 25 to 30 minutes. Cool before serving. Serves 6.

# COFFEE-MALLOW PIE

*1 tablespoon instant coffee granules*
*4 cups miniature marshmallows*
*1 tablespoon butter*
*1 (8 ounce) carton whipping cream, whipped*
*1 (6 ounce) ready graham cracker piecrust*
*½ cup chopped walnuts, toasted*

- Bring 1 cup water in heavy saucepan to a boil and stir in coffee until it dissolves. Reduce heat and add marshmallows and butter. Cook and stir over low heat until marshmallows melt and mixture is smooth.

- Set saucepan in ice and whisk mixture constantly until it cools. Fold in whipped cream and spoon into piecrust. Sprinkle with walnuts. Refrigerate for at least 4 hours before serving. Serves 8.

# GUILTLESS LIMEADE PIE

*1 (6 ounce) can frozen limeade concentrate, thawed*
*2 cups low-fat frozen yogurt, softened*
*1 (8 ounce) carton frozen whipped topping, thawed*
*1 (6 ounce) ready graham cracker piecrust*

• Combine limeade concentrate and yogurt in large bowl and mix well. Fold in whipped topping.

• Pour into piecrust. Freeze for at least 4 hours or overnight. Serves 6.

# CREAMY LEMON PIE

*1 (8 ounce) package cream cheese, softened*
*1 (14 ounce) can sweetened, condensed milk*
*¼ cup lemon juice*
*1 (20 ounce) can lemon pie filling*
*1 (9-inch) graham cracker piecrust*

• Beat cream cheese in mixing bowl until smooth and creamy. Add condensed milk and lemon juice and beat until mixture is creamy.

• Fold in lemon pie filling and stir well. Pour into piecrust and refrigerate several hours before slicing and serving. Serves about 8.

# LEMON CHESS PIE

*1¼ cups sugar*
*3 large eggs*
*½ cup corn syrup*
*1 tablespoon cornmeal*
*¾ cup sour cream*
*½ teaspoon vanilla*
*¼ cup lemon juice*
*1 (9 inch) refrigerated piecrust*

• Preheat oven to 350°.

• Beat sugar and eggs in bowl and mix well. Fold in corn syrup, cornmeal, sour cream, vanilla and lemon juice and mix well. Pour into piecrust.

• Cut 1½-inch strips of foil and cover edges of crust to keep crust from excessive browning. Bake for 45 to 50 minutes or until knife inserted in center comes out clean. Serves 8.

# CREAMY PECAN PIE

*1½ cups light corn syrup*
*1 (3 ounce) package vanilla instant pudding*
*3 eggs*
*2½ tablespoons butter, melted*
*2 cups pecan halves*
*1 (10 inch) deep-dish piecrust*

- Preheat oven to 325°. Combine corn syrup, pudding, eggs and butter in bowl, mix well and stir in pecans. Pour into piecrust. Cover piecrust edges with strips of foil to prevent excessive browning. Bake for 35 to 40 minutes or until center of pie sets. Serves 8.

# DREAM PIE

*1 (8 ounce) package cream cheese, softened*
*1 (14 ounce) can sweetened, condensed milk*
*1 (5.1 ounce) package vanilla instant pudding mix*
*1 (8 ounce) carton frozen whipped topping, thawed*
*2 (9-inch) graham cracker ready piecrusts*
*1 (20 ounce) can strawberry pie filling*

- Beat cream cheese and condensed milk in mixing bowl until smooth. Add pudding mix and ½ cup water, mix and refrigerate for 15 minutes. Fold in whipped topping, pour into 2 piecrusts and freeze.

- When ready to serve, remove from freezer and place in refrigerator for 45 minutes before slicing and serving. Spoon about ¼ cup pie filling on each slice of pie. (You could use other pie filling flavors if you like.) Serves about 16.

*TIP: Use 2 chocolate ready piecrusts. Pour 2 or 3 tablespoons chocolate ice cream topping over pie and top with chocolate shavings.*

# EASY PUMPKIN PIE

*2 eggs*
*3¼ cups (30 ounce can) pumpkin pie mix*
*⅔ cup evaporated milk*
*1 (9 inch) refrigerated deep-dish piecrust*

- Preheat oven to 400°. Beat eggs lightly in large bowl. Stir in pumpkin pie mix and evaporated milk. Pour into piecrust. Cut 2-inch wide strips of foil and cover crust edges to prevent excessive browning. Bake for 15 minutes. Reduce temperature to 350° and bake for additional 50 minutes or until knife inserted in center comes out clean. Cool. Serves 6 to 8.

# KAHLUA PIE

*26 marshmallows*
*1 (13 ounce) can evaporated milk*
*1 (1 ounce) package unflavored gelatin*
*1 (8 ounce) carton whipping cream*
*½ cup Kahlua® liqueur*
*1 (9-inch) chocolate cookie piecrust*
*Chocolate curls*

- Melt marshmallows with evaporated milk in saucepan over low to medium heat. Stir constantly and do not let milk boil.

- Dissolve gelatin in ¼ cup cold water. Remove marshmallows mixture from heat and add dissolved gelatin. Refrigerate until mixture thickens slightly.

- Whip cream and fold into marshmallow mixture. Mix in Kahlua® and pour into piecrust. Garnish with chocolate and curls and refrigerate overnight. Serves 8.

# MERRY BERRY PIE

*1 (6 ounce) package strawberry gelatin*
*1 cup whole cranberry sauce*
*½ cup cranberry juice cocktail*
*1 (8 ounce) carton frozen whipped topping, thawed*
*1 (9 inch) baked piecrust*

- Dissolve gelatin in 1 cup boiling water in bowl. Add cranberry sauce and juice. Refrigerate until it begins to thicken.

- Fold in whipped topping and refrigerate again until mixture mounds. Pour into piecrust. Refrigerate for several hours before serving. Serves 6 to 8.

# MILLION DOLLAR PIE

*24 round, buttery crackers, crumbled*
*1 cup chopped pecans*
*4 egg whites (absolutely no yolks at all)*
*1 cup sugar*

- Preheat oven to 350°.

- In bowl, combine cracker crumbs with pecans. In separate mixing bowl, beat egg whites until stiff and slowly add sugar while still mixing.

- Gently fold crumbs and pecan mixture into egg whites and pour into pie pan. Bake for 20 minutes and cool before serving. Serves 6 to 8.

# OUTTA-SIGHT PIE

1 (14 ounce) can sweetened, condensed milk
1 (20 ounce) can lemon pie filling
1 (20 ounce) can crushed pineapple, drained
1 (8 ounce) carton frozen whipped topping, thawed
2 (9-inch) cookie-flavored ready piecrusts

- Combine condensed milk, lemon pie filling and pineapple in saucepan over low to medium heat and mix well.

- Fold in whipped topping and pour mixture into 2 piecrusts. Refrigerate several hours before serving. Serves 12 to 16.

# BIRTHDAY PUMPKIN CHIFFON PIE

*The best pumpkin pie you'll ever eat!*

1 (1 ounce) package unflavored gelatin
2 eggs
1¼ cups sugar
1¼ cups canned pumpkin
⅔ cup milk
½ teaspoon ground ginger
½ teaspoon nutmeg
½ teaspoon cinnamon
1 (8 ounce) carton whipping cream
1 (9-inch) baked piecrust

- Soften gelatin in ¼ cup cold water and set aside. Use mixer to beat eggs for 3 minutes. Add sugar, pumpkin, milk, spices and ½ teaspoon salt and mix well.

- Pour mixture into large saucepan, cook in double boiler and stir constantly until mixture reaches custard consistency. Mix in softened gelatin, dissolve in hot pumpkin mixture and cool.

- When mixture cools, whip cream until very stiff and fold into pumpkin mixture. (Do not use whipped topping.) Pour into piecrust and refrigerate several hours before slicing. Serves 8.

TIP: *Original "chiffon" pies had egg whites whipped and folded into pie. Because raw eggs are not good to put in recipes, we cook whole eggs and add whipped cream. It is delicious!*

# Peach Mousse Pie

1 (16 ounce) package frozen peach slices, thawed
1 cup sugar
1 (1 ounce) package unflavored gelatin
⅛ teaspoon ground nutmeg
A few drops yellow and red food coloring
1 (12 ounce) carton frozen whipped topping, thawed
1 (9-inch) graham cracker piecrust

• Place peaches in blender and process until peaches are smooth. Pour into saucepan, bring to boil and stir constantly. Remove from burner.

• Combine sugar, gelatin and nutmeg and stir into hot peach puree until sugar and gelatin dissolve. Pour gelatin mixture into large bowl and place in freezer for 20 minutes or until mixture mounds. Stir occasionally.

• Use mixer to beat gelatin mixture on HIGH speed for 5 minutes or until light and fluffy. Add coloring, fold in whipped topping and pour into piecrust. Serves 6 to 8.

# Pecan Pie

2 tablespoons flour
3 tablespoons butter, melted
3 eggs, beaten
⅔ cup sugar
1 cup corn syrup
1 teaspoon vanilla
1 cup chopped pecans
1 (9-inch) unbaked piecrust

• Preheat oven to 350°. Combine flour, butter, eggs, sugar, corn syrup and vanilla in mixing bowl and mix well.

• Place pecans in piecrust and pour egg mixture over pecans.

• Bake for 10 minutes, reduce heat to 275° and bake for 50 to 55 minutes or until center of pie is fairly firm. Serves 6 to 8.

TIP:  *Recipe ingredient variations include using 2 tablespoons amaretto liqueur instead of vanilla. Also you could add 1 teaspoon cinnamon and ½ teaspoon nutmeg to recipe.*

# PEANUT BUTTER PIE

*⅔ cup crunchy peanut butter*
*1 (8 ounce) package cream cheese, softened*
*½ cup milk*
*1 cup powdered sugar*
*1 (8 ounce) carton frozen whipped topping, thawed*
*1 (6 ounce) ready graham cracker piecrust*

- Blend peanut butter, cream cheese, milk and powdered sugar in bowl and fold in whipped topping. Pour into piecrust. Refrigerate for several hours before serving. Serves 6.

# PINEAPPLE-CHEESE PIE

*1 (14 ounce) can sweetened condensed milk*
*¼ cup lemon juice*
*1 (8 ounce) package cream cheese, softened*
*1 (15 ounce) can crushed pineapple, well drained*
*1 (6 ounce) ready graham cracker piecrust*

- Combine sweetened condensed milk, lemon juice and cream cheese in bowl. Whip slowly at first, then beat until smooth. Fold in pineapple and mix well. Pour into piecrust and refrigerate for 8 hours before slicing. Serves 6.

# PINEAPPLE-LEMON PIE

*1 (14 ounce) can sweetened condensed milk*
*1 (20 ounce) can lemon pie filling*
*1 (20 ounce) can crushed pineapple, well-drained*
*1 (8 ounce) carton frozen whipped topping, thawed*
*2 (6 ounce) ready graham cracker piecrusts*

- Combine sweetened condensed milk and lemon pie filling in bowl and beat until smooth. Gently fold pineapple and whipped topping into pie filling mixture. Pour into 2 piecrusts and refrigerate. Serves 12 to 14.

# PINEAPPLE FLUFF PIE

*This pie is light, airy and full of fluff.*

1 (20 ounce) can crushed pineapple with juice
1 (3.4 ounce) package instant lemon pudding mix
1 (8 ounce) carton frozen whipped topping, thawed
1 (6 ounce) ready graham cracker crust

- Combine pineapple and pudding mix in bowl and beat until thick. Fold in whipped topping. Spoon into piecrust. Refrigerate for several hours before serving. Serves 8.

# PINK LEMONADE PIE

1 (6 ounce) can pink lemonade frozen concentrate, thawed
1 (14 ounce) can sweetened condensed milk
1 (12 ounce) package frozen whipped topping, thawed
1 (6 ounce) ready graham cracker piecrust

- Combine lemonade concentrate and sweetened condensed milk in large bowl and blend well. Fold in whipped topping and pour into piecrust. Refrigerate overnight. Serves 8.

# STRAWBERRY-CREAM CHEESE PIE

2 (10 ounce) packages frozen sweetened strawberries, thawed
2 (8 ounce) packages cream cheese, softened
⅔ cup powdered sugar
1 (8 ounce) carton frozen whipped topping, thawed
1 (6 ounce) ready chocolate crumb piecrust
Fresh strawberries

- Drain strawberries and set aside ¼ cup liquid. Combine cream cheese, set aside liquid, strawberries and powdered sugar in bowl and beat well.

- Fold in whipped topping and spoon into piecrust. Refrigerate overnight and garnish with fresh strawberries. Serves 8.

# Sunny Lime Pie

*2 (6 ounce) cartons key lime pie yogurt*
*1 (3 ounce) package dry lime gelatin mix*
*1 (8 ounce) carton frozen whipped topping, thawed*
*1 (6 ounce) ready graham cracker piecrust*

- Combine yogurt and lime gelatin in bowl and mix well. Fold in whipped topping, spread in piecrust and freeze. Take out of freezer 20 minutes before slicing. Serves 8.

# Sweet Potato Pie

*1 (14 ounce) can sweet potatoes, drained, mashed*
*¾ cup milk*
*1 cup packed brown sugar*
*2 eggs*
*½ teaspoon ground cinnamon*
*1 (9 inch) refrigerated piecrust*

- Preheat oven to 350°.

- Combine all ingredients (except piecrust) plus ½ teaspoon salt in bowl and blend until smooth. Pour into piecrust.

- Bake for 40 minutes or until knife inserted in center comes out clean. (Shield edges of pastry with aluminum foil to prevent excessive browning.) Serves 6.

# Thanksgiving Pie

*1 (15 ounce) can pumpkin*
*1 cup sugar*
*2 eggs, beaten*
*1½ teaspoons pumpkin pie spice*
*1 (12 ounce) can evaporated milk*
*1 (9 inch) piecrust, unbaked*

- Preheat oven to 425°.

- In bowl, combine pumpkin, sugar, eggs, pumpkin pie spice, evaporated milk and a dash of salt and mix well. Pour mixture into piecrust and bake 15 minutes.

- Lower heat to 325° and continue baking another 50 minutes or until knife inserted in center of pie comes out clean. Serves 6 to 8.

# YUM-YUM STRAWBERRY PIE

*2 pints fresh strawberries, divided*
*1¼ cups sugar*
*3 tablespoons cornstarch*
*1 (6 ounce) ready graham cracker piecrust*
*1 (8 ounce) carton whipping cream, whipped*

- Crush 1 pint strawberries in saucepan, add sugar, cornstarch and a dash of salt and cook on low heat until thick and clear.  Cool.

- Place remaining strawberries in piecrust and cover with cooked mixture.  Top with whipping cream and refrigerate.  Serves 6.

# CHERRY COBBLER

*2 (20 ounce) cans cherry pie filling*
*1 (18 ounce) box white cake mix*
*¾ cup (1½ sticks) butter, melted*
*1 (4 ounce) package almonds, slivered*
*Frozen whipped topping, thawed*

- Preheat oven to 350°.  Spread pie filling in sprayed 9 x 13-inch baking pan.  Sprinkle cake mix over pie filling, drizzle with melted butter and sprinkle almonds over top.  Bake for 45 minutes.  Top with whipped topping.  Serves 8 to 10.

# APRICOT CRUMBLE

*A bridge partner had this recently and everybody gave it a blue ribbon.  This is another one of those recipes that is really quick and easy plus really delicious.*

*1 (20 ounce) can apricot pie filling*
*1 (20 ounce) can crushed pineapple, with juice*
*1 cup chopped pecans*
*1 (18 ounce) box yellow cake mix*
*1 cup (2 sticks) butter, melted*
*Frozen whipped topping, thawed*

- Preheat oven to 375°.  Pour apricot pie filling into sprayed 9 x 13-inch baking dish and spread evenly.

- Spoon crushed pineapple and juice over pie filling.  Sprinkle pecans over pineapple, then sprinkle cake mix over pecans.

- Pour melted butter over cake mix and bake for 40 minutes or until light brown and crunchy.  To serve, top with whipped topping.  Serves 10.

# EASY BLUEBERRY COBBLER

*½ cup (1 stick) butter, melted*
*1 cup self-rising flour*
*1¼ cups sugar*
*1 cup milk*
*1 (20 ounce) can blueberry pie filling*
*Frozen whipped topping, thawed*

- Preheat oven to 300°. Pour butter in 9-inch baking pan. Mix flour and sugar in bowl, add milk and stir. Pour mixture over melted butter but do not stir. Spoon pie filling over batter and bake for 1 hour. To serve, top with whipped topping. Serves 8.

# BLUEBERRY BOUNCE

*1½ cups quick-cooking oats*
*2 cups packed brown sugar*
*1 (20 ounce) can blueberry pie filling*
*1 (18 ounce) box yellow cake mix*
*¾ cup chopped pecans*
*½ cup (1 stick) butter, melted*

- Preheat oven to 350°. Spray 9 x 13-inch glass baking dish. In medium bowl, combine oats and brown sugar and sprinkle half in bottom of baking dish.

- Spoon blueberry pie filling over oat-sugar mixture and spread evenly. Crumble cake mix over filling and spread evenly.

- Combine pecans with remaining oat mixture and sprinkle over cake mix. Drizzle butter evenly across oat-sugar mixture and bake for 35 to 40 minutes or until brown sugar looks like caramel. Serves 20.

# PINEAPPLE-BLUEBERRY DELIGHT

*1 (20 ounce) can crushed pineapple with juice*
*1 (18 ounce) box yellow cake mix*
*3 cups fresh or frozen blueberries*
*⅔ cup sugar*
*½ cup (1 stick) butter, melted*

- Preheat oven to 350°. Spread pineapple in sprayed 9 x 13-inch baking dish and sprinkle with cake mix, blueberries and sugar. Drizzle with butter and bake for 45 minutes or until bubbly. Serves 15.

*TIP: It is even better if you add 1 cup chopped pecans.*

# BLUEBERRY STREUSEL COBBLER

1 (14 ounce) package frozen blueberries, thawed
1 (14 ounce) can sweetened, condensed milk
2 teaspoons grated lemon rind
¾ cup (1½ sticks) plus 2 tablespoons butter, softened
2 cups biscuit baking mix, divided
⅔ cup firmly packed brown sugar
2 tablespoons (¼ stick) butter
¾ cup chopped pecans

- Preheat oven to 325°. Combine blueberries, condensed milk and lemon rind in medium bowl.

- In large bowl, cut ¾ cup (1½ sticks) butter into 1½ cups biscuit mix and stir until crumbly.

- Add blueberry mixture and spread in greased, floured 9 x 13-inch baking dish.

- In small bowl, combine remaining ½ cup biscuit mix and brown sugar. Cut in 2 tablespoons (¼ stick) butter until crumbly, add pecans and sprinkle over cobbler.

- Bake for 55 to 60 minutes and test with toothpick.

## BLUEBERRY SAUCE:

½ cup sugar
1 tablespoon cornstarch
½ teaspoon cinnamon
¼ teaspoon ground nutmeg
1 (14 ounce) package frozen blueberries, thawed
Vanilla ice cream

- For sauce, combine sugar, cornstarch, cinnamon and nutmeg in small saucepan and gradually add ½ cup water. Cook and stir until it thickens. Stir in blueberries.

- Serve 1 square of cobbler with ice cream on top and pour blueberry sauce over all. Serves 12.

# CHERRY-CINNAMON COBBLER

1 (20 ounce) can cherry pie filling
1 (12 ounce) tube refrigerated cinnamon rolls

- Preheat oven to 400°.

- Spread pie filling into sprayed 8-inch baking dish. Set aside icing from cinnamon rolls and arrange rolls around edge of baking dish.

- Bake for 15 minutes. Cover and bake for additional 10 minutes. Spread icing over rolls and serve warm. Serves 8 to 10.

# PEACH CRISP

*4¾ cups peeled, sliced peaches*
*3 tablespoons lemon juice*
*1 cup flour*
*1¾ cups sugar*
*1 egg, beaten*
*Butter*

- Preheat oven to 375°.

- Place peaches in sprayed 9-inch baking dish and sprinkle lemon juice over top. Mix flour, sugar, egg and dash of salt in bowl.

- Spread mixture over top of peaches and dot with a little butter. Bake until golden brown. Serves 8 to 12.

# APPLE DUMPLINGS

*1½ cups firmly packed brown sugar, divided*
*¼ cup chopped pecans*
*2 tablespoons butter, softened*
*6 baking apples, cored*
*1 (15 ounce) package refrigerated piecrusts*

- Preheat oven to 425°.

- Mix ½ cup packed brown sugar, pecans and butter in bowl and spoon mixture into each apple. Roll piecrusts to ⅛-inch thickness. Cut into 6 squares approximately 7 inches each.

- Wrap 1 square around each apple, pinch edges to seal and place in baking dish. Place remaining 1 cup packed brown sugar and ½ cup water in saucepan over medium heat and stir until sugar dissolves. Pour syrup over dumplings.

- Bake for 35 to 40 minutes or until tender and baste occasionally with syrup. Serves 6.

*TIP: For even more flavorful dumplings, add 2 teaspoons ground cinnamon or apple pie spice along with sugar, pecans and butter.*

# SWEET TREATS CANDY

## MICROWAVE FUDGE

*3 cups semi-sweet chocolate chips*
*1 (14 ounce) can sweetened condensed milk*
*¼ cup (½ stick) butter, sliced*
*1 cup chopped walnuts*

- Combine chocolate chips, sweetened condensed milk and butter in 2-quart glass bowl. Microwave on MEDIUM for 4 to 5 minutes and stir at 1½-minute intervals.

- Stir in walnuts and pour into sprayed 8-inch square dish. Refrigerate for 2 hours and cut into squares. Makes 15 squares.

## PEANUT BUTTER FUDGE

*1½ cups crunchy peanut butter*
*1 (12 ounce) package milk chocolate chips*
*1 (14 ounce) can sweetened condensed milk*
*1 cup chopped pecans*

- Melt peanut butter and chocolate chips in saucepan. Add sweetened condensed milk and heat. Add pecans and mix well. Pour into sprayed 9-inch square dish. Makes 20 pieces.

## WHITE CHOCOLATE FUDGE

*This is a little different slant to fudge – really creamy and really good!*

*1 (8 ounce) package cream cheese, softened*
*4 cups powdered sugar*
*1½ teaspoons vanilla*
*12 ounces almond bark, melted*
*¾ cup chopped pecans*

- Beat cream cheese in bowl on medium speed until smooth. Gradually add powdered sugar and vanilla and beat well. Stir in melted almond bark and pecans. Spread into sprayed 8-inch square pan. Refrigerate until firm. Cut into small squares. Makes 16 squares.

# DIAMOND FUDGE

*1 (6 ounce) package semi-sweet chocolate chips*
*1 cup creamy peanut butter*
*½ cup (1 stick) butter*
*1 cup powdered sugar*

- Cook chocolate chips, peanut butter and butter in saucepan over low heat. Stir constantly, just until mixture melts and is smooth. Remove from heat. Add powdered sugar and stir until smooth.

- Spoon into sprayed 8-inch square pan and refrigerate until firm. Let stand for 10 minutes at room temperature before cutting into squares. Store in refrigerator. Makes 16 squares.

# CREAMY PEANUT BUTTER FUDGE

*3 cups sugar*
*¾ cup (1½ sticks) butter, softened*
*⅔ cup evaporated milk*
*1 (12 ounce) package peanut butter chips*
*1 (7 ounce) jar marshmallow creme*
*1 teaspoon vanilla*

- Combine sugar, butter and evaporated milk in large saucepan. Bring to a boil over medium heat and stir constantly. Cover and cook for 3 minutes without stirring. Uncover and boil 5 minutes (do not stir).

- Remove from heat, add peanut butter chips and stir until they melt. Stir in marshmallow creme and vanilla. Pour into sprayed 9 x 13-inch pan. Place in freezer for 10 minutes. Makes 20 pieces.

# HAZEL'S NUTTY FUDGE

*The hazelnut cocoa spread in this recipe is Nutella®. If you*
*haven't tasted Nutella® before, you owe yourself a real treat!*

*1 (12 ounce) package white chocolate chips*
*¾ cup hazelnut-cocoa spread*
*1½ cups chopped hazelnuts, divided*

- In medium saucepan over low heat, melt white chocolate chips and add hazelnut spread. Cook and stir until mixture blends well.

- Remove from heat and stir in 1 cup hazelnuts. Drop by spoonfuls on wax paper; garnish with remaining hazelnuts. Refrigerate until set. Makes about two dozen.

# CHOCOLATE PEANUT BUTTER DROPS

*1 cup sugar*
*½ cup light corn syrup*
*¼ cup honey*
*1½ cups crunchy peanut butter*
*4 cups chocolate-flavored frosted corn puff cereal*

- Combine sugar, corn syrup and honey in large, heavy pan. Bring to a boil and stir constantly.

- Remove from heat, add peanut butter and stir until it blends. Stir in cereal and drop spoonfuls of mixture onto wax paper. Cool. Makes 3 dozen.

# DATE-NUT LOAF CANDY

*6 cups sugar*
*1 (12 ounce) can evaporated milk*
*½ cup white corn syrup*
*1 cup (2 sticks) butter*
*2 (8 ounce) boxes chopped dates*
*3 cups chopped pecans or walnuts*
*1 tablespoon vanilla*

- In large saucepan, cook sugar, milk, corn syrup and butter for 5 minutes or until it boils. Stir constantly with wooden or plastic spoon so mixture will not scorch.

- Add dates and cook until it forms soft ball in 1 cup cold water. Remove from heat and beat until thick. Add pecans and vanilla and stir until very thick.

- Spoon out mixture on wet dish towel to make roll. (Recipe makes 2 rolls of candy.) Keep wrapped until it is firm enough to slice. Serves 10 to 12.

# EASY HOLIDAY MINTS

*1 (16 ounce) package powdered sugar*
*3 tablespoons butter, softened*
*3½ tablespoons evaporated milk*
*¼ - ½ teaspoon peppermint extract*
*Few drops desired food coloring*

- Combine all ingredients in large bowl and knead mixture until smooth. Shape mints in rubber candy molds and place on cookie sheets. Cover with paper towel and dry. Store in airtight container. Makes 3 dozen mints.

# KARO CARAMELS

2 cups sugar
1¾ cups light corn syrup
½ cup (1 stick) butter
2 (8 ounce) cartons whipping cream
1¼ cups chopped pecans, toasted

- Combine sugar, syrup, butter and 1 cup cream in saucepan. Bring to a boil. While boiling, add second cup of cream. Cook to soft-ball stage.

- Beat with spoon for 3 to 4 minutes. Add pecans and pour onto sprayed pan. Cut into cubes when cool. Makes 3 dozen squares.

# MACADAMIA CANDY

*If you want an easy candy recipe that everyone will love, this is it. It's great!*

2 (3 ounce) jars macadamia nuts
1 (20 ounce) package white almond bark
¾ cup flaked coconut

- Heat dry skillet on medium-low, toast nuts until slightly golden and set aside. (Some brands of macadamia nuts are already toasted.)

- Melt 12 squares almond bark in double boiler. As soon as almond bark melts, pour in nuts and coconut and stir well.

- Place wax paper on cookie sheet, pour candy on wax paper and spread out. Refrigerate for 30 minutes to set. Break into pieces. Makes 2 dozen pieces.

# MICROWAVE PRALINES

1½ cups packed brown sugar
⅔ cup half-and-half cream
2 tablespoons butter, melted
1⅔ cups pecans, chopped

- Combine brown sugar, cream and dash of salt in deep glass dish and mix well. Blend in butter. Microwave on HIGH for 6 to 10 minutes, stir once and add pecans.

- Cool for 1 minute. Beat with spoon until creamy and thick, about 4 to 5 minutes. (The mixture will lose some of its gloss.) Drop spoonfuls of mixture onto wax paper. Makes 2 dozen.

# PEANUT BRITTLE

*2 cups sugar*
*½ cup light corn syrup*
*2 cups dry-roasted peanuts*
*1 tablespoon butter*
*1 teaspoon baking soda*

- Combine sugar and corn syrup in saucepan. Cook over low heat and stir constantly until sugar dissolves. Cover and cook over medium heat for additional 2 minutes.

- Uncover, add peanuts and cook, stirring occasionally, to hard-crack stage (300°). Stir in butter and baking soda. Pour into sprayed jellyroll pan and spread thinly. Cool and break into pieces. Makes 3 dozen pieces.

# NUTTY HAYSTACKS

*1 pound candy orange slices, cut up*
*2 cups flaked coconut*
*2 cups chopped pecans*
*1 (14 ounce) can sweetened condensed milk*
*2 cups powdered sugar*

- Preheat oven to 350°.

- Place orange slices, coconut, pecans and sweetened condensed milk in baking dish and cook for 12 minutes or until bubbly. Add powdered sugar and mix well. Drop spoonfuls of mixture onto wax paper. Makes 3 dozen.

# TUMBLEWEEDS

*1 (12 ounce) can salted peanuts*
*1 (7 ounce) can potato sticks, broken up*
*3 cups butterscotch chips*
*3 tablespoons peanut butter*

- Combine peanuts and potato sticks in bowl and set aside.

- Heat butterscotch chips and peanut butter in microwave at 70% power for 1 to 2 minutes or until they melt. Stir every 30 seconds. Add to peanut mixture and stir to coat evenly.

- Drop rounded spoonfuls of mixture onto wax paper-lined cookie sheet. Refrigerate until set, about 10 minutes. Makes 3 dozen.

# Sugared Pecans

½ cup packed brown sugar
¼ cup sugar
½ cup sour cream
3 cups pecan halves

- Combine brown sugar, sugar and sour cream in saucepan and stir over medium heat until sugar dissolves. Boil to soft-ball stage. Add ⅛ teaspoon salt and remove from heat.
- Add pecans and stir to coat. Pour on wax paper and separate pecans carefully. They will harden after several minutes. Makes about 1 quart.

# Sugar Plum Candy

1¼ pounds almond bark, chopped
1½ cups red and green tiny marshmallows
1½ cups peanut butter cereal
1½ cups rice crispy cereal
1½ cups mixed nuts

- Melt almond bark in double boiler over low heat. Place marshmallows, cereals and nuts in large bowl. Pour melted bark over mixture and stir to coat.
- Drop spoonfuls of mixture onto wax paper-lined cookie sheet. Let stand until set and store in airtight container. Makes 3 dozen.

# White Chocolate Salties

8 (2 ounce) squares almond bark
1 cup packages salted Spanish peanuts
3 cups thin pretzel sticks, broken up

- Place almond bark in double boiler, heat and stir until almond bark melts. Remove from heat and cool 2 minutes. Add peanuts and pretzels and stir until coated.
- Drop spoonfuls of mixture onto wax paper. Refrigerate for 20 minutes or until firm. Makes 3 dozen.

# Sweet Treats Desserts

## Candy Store Pudding

*1 cup cold milk*
*1 (3.4 ounce) package instant chocolate pudding mix*
*1 (8 ounce) carton frozen whipped topping, thawed*
*1 cup miniature marshmallows*
*½ cup chopped salted peanuts*

- Whisk milk and pudding mix in bowl for 2 minutes. Fold in whipped topping, marshmallows and peanuts.

- Spoon into individual dessert dishes. Place plastic wrap over top and refrigerate until set. Serves 6.

## Baked Custard

*3 cups milk*
*3 eggs*
*¾ cup sugar*
*1 teaspoon vanilla*
*Ground cinnamon*

- Preheat oven to 350°.

- Scald milk in saucepan. Beat eggs in bowl and add sugar, ¼ teaspoon salt and vanilla. Pour scalded milk slowly into egg mixture.

- Pour into 2-quart baking dish and sprinkle a little cinnamon on top. Bake in hot water bath for 45 minutes. Serves 6.

# CINNAMON CREAM

*This dessert must be made the day before serving.*

1 (16 ounce) box cinnamon graham crackers
2 (5 ounce) packages instant French vanilla pudding mix
3 cups milk
1 (8 ounce) carton frozen whipped topping, thawed
1 (16 ounce) can caramel frosting

- Line bottom of 9 x 13-inch baking dish with graham crackers. (You will use one-third graham crackers.)

- Combine vanilla pudding and milk in bowl and whip until thick and creamy. Fold in whipped topping. Pour half pudding mixture over graham crackers.

- Top with another layer of graham crackers and add remaining pudding mixture.

- Top with final layer of graham crackers. (You will have a few crackers left.) Spread frosting over last layer of graham crackers and refrigerate overnight. Serves 20.

# CHERRY DESSERT SALAD

1 (20 ounce) can cherry pie filling
1 (20 ounce) can crushed pineapple, drained
1 (14 ounce) can sweetened condensed milk
1 cup miniature marshmallows
1 cup chopped pecans
1 (8 ounce) carton frozen whipped topping, thawed

- In large bowl, combine pie filling, pineapple, condensed milk, marshmallows and pecans.

- Fold in whipped topping, refrigerate and serve in pretty bowl. (You may add a couple drops of red food coloring, if you like a brighter color.) Serves 8 to 10.

# BUTTER MINT SALAD

1 (6 ounce) box lime gelatin
1 (20 ounce) can crushed pineapple with juice
½ (10 ounce) bag miniature marshmallows
1 (8 ounce) carton frozen whipped topping, thawed
1 (8 ounce) bag butter mints, crushed

- Pour dry gelatin over pineapple, stir in marshmallows and set overnight. Fold in whipped topping and butter mints. Pour into 9 x 13-inch dish and freeze. Serves 6 to 8.

# CREAMY BANANA PUDDING

*This is a quick and easy way to make the old favorite banana pudding.*

1 (14 ounce) can sweetened condensed milk
1 (3.5 ounce) package instant vanilla pudding mix
1 (8 ounce) carton frozen whipped topping, thawed
36 vanilla wafers
3 bananas, sliced, divided

- Combine sweetened condensed milk and 1½ cups cold water in large bowl. Add pudding mix and beat well. Refrigerate for 5 minutes. Fold in whipped topping.

- Spoon 1 cup pudding mixture into 3-quart glass serving bowl. Top with 12 wafers, 1 banana and one-third pudding. Repeat layers twice and end with pudding. Cover and refrigerate. Serves 12 to 14.

# KAHLUA MOUSSE

*Light but rich and absolutely delicious*

1 (12 ounce) carton frozen whipped topping, thawed
2 teaspoons dry instant coffee
5 teaspoons cocoa
5 tablespoons sugar
½ cup Kahlua® liqueur

- Combine whipped topping, coffee, cocoa and sugar in large bowl and blend well. Fold in Kahlua®. Spoon into sherbet dessert glasses. Place plastic wrap over dessert glasses until ready to serve. Serves 4.

# WHITE VELVET

1 (8 ounce) carton whipping cream
1½ teaspoons unflavored gelatin
⅓ cup sugar
1 (8 ounce) carton sour cream
¾ teaspoon rum flavoring
Fresh fruit

- Heat cream in saucepan over moderate heat. Soak gelatin in ¼ cup cold water in bowl. When cream is hot, stir in sugar and gelatin until they dissolve and remove from heat.

- Fold in sour cream and rum flavoring. Pour into individual molds, cover with plastic wrap and refrigerate. Unmold to serve. Serve with fresh fruit. Serves 6.

# BLUEBERRY-ANGEL DESSERT

1 (8 ounce) package cream cheese, softened
1 cup powdered sugar
1 (8 ounce) carton frozen whipped topping, thawed
1 (14 ounce) prepared angel food cake
2 (20 ounce) cans blueberry pie filling

- Beat cream cheese and sugar in large bowl and fold in whipped topping. Tear cake into small 1 or 2-inch cubes.

- Fold into cream cheese mixture, spread evenly in 9 x 13-inch dish and top with pie filling.

- Cover and refrigerate for at least 3 hours before cutting into squares to serve. Serves 20.

# CARAMEL-AMARETTO DESSERT

1 (9 ounce) bag small chocolate-covered toffee candy bars, crumbled
30 caramels
⅓ cup amaretto liqueur
½ cup sour cream
1 cup whipping cream

- Set aside about ⅓ cup crumbled toffee bars. Spread remaining candy crumbs in sprayed 7 x 11-inch dish. Melt caramels with amaretto in saucepan. Cool to room temperature.

- Stir in sour cream and whipping cream and whip until thick. Pour into individual dessert dishes and top with remaining candy crumbs, cover and freeze. Cut into squares to serve. Serves 16.

# CHERRY TRIFLE

1 (12 ounce) pound cake
⅓ cup amaretto liqueur
2 (20 ounce) cans cherry pie filling
2 (16 ounce) cartons vanilla pudding
1 (8 ounce) carton frozen whipped topping, thawed

- Cut cake into 1-inch slices. Line bottom of 3-quart trifle bowl with cake and brush with amaretto. Top with 1 cup pie filling followed by 1 cup pudding.

- Repeat layers 3 times. Top with whipped topping. Refrigerate for several hours. Serves 8 to 10.

# COFFEE SURPRISE

*This is a super dessert—no slicing, no "dishing up".*

1 (10 ounce) package large marshmallows
1 cup strong coffee
1 (8 ounce) package chopped dates
1¼ cups chopped pecans
1 (8 ounce) carton whipping cream, whipped

- Melt marshmallows in hot coffee in saucepan. Add dates and pecans and refrigerate. When mixture begins to thicken, fold in whipped cream. Pour into sherbet glasses. Place plastic wrap over top and refrigerate. Serves 6.

# GRASSHOPPER DESSERT

26 chocolate sandwich cookies, crushed
¼ cup (½ stick) butter, melted
¼ cup creme de menthe liqueur
2 (7 ounce) jars marshmallow creme
1 (1 pint) carton whipping cream

- Combine cookie crumbs and butter and press into bottom of sprayed 9-inch springform pan. Reserve about ⅓ cup crumbs for topping.

- Gradually add creme de menthe to marshmallow creme. Whip cream until very thick and fold into marshmallow mixture. Pour over crumbs. Sprinkle remaining crumbs on top and freeze. Serves 10 to 12.

# ICE CREAM DESSERT

19 ice cream sandwiches
1 (12 ounce) carton frozen whipped topping, thawed
1 (11¾ ounce) jar hot fudge ice cream topping
1 cup salted peanuts

- Cut 1 ice cream sandwich in half. Place 1 whole and 1 half sandwich along short side of 9 x 13-inch pan. Arrange 8 sandwiches in opposite direction in pan. Spread with half whipped topping.

- Spoon fudge topping onto whipped topping. Sprinkle with ½ cup peanuts. Repeat layers with remaining ice cream sandwiches, whipped topping and peanuts. (Pan will be full.)

- Cover and freeze. Take out of freezer 20 minutes before serving. Serves 20.

# LIME-ANGEL DESSERT

*1 (6 ounce) package lime gelatin*
*1 (20 ounce) can crushed pineapple with juice*
*1 tablespoon lime juice*
*1 tablespoon sugar*
*1 (8 ounce) cartons whipping cream, whipped*
*1 large angel food cake*

- Dissolve gelatin in 1 cup boiling water in bowl and mix well. Stir in pineapple, lime juice and sugar.

- Cool in refrigerator until mixture thickens. Fold in whipped cream. Break cake into pieces and place in 9 x 13-inch dish.

- Pour pineapple mixture over cake and refrigerate overnight. Cut into squares to serve. Serves 20.

# ORANGE-CREAM DESSERT

*2 cups crushed chocolate sandwich cookies (about 20)*
*⅓ cup butter, melted*
*1 (6 ounce) package orange gelatin*
*½ gallon vanilla ice cream, softened*

- Combine cookie crumbs and butter in bowl and set aside ¼ cup crumb mixture for topping. Press remaining crumb mixture into sprayed 9 x 13-inch dish.

- Dissolve gelatin in 1½ cups boiling water in large bowl, cover and refrigerate for 30 minutes.

- Stir in ice cream until smooth. Work fast. Pour over crust and sprinkle with set aside crumb mixture. Freeze. Remove from freezer 10 to 15 minutes before serving. Serves 20.

# STRAWBERRY-ANGEL DESSERT

*1 (6 ounce) package strawberry gelatin*
*2 (10 ounce) cartons frozen strawberries with juice, thawed*
*1 (1 pint) carton whipping cream, whipped*
*1 large angel food cake*

- Dissolve gelatin in 1 cup boiling water in bowl and mix well. Stir in strawberries. Cool in refrigerator until mixture begins to thicken. Fold in whipped cream.

- Break cake into pieces and place in 9 x 13-inch dish. Pour strawberry mixture over cake. Refrigerate overnight. Cut into squares to serve. Serves 15 to 20.

# SWEET ANGEL CAKE

*This always gets rave reviews. It's a real favorite.*

1½ cups powdered sugar
⅓ cup milk
1 (8 ounce) package cream cheese, softened
1 (3½ ounce) can flaked coconut
1 cup chopped pecans
1 (12 ounce) carton frozen whipped topping, thawed
1 large angel food cake, torn into bite-size pieces
1 (16 ounce) can cherry pie filling

- Add sugar and milk to cream cheese and beat in mixer. Fold in coconut and pecans, stir in whipped topping and cake pieces. Spread in large 9 x 13-inch glass dish and refrigerate for several hours.

- Add pie filling by tablespoon on top of cake mixture. (It will not cover cake mixture, but it will just be in clumps, making a pretty red and white dessert.) Refrigerate. Serves 15 to 16.

# PAVLOVA

3 large egg whites
1 cup sugar
1 teaspoon vanilla
2 teaspoons white vinegar
3 tablespoons cornstarch
Whipped cream
Fresh fruit

- Preheat oven to 300°. Beat egg whites in bowl until stiff and add 3 tablespoons cold water. Beat again and add sugar very gradually while beating. Continue beating slowly and add vanilla, vinegar and cornstarch.

- Draw 9-inch circle and mound mixture within circle on parchment-covered cookie sheet. Bake for 45 minutes. Leave in oven to cool.

- To serve, peel paper from bottom while sliding onto serving plate. Cover with whipped cream and top with assortment of fresh fruit such as kiwi, strawberries, blueberries, etc. Serves 12.

# OREO SUNDAE

1 (19 ounce) package Oreo® cookies, crushed, divided
½ cup (1 stick) butter, melted
½ gallon vanilla ice cream, softened
2 (12 ounce) jars fudge sauce
1 (12 ounce) carton frozen whipped topping, thawed
Maraschino cherries

- Mix crushed cookies (set aside ½ cup for topping) with butter to form crust. Pour mixture in 9 x 13-inch pan and press down.

- Spread softened ice cream over crust and add layer of fudge sauce. Top with whipped topping and remaining crushed cookies. Garnish with cherries and freeze until ready to serve. Serves 12.

# TWINKIES DESSERT

1 (10 count) box Twinkies®
4 bananas, sliced
1 (5 ounce) package vanilla instant pudding
1 (20 ounce) can crushed pineapple, drained
1 (8 ounce) carton frozen whipped topping, thawed

- Slice Twinkies® in half lengthwise and place in sprayed 9 x 13-inch pan cream-side up. Make layer of sliced bananas.

- Prepare pudding according to package directions (using 2 cups milk), pour over bananas and add pineapple. Top with whipped topping and refrigerate. Cut into squares to serve. Serves 20.

# DIVINE STRAWBERRIES

*This is such a bright, pretty bowl of fruit and it's so delicious.*

1 quart fresh strawberries
1 (20 ounce) can pineapple chunks, well drained
2 bananas, sliced
1 (18 ounce) carton strawberry glaze

- Cut strawberries in half or in quarters if strawberries are very large in bowl. Add pineapple chunks and bananas. Fold in strawberry glaze and refrigerate. Serves 12.

*TIP: This is wonderful served over pound cake or just served in sherbet glasses.*

# FRUIT FAJITAS

*1 (20 ounce) can prepared fruit pie filling*
*10 small or large flour tortillas*
*1½ cups sugar*
*¾ cup (1½ sticks) butter*
*1 teaspoon almond flavoring*

- Divide pie filling equally on tortillas, roll up and place in 9 x 13-inch baking dish. Combine 2 cups water, sugar and butter in saucepan and bring to a boil.

- Add almond flavoring and pour mixture over flour tortillas. Place in refrigerator and let soak for 1 to 24 hours.

- Preheat oven to 350°. Bake for 20 to 25 minutes until brown and bubbly. Serves 8 to 10.

# ICE CREAM AND SPECIALTY SAUCES

Ice cream socials and Sunday night sundaes are fun for the whole family. These are quick and easy sauces for you to take anywhere with a half gallon of ice cream (or a pound cake). Just watch all the smiling faces.

# PRALINE SAUCE

*When you are in a hurry and want something quick and easy and*
*sinfully delicious, try this praline sauce and pour it over ice cream.*

*1 cup packed brown sugar*
*2½ tablespoons cornstarch*
*2 tablespoons butter*
*½ cup chopped pecans*

- Place brown sugar and cornstarch in saucepan and add 1½ cups water. Cook over medium-high heat until thick and bubbly, about 5 minutes.

- Add butter and pecans and continue to stir until butter melts. Tastes great on ice cream or cheesecake. Makes about 2 cups.

# CARAMEL SAUCE

*1 cup packed brown sugar*
*½ cup butter, divided*
*½ cup light corn syrup*
*2 tablespoons whipping cream*
*½ teaspoon vanilla*

- Melt brown sugar and ¼ cup butter in saucepan over medium-high heat and stir well. Bring to a boil and reduce heat. Whisk in corn syrup, cream, vanilla and ⅛ teaspoon salt.

- Boil gently for about 3 minutes and stir constantly. Remove from heat and whisk in remaining ¼ cup butter. Serve warm. Makes about 1½ cups.

# CHOCOLATE SAUCE

*¾ cup half-and-half cream*
*1 tablespoon butter*
*½ pound semisweet chocolate chips*
*¼ teaspoon vanilla*

- Melt butter with cream in saucepan over medium-low heat. (Do not boil.) Heat until thin film forms on top.

- Add chocolate and vanilla, stir until chocolate melts and mixture is smooth. Remove from heat and cool. Makes about 1 cup.

# STRAWBERRY SAUCE

*3 (10 ounce) packages frozen sliced strawberries in syrup, thawed*
*1 cup sugar*
*2½ teaspoons lemon juice*

- Blend all ingredients in food processor. Pour into saucepan, bring to a boil and cook over low heat for about 10 minutes or until bright red and thick.

- Stir occasionally to prevent scorching. Cool and refrigerate. Makes 3½ cups.

# INDEX

## Cookbooks Published by Cookbook Resources, LLC
### *Bringing Family and Friends to the Table*

*The Best 1001 Short, Easy Recipes*
*1001 Slow Cooker Recipes*
*1001 Short, Easy, Inexpensive Recipes*
*1001 Fast Easy Recipes*
*1001 America's Favorite Recipes*
*1001 Easy Inexpensive Grilling Recipes*
*1,001 Easy Potluck Recipes*
*Easy Slow Cooker Cookbook*
*Busy Woman's Slow Cooker Recipes*
*Busy Woman's Quick & Easy Recipes*
*365 Easy Soups and Stews*
*365 Easy Chicken Recipes*
*365 Easy One-Dish Recipes*
*365 Easy Soup Recipes*
*365 Easy Vegetarian Recipes*
*365 Easy Casserole Recipes*
*365 Easy Pasta Recipes*
*365 Easy Slow Cooker Recipes*
*Super Simple Cupcake Recipes*
*Easy Garden Fresh Recipes*
*& Homemade Preserves (Photos)*
*Easy Soups and Slow Cooker Recipes (Photos)*
*Leaving Home Cookbook and Survival Guide*
*Essential 3-4-5 Ingredient Recipes*
*Ultimate 4 Ingredient Cookbook*
*Easy Cooking with 5 Ingredients*
*The Best of Cooking with 3 Ingredients*
*Easy Diabetic Recipes*
*Ultimate 4 Ingredient Diabetic Cookbook*
*4-Ingredient Recipes for 30-Minute Meals*
*Cooking with Beer*
*The Washington Cookbook*
*The Pennsylvania Cookbook*
*The California Cookbook*
*Best-Loved Canadian Recipes*
*Best-Loved Recipes from the Pacific Northwest*
*Easy Homemade Preserves*
*(Handbook with Photos)*

*Garden Fresh Recipes (Handbook with Photos)*
*Easy Slow Cooker Recipes*
*(Handbook with Photos)*
*Cool Smoothies (Handbook with Photos)*
*Easy Cupcake Recipes (Handbook with Photos)*
*Easy Soup Recipes (Handbook with Photos)*
*Classic Tex-Mex and Texas Cooking*
*Best-Loved Southern Recipes*
*Classic Southwest Cooking*
*Miss Sadie's Southern Cooking*
*Classic Pennsylvania Dutch Cooking*
*The Quilters' Cookbook*
*Healthy Cooking with 4 Ingredients*
*Trophy Hunter's Wild Game Cookbook*
*Recipe Keeper*
*Simple Old-Fashioned Baking*
*Quick Fixes with Cake Mixes*
*Kitchen Keepsakes & More Kitchen Keepsakes*
*Cookbook 25 Years*
*Texas Longhorn Cookbook*
*The Authorized Texas Ranger Cookbook*
*Gifts for the Cookie Jar*
*All New Gifts for the Cookie Jar*
*The Big Bake Sale Cookbook*
*Easy One-Dish Meals*
*Easy Potluck Recipes*
*Easy Casseroles Cookbook*
*Easy Desserts*
*Sunday Night Suppers*
*Easy Church Suppers*
*365 Easy Meals*
*Gourmet Cooking with 5 Ingredients*
*Muffins In A Jar*
*A Little Taste of Texas*
*A Little Taste of Texas II*
*Ultimate Gifts for the Cookie Jar*

www.cookbookresources.com
Toll-Free 866-229-2665
Your Ultimate Source for Easy Cookbooks